PRAISE FOR *BECOMIN*

From students and trainees:

Becoming a Teacher is a wonderful read and a perfect 'new teacher' gift. Alan's personal reflections are not only funny but also comforting. He finds the funny side of the mishaps we all experience, from training year and beyond! The book is easy to navigate and covers a great range of topics too, yet there is no pressure to read the entire book – you can dip in and out of it regularly with ease. Its chapters are of a good length and when you get stuck in, you find yourself at the end of the chapter and wanting to read more.

Katarina Pillai, primary school ECT, LETTA Trust school

The introduction to this book is so powerful that it reminds me why I chose this profession. I love that its content isn't at all patronising and has a sense of humanity and relatability in its coverage of the topic of ethics. The message is that it's OK to make mistakes, as we are all human, and from mistakes comes great learning and character building – something we are not reassured of enough as new teachers. *Becoming a Teacher* is inspiring to read and it makes you want to be a better teacher.

Natasha Ryan, Secondary PGCE student, Middlesex University

The style in which the book is written is fantastic. Alan's stories of his own experience really grab the reader and he kept my attention throughout.

Michaela McCaugherty, Secondary PGCE student, University of Sunderland

This is an engaging and very thought-provoking book that would have been great to have had right at the beginning of my journey into teaching. Alan asks questions and encourages the reader to think for themselves, while also providing a genuine account of the experience of teaching. Absolutely brilliant.

Patricia Duncan, Secondary PGCE student, University of Worcester

I thoroughly enjoyed reading *Becoming a Teacher.* I'm even drawing on some of it in my job applications! But the best part for me is how Alan manages to connect all the guidelines, procedures and protocols around being a teacher with real-life stories. Some even brought a little tear to my eye! Alan's words remind me of the writing of James Herriot, in being very honest and showing teaching for what it is – and he also discusses topics not found on my PGCE course, such as how to manage criticism.

Michael Walker, PGCE student, University of Sunderland

There is so much in this book I wish I had been able to read before starting my training. *Becoming a Teacher* is an invaluable guide for trainees and teachers alike.

Maisey Hodges, Secondary PGCE trainee teacher, Northampton TTP

I love this book. It is a great and engaging read, and very relatable to the experiences of Scottish teachers. I have taken away a lot from it that I can apply to my practice and how I look at the teaching profession. Thank you!

Megan Turnbull, primary probationary teacher, East Renfrewshire

This is a really useful book as it gives an authentic insight into teaching, and not just the 'fluffy' stuff that we are often shown at university. It strikes a great balance between personal experiences and theory, and it's full of knowledge that would be really helpful for ECTs too.

Chris Griffiths, PGCE student, Cardiff University

I thoroughly enjoyed reading this book and was really inspired by the concept of a good teacher being recognised by the values they model. The historical perspective provided is very interesting too, and I also appreciate the reassurance that the challenges I will face as a teacher will build my character – this sends out a message of 'keep going' even if you feel you are not at your best at that particular time. I think the book inspires student teachers to uphold codes of practice and standards, not just as a professional prerequisite but also as a moral responsibility.

Eilidh Macpherson, Secondary PGDE student, University of Strathclyde

From lecturers and tutors:

In an environment where the teacher dropout rate is high, this thought-provoking book will offer much support to teachers during their early years. I certainly would have appreciated having it during my PGCE and ECT years. The format is perfect to guide discussions with mentors and also to enable ECTs to reflect on a variety of issues they will be confronted with. That said, I also think it would be a valuable read for more experienced teachers.

Maddy Fowler, ECT, London

I will be honest, when I first started reading this book I thought: 'What have I done? I can't possibly read an entire academic book.' Well, let me tell you that I was wrong! It is written very thoughtfully without lots of references or jargon, and I really enjoyed how Alan includes anecdotes from his teaching days and time as a head teacher. It really is thought-provoking but also very readable, so you can put it down and pick it back up again without losing your thread. I would highly recommend this book for those who are only just starting their teaching journey or halfway through it like me. *Becoming a Teacher* is a brilliant book and I think Alan's words, thoughts and pearls of wisdom will stay with me and support me throughout my career.

Hannah Mitchell, second-year student, Primary BA QTS, Edge Hill University

I very much enjoyed the interactivity throughout this book, where the reader is encouraged to reflect upon and consider a variety of issues as well as draw lessons from the personal experiences of Alan himself. This offers a personal touch and makes the book easy to relate to. Alan highlights the pressures of teaching, but not to the point that it would put off any aspiring trainees; if anything, it will give them a sense of purpose and an understanding of the challenges that lie ahead. Ultimately, we as teachers are role models – and that's something, as emphasised by this book, that I am proud to be a part of. I will certainly be keeping a copy for use in my career.

Daniel Strachan, primary school ECT, South Farnham School

Becoming a Teacher gripped me from the first page and at times I had to drag myself away from reading it. I love the personal stories that make your heart drop as you ask, 'What if I were put in that situation?' I found the 'Discuss and reflect' sections very helpful too – they made me think about my own teaching and I found myself using the questions as talking points within my department at school. The discussions that ensued have helped me see teaching from the perspective of my more experienced colleagues.

Bryher Freight, secondary school ECT, Cornwall

I found this book extremely interesting. It is very easy to connect with Alan's writing, and his personal anecdotes are motivating, inspiring and moving in bringing the book to life. Alan covers broad themes and ethical conundrums related to building character, relating it to professional development and reminding us why we should take certain actions for the betterment of the pupils and communities we serve. The story concerning one of his students' attitude towards Anne Frank's diary resonated with me as I teach within an inner-city school in Greater Glasgow – and I'm all too often faced with sectarian views which can at times be difficult to confront. Alan reminded me that it is ethically and morally right to tackle controversial issues in a way that does not lead to further provocation. I think *Becoming a Teacher* is a fantastic book that could be described as a go-to guide for anyone joining the teaching profession.

Sarah-Jane Hamilton, fourth-year MEduc student, University of Glasgow

At university we tend to focus on specifics with relatively little time for aspects such as ethics or morality, so this book helps to develop a teaching philosophy and to determine what defines you as a teacher. *Becoming a Teacher* is incredibly insightful for both ECTs and more experienced teachers, and will help develop wider perspectives on teaching.

Amelia Sowden, Primary BA QTS student, York St John University

Becoming a Teacher explores a variety of issues and provides direction on how to effectively navigate them. Alan gives indispensable support by sharing and examining his own teaching, but it is his reflections upon his own values that are so fascinating and relevant to anyone involved in education.

An excellent book that gives everyone food for thought, and an essential and invaluable resource for new and experienced teachers.

Aimee Lascelles, PGDE student, University of Dundee

I was hooked from the start – the tone, the way it sets out exactly what the book aims to do, how it is structured to enable the reader to dip in and out, and much more. There is great use of further and recommended reading per chapter too. I particularly enjoyed the section on teaching and theory, as I found myself drawn into the question of whether we are reliant on the theory to underpin practice. I also enjoyed reflecting on the incident of children climbing high up in the tree and what the teachers were trying to achieve. This engaged my whole household in an interesting discussion!

A thoroughly thought-provoking read and a pleasure to engage with.

Amelia Shimells, Primary BA QTS student, York St John University

While reading *Becoming a Teacher* I found myself reflecting on my own beliefs and politics, and I really liked this. Alan's honesty and transparency makes it easy to imagine oneself in the situations described in the book, and to consider what one's own reactions might be to similar situations – such as going on strike, which really challenged my thinking. I enjoyed the discussion and reflection sections too, as being confronted with specific questions was really thought-provoking. The book is also helpful in relieving anxieties on how to handle situations in the classroom, and offers a perspective of teaching backed by a wealth of experience and honesty.

Nicole Larkins, primary school trainee teacher, South Farnham SCITT

What I love about this book is that everything is presented from authority and experience, not merely opinion. When Alan tells the story of the troubled child and the father who beat him in front of him, he doesn't waste time stating 'obviously, this was wrong' but instead allows us to process how we, as teachers, might respond in this situation. I was initially terrified of the numerous pages of appendices, but Alan clearly states how to approach them and why. I therefore enjoyed the debate on 'Britishness'. This was introduced during my secondary school days and I remember we hated how it was presented; however, Alan provides a very good argument for how 'British values' should be explored in schools – and now I will take his insights on board in my own teaching.

Nathan Alexander Kennedy, Secondary PGCE student, University of Sunderland

I highly recommend *Becoming a Teacher* as a core course text. It will be an invaluable companion for trainees throughout the PGCE year and support them during their ECT years too, and even for those contemplating a teaching career and preparing to apply.

Michelle Wormald, Programme Director – Secondary PGCE, University of Hull

What is appealing about Alan's book is that it encompasses so many crucial aspects of ITT. Not only does it relate to key legal elements of the role but has clear links to the Teachers' Standards and professional and personal attributes and values – essential for all teachers. We will be providing all of our trainees with a copy of the book at the start of our training programme.

Stuart Russell, Director of ITT, Kent and Medway Teacher Training

This book is much needed in the ITT sphere, where new teachers grapple with the complexities of what it means to be a teacher. We will definitely use *Becoming a Teacher* with our ITT students, adding it to the essential reading list for professional studies.

Professor Anna Lise Gordon, Director, Institute of Education, St Mary's University, Twickenham

Alan tackles a wide range of issues brilliantly in his book, with an extremely engaging style – covering topics that are of real significance and importance but are also very challenging.

Janet Limberg, Course Leader and Programme Manager, Somerset SCITT

Becoming a Teacher has tremendous merit and value, providing a key point of reference for students. Alan addresses sensitive issues in depth – issues that often cause confusion and uncertainty among trainees and ECTs. The book's format also aligns with the way we encourage trainee teachers to approach their studies, which is to critically analyse and evaluate their practice and search for ways to strengthen and confirm their evolving teacher identities – so it will also appeal to all early career teachers.

Suzanne Allies, Senior Lecturer, School of Education, University of Worcester

I would encourage all trainee teachers to read this book. Alan draws on his own experience to highlight the practical implications of each topic, making it relevant to all teachers, not just trainees. It should be an essential text for all ITT courses.

John Taplin, Programme Facilitator, Northampton TTP

Alan's work has consistently been evaluated at a high level by our PGCE cohorts. We would certainly recommend his book to our PGCE trainees.

Harriet Rhodes, Faculty of Education, University of Cambridge

Alan Newland's sessions are challenging, relevant and important. They inspire our trainees to connect with the core purpose of being a teacher. His book will now be part of our core curriculum.

Ben Sperring, Director, LETTA Teaching School

The content Alan covers in *Becoming a Teacher* is key to enabling trainees to understand their responsibilities as teachers and providing an awareness of professional ethics and British values. Having scenarios for them to reflect upon engages them quickly and raises the key questions concerning them. I will include it in pre-course reading.

Eluned Pickup, Senior Teaching Fellow, PGCE Programme, University of Southampton

We very much endorse Alan's book and are really excited by it. The book's structure provides a great core text for our course and tutors. It is a critical discussion about professionalism – examining the legal, ethical and moral issues, as well as a positive understanding of the Teachers' Standards and fundamental British values, very much supporting the development of those new to the profession.

Davinder Dosanjh, Executive Director, Leicestershire Secondary SCITT

We will be including this book on our pre-course reading list.

Dr Bryony Black, Director of ITE, University of Sheffield

What Alan does in this book is nothing less than magic. With admirable empathy and calm he presents the most difficult and controversial but highly relevant topics, delivering key messages clearly, bravely and with tangible impact without ever sounding patronising, judgemental or confrontational. To have his wisdom on our bookshelf now will be invaluable both for me and my trainees.

Isabella Mora, ITE Programme Leader, 2Schools Consortium

Becoming a Teacher will without question be a core text for our teaching on professional knowledge and pedagogy.

Gareth Evers, Professional Studies Tutor for PGCE Programmes, Middlesex University

I certainly recommend this book for our pre-course reading list.

Juliet Pearce, Director, Hampshire SCITT

Becoming a Teacher really supports the work we do around professional values and teacher identity, and it will be a very useful addition to our reading lists across all of our programmes.

Keither Parker, Associate Head (Education), York St John University

The publication of this book is great news for all our ITE programmes and for our master's level modules.

Kate Brimacombe, Programme Area Leader – Postgraduate Primary ITE, Plymouth Marjon University

I will most certainly be using this book on our courses. The narrative style is lively and refreshing, and portrays a frank and honest discussion of the challenges that teachers face through real-life and authentic anecdotes. It prompts reflection and debate on a number of issues, some of which move us from our comfort zone, but everything is grounded in the real world. I particularly like the reference to character and values and the implications this has for becoming a teacher. I also think its constructive look at fundamental British values and the Teachers' Standards is much needed and long overdue. There are few books that critically examine the profession in this way.

Alison Hales, Senior Lecturer, School of Education, University of Greenwich

Alan delivers brilliant, thought-provoking sessions about professionalism. Our trainees always thoroughly enjoy hearing him speak, and I too always learn a lot from him. Now it's good to have his wisdom and experience packaged together in this book.

Louise Leigh, Director, King Edward's Consortium SCITT

There is very little on the market that covers the wide range of content that Alan covers in *Becoming a Teacher*. We fully support this book and recommend it as part of our professional studies, school placements and to all our professional mentors. It will be a core text and essential reading for those coming on to the PGCE course.

Edmund Boyle, Head of ITT Partnerships, St Mary's University, Twickenham

We are very happy to be adding this book onto our essential reading list. Professionalism and teacher identity is a crucial area for ITE courses, and yet it is one of the hardest areas to instil understanding. I look forward to using this book and signposting our trainees to it as an area of critical importance.

Dylan Gwyer-Roberts, PGCE Secondary Programme Leader, Bath Spa University

The quality of Alan's work is well thought through and presented – and, with the increasing use of online tutorials, a course reader like this will be a great stimulus for group discussions.

Sharon Chester, Director, Lincolnshire SCITT

We've always found Alan's visits and video lectures really useful, so to include his book on our ITE courses will be great.

Damienne Clarke, Deputy Course Leader, PGCE Primary, Birmingham City University

Full of both practical and philosophical advice that is really useful to student teachers, *Becoming a Teacher* is more than essential reading.

Alistair Ross, Emeritus Professor, London Metropolitan University

Alan's style of writing is very clear and engaging. I like the anecdotes he includes that help contextualise issues. The topics he covers delve into a variety of implications for a teacher's career and are an essential part of a teacher's training.

Kate Sida-Nicholls, Secondary PGCE Course Leader, Suffolk and Norfolk SCITT

This book is an exceptionally timely addition to the essential reading for anyone hoping to become a teacher and even for those moving from classroom teaching to senior management. Never has a book which addresses the fundamental questions of what it is to be a teacher been more apposite. I regard *Becoming a Teacher* as a must-read text.

Professor Ruth Merttens, Director, Hamilton Trust

BECOMING A TEACHER

the legal, ethical and moral implications
of entering society's most fundamental profession

ALAN NEWLAND

Crown House Publishing Limited
www.crownhouse.co.uk

Published by
Crown House Publishing
Crown Buildings, Bancyfelin, Carmarthen, Wales, SA33 5ND, UK
www.crownhouse.co.uk

and

Crown House Publishing Company LLC
PO Box 2223, Williston, VT 05495, USA
www.crownhousepublishing.com

First published 2021.

British Library of Cataloguing-in-Publication Data
A catalogue entry for this book is available from the British Library.

Print ISBN 978-178583568-1
Mobi ISBN 978-178583581-0
ePub ISBN 978-178583582-7
ePDF ISBN 978-178583583-4

LCCN 2021939371

Printed and bound in the UK by
TJ Books, Padstow, Cornwall

For Evelyn, Reginald, Pamela and, of course, Monique.

PREFACE

This book is about the values of teaching and the virtues of being a good teacher – what I call a teacher of character. In the last twenty-five years there has been a damaging over-emphasis on the skills and efficiency of teacher competence and an underemphasis on the values and virtues of good teaching. It has become more important to be able to *describe* a good teacher by their performance – of what a teacher teaches – than to *know* a good teacher by the values they model and demonstrate. In my view, this is a mistake. The role of being a teacher requires at least as much public trust (and probably much greater moral responsibility) than any other profession I can think of. In this book I will ask a series of questions: what roles and responsibilities must a good teacher accept? What kind of a person must a good teacher be? What kind of values must they subscribe to? What kinds of virtues must they display and demonstrate? What kind of character must they develop in themselves and their pupils? In other words, if you are a teacher, who are you?

You will be questioned and tested every day when you attempt to impart values to your pupils: every time you select or exclude topics to discuss; every time you insist on an accurate answer rather than a fantastical one; every time you correct a child's misbehaviour rather than tolerate disobedience and impertinence. The ethical and moral dimensions of what you do cannot be ignored or avoided, so it is better that we try to make them more transparent and therefore subject to conscious control.

In writing this book, I have included two preparatory chapters exploring fundamental characteristics of teaching as a practice and teaching's relationship to professionalism to lay the foundations for subsequent discussion, but my principal endeavour is this: firstly, I will explain the key elements of a teacher's legal responsibilities and how you can exercise that new-found authority with confidence. I am regularly struck by how often teachers (including those with experience) are confused and nervous about the exercise of their powers – what they think they can and cannot do; the extent of their disciplinary powers to punish; whether they are even allowed to touch children, let alone search them or use force or restraint where necessary. Chapter 3 on your legal responsibilities and powers will explain all this and reassure you.

Secondly, I will help you to develop an understanding of, and articulate a commitment to, a professional ethic that will inform your identity as a teacher. This begins in Chapter 4 and continues in other sections of the book. I will ask you to think about the key principles of teaching; to identify the characteristics of professional status and practice; to define a profession in your own terms; and to decide whether teaching actually fits within the definition you have given yourself. I will address ethical issues specifically related to the teaching profession – in particular, those that emerge as an outcome of having an ethical code that straddles personal as well as professional values, including 'fundamental British values' and the complex issues teachers must face when dealing with the promotion of tolerance, free speech and identity.

Thirdly, as each new generation of children must be taught the difference between right and wrong, teachers play a key role as agents in cultivating moral understandings. Chapter 5 therefore discusses morality at some length. Teachers must enlist, persuade and secure young people's commitment to those moral standards and get them to believe that they are justified. I want to help you realise the nature of your own moral agency as a teacher by exploring the scope of your own private and public behaviours, and where and when they should be delineated. Where the boundaries lie between your personal and your professional life is a fascinating but complex discussion.

Finally, in Chapter 6 I want you to appreciate the extent to which the challenges of becoming a good teacher are, in themselves, character-building. Your own demonstration and modelling of virtues is part and parcel of becoming a teacher of character, but it is a process racked with ambiguity and challenge. The questions I raise in this chapter are intentional and self-conscious as a necessary part of the process for realising your character as a teacher and resulting in the ultimate acquisition of what Aristotle called 'practical wisdom'.

Don't be intimidated by the mention of Aristotle. This is not a book about Greek philosophy, nor is it even an academic book as such. I have included many activities and appendices which will help you to understand the ideas behind becoming a teacher of character, both in the sense of developing your character and of teaching character as a subject. Some of the appendices are quite extensive in that they allow the reader to explore some issues in much greater depth. For example, had I included all the discussion points related to fundamental British values in the chapters on ethics and morality they would have become very unwieldy; much better in my view to consider the essentials in the main text and examine deeper issues as advanced study later in the appendices.

The book is written in my voice. It is largely an account of personal professional experiences and in some ways could even be described as part-memoir. The style is very direct – addressing the reader in the first person in a deliberate way for reasons that are quite intentional. People have often asked me if all the anecdotes I use are true. Indeed they are. Their apparent implausibility to some is not that they are tall tales, but more a reflection of the dramatic changes in attitudes and values over time. If my tone occasionally sounds paternalistic or long in the tooth, implying that 'In my day, we did it like this …' or 'Years ago, we could do this, that and the other …' it is not to be inferred that I think things were better in former times. Quite the opposite. I merely want to illustrate and emphasise the contrast in values – both professional and societal – that I hope will inform the discussion and encourage you to reflect.

I therefore use a lot of anecdotes – unapologetically. I hope that some of them will motivate, inspire and sometimes move you. Aristotle believed that stories have the power to illuminate human motivation and morality in ways that scientific sources are not necessarily equipped to do. He believed that the development of emotion through story was crucial to the development of moral virtue. Besides, they are entertaining! However, I want the book to feel like it is a conversation with the reader. I want it to be accessible but intelligent and serious. Although I am addressing important professional issues – the fundamentals of this most fundamental of professions – I want to engage the reader in thought, reflection and discussion. I hope the informality of the tone does not grate with the seriousness of the content. I frequently, for example, refer to children as 'kids', which some might regard as unprofessional in itself. You may find that university lecturers or training tutors disapprove of you using the term in a professional context. I am not challenging that; I respect their view. But, for me, it is about the context of language usage. I leave it for others to judge whether my references to children as kids is ever demeaning or patronising. It is certainly not intended.

While I have used references, footnotes and citations, I have tried to minimise these so as not to clutter the text, including them where regard and acknowledgement is due to those who have written extensively about these issues and about whom you may be interested to read further. Above all, though, I want this book to flow like a story. The appendices are intended to provide a number of things: an opportunity for additional reflection on some extremely complex topics that are very high on the agenda of the teacher training requirements, yet find so little time devoted to them on courses or discussed critically with confidence; opportunities to provide practical help and resources for the teaching of fundamental British values through spiritual, moral, social and cultural education and the logical extension of this, virtues and character education; and, finally, an opportunity to compare and contrast the professional codes of other countries and help readers in those countries to situate the themes of this book within their own context.

The book is primarily targeted at trainee teachers – those on school-centred initial teacher training (SCITT) courses or university-led undergraduate or postgraduate courses. As much as the principal audience for this book is trainee teachers, there are wider audiences who will doubtless be interested too – indeed, many very experienced teachers told me (on reading drafts of the manuscript) that it was 'a book for all teachers'.

Tutors and lecturers will find it useful, perhaps, for initiating debate or posing questions in seminars and tutorials. I have therefore included dozens of activities – marked as 'Discuss and reflect' boxes – which can be used either as one-off discussions or as a series of related questions for seminars. These are best used by groups of trainees to initiate discussion, but if you are reading this book alone, then use them as points at which to pause and reflect.

Mentors inducting early career teachers will find the book very useful too. Senior leaders responsible for continuing professional development (CPD) in schools are another relevant audience. There is a lot for teachers of all ages and experience – especially the discussion scenarios, many of which address a range of fascinating issues related to legal, ethical and moral dilemmas in teaching.

The book is structured and formatted to allow the reader to dip in and out. If you choose, you don't even need to read the book from the beginning through to the end – although, of course, I hope you will read it all in due course. Instead, you may wish to read only one particular section and focus on that for now. Any chapter can be taken as an entity in itself for specific study or group discussion. I think the sequence of chapters dealing with legal, ethical and moral issues has some merit logically, although it is not necessary to read them in that order. For that reason, you will find that I make similar points more than once, but (I hope) from a variety of perspectives. This has been a conscious decision, either because I know the book will be read in parts or because the complexity and importance of the issues warrants examination or illustration from a number of different standpoints.

While the book has been written from the perspective of the teaching profession in England, teaching professions in most English-speaking countries are, although far from identical, very similar. For readers outside the UK, the book will provide a fascinating contrast and reflection on how the scope and extent of teaching professionalism emerges and evolves from a particular society's politics, history and culture.

One of my central aims, therefore, is to frame a debate about teaching's fundamental moral purpose. I will ask a lot of questions. I will challenge you personally to consider justifiable answers. I will help you to explore categories and characteristics that define teaching technically – referring to its legal and ethical codes – but go on to discuss how teachers must grapple with the personal and professional dilemmas of competing moral values. I will challenge you to define and apply the virtues shaped by your experience of working – day in, day out – in a classroom full of diverse and challenging young minds. Finally, I want you to imagine how such testing experiences will develop you into a teacher of character and, ultimately, one of practical wisdom too. I hope you enjoy the experience.

ACKNOWLEDGEMENTS

For their support in critically reading the earlier manuscripts I would like to thank: Bryony Black, Jenny Bosworth, Davinder Dosanjh, Anna Lise Gordon, Rien Haest, David James, Louise Leigh, Ruth Merttens, Jenny Murray, Eluned Pickup, Harriet Rhodes, Alistair Ross, John Taplin, Katy Wilkins, Guy Willems, Justin Woolliscroft and a number of others who would prefer to remain anonymous. Their constructive comments and contributions at a formative stage improved this book immeasurably. Any errors I let slip through are, of course, entirely my responsibility. A special mention needs to go to my editor, Emma Tuck, who has done a brilliant job of lubricating my clunky prose.

My thanks also go to: Suzanne Allies, Julie Bostock, Brigitte Boylan, Kate Brimacombe, Sharon Chester, Damienne Clarke, Allan Dick, Patricia Duncan, Caroline Elbra-Ramsay, Gareth Evers, Maddy Fowler, Bryher Freight, Chris Griffiths, Dylan Gwyer-Roberts, Alison Hales, Sarah-Jane Hamilton, Claire Harnden, Maisey Hodges, Ruth Hollier, Nathan Kennedy, Nicole Larkin, Aimee Lascelles, Janet Limberg, Eilidh Macpherson, Michaela McCaugherty, Jo McShane, Banna Millar, Hannah Mitchell, Isabella Mora, Keither Parker, Juliet Pearce, Alison Pemberton, Katarina Pillai, Stuart Russell, Natasha Ryan, Amelia Shimells, Kate Sida-Nicholls, Harvinder Singh, Amelia Sowden, Ben Sperring, Amy Strachan, Daniel Strachan, Megan Turnbull, Michael Walker and Michelle Wormald.

For their willingness to assess the book proposal, help me with technical matters of expertise or understand and navigate teaching professions in other parts of the world, I would like to thank: Ian Avent, Pauline Barnes, Anne Beitlers, Ed Boyle, Julie Brierley, Vanitha C., Mindy R. Carter, Agnes Chigona, Vanencia Chiloane, Viv Ellis, Deanne Fishburn, Donna Fogelsong, Michael Fullard, Alex Gunn, Lesley Hoskin, Robyn Ilten-Gee, Joni Kolman, Alan Lawton, Bruce Maxwell, David Montemurro, Kelly A. Parkes, Leonie Paulson, Margaret Plunkett, Ozlem Sensoy, Shaheen Shariff and Trevor Thomas Stewart.

For all the things I have learned about teaching, education and the development of my own character over the last four decades, my thanks go to: Isabelle Alexander, Desmond Awoonor-Gordon, Richard Crease, Sue Creber, Dolly Day, Jeni Durowoju, Dave Edwards, Ruth Edwards, Duane Emmanuel, Jane Garfield, Clee Griffiths, Elizabeth Haines, Olive Irwin, Tozun Issa, Lorna Jarrett, Emma Lewenden-Strutt, Barry Lewis, Sharman Masterson, Ruth Merttens, Lissa Paul, Nicola Robinson, Alistair Ross, Leon Tong, Hardeep Kaur Virdee and, of course, Maxine Williams herself and all the children – too numerous to mention – to whom I wish I had been a better teacher.

CONTENTS

Prologue:

THERE IS ALWAYS ONE … THE MAXINE STORY

If you are going to become a teacher, you will soon have lots of great stories to tell. Let's start with one of mine – it is absolutely true. It begins in the first few weeks of my very first term, way back in September 1979. I lost a child on the London Underground. Beat that for a way to embark on your teaching career.

I had just finished my teacher training in London. I'd had a really good final teaching practice in a nice suburban school. I had taught a 'topic' – as we called it in those days – on dinosaurs. Kids love dinosaurs. Diplodocus, Pterodactyl, Tyrannosaurus rex and all that – terrifying and great fun. I had collected some nice resources – books, dinosaur models, posters and so on – and finished my teaching practice with a merit award. I was pleased with myself. When I got to my new school in Hackney, East London, I found that I had been given a lively Year 6 class (and we all know what it means when a class is described as lively, right?) and so I knew I had to get them onside pretty quickly. I thought it might be a good idea to repeat my dinosaur topic. After all, why reinvent the wheel? I had all these lovely resources and ideas. I could use them again and get off to a flying start with my new class. Then I had an even better idea: I would take them on a trip to see the amazing life-size exhibits of dinosaurs at the Natural History Museum in South Kensington. That would *really* get these kids on my side.

In those days, getting to the Natural History Museum from Hackney involved a bus ride to King's Cross followed by a Tube ride all the way across London. I don't know if you have ever been to King's Cross Underground station, but it has undergone a transformation in recent years. It needed it. Hundreds of thousands of people pass through that station every single day. It is an easy place for someone to get lost …

Imagine the scene. There I was, about six weeks into teaching, with thirty 10- and 11-year-old kids. I was on my own (except for a mum who worked part-time at the school – known in those days as a 'lady helper'!). We are on a platform at King's Cross Underground. Everyone is excited. It is a day out for us all. The kids are chatting and laughing; their main focus is comparing what sandwiches they have brought for lunch. I spot that the first train coming is not going in our direction, so I am calling out to the kids: 'Stand back, everyone! It's not our train!' I am trying to make myself heard above the bustle of the commuters – it is still only 9.30am, for heaven's sake. I am disco-dancing up and down the platform trying to keep the kids back from the edge: 'This is not our train, everybody! Stand back! Stand back! It's not our train!' Just as I think I have got the situation under control … I haven't.

There is always one, isn't there? It is Maxine. She is a lovely kid but she is not taking a blind bit of notice of me – she is on a day out with her friends and full of excitement. The train comes in, the doors open and she jumps on thinking everyone is going to follow her. The kids are shouting: 'Maxine! Get off, it's not our train!' She turns, but in the pushing and shoving of commuters getting on and off, it is too late. Before she can reach the doors, they close.

This incident happened over four decades ago, but I have never forgotten her face. Have you ever seen that painting by the Norwegian artist Edvard Munch called *The Scream*? Well, her face looked just like that.

Now, I want you to pause for a moment with that image in your mind's eye. Do you think it is funny? You can be honest – I am big enough to take you laughing at me. Or perhaps you are thinking, 'My God, what a nightmare. I hope that never happens to me!' Whatever is going on in your mind, here is a question for you to contemplate: how do you think the kids reacted in that moment?

With horror? Shock? Panic? Maybe a few tears? Perhaps even one or two of them laugh nervously out of fear? If you think some reacted with laughter, then you are only half right. It wasn't just laughter. It was more like hysterical cackling – and it wasn't just some of them. It was all thirty kids screaming with raucous, uncontrolled hilarity. 'Maxine! You idiot!' they shouted, running after her, chasing the train down the platform for as long as possible before it disappeared into the darkened tunnels of the London Underground. I was the one petrified and in a state of horror, shock and panic – not least because I didn't even know where the train was going. These days there are information boards, regular announcements, bright lights, CCTV, help points and friendly people in blue uniforms everywhere. Back in 1979 there was nothing – London Underground stations were dark and dingy places. You had to go back up to street level to find someone to help.

While the kids were rolling about laughing, I was chasing back and forth trying to calm them down and gather them together. 'Mr Newland, what are you going to do now?' they roared hysterically. They thought it was great. Even my lady helper couldn't suppress her giggles, so she was no help at all. Finally, after a couple of minutes, I managed to settle the kids enough to leave them with her while I went to get some assistance. Just as I was about to set off, somebody walked round the corner and gave me one hell of a shock. A policeman? Wrong. The head teacher? Wrong again. Maxine's parents? Nope (although I will tell you about Maxine's mum in a minute).

Well, you may or may not be surprised to learn – it was Maxine. Now, before you think she has pulled off some kind of David Blaine-type optical illusion, the next stop along the line is Euston Square, only fifty seconds away. She had obviously jumped off the train there, ran over the footbridge, spotted there was a train coming back in the opposite direction, got straight on it, no doubt with the balletic dexterity she did the first time, and – I kid you not – she was back with us in about three minutes. OK, four. Tops. She returned so quickly the other kids hadn't even finished laughing.

Phew! Was I relieved! Off we went to the Natural History Museum and had a great day. We ate our sandwiches. We saw Dippy the Diplodocus and got a fantastic tour of the dinosaur exhibits from the education staff. They drew some fabulous pictures. We learned so much about dinosaurs – it was amazing. Of course, when I got the kids back into class I asked them to write about 'all the wonderful things you've learned about dinosaurs from the Natural History Museum'.

What do you think they wrote about? Yeah, you guessed it. All they wrote about was Maxine getting on the wrong train. But I will tell you this – and this might surprise or even shock you – it didn't even enter my head to report the incident to the head teacher. I have often wondered why. You would think that losing a child on the London Underground is a fairly reportable incident, wouldn't you? Over the years, having reflected on it, I have concluded that in a funny sort of way nothing *really* happened. Yes, I know I lost a child; you don't need to remind me. But there was nothing much to report. Maxine wasn't hurt. She wasn't even upset. Maybe she was a little embarrassed for a few minutes because the other kids were laughing at her, but nobody, including the children, saw it as an issue.

Fast-forward twenty years. It is 1999 and I am now the head teacher of a primary school in Hackney. My Year 6 teacher is planning to take her twenty-four kids to the Natural History Museum because – yes, you have guessed it – she is doing a class topic on good old dinosaurs. How many adults do you think she is taking with her on this trip? Four? Five? Actually it is six. The school's health and safety policy (I hadn't even heard the phrase 'health and safety' back in 1979) required a minimum of four adults – and, of course, this time most of them are not lady helpers; they are trained and qualified teaching assistants. There are also two parents who won't let their children go on the trip unless they are in attendance.

The teacher – a fantastic young woman with bags of energy and ideas, who had already spent her weekend doing a reconnaissance visit to the museum, plus completing a risk assessment and insurance forms, collating permission slips and planning some lovely activities – sets off to the Natural History Museum with twenty-four kids and six other adults. She takes the bus down to King's Cross to get the Tube to South Kensington. They get onto the platform of the Underground … and guess what happens? You think that this time maybe a teacher gets on the wrong train? No. One of the parents? Not that either. And no, before you say it, Maxine has not grown up to be one of the parents (I have heard that wisecrack a hundred times).

Believe it or not, exactly the same thing happens – only this time, it isn't *one* child, it's *four*! In spite of the fact that the kids are all in baseball caps and hi-vis vests and organised into groups with an adult standing next to them. When the train pulls in, the teacher is calling out: 'It's not our train, everybody! Stand back! Stand back!' But are they listening? Of course they aren't. They are on a day out with their mates and as excited as bees on a lavender bush. The train doors open, a group of girls jump on thinking everyone will follow them. The other kids are shouting: 'Get off! Get off! It's not our train!' Before they can, in the melee of pushing and shoving, the doors close and the train moves off.

What do you think the reaction of the other kids is this time? Laughter? No. Not even close. This time it is pandemonium. There is screaming, crying, hysteria – not just from the four on the train but also from the other twenty children on the platform, including half of the adults. There are no dinosaurs this time. Instead, there is a full-scale search and rescue operation because these four girls didn't do what Maxine did – jump off at the next stop and come straight back. Oh no, they were so freaked out that they stayed on the train until the end of the line. And this was the Metropolitan Line. It terminates thirty miles away in Buckinghamshire!

Meanwhile, I am at school. Mid-morning I get a telephone call. 'This is the station manager at Amersham. I've got four of your girls here. What do you want me to do with them?' I sent out a teacher in a taxi to bring them back. They return later that afternoon with no harm done. The next day I got those twenty-four kids together and asked them: 'How many of you have been on the London Underground before?' I was amazed. Out of twenty-four Hackney born-and-bred kids, only eight had ever been on the London Underground. Now, that is a change of lifestyle for you, isn't it? Twenty years previously, 10-year-old Maxine had taken herself off to school every day using buses and Tube trains without the slightest fear or hesitation. She had obviously gained knowledge of the system, developed a sense of direction and worldliness and, most importantly, the confidence to deal with a situation herself if something didn't quite go to plan. This group of kids – it isn't their fault and I am not blaming them – didn't have what Maxine had. Nearly all of them lived within three hundred yards of the school but their parents were regularly driving them to and from school every day. They weren't building up that worldliness, confidence and ability to assess risk – and deal with it – in the way Maxine clearly could.

The reason I relate this story is not because of the reaction of the children but because of the reaction of their parents. As I said earlier, I didn't mention the first incident to my head teacher – a wonderful man who had a huge influence on me and who would not have been censorious or judgemental even if I had. It is just that I never thought of it. I never thought of telling Maxine's mum either, although I remember Maxine's mum as well. She was about six foot two. A matriarchal Jamaican woman whose attitude to her kids and school was something like: 'You behave yourself in school and do what your teacher tells you!' If I had told Maxine's mum, I think I know what her reaction would have been. She would have probably given Maxine the hairdryer treatment for 'not listening to your teacher'!

The parents of the second group of kids were very different. Within hours of the news getting out, I had about a dozen of them outside my office giving me earache. 'Why hadn't we done this, that and the other?' 'Why hadn't we organised a coach?' 'Why had we exposed the children to the hazards of the London Underground?' One by one, I calmed them down, explaining that the teacher had planned the trip perfectly well. Nobody was hurt, these things happen and so on.

Nevertheless, I went home that night feeling quite depressed. Here was a talented, hard-working and conscientious young teacher who had only been in the job for a year. She had planned a fantastic educational trip for her class and it went wrong through no fault of her own. Now the only thanks she seemed to be getting was criticism from people who I thought should know better – parents; people who you might think would understand that when you take kids on an outing, things don't always run smoothly. Reflecting on it later that evening, I realised that judgement was unfair. Why? Because these days we all do it – we are all much more ready to voice our thoughts and opinions than we once were. In many ways, that is a very good thing. I do it myself occasionally in restaurants, both when the food and service is excellent and when it isn't up to scratch. We should give feedback – positive as well as constructive. But the incident also made me reflect on the changing nature of the relationship between professional groups like teachers and their 'clients' – in our case, parents – and how that relationship has changed over the years and how it continues to change.

A transformation in ethical expectations has affected nearly all professional groups, not just teachers. In fact, a better illustration of this phenomenon is the medical profession. You may be too young to remember this, but I can tell you for a fact that twenty-five years ago doctors were treated almost like gods. Few people ever questioned the judgement of a doctor. In those days, most of us went to our GP, meekly reported our health issue, gratefully received our prescription (illegibly handwritten) and scurried off to the chemist to get our medicine. Now, when I see my doctor, I expect to be engaged in a conversation. I expect to ask questions and get some understandable answers in plain English about the issues affecting my health. I expect to be involved in the decisions and options about any treatment that might be required.

When I was a young man, the public were far more deferential to the likes of doctors, lawyers, accountants, architects, engineers and, believe it or not, teachers. These days we, the public, are still largely respectful to these professions, but we now expect, quite rightly, that professional people are accountable for their actions, especially when they take important decisions on our behalf. On reflection, I think that is what these parents at my school were doing – asking questions and making me, as the head teacher, accountable for the decisions that had been taken on their behalf. It was a challenging episode, I grant you, but it was one that parents have a right to expect as part of their relationship with people like teachers.

The point here is not, I repeat not, to alarm you. This is not a story that should deter you from taking children out on school trips; quite the opposite, in fact. Take kids out as much as you can. They love educational visits and learn a lot from them, especially when they are well planned, focused and challenging. When children get a little older, you may be lucky enough to take them on a residential visit somewhere, perhaps to an outward-bound centre or on a geography field trip. I can assure you that they will come back different people. You will find your working relationship with them has changed too. Don't be deterred.

This story illustrates how society's expectations change. You are about to enter the teaching profession – a profession that will be a different place in ten or fifteen years' time, with different legal, ethical and moral expectations. It will be different again in twenty-five or thirty years. Change is inevitable. We have to accommodate change and, where we can, try to embrace it. So, I tell you this not as an ex-head teacher reminiscing about the long-lost good old days that, in reality, never were. I tell you because, as members of a well-regarded professional group – teachers – you will be the highly trained, highly educated experts who are best placed to inform the necessary changes that may be in the best interests of the children and their parents, whom we should think of as our clients – the people we are here to serve.

I want you to reflect on the Maxine story as you read through the rest of this book and I ask you a series of questions and engage you in some thinking and discussion about the nature and challenges of becoming a teacher. Not just any teacher, but a *teacher of character*. If you are in the profession for any length of time, you will experience an incident like the one I did with Maxine. When you do, you will be tested to make decisions – sometimes in the spur of the moment, sometimes under huge pressure, sometimes when there is more than one right answer and more than one justified response to resolve an issue. In such circumstances, your character both as a person and a teacher will be built. That character will also be the model you demonstrate to the children you teach.

Chapter 1

WHAT IS TEACHING?

Our intelligent minds have evolved to target objects. From aiming spears while hunting animals in the forests and savannahs in prehistory through to launching projectiles and rockets at real or potential enemies today, we have needed to learn to target. We aim at metaphorical targets too: destinations on a map, dream jobs, or gods in their heavens. We need goals in our lives. Unless we keep track of where we are and how we intend to move from one place to the next in pursuit of our goals, we soon lose our ability to navigate.[1] Teachers (and loving parents) show us things we haven't seen before, point out new dimensions of the things we have, and present confusing stuff in understandable and manageable ways to help us learn some of the crucial skills that enable us to orientate ourselves towards a given goal. Eventually, we become more adept and gradually take over these skills to steer and pilot ourselves to reach these goals independently.

Another lesson from the London Underground

I was on a Tube train in London some years ago when a father got on with his son, a boy of no more than 5 or 6 years old. I can't say this account is word for word because it happened a long time ago and I didn't record it, but these are the parts I remember vividly. Within a minute or two the boy was looking up at the linear diagram above his head showing the stations on the Piccadilly Line of the London Underground. The father noticed his son's interest and said: 'That's the map of all the stations on the Piccadilly Line. It's so we know where to get off.'

'Where are we getting off?'

'Knightsbridge. Can you see where it says Knightsbridge?'

The boy shook his head, so his father pointed it out.

'See? It says *Knights … bridge*,' underlining the syllables with his finger.

'Why do you think it is called Knightsbridge?'

1 See Jordan Peterson, *Twelve Rules for Life: An Antidote to Chaos* (London: Penguin, 2018), ch. 4.

'I don't know – does a knight have a bridge there?'

'Maybe,' replied the father, amused. 'It's a good question. He may have at one time. Can you count how many stations we've got to go until we get there?'

'Where are we now?' asked the boy.

'Here ... at King's Cross. Look, *King's ... Cross*.'

'Why is it called King's Cross? Did a king have a cross there?'

The father laughed again. 'Yeah! He did actually.'

'Why?'

'In the olden days, people travelling to London on horses or on foot needed to know they were getting close to the centre of the city, so there were crosses to mark the way.'

'Really?'

'Yeah. Look, here's King's Cross and here's Knightsbridge. Let's count the stations ...'

At that point, the boy moved to climb onto the seat to see the diagram better but his father told him to get down. The boy asked why he couldn't stand on the seats and his father replied: 'Because people have to sit on these seats and they don't want to sit where your dirty feet have been.'

For the next minute or so the father pointed at the stations and read the names as the boy counted them. When he had finished, the boy went back to Covent Garden – one of the stations pointed out by his father.

'Does that say "garden"?'

'Yes.'

'Is there a garden there?'

'Not any more,' replied his father. 'But I think there was once.'

'What's a covent?'

'Another name for a convent, I think. That's a place where nuns live.'

'What are nuns?'

'Women who love God, pray a lot and do good things for poor people. But it doesn't say *Convent* Garden – it says *Covent* Garden. See, there's no "n" in it. If there was an "n" there (pointing), it would say convent.'

At that point another passenger, equally entertained by this masterclass of paternal tuition, pointed out to the little boy: 'Actually, you're right! There was once a convent in a garden there, and that's why it used to be called Convent Garden!'

The boy's face lit up and he looked at his father with a satisfied grin. His father laughed. It was my stop. So I got off.

This father may have consciously learned some teaching techniques – questioning, counting by pointing, sounding out letters and syllables – or he simply may have intuited the behaviours of how to pass on skills and knowledge, motivated by his love for his child. But it wasn't just skills and knowledge the father was passing on; he was passing on morality too. At the point where he corrected his son's attempt to stand on the seats, he explained why he shouldn't – thus regulating the behaviour the boy ought to display and thereby passing on virtues and values. Either way, the father was doing a brilliant job at *teaching* his son.

Humans developed teaching – the process by which to educate – to answer the questions that only humans ask. As far as we know, human beings are the highest developed proponents of the ability to consciously question and then set targets from which to learn. As far as we know, no other species has been able to refine the practice of teaching and educating its young to the extent that humans have: the passing on of skills to use tools, the wisdom to imbibe knowledge, the development of reasoning and judgement, the refinement of perception and intuition and, above all, the constant asking of the question 'why?'[2]

Teaching as a calling

What teachers teach and what children learn is not solely focused on the cognitive. It is also about how to want, to feel, to do and to be. I often hear trainee teachers tell me that teaching is a 'vocation'. I understand what they mean, but sometimes I think they confuse this with modern connotations of the word, which focus on training in the practical application of skills. The word vocation comes from the Latin *vocare* meaning 'a calling', which referred to a religious 'calling to serve God', as a priest might. The

2 See Yuval Noah Harari, *21 Lessons for the 21st Century* (London: Jonathan Cape, 2018), ch. 19.

word has also evolved to express a sense of purpose that others, such as doctors, nurses and teachers, might feel about their role in society. What they do is not just a job, it is a mission.

A person with a deep sense of vocation, therefore, is someone who is not dependent on constant positive reinforcement. If you are hoping your class of children will thank you every day for the wonderful lessons you teach them, you are probably going to be disappointed. You will almost certainly not get a daily adrenalin rush of triumph at witnessing some cognitive leap forward. There will be times when you may not even feel much sense of satisfaction. I once went a whole year feeling frustrated, undervalued and, I admit, angry – but I went home every night still knowing I was doing a job that was intrinsically good.

For the majority of the children you will teach, any realisation that you have done a good job may come as a reflection later in their life, when it is probably too late for them to tell you. They may suddenly remember a moment in your class when they recall the patient way you showed them for the umpteenth time how to tie their shoelaces or the gentle, sympathetic tone you used in order to explain an arithmetical procedure, or the excitement triggered by the passion you had for history, geography, science or sports. It may even come as late as when they are themselves parents, perhaps trying to teach their own children something for the first time. During the various lockdowns of the COVID-19 pandemic, it struck me how often parents appeared on television and radio singing the praises of their children's teachers; until they had to 'homeschool' them, they hadn't realised the extent of the knowledge and skills required and the sheer hard work involved in teaching children.

This is an important conceptual lesson for a teacher, or indeed anyone in any profession. Most of the really important fundamental achievements in human existence occur over a generation or longer, not in the timeline of a day, a month, a year or even a working life. We must satisfy ourselves that we are committing to a generational process that transcends our lifetimes. The brevity of our lives as teachers is compensated for by subscription to a historic commitment. Your teaching, as technically proficient as it may be, is not merely about passing on skills and knowledge or even creating opportunities for experiences that enable growth and reflection. Your teaching contributes significantly to the development of moral values: the knowledge of the difference between right and wrong; the ability to choose between right and wrong; the capacity to select and employ a range of virtues that will form the kind of character that can stand up for right and stand against wrong.

This book makes the claim that teaching is a profession (a discussion we will address shortly), but that is not an assumption you should take for granted. Indeed, whether teaching is a profession or not has been a hotly contested notion at times, not least in recent decades. In many ways, professions are a particular construct of a society at a given time and place, and teaching is no different. The demise of communism at the end of the 1980s resulted in the liberal-democratic model of government dominating the global stage. It also heralded a new and rampant age of neoliberal economics. In my view, both of these phenomena have had huge implications for the way professions in general, and teaching in particular, are perceived and new ones conceived (just look at the professions that have emerged from the new generation of tech giants in the last twenty-five years: front- and back-end developers, app and user interface designers, community and content managers and more). Established professions like medicine, law and teaching have not escaped the effects of political change which have included the intense scrutiny and questioning of professional standards and autonomy. In recent years, senior politicians in the UK (including successive secretaries of state for education) have chosen to speak of teaching as a 'craft' one minute and as a 'profession' the next, judging when they think it politically expedient to do so.

Unlike the parent with his son on the Underground train, teachers teach in a systematic, scientific and technical way. The demands of imparting skills and knowledge to a class of thirty children requires different techniques than with a single individual. But a good teacher soon learns to think of her class as if she were talking to an individual – a technique that charismatic orators know well. Firstly, speak to an identifiable individual within a large audience – capture their attention, engage them with a compelling narrative and complement it with appropriate gestures and expressions – then replicate this with another audience member, then another and so on. This is what good speakers do with an audience and what good teachers can learn to do with a class.

Teaching as analogy

When I am speaking to my audiences, I will often draw analogies with other professions and their practices. There are times when I compare teachers to soldiers, for example, not because we think of children as 'the enemy' but because teaching requires courage, sometimes enormous amounts of it, to go out and face adversity and even conflict every day. But we still do so, as a *duty*. I sometimes compare teaching to acting. Again, not because I think teachers are creating illusions or fictional states of being in which their audience is expected to suspend disbelief (which they are), but because teachers must train for and prepare to engage minds in extended states of elevated consciousness and imagination. They must motivate and inspire, rousing an audience (their class) to an emotional response and creating a desire to want to know more once they have left the theatre (the classroom). They must learn their lines and know the script (their subject knowledge) both in the immediate sense of what they are about to teach but also by knowing the wider context – in the same way that an actor must know the wider context of a character, a playwright and a play. There is a significant dramatic and artistic dimension to teaching. A colleague of mine even believes that in order for teachers to teach, it is not possible for them to be themselves; they must create a version of themselves, a persona, that they find a way to 'act out'. Whatever the psychological dimensions to the role, teachers should recognise, like actors, that they must engage the imaginations of their audience and bring expression, creativity and flair to their performance.

In spite of these strong parallels to performance art, teaching is still much more than even this. How teachers teach and how children learn is not merely systematic, scientific and technical; nor is it just about acquiring information, knowledge or understanding; nor evaluating claims and discerning truths. What teachers teach and what children learn is much more than all these things – it is about how to know your desires, how to evaluate your feelings, how to know what to do, when to do it and, above all, to know how to be.[3]

Teaching and secularism

Evaluating feelings, knowing what to do, when to do it and how to be brings me to the idea of secularism and its relationship to teaching. I do not want to suggest that I am privileging secular perspectives of teaching over religious ones; indeed, I refer to and endorse a variety of faith-based ideas later in the book. The Israeli historian and social philosopher Yuval Noah Harari has written interestingly about this topic in ways that have much to say about teaching, and they are relevant at this point.[4]

Secularism is first, and perhaps foremost, a commitment to a rational *truth* based on evidence and observation. It does not sanctify any single person, group or idea as the sole arbiter of truth but seeks to reveal truth from wherever it comes. If you are a primary school teacher, you may take young children's naive understanding of truth for granted. Don't. If you are a science or a humanities teacher, you won't need to be persuaded about the centrality of such a fundamental value in what you are trying to teach. But, as we have seen, teaching is not just about curriculum subjects; it is about how people know the truth of their desires, their feelings and their being.

Secularism is imbued with a commitment to *compassion* – an understanding of the harm inflicted by suffering. This is not to suggest that those with religious faith do not have compassion – of course they do – but secularists ask questions of issues like suffering in a different way. They do not ask: 'Does God want this?' or even 'Why is God

3 See Michael Hand, *A Theory of Moral Education* (London and New York: Routledge, 2018), p. 30.

4 Yuval Noah Harari's trilogy on the expanse of human history is highly recommended: *Sapiens: A Brief History of Humankind* (London: Penguin, 2011), *Homo Deus: A Brief History of Tomorrow* (London: Penguin, 2015) and *21 Lessons for the 21st Century* (London: Jonathan Cape, 2018) all have fascinating insights about the relationship of faith to secularism and the way values have been passed on through culture and teaching.

allowing this?' but rather: 'What harm is being done?' As a teacher, try to make rules that the children will see as rational and compassionate; rules that try to prevent harm or ensure fairness, not ones that appear only to enforce authority or conformity.

Secularism claims to have a particular commitment to *equality* – its advocates are suspicious of hierarchies. To them, suffering is suffering whoever experiences it. Knowledge is knowledge whoever discovers it. They do not privilege the experiences, discoveries or history of a particular group or nation; although they may be proud of the uniqueness of their own nation, they don't confuse uniqueness with superiority.

Secularists also believe that we cannot seek truth or a way out from suffering without having the *freedom* to think, question, investigate, doubt and challenge. Teaching in modern British schools is not a didactic affair, although it was at one time. Now, there is no place in schools for a Thomas Gradgrind, imparting only 'facts'. Teachers and children must be free to challenge and test facts.

It therefore takes *courage* to employ these values, especially when we meet ignorance, prejudice and bigotry. The loss of one truth to another more refined truth is not a threat to a secularist. A secularist will not turn violent because their truth starts to crumble. Teachers should not, and indeed must not, feel threatened because pupils respectfully and intellectually challenge the basis on which, for example, school rules are made. We must not feel undermined by children coming into school with better knowledge and skills in web design or computer coding. However, we should not and must not shy away from ethical and moral challenges that might come from the ignorance and prejudice of any cultural community.[5]

Finally, secularists cherish taking *responsibility*. They believe that the solutions to human problems are within the agency of human beings. This does not mean that religious people or nationalists cannot or do not believe in human agency. They can and do, but a secular education teaches children to distinguish appropriate categories of truth from belief. Most religious people and religious communities can recognise the fundamental importance of this distinction too, but teachers must be alert to the challenges posed by people who do not hold secular values.[6]

5 I clearly remember the doubt and uncertainty – or perhaps the absence of courage – that teachers like me (and those in the police, medical and social work professions) displayed as knowledge emerged about the prevalence of female genital mutilation being perpetrated in some cultural and faith communities in the UK in the 1990s. The dominant belief at the time was, firstly, to misname a crime by referring to it as 'female circumcision' and, secondly, that professional authorities had 'no right to interfere' in the cultural and religious practices of minority communities. This was both a confusion of secular values and an abdication of moral courage.

6 For more on secularism and education, see Harari, *21 Lessons for the 21st Century*, ch. 1.

I say all this as a person of religious faith myself, but we must be alert to the distinction between faith and fact, spiritual and temporal, emotional and rational. Religious truth is valid truth, but it is not in the same category as objective truth which is established by empirical evidence and facts. Teachers can teach both kinds of truth honestly and with ethical and moral conviction, but we must call out the distinction and teach our pupils to know it too.

Discuss and reflect

- How does teaching on the basis of secular values cohere with, or diverge from, teaching on the basis of faith-based values?

The difference between teaching and education

Obviously, teaching and education is not the same thing. A child can be taught the mysteries of astrology, mindfulness, Zen Buddhism and the art of motorcycle maintenance, but that is not an education. They might be taught to pick pockets, forge documents or embezzle funds. That is not an education. Being taught only mathematics, to the exclusion of everything else, is not an education either. Acquiring an education, therefore, implies both an initiation into a generalised culture and the achievement of a specific set of outcomes of understanding, which include a wide range of complex, rational and cognitive challenges deemed worthwhile and valuable by society.[7]

In contrast to an education, indoctrination is an inculcation of belief without understanding or willingness to evaluate those beliefs. I have heard some people claim that teaching is mere indoctrination. The answer to such people is that it is not. Not if teaching relies on rational justifications for propositions that are held to be true. Not if it proposes standards that are held to be justified by regular testing and verifying. Not if ideas are open to revision and correction. Indoctrination is the reverse of all that; it is cajoling, bullying and seduction into beliefs that lack the force of relevance and argument.[8]

7 For more on teaching and education as initiation, see Richard S. Peters, *Ethics and Education* (London: Unwin, 1974), ch. 1.

8 See Hand, *A Theory of Moral Education*, p. 6.

Teachers therefore have a moral purpose too. Should society give public recognition to someone who teaches others to steal or embezzle? No, they should not. Should society publicly recognise someone who teaches astrology, crystal healing or Zen Buddhism – subjects that cannot be rationally justified, tested or verified? No, they should not. Even someone who teaches mathematics to the exclusion of all else is not publicly recognised as a teacher but as a tutor. An education includes the teaching of subjects that are rationally justifiable, testable and verifiable, where learning is acquired through formal and informal initiation into a wider moral culture, lending weight to the idea that an education is both taught and caught. (Although, there are some curriculum subjects, like mathematics and music, that are much more effectively taught rather than caught.) Nevertheless, an education requires the initiate to subscribe to moral standards as part of their initiation. Teachers are not, therefore, trainers or coaches, and nor are they instructors or tutors. They are *educators* (from the Latin root *ducare* – 'to lead out').

As a naive young teacher, it took me some years before I realised this. I undermined my own professionalism by mistakenly promoting the idea (very fashionable at the time and still heard in some quarters) that teaching is really about facilitating and enabling children to learn. For a long time, I saw myself as someone whose role was to reveal diverse but equally valid versions of knowledge, narrative interpretations of history and social constructions of truth, so that children could choose which they thought best fitted their background and culture. I thought this would be hugely empowering for them. I also thought they would see the point in education if they could only assemble their own definitions of knowledge rather than have this foisted on them like some oppressive cultural hegemony. It sounds incredibly unsophisticated and dewy-eyed now, but I was far from being the only one.

The political contexts of teaching

Educational debates in the 1970s and 1980s seemed all-encompassing and all-consuming, often ideologically divisive and at times uncompromisingly authoritarian. It sometimes felt as if you had to be on one side or the other: a traditionalist or a progressive, a die-hard believer in either comprehensive schools or selective education. The ideological nature of teaching seemed to apply to every subject, even down to teaching 5-year-olds how to read. Indeed, this was one of the most fiercely fought battlegrounds. You were either in the revolutionary vanguard for teaching reading with 'real books' or you were an incorrigible conservative forcing phonic methods and 'reading schemes' on the poor little beggars. I was in the former camp, convinced that children's language and literacy emerged through organic reading and writing activities. Teachers like me never used the word 'literacy' – it was always 'language development'. As a teacher in the 1970s, 1980s and even well into the 1990s, you felt yourself to be either behind the barricades or in front of them, but never in-between. Today, I see the world – and teaching – in much more complex and nuanced terms. A good teacher must resolve the tensions between educational ideals on the one hand and institutional and political realities on the other.

While I never abandoned the idea that, above all, I wanted children to discover a lifelong love of learning, I now see teaching as a much more graduated and varied set of skills and knowledge, which has within it a distinct ethical and moral purpose. It involves generating – and passing on – established values and cultural norms to young, aspiring citizens. If being a teacher meant merely facilitating or enabling children to learn, would it be necessary for teachers to have even half the skills, knowledge and qualifications currently required? I think not. Even within the teaching profession, which is relatively un-hierarchical compared to some, there are hierarchies of skills and knowledge that differentiate teachers in different subjects and phases. Indeed, without underestimating either, you could reasonably ask whether an early years teacher really needs the same specialist subject knowledge and qualifications as a teacher of, let's say, A level physics. While there is a wealth of research showing the importance of the early years as the foundation of successful learning, it has also been argued that an early years teacher's professional knowledge is underpinned by principles more heavily weighted to that of a craft, being focused on effective oral communication, personalised classroom management and organisational skills.

If certain areas of teaching are more like an art than a science, more like a collection of craft skills than a matrix of responsibilities and accountabilities, then some people argue that teaching is more resistant to being codified and professionally described and less easily transferred from one person to another through professional training.[9] For others, teaching is more than mere expert subject knowledge and the application of acquired technical skills; it is an indefinable cocktail of personality, character, intuition and on-the-job experience.

Teaching risk

The children coming into our schools now are perhaps (at least on a strictly physical level) the safest in history: school buildings and facilities are secure and maintained to high standards, children have little risk of accidents that will seriously injure them, there is markedly less risk of personal danger such as fighting (which was commonplace thirty years ago) and there is little risk of unsupervised exposure to strangers. However, in spite of all this there is a widespread feeling that, with regard to both

9 See, for example, Elizabeth Campbell, *The Ethical Teacher* (Milton Keynes: Open University Press, 2003) and David Carr, *Professionalism and Ethics in Teaching* (Abingdon and New York: Routledge, 1999).

physical and mental resilience, children are much more vulnerable than they once were. Rates of obesity, mental ill health, depression, self-harm and even suicide are reportedly at all-time highs among the young.

While these are real concerns that cannot be ignored or downplayed, teachers – like parents – ultimately have to decide whether their purpose is to make children safe or make them competent. Of course, you would want to answer both, but the choice between the two is not always straightforward. Reducing risk to the extent they are unlikely ever to have an accident makes them safe but incompetent. Exposing them to calculated, non-neglectful risk, and encouraging them in that pursuit, builds competence and confidence. It also builds character. If we protect children too much from their own inevitable foolishness, they will be completely unprepared to look after themselves when they leave our protective embrace and go out into the world, as they ultimately will. When we overprotect, we often do more harm than good. As caring teachers, as with loving parents, we need to be strong enough to advocate for children taking risks that equip them primarily for a competent life, not necessarily for a safe one.[10]

'OK, what do we do now?'

A colleague and I had organised a school journey to Yorkshire. The five-day trip included a stay at the youth hostel in York which then had a sprawling garden with some vast old oak trees with thick branches that drooped to ground level. We arrived – thirty kids, two teachers and other adults – after a tiring train journey up from London. As soon as the kids saw the garden they wanted to play in it.

We managed to herd them first to the dormitories, allocated beds, got them to unpack a few things and then submitted to their pleas to let them play in the expansive but safely walled garden before supper. My colleagues and I spent a few minutes unpacking our bags, checking the facilities and confirming arrangements with the hostel manager. We made our way down to the garden where we could already hear the delighted screams and shouts of children playing joyfully outside.

As we arrived on the steps leading down from the house to the garden, we could see that the lawn was empty – not a single child was visible. But we could hear them! Every child in the class – all thirty of them – was climbing somewhere

10 For more on analogies with parenting, see Rule 5 in Peterson's *12 Rules for Life*. I will say more about the analogy of the responsibilities of a teacher being like that of a responsible parent in Chapter 3.

among the enormous oak trees at the bottom of the garden, one of which was taller than a three-storey building. The kids were shouting: 'Look, Sir! Look! We're in the trees!' I looked up. In front of me was a sight that reminded me of a tree heavy with ripe fruit, only this time, the fruit was 10- and 11-year-old children dangling from the branches. Right at the top was a child shouting: 'Sir! Look at me! I'm king of the world!'

There are very few occasions in life when your heart really does skip a beat, followed by it racing like an over-wound alarm clock, but both of these sensations were my immediate bodily reaction. I was genuinely experiencing a panic, silent and repressed though it was. I tried not to scream out: 'For goodness sake! Get down! Get down!' I turned to my stunned colleagues, both of whom were agog at the sheer ability of the children to climb such enormous trees with the gymnastic dexterity they had never shown in PE lessons back at school.

'OK,' I said to my colleagues, as the senior member of staff, and as calmly as I could, 'What do we do now?'

'Shout at them to come down?' proposed one.

'How about we tell them that supper is ready?' suggested the other. 'That'll bring them down.'

Either of those suggestions could have led to a precipitous rush that might have resulted in disaster, so I decided to pause for a moment and gather my thoughts. I then called up to the assembled throng.

'Please be very, *very* careful, everybody. Climb only on the branches that are thick – so thick they don't even wobble or shake. Don't get in each other's way. Don't go any higher than you are now. Supper is being served in five minutes ...' (which was a blatant lie).

The three of us stood and gawped, hoping and praying that we would survive the next five minutes without a child falling from some of the largest oak trees I had ever seen in my life. Gradually, one by one, they descended – running to us, excited, elated and, as I think now, forever changed.

After supper, the child who had shouted to me from the very top of the tree came over, still thrilled by his achievement, and said to me: 'Sir! I could see the whole world from the top of that tree – I really could!'

Discuss and reflect

- What should teachers ultimately try to achieve – to help children find happiness or to help children find meaning?

Teaching and theory

In England in recent years, there has been a proliferation of employment-based routes into teaching, such as School Direct and SCITTs. These are courses where trainees spend the vast majority of their time in school, teaching in classrooms and gaining practical hands-on experience, with relatively little in the way of theoretical study. This has revived debates about 'theory dependent' and 'theory independent' conceptions of professional practice. It begs the question: are all professions reliant on theory to underpin their practice? The practical skills of a brain surgeon, for example, are by no means independent of the knowledge of biological and physiological theory. Can you argue the same for teachers? Would I risk my child being taught by a talented, inspirational teacher who had never studied Piaget or Vygotsky? While I think my child's teacher would be much the poorer for not having done so, I probably would. Would I risk having my child being operated on by a brain surgeon who had not acquired a thorough grasp of human physiology? Definitely not. However you define a profession,[11] I think it is important that teaching as a practice is able to define itself, both now and in any way that society demands in the future.

However, I am also convinced that teaching should not over-reach itself and make claims that it will struggle to substantiate. For example, teachers should be aware of being drawn into fads and fashions (as I was) that purport to add quasi-theoretical, overly academic or even absurdly professional dimensions to what they do. From classroom-based action research to kinaesthetic learning and from Brain Gym to mindfulness, there have been a lot of well-intentioned fads that have come and gone. While it is the mark of professional people to look constantly for better ways to practise their trade, keeping on top of the fundamental principles of teaching will occupy your time quite well enough – and be the best driver to improve your overall performance. Just try to be a *good* teacher. That is enough for now.[12]

11 We will come to an extended discussion of this in Chapter 2.

12 I don't want to get into a discussion here about the use or definition of the term 'good', either as a measure of performance or as a moral qualifier, or 'good' versus 'outstanding' as set out by the inspection agency Ofsted. It is self-evident that not every teacher or school can be outstanding, otherwise the term is rendered meaningless. However, it is possible for every teacher and every school to be good.

Of course, skills are by their nature developmental and teachers can be technically incompetent. They can be found lacking in the ability to manage or exert their authority over a class or have inadequate knowledge to teach a subject. They can lack organisational ability or basic communication techniques. They may simply not have the personality for it. Being a lovely person is not a qualification to teach. After all, it requires a robust personality (to say the least), and sometimes a thick skin and an element of ruthlessness, to cope with the physical and emotional demands of young people challenging your authority every day. If teaching is indeed a profession, we need to be able to articulate clearly what the defining features of the activity are: what our mission is, what it is we do and why society should give it special recognition. We also must know what its best practices are and how we recognise its best practitioners – our standards. Finally, we need to know what our ethical identity is – how we recognise what the right thing to do is, where to draw the lines, when and why not to cross them.

There is a lot to consider. Let's make a start.

Chapter 2

IS TEACHING A PROFESSION?

How would you define a profession? What are its characteristics? Is teaching a profession? I ask these questions of the trainee teachers I meet when I give lectures at universities and training centres around England. I get a fascinating range of responses that reflect dominant as well as changing values. I like it when people take me to task about my own assumptions too – it keeps my arguments sharp and stops me taking them for granted.

There are a variety of challenges to the concept of a profession in the modern era, so it is a worthy topic for scrutiny. The first thing I do with my audiences is to reassure them that I am not trying to impose any preconceived definitions. The point of the question is for them to think about and challenge their own assumptions and try to define the profession in their own terms. It isn't a trick, although clearly I have a view on the subject that I am prepared to put to them, drawing together threads.

I suggest to trainees that when they start to consider the question, they may find it useful to think of a profession that is not teaching. Whatever they define as a profession will do: they can think of an established one (like medicine or law) or they can widen the notion and bring in other trades (like builders, plumbers, hairdressers, electricians or IT managers). I ask participants to come up with at least seven or eight characteristics of what they think constitutes a profession and to discuss it with each other. At the end of ten minutes or so, I stop them and get some feedback on what they have talked about, reassuring them that they can say whatever they like. They are free to challenge and even reject the whole concept if they want to. I will challenge some of the things they say, but only in a spirit of robust debate. Here is an encounter I had a year or so ago.

'Worr'about footballers – derr professionals, aren't dee?'

If you have ever heard one of my talks live and you have an ear for English accents, then you will probably recognise where I am from.[1] In spite of living in London for forty years, the traces of my Liverpool accent are still very evident. I am proud of that, of course.

1 Recorded versions of my lectures (without audiences) are available to view at www.newteacherstalk.com.

I happened to be doing a session at a university in my home town a couple of years ago discussing this very topic, 'What is a profession?' with an audience of over 200 postgraduate trainees. I thought I was on home ground … Then a voice from the back of the large lecture theatre called out: 'Worr'about footballers – derr professionals, aren't dee?' (Translation: What about footballers – they're professionals, aren't they?)

'Well, if you say so,' I said, rather haltingly, surprised by the sudden intervention. 'If that's your definition of a profession, that's fine …'

'Well, they are, aren't they!' he shouted back (keep the Liverpool accent going in your head). 'They call them "professional footballers" for a reason, don't they? So they are, aren't they?'

'If you think footballers are members of a profession – and that's a definition you are happy with – OK …' I paused for a moment and asked my rather voluble audience participant a couple of follow-up questions.

'Which football team do you support?'

'Liverpool!' he shouted back.

'OK,' I said. 'Then you'll know that Liverpool had a player playing for them a few years ago – a guy by the name of Luis Suárez?'

Now, for those of you who are not football fans, Suárez is by any reasonable measure still one of the world's top footballers (at least at the time of writing). He went on to play for Barcelona and Atlético Madrid, two of the world's top football clubs, and has been rated as one the world's top thirty football stars.[2]

'When Luis Suárez was playing for Liverpool,' I continued, 'indeed, both before and after, he was banned three times for biting his opponents. He was banned twice for racially abusing them.'

Some people in the audience, presumably those who were not Liverpool or even football fans, looked quite shocked. I even heard one person gasp.

'Now,' I said, 'what do you think would happen to you if you bit a child in your class or bit one of your colleagues in the staffroom?'

2 See *The Guardian*, The 100 Best Male Footballers (20 December 2019). Available at: https://www.theguardian.com/global/ng-interactive/2019/dec/17/the-100-best-male-footballers-in-the-world-2019.

There was laughter from some, incredulity from others and a shocked silence from most.

'What would happen to you if you racially abused one of your pupils?' I asked. There was still no answer from the audience or my stentorian contributor on the back row. 'You'd be out,' I said quite definitively. 'You'd be out of this profession, and I can assure you that you wouldn't get back into it either. You wouldn't get an eight-week ban on full pay the way Luis Suárez did.' You could hear a pin drop in the lecture theatre.

'Now, you can call footballers professionals if you want to, I haven't got a problem with that,' I said, looking up at the back of the hall. 'If that's your definition, that's one you'll have to live with. But the levels of accountability to which you will be held is a world away from the levels of accountability that Luis Suárez and his ilk are held. That's not a bad thing. That's a very good thing.'

Discuss and reflect

- What is a profession?
- Identify seven or eight characteristics of a profession.
- How can a profession be distinguished from a job, if at all?

You may find it useful to ignore teaching for this activity. Try thinking of another job or role that you consider to be a profession.

I leave students and trainees talking about this, usually in quite an animated way, for a while. Some hit barriers very quickly, stalling on issues of terminology: 'Is being a "professional" the same as being "a member of a profession"?' Others will go down a cul-de-sac: 'Are footballers professionals?' or 'Does professional status depend on the level of pay?' which, in the end, are really distractions. Some people reflect on a previous career, like working in retail at management level or managing IT infrastructure, and argue convincingly that this is professional work. I am never disappointed by what crops up. After ten minutes or so, people contribute a list of items (presented in the pages that follow in no particular order) that we can start to unpack.

1. Specialist skills and knowledge

Some people make the point that a profession involves acquiring a specific set of specialist skills and knowledge. It usually occurs to some of the trainees fairly quickly that if they are training to be early years teachers, the knowledge and skills they attain will be quite different from those acquired by their secondary (high school) colleagues (who are sometimes sitting in other parts of the same lecture hall). However, while teaching does have a common set of characteristics, it goes without saying that teaching 5-year-old children to read is a very different activity to teaching Shakespeare's tragedies to 17-year-old pupils on the threshold of university. The knowledge and skills that underlie such practices are obviously quite distinct. It is therefore reasonable for the public to expect that someone who claims to be a member of a profession would have possession of highly developed specialist skills and knowledge to which not every Tom, Dick and Harriet has access. But how do these so-called professionals obtain this body of specialist skills and knowledge?[3]

2. Training

Training is a characteristic that people recognise very quickly as being necessary to professional status. While it may seem obvious, I nevertheless point out to my audiences that professional training is exactly what they are engaged in right now – a course designed to acquire specialist skills and knowledge, such as a Postgraduate Certificate in Education (PGCE) or a Bachelor of Arts (BA) with qualified teacher status (QTS). Professional, not just academic, training is what doctors, dentists and nurses must do; they embark on training courses that combine theoretical knowledge with practical skills and hands-on experience. Such courses either last a long time (five or six years in the case of doctors) or they are intensive (like a one-year PGCE on the back of an academic degree). Some teacher training courses (such as three- or four-year bachelor degrees with QTS) combine academic study with professional training. Following up, I ask my audiences another seemingly obvious question: 'Can anyone get on a training course, such as the one you're on?' They rapidly realise that they are undertaking a course that has access barriers and is, in fact, highly restricted.

3 It is important to note here, especially as a point of encouragement for new teachers, that some teaching skills take a long time to develop. You will need to be patient. Some skills take time to become effective and you will need to live with that frustration. Some skills ebb and flow with different children, different classes and at different times of your career. You will need to be tenacious but acquire the virtue of forbearance in relation to the development of your own teaching skills.

3. High standards of education

Everyone knows that to access a training course for an established profession such as law, medicine, engineering or accountancy, they will need a high standard of education just to apply for it. That usually means educational qualifications from school such as A levels or Scottish Highers, or a university degree to access a postgraduate course. Most trainee teachers in the UK are training on postgraduate routes (either at a university or a school-centred training provider) so they need a degree to get onto the course. A degree is the minimum requirement for entry. Just pause with that thought for a second: a degree as the minimum. That is a pretty high minimum when you come to think of it.

For teachers in England, even a degree is not sufficient. Anyone wanting to become a teacher there must have GCSEs in English, maths and (depending on your specialist subject) a science subject too. They also have to assure their training provider that their skills in literacy and numeracy satisfy the exacting standards of the Department for Education. As I indicated earlier, some (currently about 15 per cent) acquire QTS via an undergraduate route,[4] so they will do a three- or four-year BA degree with QTS. This route is designed to gain degree standard education while at the same time acquiring the practical, specialist skills and knowledge required of a professionally qualified teacher. When people are awarded their BA degree – which is an educational qualification – they are also awarded qualified teacher status – which is a professional qualification.

In recent years, employment-based routes have become more popular; currently about 53 per cent of those entering teaching in England choose this route.[5] While trainees still attend lectures and complete written assignments on the theoretical aspects of teaching (and many will do a PGCE at the same time), they feel that the greater proportion of hands-on experience they get from being based in schools equips them better to meet the practical challenges they will soon face.

4 HM Government, Initial Teacher Training Census – Academic Year 2020–21 (3 December 2020). Available at: https://explore-education-statistics.service.gov.uk/find-statistics/initial-teacher-training-census/2020-21.

5 HM Government, Initial Teacher Training Census – Academic Year 2020–21.

4. Experience

Experience in itself is not a qualification, of course, and nor is it necessarily a professional characteristic. While experience is an essential part of any practical training, particularly for vocational 'direct contact' professions like social work and nursing, experience per se cannot be a criterion for qualification. We do not qualify doctors, nurses, lawyers, engineers and others on the basis of experience alone, however relevant or appropriate the experience may have been. On the other hand, imagine being treated by a doctor who had no prior experience of treating patients in a hospital but had been allowed to qualify from medical school? Would we allow an engineer who had never been on-site to supervise the construction of a building? No, that is why a period of apprenticeship or induction, where you work alongside qualified and experienced people, is important. We will come to that on page 27.

You may feel, as I did, that the amount of experience you have had by the end of your teacher training course is woefully insufficient to prepare you for the rigours of full-time professional practice. Nevertheless, it will be judged as 'just enough' to equip you with sufficient competence and confidence to go out there and make a start. Hopefully, you will demonstrate not just a minimum level of competence and confidence, but you will assure your clients (the children and their parents) that you are committed to the task, including a level of dedication, even passion, for what you are trying to do. The public expects not only that you have a firm grasp of all the technical aspects of teaching, having acquired the relevant skills and knowledge, completed training and gained qualifications, but that you also show essential personal qualities and attributes that give your clients the confidence that you deserve to be in the position you are in. The public needs to trust you when they put their children in your hands.

5. Commitment, dedication and passion

The public have a legitimate hope (if not an expectation) that professional people are committed, dedicated and passionate about what they do. In my view, these virtues are not complementary to professional status; they are essential. Nor are they mutually exclusive; they are interlocking. Don't underestimate this. If I was lying on an operating table about to go under a surgeon's knife, I would like to think that he or she was committed, dedicated and passionate about attending to my urgent medical needs. I would hope and expect that a barrister who has taken on my case – defending me on a charge of, let's say, murder (I am being hypothetical here!) – feels committed, dedicated and passionate about defending me to the best of his or her ability.

As members of the public and as potential clients, we assume that our professionals have commitment, dedication and passion as part of their professional make-up. It is a key clause in the contract of trust we have with them. I haven't been a schoolteacher (in the sense of being a class teacher) for many years, but when people ask me what I do for a living, I still rather proudly say, 'By profession, I'm a teacher.' Being in a job that you feel dedicated to and passionate about will become part of your professional persona, part of your identity and part of who you are.

However, commitment, dedication and passion are not enough in themselves. While they may be necessary, they are not sufficient. You cannot be a dentist just by being committed, dedicated and passionate. You have to have the education, training, specialist skills, knowledge and qualifications. These are the requisites that make up one half of the equation. I don't know about you, but I don't want to put my trust in a dentist who is merely passionate about my teeth. I want to go to a dentist who has been at medical school for six years, passed all her exams at the end of an exacting practical and academic training course and is fully qualified. I want to go to a dentist who has letters after her name, engraved on a brass plaque outside the door of her surgery, declaring to the public that she is fit to practise. It doesn't stop there either. Don't think that because you have got a degree and a PGCE with QTS that it will be enough to rest on your laurels. You won't be able to say: 'Great! Now I've got my degree, I've got my PGCE, I've got my QTS ... just let me get on with the job for the next forty years ...' Not on your life!

6. Apprenticeship, probation and induction

In all professions, there is a period of induction or probation to put you through an initial test of competence. In teaching, it is currently an induction period as an early career teacher.[6] All established professions do this: doctors must serve as 'junior doctors' on a foundation programme for two years on hospital wards working all the hours God sends; barristers do time as a 'pupil' working under the supervision of an experienced barrister in chambers; solicitors must find a legal practice that will sponsor them on a 'training contract' and so on. These are all akin to an apprenticeship period where you are not only supervised, but also supported, guided and allowed time to continue training in key personal areas and develop your fledgling skills. You will have an induction mentor who will – or should – look after you and make sure you get the non-contact time to which you are entitled, who will have regular sessions with you and enable you to feel confident to raise issues. Perhaps, most importantly, they will be – or should be – your advocate in the school.

6 The Early Career Framework – a two-year period of induction and CPD – was fully introduced for early career teachers in 2021.

New teachers need to feel they are free enough to make basic mistakes and learn from them, as I did when I was a probationary teacher. We can learn by our errors, especially if we are helped to reflect on them and put in place strategies to correct them in future. In my view, learning from your mistakes is an adage that needs reviving – not just for our pupils but for the teaching profession in general. These days, the stakes are very high and schools expect early career teachers to come in and, to quote that awful phrase, hit the ground running. That is all very well, but many of us hit the ground and sometimes stumble. That doesn't mean we won't get up and rejoin the race, but if we are frightened that we will be disqualified just because we falter at the first hurdle, then we won't take the risks necessary to truly learn.

Hopefully, your induction period will be a time when you can feel that your learning and development is scaffolded by your mentor and more experienced colleagues. When you do eventually pass your induction period, the idea that you can cruise through teaching on a following breeze could not be further from the truth. Professions like teaching expect their members to continually engage in professional learning throughout their career.

7. Continuing professional development

Some professions not only expect their members to engage in CPD, they formally require it. If you are a solicitor, for example, you will need to provide evidence to the Solicitors Regulation Authority that you have engaged in professional development every few years just to maintain your registration. Nurses, dentists, engineers, accountants and ophthalmic opticians all need to submit a record of their CPD to their professional body. Failure to do so could lead to them being deregistered and ultimately deemed unfit to practise. The teaching profession has had a fierce debate about this over many years. Currently, teachers are not formally required to do CPD as a necessary function of their professional status, although the new Early Career Framework (ECF) will formalise it to a degree hitherto unknown.[7] When the idea of regulated CPD had been suggested in the past it had been opposed, sometimes by trade unions demanding that the government stump up the money to fund it. Schools have limited budgets and must pit employing teachers against developing teachers. Most schools find a way to balance this, but in some the latter does not always prevail.

7 The ECF is designed to support early career teacher development. From September 2021, it sets out what early career teachers (ECTs) will be entitled to learn about and how to acquire the skills and knowledge to implement it. The framework includes sections on behaviour management, pedagogy, curriculum, assessment and professional behaviours. The support package includes: funded 5 per cent time-off timetable in the second year of teaching, in addition to the existing 10 per cent in the first year; a range of curricula and training materials; funded training and funded time for mentors to support early career teachers.

Cyclical teacher shortages and recruitment crises have weakened the resolve of successive governments to enforce the idea on teachers and schools, but it is a debate that will inevitably re-emerge.

The desire to engage in CPD is not resisted by teachers or by unions, especially where they see it as a beneficial and genuine learning experience. The trouble with much professional development in recent decades, however, is that it has come on the back of government-initiated strategies. Additionally, there has been the perception that an overemphasis on generic training, such as safeguarding or first aid, has not responded to local needs. Too often, teachers have felt that they are being trained merely to deliver the latest government initiative rather than truly develop their skills and knowledge as autonomous professionals.

The vast majority of teachers want to learn as much as teach. This is especially true for new teachers. As an early career teacher keen to learn, you will want to visit the classrooms of experienced and talented colleagues to watch how they do things, which is often the best form of CPD. You may want to go on courses to improve your practical or professional skills, like the National Professional Qualification for Middle Leadership (NPQML). You might even want to continue academic study long term, doing an MA or eventually a doctorate. Why not? These extended periods of academic study might inject your career with new vigour, as they did for me. I did two master's degrees while I was a schoolteacher, ten years apart, and both gave my teaching (although not necessarily my career prospects) a massive boost.

The question of whether having a higher degree like an MA will improve your career prospects is a complicated one. I never felt that either of my MAs made me more 'marketable' as a potential employee or candidate for a specific position. I think that most employers in schools – head teachers and governing bodies – are more concerned with high performance, competence and relevant experience than higher degree qualifications. However, having a higher degree does indicate to employers both your willingness and commitment to develop. It shows that you expect something of yourself, and that in itself is a professional characteristic.

One of the easiest ways to take control of your own CPD is to be an avid reader. There is a wealth of good books and journals on education and teaching topics. As a busy teacher, you may feel you don't have the time or the opportunity to go on courses, but you can always find time to work your way through more of that reading list you never got to the bottom of during your teacher training.

A wider point about professional development is that of expectation. A clear characteristic of being a member of a profession, as opposed to doing a job, is the professional attitude and mentality that you will bring to it; not only the desire to continue your learning and development but the expectation of your commitment to do so. As I have suggested, as a professional person you will naturally want to engage in CPD because, as we all know, learning is vital to human flourishing. You will also want to do it for the satisfaction it gives you: learning new practical skills and taking on fresh knowledge and ideas. Perhaps, in certain circumstances, it will improve your prospects for promotion and seniority. All of these are bankable reasons to want to do it. Having said all this, expectation comes not just from your professional attitude but from other quarters too.

Your employer has a right to expect you to undertake CPD. Schools will require it (perhaps as a result of a government initiative or strategy, such as a focus on raising standards in maths or literacy, technology or safeguarding, or whatever is the current perceived priority). You may suddenly find that half of the school's staff meetings and training days are given over to whatever that is. Whether or not the subject being focused on is your priority is another matter. There are some serious issues about how much learning and development actually happens when teachers don't 'own' their CPD, but there is no doubt that you will be expected to engage, professionally, in making it a success, even if, secretly, you are bored rigid by it.

The imposition of an external focus might be the result of a critical factor, like an unfavourable Ofsted inspection which imposes special measures on the school. If that is the case, you will find there is very little of the school's resources that are not directly or wholly consumed by those priorities. Schools have a right, and an obligation, to set their own priorities for strategic development. You are an employee, after all, so schools have a legitimate expectation that you will support their priorities. Indeed, it is your professional duty to do so. Don't necessarily expect a head teacher to indulge your desire to bring in a yoga teacher, however convincingly you may argue the case that it will benefit the pupils' or your own well-being, if the school's literacy provision or mathematics teaching has been judged inadequate by Ofsted. This is not a personal judgement, merely a reflection of the practical reality and pressures.

While your employer may be persuaded to enrol you on a deputy headship training course, they may want some reassurance that on completion the first thing you don't do is apply for a deputy headship somewhere else, fast-tracking your career and benefiting another school as a result. Most schools are very supportive of management development courses even if it does result in people subsequently leaving; but not all, so be sensitive to the school's ability to support you. By contrast, in many countries you would be contractually obliged to remain in post for some years as 'payback' to the school. Clearly, employers also have a duty to support your development. The problem is that they will always have intense and competing claims on their time and resources. Sometimes you will feel frustrated by that. Don't hold your breath if you think that by being patient and waiting your turn you will be able to go on the course of your choice. You may not. If you want yoga as part of the school's CPD offer or if you aspire to be a deputy head, don't wait for the school's priorities to align with yours – get out there and take responsibility for your own CPD.

The presumption that you will continually learn and develop comes from a wider group of stakeholders than just your employer. In a profession, colleagues have a legitimate expectation that they will engage with one another and that they will also engage with CPD. If you become incompetent because you have not kept up to date with developments – such as the latest GCSE or A level specifications – that incompetence has significant implications for others; it can damage the reputation of your school and your colleagues.

By contrast, in many jobs, such presuppositions are not at all entrenched. This is not to disrespect anyone doing a 'job' – we all go to work wanting dignity and recognition for our hard work – but there are self-evidently different levels of expectation in different jobs. In my work experience over a lifetime, I have worked with many people who have few or no qualifications at all, little required training and a low level of responsibility, yet they have displayed high levels of commitment, dedication and professionalism. However, in many jobs you wouldn't be unduly concerned if one of your colleagues had not been on a refresher course recently; that is a concern for the supervisor or manager. In some jobs, you wouldn't concern yourself about how efficiently or effectively your colleagues were working, as long as their inefficiency doesn't directly impact upon you; again, that is your line manager's responsibility. You might have a view about their lack of ability or inadequate training, and you might even make a supportive offer of help occasionally, but you wouldn't be responsible. Alternatively, you might think them lazy or feckless. Whatever your view of an inefficient colleague, it is the responsibility of your manager to address the issue.

However, as a professional person you are called on to think and respond differently. Leaving a teaching colleague to perform incompetently, even lazily, carries with it the implication that you condone such behaviour, and that has implications for your reputation as well as theirs. Continuing to learn, develop and perform at the forefront of best practice – and therefore being seen as having a shared responsibility for such – has potential repercussions not just for you, but for your immediate colleagues, your school and the profession as a whole.

Finally, the general public – or perhaps that section of the public we could reasonably call our clients: the children and their parents (or carers) – have an expectation that we regularly engage with CPD. I think it is unlikely that on any given day your pupils will come into school wondering whether you have been on a course recently, but they and their parents will assume implicitly that you are keeping on top of your game – staying abreast of the latest methods and techniques and at least being aware of new research that helps teachers to perform at the forefront of best practice.

As members of the public, it is an assumption and expectation that we have of other professions too. Imagine going to your GP, for example, and discovering that she had not attended any clinical training or refresher courses for years or read a medical journal in that time. I think we would all be justifiably outraged. We might even complain to the General Medical Council (GMC) that our doctor had become unfit to practise. Professional people are expected to stay sharp and keep abreast of developments, not just for our own benefit – to gain future promotion and advancement – but also for the benefit and interests of the public we are here to serve.

8. Professional bodies and regulation

As we have just mentioned the example of the GMC, let's explore the role of professional bodies and their purpose in regulating professions a little more. Primarily, professional bodies exist to regulate the competence and conduct of a profession. The GMC – which is the statutory body that registers and regulates medical practitioners in the UK – has been in existence for over 160 years. Interestingly, the idea of a General Teaching Council was mooted around the same time, although it wasn't established until September 2000.[8] Established professions such as medicine, nursing, law, dentistry, accountancy, engineering and others all have professional regulatory bodies that maintain a register of those qualified and fit to practise.

Indeed, it is not just a matter of professional ethics that someone qualified to be a nurse, for example, maintains registration. With many professions, it is a matter of the law too. It would be illegal to practise as a nurse without being registered with the Nursing and Midwifery Council, just as it would be illegal to practise as an unregistered social worker, dentist or solicitor. That is not true for all professions. Architects, for example, can choose whether to register with the Royal Institute of British Architects before going into practice. Although many architectural practices require employees to register as a condition of employment, it is not the law.

The criticality of the role is obviously a key point in how much statutory regulation is involved. Nurses and doctors are concerned with a major public interest issue: the nation's health. This is a critical issue, as we all pay taxes towards the NHS, so it is legitimate that statutory regulation is involved. However, there is some debate about what constitutes a 'critical role' in society. It is not a legal requirement for structural or civil engineers to register with their respective professional bodies in order to practise, yet the construction of bridges and buildings (whether in the public or private sector) is of huge public interest, so it is imperative that the highest ethical and technical standards are maintained in the engineering and architecture professions. Even when relatively little of our taxes go directly towards a sector, such as accountancy, we

8 The Conservative-led coalition government abolished the General Teaching Council for England in March 2012. It operated for a mere twelve years.

expect high standards of probity in the public interest. The profession of accountancy therefore plays an active voluntary role in reassuring the public through rigorous regulation of its members on the basis of its ethical code.

You may now be wondering why teaching does not have an independent, professional regulatory body on the model of other professions.[9] As I pointed out earlier, England did have one – the General Teaching Council (GTC) – and I used to work for it. Any discussion about why teaching no longer has a professional regulatory body is obviously going to be highly politicised (given that it was abolished by an Act of Parliament with little opposition), so I am not going to spend any time repeating arguments that are now part of history. But it is worth considering whether teaching is still a profession when it does not have an independent, professional regulatory body like other professions do.

Discuss and reflect

- Should teaching have an independent, professional regulatory body?
- What is the difference between a union and a professional body?

9. Codes of practice

Professional bodies regulate their members by conceiving and publishing ethical codes of practice. These are sometimes called codes of ethics or codes of conduct. Such codes serve several purposes, including affirming the values of the profession to its own members, providing a broad set of criteria for regulating them, and telling the public what values and ethical standards they have a right to expect from members of that profession.[10] Indeed, the codes of practice of many professions are prominently displayed on their websites and are intended to show the public what the profession is about and what the public can expect from them.

9 The Chartered College of Teaching is a professional body for the teaching profession but it has no regulatory role. It is a voluntary, membership-based organisation that began operating in January 2017. Its aims are to support teachers' professional development, promote and share evidence-informed good practice, and recognise excellence. Currently its membership is small but growing.

10 We will examine and discuss the code for teaching in England, the Teachers' Standards, in Chapter 4.

Many professional codes of practice emphasise 'duty to the client', stating something like: 'We put the interests of our clients first.' This seems like an impressive way of trying to impress your clients, but is it always true? Occasionally, sadly not. Professional bodies, especially in the case of established professions such as medicine, law and nursing, have important disciplinary committees which deal with cases of incompetence or misconduct in relation to the derogation of a duty of care, a diminution in fitness to practise or an allegation of professional misconduct. These cases are relatively rare, but the penalties for putting personal interests ahead of your clients are harsh, including suspension or being struck off the professional register.

Some professions will be in the full, unmerciful glare of the media's attention when such cases do occur. Derogation of competence or conduct could extend into the realm of illegality too. If a dentist is accused of serious malpractice that caused physical harm to a patient, for example, they might not only be professionally culpable – such as being struck off or suspended by the General Dental Council – but they may also find themselves the subject of a criminal investigation. In professions like teaching, where the care of children is paramount, responsibilities are therefore critical.[11] Finally, professionals convicted of serious criminal offences can find themselves struck off their professional register for bringing the profession into disrepute – a topic we will explore in Chapter 5.

10. Responsibility

As we have seen, most of us go to work wanting to contribute, make a difference and be recognised and rewarded for our hard work; that is a given, whether you are a refuse collector or a brain surgeon. However, it is also self-evident that some jobs carry more responsibility than others. This is not to denigrate some types of work but merely to describe it objectively. Some jobs require slavish repetition (although these are rapidly being replaced by machine learning and artificial intelligence). Some jobs are routine or menial, in that they require unexceptional levels of competence or adherence to a basic standard that most people would have the physical and mental capacity to complete without much training. An example of this would be working as a care worker, shop assistant or delivery driver.

This is not to say that relatively unskilled jobs don't have a great deal of responsibility – they do. Care workers must be sensitive communicators, conscientious, assiduous and skilled in attending to the washing, dressing and eating needs of the elderly and disabled. Their huge ethical and moral responsibilities were more than admirably demonstrated by their commitment, dedication and sheer courage during the

11 We will discuss the duty of care of teachers in Chapter 3.

COVID-19 coronavirus pandemic. That crisis also revealed the previously undiscovered moral agency of shop assistants, delivery drivers, refuse collectors, postal delivery workers and many others. Those working in supermarkets, for example, tenaciously maintained essential food supplies in the face of very stressful and hazardous working conditions.

Other jobs too – like bus drivers – have levels of responsibility above the general norm (these workers displayed similar courage during the pandemic). Even in normal times, driving a bus is a fairly responsible job which requires handling a large vehicle and navigating it safely through busy traffic, making sure that the hundreds of passengers who get on and off every day do so safely. It calls for skill, care and diligence. While the roles of care workers, shop assistants, delivery and bus drivers can be seriously responsible, they are not usually complex. For example, they don't require autonomous and accountable decision-making, high levels of theoretical knowledge or the ability to respond to a nexus of compound or composite demands with a variety of intellectual as well as technical skills.

By contrast, professional roles usually do. They are characterised by responsibilities that are both weighty and involved. When you become a qualified teacher and turn up for your first job at your new school, the head teacher is not going to welcome you through the doors and merely introduce you to the lovely new furniture or a bank of computers for which you will be responsible. No, looking after furniture and equipment won't be your key concern. The head teacher will (hopefully) welcome you to your new school and introduce you to the children – your clients – they want you to educate and whose well-being they want you to promote and safeguard. If you are in a primary school, you will be reminded of this almost every day when parents come into school to hand over to you the beings they most love and cherish: their children. They say (at least implicitly): 'Here you are … I trust you to take responsibility for my child – the most precious thing in my life. Please educate them, look after them and return them safely to me at the end of the day.' That is a pretty big responsibility.

In schools, professional responsibility is sometimes shared with people like teaching assistants, especially where they have been trained to high standards and gained qualifications. Many schools give teaching assistants quite a lot of responsibility – taking on teaching roles with individual children, groups and sometimes covering classes when teachers are absent. I accept that other staff members in schools have key responsibilities, but it is the qualified teacher who is recognised as having the ultimate responsibility. Teaching assistants are (or should be) always under the direction of a qualified teacher. It is the qualified teacher, not the teaching assistant, who is *in loco parentis* – 'in place of the parent' – a concept we will explore in the next chapter. When you take a group of thirty children out on a visit to the Natural History Museum (or wherever), and you return with only twenty-nine (like I nearly did), it is not the teaching assistants or learning mentors who will have to answer the awkward questions that the head teacher and parents will be asking. It is the qualified teacher who will have to face the music, while the teaching assistants and learning mentors will be on their way home and breathing a huge sigh of relief.

Don't think of responsibility as something onerous. It may be the very thing that motivates and focuses you. It will certainly be a domain where there are worthy and meritorious principles competing with each other that will challenge your decision-making skills and where people are relying on your good judgement. Responsibility is not a burden, it is a privilege, and a character-forming one at that.

11. Accountability

All this weighty and complex responsibility has a necessary flip side. You will need to accept wide-ranging accountability as well. Professionals are accountable to a lot of other people and to other stakeholders. I see it as two sides of the same coin, at least in liberal democracies where accountability is more likely to be democratically institutionalised. The more weighty and complex your responsibilities, the more extensive the accountability to those you serve.

Discuss and reflect

- Who are you accountable to as a teacher? Make a list.

You have probably compiled a long list! Let's start with the children. They will come into class every day and ask (literally or metaphorically), 'What are we going to do today, Miss?' or 'Sir, you forgot to mark my homework!' Even young children will make you feel accountable.

Then there are the parents and carers. Secondary schools are different to primary schools in that, unless there is a problem, most parents are generally not well known to most secondary teachers – at least, not until parents' evening comes along. It is not like this in primary schools. As a primary school teacher, you will see parents bringing their kids into school every morning, handing them over to you and saying things like: 'Johnny didn't bring his reading book home last night. That's the third night in a row he hasn't brought his reading book. Why hasn't he got a reading book?' You will need to provide an answer.

You will be accountable to your line manager too – this is your head of department in a secondary school or the head teacher, deputy head or head of phase in a primary school. They will be asking questions like: 'Can I see your planning for this half term, please?' and 'Show me what you will be doing with the children this week.'

You will also be accountable to your employer. These days that is more likely to be the school's governing body than the local authority, but there will be occasions when they will ask you to speak to a subcommittee of the school's governing body, perhaps on a curriculum matter or pastoral initiative once you become a curriculum coordinator, head of department or head of year. Sometimes the governors will want to consult staff about the school's equality or behaviour policies and may invite you to attend a committee meeting as a staff representative.

And how could we forget Ofsted? The Office for Standards in Education is an arm's-length government agency, technically independent, but whose appointed role is to go around the country and inspect the quality of teaching, learning outcomes and overall level of education children receive. And, boy, do teachers feel accountable to them!

Finally, as we have seen, although you are not directly responsible for your colleagues' competence, conduct or professional development, you will feel some accountability towards them as they will towards you. No one who regards himself or herself as truly professional would turn a blind eye to persistent incompetence or evidence of serious professional misconduct. Teaching is a collegial profession, so accountability has a collegial dimension. Many schools consciously and systematically share planning, preparation and other aspects of workload as a way of encouraging their staff members to be accountable to each other.

12. Trust and role model status

As we have noted, children are by their nature vulnerable and relatively powerless. They are taught to distrust strangers. Yet, we ask millions of parents to turn over their children every day to people who are virtually unknown to them. This enormous burden of trust must therefore come with enormous responsibility not to abuse it by over-reaching our authority. Instead, we need to establish relationships based on mutual respect and approach our duty of care with diligence. We are expected to ensure that children are protected from harm while in our care; therefore, a breach of trust is a catastrophic failure.

Professional people are trusted implicitly. Teachers are seen as role models in a way that few other professions are. Trust and role model status are difficult to define, but it is interesting that virtually every audience I speak to acknowledges this point willingly and without question. Society does not (and should not) expect teachers to be faultless; we are not angels or saints. But society does have a right to expect teachers to be role models. In all my years in teaching, I have yet to meet anyone who has seriously contested that canonical precept.

Challenging the notion of professionalism and professions

Over the years that I have been doing lectures and leading sessions on this topic with trainees, there have been many fascinating challenges to the ideas raised above. Some people, while accepting their status as a role model, will contest the whole notion of a profession. Indeed, some will invoke the dictum of George Bernard Shaw that 'all professions are conspiracies against the laity'. Occasionally, I even find myself agreeing with some of the sympathies expressed. For example, a trainee in one of my sessions once complained that if teaching really is 'the best job in the world', then why isn't it better paid? We all laughed at that. Other trainees feel that the presumptions of professional standing are another way of stratifying elites and reinforcing class status. Some argue that the professions are anachronistic in the modern age where, in many sectors of life, 'the customer is king' and power is in the hands of consumers who are able to move their custom from one provider to another at the click of a button. Indeed, I have heard people say that so-called communities of interest, especially those that can garner millions of people online, are the way that standards are regulated in the internet age – via customer reviews or 'likes' on sites like Amazon, Tripadvisor and Trustpilot.

In recent decades, the scope of the words 'professional' and 'professionalism' has widened and they are now used to describe a broad variety of people simply doing their job well. These days, everyone is potentially a professional by virtue of basic competence, irrespective of the qualifications they hold or how (adequately or inadequately) they were trained for the (skilled or menial) responsibilities they take on or the (high or low) standards of the (excellent or poor) quality of the service they provide. If I go to a supermarket and I am served by a real human being (rather than a self-checkout bot) in a way that is not up to my expectations of politeness or helpfulness, I might complain that 'The checkout assistant was very unprofessional', referring to nothing worse than a sullen attitude, the absence of a smile or the lack of an offer to help pack my shopping bags. While I think that it is reasonable to be served with a smile and the offer of some help, I am not sure we are being fair to anyone by expecting such a service to be defined as 'professional conduct'.

I am not trying to impose my definition of what a profession is, or is not, on you or anyone else. My job here – as is in my lectures – is to challenge you to think about the question and decide the matter for yourself. However, I believe this is an important question to consider at the point at which you may be entering teaching because, whether or not you agree, there is no doubt that many of your clients will consider teaching as a profession. Conversely, there will be some who do not, so you should be armed with a list of claims to argue your case, if and when those challenges arise.

Trades vs. professions

Some jobs do tick a lot of the boxes we have been using to define a profession. We discussed professional footballers earlier, but a much more interesting example in my view are those jobs we used to call trades – electricians, plumbers, carpenters, hairdressers, gas fitters, car mechanics, secretaries and so on. The people who do these jobs satisfy many of the criteria we have been talking about: they have training, skills, knowledge and qualifications; they are often members of professional associations; and they adhere to codes of practice that assure the public of the quality of their work. If you are an electrician or a gas fitter, for example, you cannot ply your trade unless you are properly trained, qualified and registered with the appropriate professional regulatory body. It is illegal to attempt to 'pass off' as an electrician or a gas fitter. Society needs competent and qualified electricians and gas fitters – for obvious reasons of public safety and confidence. To my mind, qualified trade practitioners come close to owning the characteristics of an established profession. However, I still think there is a key distinguishing factor between the likes of electricians, hairdressers and car mechanics on the one hand, and doctors, lawyers and teachers on the other. I will illustrate my point with reference to my own car mechanic.

'Have you got any qualifications in car mechanics?'

I have a fantastic car mechanic whom I have been going to for years. He is brilliantly professional – and I don't need to put those words in inverted commas. He has fantastic skills, knowledge and experience going back decades. A couple of years ago, I was chatting to him about the talks I do to trainee teachers. I asked him, just as a matter of interest, 'Do you have any qualifications in car mechanics?' His reaction surprised me. He laughed out loud. 'Look mate, I left school at 16 without any qualifications. I inherited this business off my dad. I've been mending cars since I was a kid. I'm passionate about mechanics.' Needlessly justifying himself, he added: 'Of course I keep up with changes – everything is electronics these days. I go on courses and whatnot. I get inspected as well, to keep the MOT badge and things like that. But I haven't got any qualifications in car mechanics, if that's what you mean.'

For the last twenty-five years I have been taking my car to a man who has no qualifications in car mechanics! Should I be worried about that? Well, no, I am not worried at all, and I never have been. I know from experience that this guy is an excellent car mechanic and he has never given me reason to doubt it. I haven't the slightest hesitation in taking my car to him. However, I feel differently about my child's teacher. I want the person standing in front of my child to be properly trained and qualified. That is my expectation.

My car mechanic is a very nice guy, but for all the years I have been going there, I know very little about him. For all I know, he could have a conviction for dealing Class A drugs. Should I be taking my car to someone who might have a conviction for dealing drugs? My attitude is this: I am taking my car to be serviced, not to judge the man's morals. Of course, I wouldn't approve if he did have such a conviction, but as long as he isn't stashing drugs in the back of my car while he is servicing it, the question of his personal morality doesn't seem relevant. However, if I discovered that my child's teacher had a conviction for dealing Class A drugs ... well, that would concern me. Not that I would be unforgiving of someone who had done something stupid in their youth. We all do silly things we regret and we all deserve a second chance. But I would want reassurance from such a person that their wayward behaviour was now a thing of the past.

I think this reflects a much wider public attitude. Yes, we should give due recognition to high levels of skill and knowledge that have been acquired through on-the-job experience, such as being apprenticed as a car mechanic. And, yes, we should give due recognition to the training, qualifications, adherence to codes of practice and membership of trade associations that make their members accountable. But I think the public is expecting a little bit more from the likes of doctors, nurses, lawyers and teachers. What that 'little bit more' actually consists of is quite difficult to define, but I think it comes back to the notion of being a role model, where high levels of public trust are invested in your character as well as your competence.

So, what's the verdict? Is teaching a profession?

As I stated earlier, I am not trying to impose my definition of a profession on you. What I am concerned to do here is raise some awareness about the characteristics claimed, the justifications made and the issues surrounding them. I want you to decide for yourself what a profession is and whether or not teaching is a profession. This is not a rhetorical question, but a rather important one for you to consider. The answers you form in your own mind, not the ones you might rehearse to a university tutor or head teacher at a job interview, are crucial. They will determine how you see yourself in the coming months and years. Even more importantly, they will determine a lot about how you try to manage other people's expectations of you in this role – and that comes with challenges, sometimes direct and serious ones.

The philosophical and political context

In the 1960s and 1970s, issues emerged from both the political left and right about the perceived status of the established professions and the rhetoric around them. The left became increasingly suspicious of the threats to professional autonomy posed by the growth of managerialism and bureaucratisation. The right cited the primacy of 'client interest' (and later 'consumer interest', which in our case is pupils and parents) over what it referred to as the 'producer interest' (in our case, teachers and their advocates – the teacher unions).

The 'traditionalist' view of teaching is that teachers are custodians and purveyors of a specific set of values and key agents for the transmission of culture. Fundamentally, teachers are people who can be – or should be – looked up to as exemplars of the highest standards of a society's principal values and culture; people who possess not just skills and knowledge but a range of virtues. However, there is a natural tension between those who think that teachers are and should be purveyors of a society's value system and those who think teachers should maintain a value-neutral and independent stance.

Educational 'radicals' and 'progressives' (usually on the left but not exclusively) challenged and resisted the notions of bureaucratisation and managerialism that came with professionalisation, on the grounds that it undermined professional autonomy and even dehumanised the education process. Some, including various generations of politicians – of all persuasions – conceived of teaching not as a profession but as a trade or craft with a restricted set of skills, knowledge and contractual obligations.

Personally, I prefer the notion that a profession is essentially a community of shared values. This definition embraces the idea of common purpose with colleagues and peers, and the importance of trying to improve your own practice through continuous development and working collegially. It also extends to having a defined role set out in a code of practice, a common technical language, a belief in reflective practice and a commitment to the regulation of yourself and your colleagues based on the standards you profess to uphold.

Clearly, then, a body of people that claim to be a profession must:

- Provide an important public service.
- Involve theory as well as practice in what they do.
- Submit to regulated recruitment and discipline.
- Demonstrate a high degree of autonomy and independence of judgement.
- Display values and attitudes commensurate with the rights of, and obligations to, their clients.
- Reflect motives that are designed to elevate the interests and needs of the public generally.

In my view, any profession worthy of its name must include all these things. An individual who claims to be a member of a profession but who lacks these virtues or this commitment, however skilful or knowledgeable they are, is not ethically fit to practice.[12]

Emmanuel Kant, the eighteenth-century German philosopher, referred to a morally grounded 'categorical imperative' that distinguishes the particular agency of some people (he did not use the term 'professionals', but let's call them that) compared to the absence of agency in others (let's call them 'non-professionals'). In other words, we have the basis for a profession where such a necessary provision contributes to human flourishing – such as the application of healthcare, justice and education – or where its lack contributes materially to human impoverishment – such as disease, injustice and ignorance. While we are at it philosophically, Aristotle had something to say on this too. He asserted that, at least in principle, there are some activities that we should deliberate on carefully as means rather than ends. He argued that a doctor does not deliberate whether he or she should heal, but only how to heal; a lawyer does

12 For more on definitions of a profession, see Campbell, *The Ethical Teacher*; Carr, *Professionalism and Ethics in Teaching*; and Meryl Thompson, *Professional Ethics and the Teacher* (Stoke-on-Trent: Trentham Books, 1997).

not deliberate about whether he or she should promote justice, but only how to promote justice; and a teacher does not deliberate about whether a child should be educated, but only how.

Compare this to the activities of the trades, as we did earlier. As I hope I have made clear, this is not to demean or denigrate other kinds of important work, but to describe, as comparatively fixed, the basic goals of activities like plumbing, joinery, catering, hairdressing and car mechanics. The essential questions about the efficient and economic achievement of the means and ends are comparatively technical. A service is being provided: repair a boiler, fit a kitchen, cook a meal, cut and style hair, service a car. By contrast, the practices of medicine, law and education have a philosophy that is not applicable to a trade. Society asks itself some fundamental questions about these practices, such as: 'What does healing the sick mean?' 'What does justice mean?' 'What does education mean?' and 'What is the scope of such a practice in a civilised society?' We don't ask these fundamental questions, or need to ask them in the same way, about plumbing, hairdressing or car mechanics.

Do professions go on strike?

Some years ago, I was at a drinks party one Saturday evening in the neighbourhood where I live. There I was, standing around, drinking wine and chatting to my neighbours. I was introduced to a guy I didn't know, who asked me what I did for a living.

'By profession, I'm a teacher,' I said, being genial.

He laughed.

'Did I say something funny?' I enquired.

'Oh, I didn't mean to laugh,' he said (although clearly he did), 'but I hear this a lot from teachers. I'm sorry, teaching is *not* a profession.'

I was astonished: 'Why do you say that?'

'Because teachers go on strike,' he said. 'Professions don't go on strike.'

'Don't they?'

'No,' he said, quite firmly. 'Look at the codes of conduct of any established profession and see what it says: "We put the interests of our clients first." If you're going on strike for better pay, better pensions or better working conditions,' he said, and there was a tone of disdain in his voice now, 'then you're not putting the interests of your clients first, are you? You're putting *yourself* before the interests of your clients.'

Now, I must admit that I was very challenged by his remarks. For the next ten minutes we had a rather interesting, even quite animated, discussion about whether teaching met the criteria for being a profession. At that point, I had been teaching for nearly twenty years! Now someone had come along out of the blue and told me, 'Teaching is not a profession.' Suddenly, I was challenged to find good reasons why I thought it was.

Is going on strike unprofessional? Not to me. I did it three times in the 1980s. Twice because of what I perceived as unjustifiable cuts to the national education budget, which I was convinced would be injurious to children's life chances. Once for better pay, based on the argument that good graduates would not be attracted into teaching while pay levels were so comparatively low. I didn't take a cavalier attitude to going on strike, but as a young, single man without responsibilities (as I was at the time), I was very focused on what I thought was the moral justification for my actions.

The day before one of the planned strikes, just as I was leaving school, a father of a child in my class approached me as I was getting into my car.

'Oi! Are you lot going on strike tomorrow?' he called out as he approached. I could tell by the tone of his voice that this wasn't a casual enquiry.

'Yes, I'm afraid so …'

'What's it about this time?' he said bluntly.

'Better pay.'

'Better pay! You're joking, aren't you?'

'No. I'm afraid not …' and I began what must have sounded like a rather patronising rationale for why I thought it was necessary. 'We're protesting to government about the low levels of teacher pay … we can't attract good graduates into teaching … we can't recruit good teachers into the inner-city … blah, blah, blah.'

'Don't give me that sob story!' he interrupted. 'You lot are better paid than I am! And you don't have to work on a building site in all weathers either! I'm having to take a day off work tomorrow and lose a day's pay to look after my kids while you lot are out protesting!'

I drove home that night reflecting on what he had said. Not that his remarks didn't apply to parents of all social backgrounds, of course, but it did weigh on me heavily how much impact losing a day's pay might have on a working class family in Hackney who could ill afford it.

Discuss and reflect

- Are there justifiable reasons why professional people, dedicated to the interests of their clients, might go on strike? In your view, what are those reasons?

Such challenges are going to happen to you, perhaps in different contexts and circumstances, but they will come. I am not telling you that you should never go on strike, but the parents and children you teach deserve an explanation about why you are prepared to do it – a compelling one. That explanation may be something like: 'We can't attract good people into teaching unless we can compete on salary with other graduate professions' or it might be: 'The lack of resources means we can't deliver the standard of education that you and your children deserve' or even: 'I'm sorry, but I can't live on the salary I'm currently paid!' Whatever your reasons, they need to be credible, reasonably justifiable and relate to your professionalism.

If you think teaching is a profession, start rehearsing your arguments.

Chapter 3

THE TEACHER AND THE LAW – THE TEACHER YOU MUST BE

Teachers not only have wide-ranging legal responsibilities but they have wide-ranging authorities too, endorsed by statute, which give them the power to impose discipline and punishment (including, where necessary, the use of reasonable force). However, while the intention of this chapter is to provide information about your legal responsibilities and authorities as a teacher, above all it is intended to reassure you. It is not intended to alarm you. I will not be lecturing you: 'You mustn't do this! You mustn't do that! You mustn't touch children!' and so on.

There is quite enough scaremongering in the guise of 'advice' that does little more than drain confidence from people who we want to be excited about working with children, so I am not going to contribute to that fear. However, teachers do have significant legal responsibilities, which if abdicated could make them answerable to allegations of neglect. This is particularly true in relation to the quality of care they give to children. In order to make sense of these complex and weighty responsibilities, I want to make the case for revitalising the notion of being *in loco parentis* – accepting responsibilities like those of a responsible parent.

You may find that I repeat some advice quite often in this chapter. The reason for that is because, in my experience, it needs repeating. So, forgive me if I seem at times to be hammering home some points with sledgehammer-like iteration. If you remember it, you will thank me for it.

This chapter sets out calmly and sensibly the key legal responsibilities and authorities most relevant to you. They are:

- Recent legal statutes (in other words, the laws of the land).
- Old and established English common law precedents (which often emphasise that which is considered 'reasonable' in any given situation).
- Contracts of employment.

I will again raise points to discuss, reflect on and debate, so please use the discussion panels to pause, think and talk about the issues with fellow trainees or colleagues if you have the opportunity.

Duty of care

Discuss and reflect

I referred briefly to duty of care in the last chapter.

- What is a teacher's duty of care? Come up with a sentence or paragraph to describe it.
- Consider the scope and extent of a teacher's duty of care. Does it, for example, extend beyond the school grounds or beyond the school day?

Imagine you are doing your Saturday afternoon shopping on the local high street. You see some children from your school. They are sitting in a bus stop and smoking cigarettes.

- Would you do anything about it? Should you exercise a teacher's duty of care in this situation?

Before we assess the issues relating to whether you would deal with a group of children from your school seen smoking, let's start with some definitions and general scoping around a teacher's duty of care and go back to the three categories I have just mentioned: statutory, common law and contractual.

Statutory duty of care

Believe it or not, in spite of all the weighty and complex responsibilities teachers have, the legal description of these responsibilities is surprisingly vague. For example, Section 11 of the Children Act 2004 requires teachers to have regard for the need to safeguard and promote the welfare of children when carrying out their work.[1] There are a number of references to a teacher's duty of care being defined as what is considered 'reasonable' in the circumstances. Not very specific, is it? But note the word reasonable; you are going to come across it a lot in the following pages. When I lead

1 A summary of teachers' safeguarding responsibilities under this Act (and others related to it) appears in Department for Education, *Keeping Children Safe in Education (2020): Statutory Guidance for Schools and Colleges* (2020, updated January 2021). Available at: https://www.gov.uk/government/publications/keeping-children-safe-in-education--2.

discussions on this in training centres and universities, the general consensus I get from audiences (after allowing them time to discuss the question) is that a definition of a teacher's duty of care includes things like:

- Providing for a child's educational needs as well as their physical, emotional, psychological and mental welfare.
- Furnishing a safe and secure learning environment.
- Caring for a child's needs both in and outside of school – bearing in mind that a teacher is not a parent but has responsibilities to look out for and report signs of neglect or abuse.

In all the sessions I have done over many years, nobody has ever said: 'I just want to teach my class, go home and forget everything until the next day.' In the UK, our educational culture has evolved a very wide interpretation of the notion of duty of care. Personally, I find it quite inspiring that we embrace such a professional culture. It is not true of all countries or for all professional, ethical codes related to teaching – at least not to the same extent. There are countries that have a much more constrained and tightly defined view of what a teacher's duty of care entails, which does not reflect a lack of personal dedication or commitment but is more about contractual obligation. Here in the UK, we accept a wider interpretation that, in my view, enhances our role and fits with the idea of being like that of a parent (which we will come to shortly).

Common law duty of care

English common law and its origins go back almost a thousand years.[2] It has helped to introduce and establish the notion of what is reasonable in terms of the limits of legal responsibility. While it might seem vague and unspecific in modern parlance, this was a massive leap forward in establishing a rule of law, which ultimately (admittedly centuries later) led to notions of universal human rights. The roots of concepts like what is reasonable and defensible action emerged from such historical milestones as the Magna Carta (1215) through to the protection of the individual against the state and the articulation of liberties in constitutional documents like the Petition of Right

2 English common law is the body of law developed primarily from judicial decisions (in other words, judges), based on custom and precedent, unwritten in statute or code. It constitutes the basis of the English legal system.

(1628) and the Bill of Rights (1689), and on down to the judgements made by the UK Supreme Court in the twenty-first century. Even today, where and when a case of a teacher's duty of care is examined or tested (which is extremely rare) a court will ask:

- Did the teacher behave in a way that a caring and responsible parent would?
- Did the teacher take reasonable steps to avoid exposing pupils to foreseeable dangers with which those children could not reasonably be expected to cope? (While, all the time, making allowances for the fact that taking responsibility for the management of thirty children is of a different order than taking responsibility for managing children within a family.)

In extreme and unusual circumstances, a court might test the extent to which any failings or neglect might have occurred, although in reality this examination is much more likely to be focused on the collective or institutional failings of a school rather than an individual teacher. For example, a child may have been injured in an accident caused by furniture or equipment failure. This would probably be seen as the collective failing of the school (sometimes known as 'vicarious liability') in not maintaining its furniture or equipment to a safe standard. As a new teacher, you should be reassured that unless there is clear evidence that you have failed to prevent harm through a reckless level of negligence, then it is very unlikely that you will be culpable for neglect as an individual.

A teacher, regardless of age or experience, will be expected to have considered the level of risk to which the children were exposed. For example, was it commensurate with what the teacher knew about the levels of sensibility, maturity and skill of the pupils in the context in which they were being taught? It seems blindingly obvious, but you must take into account the fact that not all your pupils can cope with the same degree of risk. You only have to observe a class of 5- or 6-year-olds climbing the PE apparatus for the very first time – their levels of confidence and skill will vary enormously. Clearly, what is considered a reasonable duty of care in preventing harm and neglect, and any resulting liability, will be informed by the circumstances in which you are teaching. This will include:

- **The subject or the activity being taught.** Teaching 6-year-olds gymnastics is patently more hazardous than sitting them on the classroom carpet and reading them a story. Teaching 15-year-olds practical chemistry or dissecting specimens in biology is clearly more risky than studying a Shakespeare play or conjugating French verbs.
- **The age, dexterity and maturity of the children.** A reasonably responsible teacher would not (I hope) introduce sharp knives or potentially dangerous tools for the first time to a group of 7-year-olds in the same way as they might

introduce them to a class of 12-year-olds. Relationships and sexuality wouldn't be discussed with a class of 10-year-olds in the same way that they would with a class of 16-year-olds.

- **The available resources and furniture design.** If you are an early years teacher you will be immediately aware of furniture design that is inappropriate for the age group. There won't be (or shouldn't be) tables with sharp corners or chairs too high for the children to sit on. If you are a science teacher and your lab has a limited number of Bunsen burners, you will be much more alert to the way you manage the pupils and how safely you can demonstrate and engage them in scientific techniques.

- **The size of the class.** Doing any kind of practical activity with a class of up to thirty pupils (let alone hazardous activities involving tools, hot ovens or naked flames) is a very different proposition in terms of planning and preparation than doing the same activity with a small group of five or six children.

Before you set your default risk mode to the lowest common denominator and avoid any kind of hazard, you should be reassured by the fact that in the event of any accidents, if teachers take all reasonable steps to ensure the safety of their pupils, it is very unlikely that they will be held to be negligent. As I mentioned earlier, and want to emphasise again, negligence could arise if there is a serious failure to prevent harm to a child, although this is more likely to be a collective or institutional failing rather than an individual culpability.

During my first two decades in teaching (the 1980s and 1990s), many schools around the country had fallen into a parlous state of disrepair. In two cases I can remember in the boroughs where I taught in East London, part of a ceiling fell onto the floor of the school hall only minutes after a whole-school assembly had finished. In another, a large sash window – ten feet in height – fell from its frame onto the (thankfully empty) school playground. Obviously, these were issues relating to the maintenance of the school and were therefore the responsibility of the local authority at the time. These days, the responsibility is much more likely to be down to the governing body of the school or the academy trust.

However, schools are by their nature potentially hazardous places – and quite right too. Exciting things should be going on all the time to physically and mentally challenge young people; that is the function of schools. Of course, both you as an individual teacher and the school as an institution must take all reasonable steps to make it as safe as possible. Try to foresee the possibility of accidents and minimise the risk of them happening, but do not design and plan your teaching to avoid risk altogether. Risk is unavoidable where challenge exists. This is a matter of common sense rather than the application of specialist skill or knowledge. I implore you not to avoid risk but to challenge children – and manage and minimise risks where you can. The good news is that when you take all reasonable steps to do so, the law will protect you.

Contractual duty of care

The School Teachers' Pay and Conditions Document (STPCD) sets out the twenty-nine statutory duties of a teacher.[3] This is a national agreement between teachers and employers that goes towards forming the contract of employment between the two. Most of the (approximately) 450,000 teachers in over 24,000 schools in England work to this document, but check with your employer. The STPCD doesn't necessarily apply in academies and free schools, although contracts are often very similar. You may find there are small but important stipulations in your employer's contract referring to planning and teaching lessons and schemes of work, assessing and monitoring progress, and promoting safety and well-being.

Another dimension to contractual definitions of duty of care is that most schools have adopted formal codes of conduct into employment contracts, usually from the previous functions of local authorities. As if the STPCD, the Teachers' Standards, the Ofsted Framework and goodness knows how many Education Acts weren't enough, these school codes of conduct set out the standards and expectations for ethical behaviour both within and sometimes outside of school. If your school has a code of conduct, and it probably does, read it. Indeed, ask for a copy if you don't have one. Normally, you will be asked to sign and accept a code of conduct when you start work. It is likely to include:

- The school's policy on physical contact with pupils, particularly with reference to vulnerable children with special needs.
- Interactions with pupils and the appropriate use of language and teaching materials.
- Arrangements for meeting or communicating with pupils outside of school hours, particularly via mobile phones or social media.
- The use of school property for private use or the potential impact of undertaking activities outside school.
- The acceptance of gifts or hospitality.

3 Department for Education, *School Teachers' Pay and Conditions Document 2020 and Guidance on School Teachers' Pay and Conditions* (September 2020). Available at: https://www.gov.uk/government/publications/school-teachers-pay-and-conditions.

- The disclosure of confidential information and data relating to pupils.

These customised codes of conduct are almost always universally imposed from above and usually focus on foreseeing negative possibilities. While I understand and sympathise with the pressures on head teachers and schools, such codes contribute to a negative accountability culture that does nothing to inspire teachers. More than that, as they are often negatively couched, they arguably undermine the whole notion of a professionalism that should come from within – the nurturing of a community of shared values that inspires teachers to achieve their full potential on behalf of children.

'Last night my teacher was drinking beer with my dad!'

In mid-career, I ran the school football team for several years. I involved parents in training sessions: they washed the kit and helped me ferry the kids to and from matches. They loved it and their kids loved it too.

One evening after an away game, the dad of a particularly challenging boy (who was in my class) was helping me to drop off the kids at their homes. I was keen to have him involved because it clearly made a difference to his son's motivation and behaviour in school. After we had dropped off the last child (and by this time it was well into the evening) he said: 'Come and have a cup of tea before you go home.' I thought it was a kind offer, so I accepted. I entered his home, his wife greeted me warmly and his embarrassed but excited son moved the cat off the sofa. We all chatted about the game (we had lost) and I sipped a very welcome cup of tea after a long day. But before I knew it, the boy's mum had made me a sandwich and his father was taking a couple of beers from the fridge and prising off the bottle tops.

Now, what is happening? Am I about to cross a boundary? Is there a risk to be managed? Or a different judgement to be made? On the one hand, I could accept their hospitality. But Little Johnny – as nice a boy as he was – might go straight into school next morning and tell all his friends: 'Hey, Mr Newland was in our house last night drinking beer with my dad!' and I would be left to deal with the possibly damaging perceptions that might flow from that. On the other, I could politely decline and risk causing offence to parents I wanted to remain actively involved in their child's schooling.

What do you think I did? What would you do in that situation? Accept the sandwich and decline the beer? Decline both? Make your excuses and leave? You might do one of these, and I wouldn't blame you if you did. What I did was to accept graciously the hospitality that I judged was well intended and genuinely offered. Little Johnny didn't go into the playground the next morning and blab to his mates. His parents remained actively involved in the school until the day he left.

There are always risks to be evaluated and judgements to be made. If you make them in the best interests of the children and their families, I think you will be able to live with them. As I did.

In loco parentis

For those of you lacking a classical education (and that includes me), *in loco parentis* is Latin for 'in place of the parent'. It is thought by some in the legal arena to be an archaic term since the Children Act 1989 gave children an independent legal status. The term 'duty of care' has been used much more regularly since; however, *in loco parentis* provides teachers with a very helpful if not hugely positive and inspiring analogy for understanding the nature of their duty of care.

The notion derives from a court ruling dating back to 1893 that 'the schoolmaster is bound to take care of his pupils as a careful father would'.[4] Don't be put off by the archaic Victorian language but focus on the idea – one that retained a valuable currency for many decades. By the 1960s, courts regularly upheld that the 'standard of care' expected from a teacher to be that of 'a person exhibiting the responsible mental qualities of *a parent in the circumstances of the school, rather than home life*'. Just as useful and encouraging for teachers was the idea that being *in loco parentis* acknowledged that 'the "sturdy independence" of a child is to be encouraged and that classroom activities may present the occasional risk'.[5]

In my view, the idea of being *in loco parentis* is both inspiring and reassuring. Even if you are not a parent, we all have a reasonable understanding of how a responsible parent would behave in most situations. It is a very helpful and encouraging way of thinking about your duty of care as a new teacher. In recent decades, rather than inspiring young teachers to see themselves as being a responsible agent in place of the parent, the law has focused on negatively identifying bad behaviour with a strong emphasis on deterrence.[6] This has created a climate of extreme caution, even fear, and has resulted in a widespread loss of conviction and self-belief, especially around

4 See Williams v Eady (1893) (10 TLR 41).
5 See Jon Berry, *Teachers' Legal Rights and Responsibilities: A Guide for Trainee Teachers and Those New to the Profession* (St Albans: University of Hertfordshire Press, 2013), p. 6 (original emphasis).
6 For more on this, see Kate Myers with Graham Clayton, David James and Jim O'Brien, *Teachers Behaving Badly: Dilemmas for School Leaders* (Abingdon: RoutledgeFalmer, 2004), ch. 5.

physical contact and the full application of duty of care. Teachers themselves, and especially those in senior positions who are highly sensitive to a school's reputation, have unwittingly diluted confidence in the operation of professional judgement out of fear of accountability if they get it wrong.

Ask yourself ...

When you find yourself planning or teaching an activity where the risk of an accident happening is greater than average, or you think your duty of care might be tested, or questions might be asked about how you planned and prepared, then ask yourself: what would a responsible parent do now?

If you do what a responsible parent would do – that is, demonstrate care and show you have done what is reasonable to prevent a foreseeable accident and respond and act in the way a responsible parent would if an accident happens – then you are, in almost all conceivable circumstances, acting to safeguard and promote the welfare of the child. Acting *in loco parentis* is, in almost all conceivable circumstances, fulfilling your duty of care. If you are behaving appropriately *in loco parentis*, then the law will protect you from allegations of neglect. Be reassured by that. Don't let the fear that a child might have an accident be the sole reason for denying them the right to experience risk and challenge. Exposure to risk and challenge develops character in the child and character in you as a teacher. It is the golden thread running through this book.

Duty of care and out-of-school activities

Schools are generally routine places where timetables and behavioural norms quickly become established and habitual. Children know the expectations of school life even if they don't always abide by them. They know they should walk (not run) in the corridor, not push and shove each other, keep the noise down, sit in rows or islands at desks and tables and so on. Schools are all about routine, order and limits.

The moment you take kids out on an educational visit, all that routine and order goes straight out of the window. Outside of school there is hazard everywhere. The noise and motion of cars, lorries, buses and trains, and people bustling hither and thither. The kids suddenly get excited and distracted – and that is even before you have arrived at the theatre, museum or activity centre. Oh dear, I have just reminded myself of the Maxine story, and now I have thought of another one too.

'I wanted to thank you for bringing me on this trip'

Darren (not his real name) was a troubled little boy in my Year 6 class. His father was in prison and his mother was struggling with drug and alcohol problems of her own. She was trying to bring up two kids as a single parent. I could see that Darren was both intelligent and perceptive, but serious misdemeanours were his way of distracting himself from the daily family turmoil that surrounded him.

We were doing the Second World War as a topic from the history curriculum. I was reading *The Diary of Anne Frank* to the class as part of a series of activities that they were thoroughly enjoying: dressing up in 1940s clothes, cooking with food rations and listening to the testimonies of elderly people who had been evacuated as children their age. During my lesson preparation research, I discovered to my delight that Anne Frank's stepsister, a woman named Eva Schloss (by this time in her sixties), had moved to London after the war, had married and had a family, and was living only a few miles from the school. Through a publisher, I wrote to her and asked whether she would visit my class and talk to the children about her experiences of the Second World War, which, being Jewish, had included going into hiding, being interned in a concentration camp, and losing her father and brother to the gas chambers, so they were remarkably similar to Anne Frank's own.

When she accepted the invitation, it was Darren who had the brilliant idea that we should make a video of Eva's visit. To cut a long story short, I put him in charge of directing and filming Eva's talk. He showed a natural ability with a camera and produced a moving and inspiring historical testament.[7] While Darren responded brilliantly to the challenge, it proved to be a brief respite from his behavioural infractions, which were sometimes serious.

As the end of the summer term approached (and the topic on the Second World War), I organised a visit to the Anne Frank House in Amsterdam. It was a fitting climax to a project during which the children had excelled. They were soon to be leaving the school, so an excursion abroad was a nice way to end their primary school careers. It was a four-day trip involving a long coach journey from East London, a cross-Channel ferry, overnight stays in a hotel and various visits to museums and historical sites around Amsterdam, all related to Anne Frank. My head teacher at the time, Richard Crease – a generous, supportive and very responsible man – asked me whether I intended to take Darren. I said tentatively that I would. Richard looked uncertain, questioning the wisdom and reminding

7 You can view this film at www.youtube.com/watch?v=4ubyZVyHpPQ.

me of Darren's unstable behaviour, his difficulties managing stressful situations and the number of times he had been accused of taking or damaging other people's property. He suggested I think about it overnight.

I won't say I had a completely sleepless night but I did think about it long and hard. The next day I went back to Richard and said that I had decided to take him. In order to reassure him, however, I would make sure that Darren stayed by my side the whole time. Richard, excellent head that he was, looked at me and said: 'OK, I'm not sure that would've been my decision, but I'll back you on it. I just pray he doesn't let you down.' When the news got out, a number of my colleagues came to me with undisguised incredulity asking: 'You're not taking Darren to Amsterdam, are you?' I must admit their reactions led to some momentary doubts.

On the morning we departed, Darren and his mother arrived at school first. She delivered him to me personally and left him with the words: 'Behave yourself now, Darren – and remember you're to stay with Mr Newland at all times.' He nodded silently. I knew that would be a tall order. Things started well. On the coach to Dover, Darren was the picture of a well-behaved boy. Then we got on the cross-Channel ferry. By now, it was a beautiful, warm summer's day and a fresh breeze was blowing. The kids wanted to walk around the decks and enjoy the sea air and the swaying of the boat on the open sea, which most of them had never experienced before and was exciting. I organised them into groups with various adults to accompany them. I trusted them to behave as they went off to explore and look out to sea.

I sat with Darren in the rather stuffy passenger lounge trying to make conversation. After a while, we ran out of things to talk about and he asked me if he could go to the toilet. I didn't want to behave like his jailor, so I let him go on his own. I sat reading my newspaper, occasionally interrupted by children thrillingly reporting the rolling of the boat and the windy conditions on the English Channel. Suddenly, I realised that Darren should have been back by now. I went to find him but he was nowhere to be seen. Just as the first thoughts of self-reproval crept into my mind, I saw a man in a naval uniform walking towards me holding Darren by one hand and a plastic bag in the other. The bag had the words 'duty free' on it.

'Is this your teacher?' said the officer sternly. Darren nodded. 'I just wanted to be sure,' he said addressing me. He introduced himself as the purser. 'This young man asked me to buy something for him in the duty-free shop ...' holding up the bag. 'I needed to check he was telling the truth about why he insisted he had to buy it.' The purser handed the bag back to Darren and walked off. Darren held it out to me. 'It's for you,' he said. I took the bag and looked inside. By chance, or perhaps the diligent investigation of his mother, it was a large bottle of my favourite single malt whisky. 'Me and my mum wanted to say thank you for letting me come on this trip,' he said.

The moral of the story? Don't think the law is there to stop you doing things or to try and catch you out. Be responsible, but be willing to take risks in order to create challenge, adventure and moments that the children – and you – will never forget.

Before you start taking kids out on educational visits, you will get some induction (if not training) on how to do it. You will certainly go out first with an experienced teacher, be shown how to complete a risk assessment, plan the visit according to school or local authority protocols, obtain permission slips and any additional insurance (if that is necessary), don the kids with high-vis jackets and brightly coloured baseball-style caps and so on. The point I want to reiterate here is the basic concept of doing what is reasonable to keep them safe.

Don't think that just because a child has a history of challenging behaviour they can never be trusted to go on a school trip. Being given the trust and responsibility usually denied them might be the catalyst that turns them around. Think like a responsible parent and do what he or she would do. That is how to fulfil your basic duty of care.

Finally:

- Be assured that there is no legal liability for any injury sustained by pupils unless there is proven negligence on your part.
- Being *in loco parentis* satisfies your responsibilities for duty of care and absolves you of almost all conceivable liabilities for neglect.
- Liability goes with fault. In the case of an accident, where no one could reasonably foresee that accident happening, then no single individual bears liability.

Checklist for planning out-of-school activities

- Read the school's policies on risk assessment and planning outdoor activities and any advice that your local authority or academy trust might provide.
- Check the qualifications and credentials of the outdoor activity provider (i.e. the activity or outward-bound centre).

- Assess whether the planned activities are commensurate with the skills and physical and emotional maturity of the pupils.
- Make parents aware of any foreseeable risks involved in the activities.
- Consult the advice provided by:
  - Council for Learning Outside the Classroom (www.lotc.org.uk)
  - Health and Safety Executive (www.hse.gov.uk/services/education/school-trips.pdf)
  - Outdoor Education Advisers' Panel (www.oeapng.info)
- Read any subject association advice on planning outdoor activities.

What are your responsibilities outside of school? Coming across smokers and drinkers

Let's get back to those pesky smokers sitting at the bus stop – remember them? (I've got some underage drinkers in a pub for you to meet in a moment as well!)

If you discussed or even just thought about the question I set at the beginning of this chapter, you may have decided that a number of options presented themselves. For the sake of argument, the kids smoking cigarettes are under the age of 16, so technically what they are doing is illegal (although, of course, this is not a matter the police would normally be concerned with as, understandably, they have more important things to do). Keep in mind your legal responsibility to be *in loco parentis* and to do all that is reasonable to safeguard the children who are in your care. Let's examine some options you might have considered.

Option 1

You may have decided that the best thing to do was report the matter to a more senior or experienced colleague back at school on Monday morning. The head or deputy will surely want to know if kids from the school are doing something that is harmful to their health and well-being. You will probably know by now that all schools have a designated safeguarding lead (DSL) who has been trained and is responsible for issues like this. When you go on teaching practice or get your first job, find out who that person is. They will know exactly what to do. They may want to speak to the children involved, reminding them of the health issues around smoking, and they may also speak to their parents.

Are these reasonable responses? Yes.

Option 2

You may have thought, 'Hmm, best not confront these kids – after all, they're not actually on the school premises or even in school uniform. I don't know these kids very well either, so I don't want to have a situation on my hands that I can't handle. They might even kick off and give me a mouthful of abuse and tell me where to go! Best thing to do is just report it to the head or DSL on Monday morning.'

Is this reasonable? Yes.

Option 3

You may go into school on Monday and decide not to say anything directly to the kids involved, but after reporting it to the head or DSL you plan some specific educational responses. If you are a primary school teacher you might have the flexibility to produce a series of sessions on health and well-being, focusing on the dangers of smoking. If you are a secondary teacher you might use your tutor group time to address the issues of smoking or perhaps plan a school assembly on the topic.

Are they reasonable options? Yes.

Option 4

You may go into school on Monday and not only report what you saw to the head or DSL, but have a quiet word with the children as well (depending on your existing relationships), perhaps saying something like: 'I was really disappointed that I saw you smoking on Saturday. You know that's a silly thing to do, don't you? Smoking is very bad for you. You don't want to damage your health, do you?'

Reasonable? Definitely.

Option 5

You may decide to look the other way, pretend you didn't see a thing and get on with your Saturday afternoon shopping, satisfied in the knowledge that you can't possibly be a teacher twenty-four hours a day and, anyway, this is your precious weekend!

Is that reasonable? No.

The very least you can – and must – do is go back to school and report it to someone who has formal responsibility. What if the child had seen you? Walking away and doing nothing is sending them a very clear message that you don't care. As a bare minimum, if and when you see a child doing something they shouldn't be doing outside of school (especially if they have seen you) is to give them the 'evil eye'. This is the look that says: 'I've seen you. I'm not going to do anything now, but I'll be dealing with it back in school on Monday.'

As a trainee teacher, or even as an early career teacher, you probably won't know the kids very well and you may feel that you aren't sufficiently established in the school to have the air of natural authority that more experienced teachers seem to have. Of course, you will be nervous about saying or doing anything there and then, of not being able to control a situation if it escalates and they react negatively or even aggressively. That is understandable. But in a few years' time, when you may have been a teacher at the school for four, five or six years, you will know these kids and their families well, and you will be an established teacher with considerable cachet, authority and respect. When that is the case, you may well consider the following option.

Option 6

You may think about going over to these kids and saying: 'What on earth are you doing a silly thing like that for? You know that smoking is bad for you. Why are you harming yourself?' Would that be the wrong thing for a teacher to do? A lot of people in my audiences aren't sure – they think they aren't allowed to challenge kids outside of school.

Let's go back to the definitions of duty of care that we considered earlier. There are the informal definitions that focus on caring for a child's educational needs, as well as their physical, emotional, psychological and mental needs, both in and outside of school. Then there are the legal ones that refer to being *in loco parentis* – behaving as a responsible parent would in the circumstances. We can test these definitions now.

Would a responsible parent challenge their own child if they saw them smoking? The answer is, of course, yes. Now, you might say: 'But these aren't my children. It's outside of school and outside of school hours' or: 'These kids might tell me it's none of my business. They may say: "Get lost, Miss! This is my Saturday! I'm not in school now. I can do what I want!"' Yes, they might say that, but it doesn't mean that challenging them is the wrong thing to do. It isn't. If you believe that your duty of care as a teacher is to care for a child's physical, emotional, psychological and mental needs both in and outside of school, then challenging children when you see them doing something wrong is the right thing to do.

If you choose that option, the good news is that the law is on your side. Why? Because you are behaving as a responsible parent would in the circumstances – *in loco parentis*. Of course, don't turn a reasonable challenge into a full-blown confrontation where a heated argument ensues. That would just inflame the situation. And don't try to wrestle the cigarettes out of their hands. That would be assault. The law would not protect you in those circumstances. I am not telling you to take this option if you are uncomfortable with it, but if you are behaving as a responsible parent would, then legally you have nothing to worry about.

But I haven't finished yet!

You might get into school on Monday and be met with an angry parent: 'What are you doing poking your nose into my child's business on a Saturday afternoon? What my kids do in their own time is nothing to do with you!' What would be your answer now? Well, your answer could be: 'Actually, Mr or Mrs So-and-So, it is my business – in the sense that I am your child's teacher – and I have a responsibility to act when I see them doing something that is bad for their health or well-being. So I challenged them. I didn't tell them off. I didn't try to take the cigarettes. I didn't try to march them off anywhere – but I did challenge them. I'm sorry if I don't have your support for doing that – which is to behave as a responsible parent would in the circumstances – but, with respect, that won't stop me doing my job when I see your child doing something harmful or wrong.'

Of course, this is not the kind of conversation you are likely to have as a new teacher (and in fact, 99 per cent of parents will thank you rather than admonish you). Your head or deputy head should be handling difficult conversations with parents, but such conversations will happen in your career. When they do, avoid using confrontational or inflammatory language and try to de-escalate any conflict – but don't abdicate or deny what is your responsibility. Ultimately, parents and children, even the ones who resisted what you did, will respect you for it. Routinely, schools (through the DSL) will normally alert parents when a child's behaviour outside of school has caused concern, so all the relevant parties are forewarned of the issues. As I said, most parents will appreciate the duty of care you are willing to apply to their child even when they are not in school.

Once again, this is not to imply that you should necessarily choose option 6. There is no legal obligation on you to intervene at that moment if you decide not to. You may consider that it isn't a reasonable option given the circumstances. That will be your professional judgement. But if you did decide to intervene and behave as a responsible parent would, then the law will be on your side. The only wrong thing to do is nothing at all. Doing nothing is not an option for a professional person.

Discuss and reflect

- You are in the pub on a Saturday evening having a drink with your friends. You see some kids from your school. They are all 16 or 17 years old but they are drinking alcohol. What should you do?

'I'm not a teacher twenty-four hours a day and it's not my responsibility'

I was at a university in the North of England and had an interesting plenary session around the issue of underage drinking. One of the trainees put up his hand and said: 'I wouldn't do anything if I saw kids from my school drinking in a pub.'

'Really?' I asked.

'No. It's my Saturday night. It's my social time. I'm not a teacher twenty-four hours a day and it's not my responsibility.'

'OK,' I said. 'Can I test that?'

'Yeah, go on,' he said, up for the challenge.

'What if the kids were getting drunk? Would that matter?'

'No,' he said. 'That's their lookout.'

'Would you mention to the pub landlord that these kids were underage?'

'No, that's his job, not mine.'

'You know these kids from school. They know you. Would you go over and say something like: "Come on, lads … or come on, girls … you shouldn't be drinking alcohol. Out you go."'

'No, it's not my responsibility.'

'Not even if they were getting intoxicated?'

He shook his head.

'OK. Let's imagine a fight breaks out. They start throwing tables and chairs and it gets pretty ugly. Would you try and intervene to calm things down, knowing that you might have some influence over them as their teacher?'

'No,' he insisted.

'One of these kids is hit with a bottle across the face. It smashes. There's blood everywhere. The police and ambulance service have to be called. Do you feel any sense of responsibility or regret that you didn't intervene earlier?'

'Nope.' He was adamant.

'OK,' I said finally. 'Let's imagine that I'm the parent of this child who has been hit with a bottle. I find out that you were in the pub on the Saturday night. I come into school on Monday morning and I confront you, saying: "You're my child's teacher! You saw him drinking alcohol when you knew he was underage. Now he's got into a fight and someone has smashed a bottle in his face and scarred him for life!" What would you say to me?'

The trainee looked at me and replied quite confidently: 'This is what I would say to you: "Where were *you*? You're the parent, *not me!* Where were *you* while *your* son was out drinking and fighting in a pub on a Saturday night? I'm not your child's father, *you* are! Take responsibility."'

I thought that was a brilliant retort. Not only is it clever, it is also a perfectly defensible legal position to adopt, and you can adopt it if you want to. There is nothing that requires you as a teacher (or indeed, as a citizen) to intervene if you see someone breaking the law. This trainee went on to explain and justify himself: 'I draw a line,' he said, 'and I'm not crossing it. I'm keeping strict boundaries between my personal and professional life. We're always being told by our tutors not to have any kind of inappropriate relationships with our pupils, so I'm not going to confuse issues by crossing a line and getting involved in other people's business in my own time.' He added, 'And d'you know what else? I'm not letting people cross the line from the other direction either and allow them to have unrealistic expectations of me outside of my working life.'

I thought this guy made a very compelling and convincing case for his position. He knows he doesn't have any legal obligation to intervene and he is prepared to defend that position, even under pressure.

The problem for that young man, and for all teachers, is that there are millions of people who have a different expectation – one that is not formed primarily by an understanding of the legal or contractual obligations of teachers, but by the moral obligation they think we should have. I believe, although I have no evidence for this view, that the vast majority of the general public would expect a teacher to do something if they saw a child (especially a pupil) at risk of danger or neglect.

Of course, exactly what is expected of them is not clear, and that is where these issues get a little complicated. To clarify in a case like this, I suggest we go back to the definitions of doing what is reasonable in the circumstances for safeguarding the child and behaving as a responsible parent would. However, you should keep in mind the legal, moral and ethical distinctions as you go through this book and as you go through your career as a teacher. They are not always clear-cut, as we have just seen, but they will stand you in good stead when making considered and well-informed judgements.

Physical contact with pupils

The first thing I would like to say about the issue of physical contact is that the most profound contact teachers can make with a child is to smile – as an introduction or greeting or as a gesture of confidence, consolation, comfort, encouragement or reassurance. Although a smile is not really physical, it is a very visceral gesture, evoking deep emotional responses that are likely to build bonds of trust and faith.

Having said that, issues around physical contact have multiplied and intensified in recent years. In 2013, the Department for Education's revised guidance to all schools on physical contact included the following statement: 'It is not illegal to touch a pupil. There are occasions when physical contact (other than reasonable force) with a pupil is proper and necessary.'[8] This reminded schools that when teachers are doing their jobs properly, they will normally and systematically engage in a variety of forms of physical contact with their pupils. And not just occasionally either. Depending on the phase or the subject being taught, it might be regular or even constant. This seems a

8 Department for Education, *Use of Reasonable Force: Advice for Headteachers, Staff and Governing Bodies* (July 2013), p. 8. Available at: https://www.gov.uk/government/publications/use-of-reasonable-force-in-schools.

statement of the blindingly obvious to most sensible people. The reason the Department for Education may have felt it necessary to issue such guidance might have had something to do with the fact that thousands of schools around the country had policies (and still do) stating that staff should avoid or minimise physical contact with pupils.

How have we come to a situation where there is so much distrust? Any allegations of inappropriate, especially sexualised, touching would, of course, be emotionally devastating for the pupil and professionally catastrophic for the teacher. The reputation of the teacher and the school would suffer irreparable damage whether or not the accusation had any credence. In this sense, it is perfectly understandable that some teachers, schools and teacher unions have taken highly cautious, even extremely defensive, positions on this issue. But is extreme caution the appropriate response? In my view it is misguided. We will come to the reasons shortly.

Discuss and reflect

- Make a list of all the occasions when physical contact with your pupils is both proper and necessary. (Take your time – this is quite a long list.)

Sometimes when I am leading sessions, I phrase this question slightly differently (I am being a little mischievous). I say: 'When is it proper or even necessary to touch children?' I can see half the audience recoil in horror as though I am suggesting something sinister. It is curious and very sad to consider how, as a society, we have got ourselves into the insane position of believing that such a question could sound sinister. But, of course, it does; 'touching children' is a phrase that has come to sound ominous and forbidding. This is an illustration of how our normal human interactions are in danger of becoming abnormalised.

This phenomenon is not exclusive to the UK; it is true in most countries across the Western world. Issues around physical contact, not just between adults and children but also between adult men and women, have become highly problematic. The reasons for this are often rooted in legitimate concerns. The abuse that many people have suffered, often in silence and over many years, either as children at the hands of responsible adults or as adults at the hands of manipulative authority figures, is now coming to light as never before. The courage of those who decide to speak out is very considerable, and their attempts to bring those responsible to account – and in some cases to justice – means embarking on a difficult and perilous path that is not undertaken lightly. Their bravery is to be acknowledged and applauded.

However, as far as teachers are concerned, the urgent and legitimate duty to protect children from harm and keep them safe from abuse has somehow got confused with the equally legitimate need for teachers to apply a responsible duty of care. There are areas where these two concepts overlap, of course, but keeping children safe from abuse on the one hand and applying a duty of care on the other are two discrete notions. Protecting children from harm is an essential part of your role as a teacher, but that duty is much greater than simply protecting children from harm. Teachers have wider care responsibilities too which will involve touching children, sometimes on a regular basis.

Physical contact with other people, including children, is an appropriate and often necessary thing to do. In many ways, it is a desirable thing to do too. Clearly, the customs and mores of our culture and society shape the way that such touching takes place; you only have to go on holiday overseas to see how some things we take for granted in the UK are not acceptable forms of behaviour in other countries. Of course, we should be sensitive and respectful to others. Of course, we should be cautious about social and cultural norms of behaviour around physical contact. We have grown up respecting other people's personal space (or we should have), so we should not invade that personal space or impose ourselves on others without making a reasonable assumption that such impositions will be greeted with consent. Physical contact is a normal and regular part of human life – with all due respect to people who, for one reason or another (such as a disorder like autism), might need or want to avoid it.[9]

However, there are rules. The problem is that within any given culture most of these rules are unwritten and assumed. As a teacher in a school in the UK, you are operating within a particular subculture that has additional rules about all kinds of things, with physical contact being just one of them. That means taking responsibility to operate within these social and cultural rules – being confident about coming into physical contact with your pupils for necessary, proper and appropriate reasons – and not shying away from the responsibility when it arises.

In recent years, I have heard experienced teachers, mentors and advisors telling new teachers 'not to touch children unless it's an emergency' or 'only if you need to restrain them from fighting'. I have also heard teachers being advised to 'never be alone with a pupil' and 'always have another adult present or in an adjacent room'. This advice is given to male teachers in particular, many of whom are already scared witless about being an adult male in a classroom half full of adolescent girls. Remember the maxim we discussed earlier: the principal legal responsibility of a teacher is that of carrying out a duty of care *in loco parentis*. Behave as a responsible parent would. That is a legal responsibility as well as an ethical and moral lodestar.

9 The COVID-19 pandemic highlighted our need for regular physical contact as a way of normalising and enriching social interactions.

Allegations of inappropriate contact

A report prepared for the Department for Education in 2012 found that the number of allegations against teachers for inappropriate physical or sexualised contact was around 2,800 cases a year.[10] It sounds like a lot, but let's put that figure into context.

Most of these are not cases of alleged sexual contact but incidents where teachers have been accused of behaviour bordering on or involving physical assault. I am not condoning this behaviour, but professionally trained people (including nurses, doctors, police and prison officers, firefighters and social workers) do sometimes lose their composure with their clients or those they are trying to help, particularly in moments of extreme stress. It may happen when their intentions to help are met with impertinence, rudeness, insults, provocation or even outright assault. Sometimes their reaction to this includes pushing, shoving, mishandling or physical assault. Of course, such behaviour is incompatible with a professional ethic, but losing your temper is a human reaction to fraught circumstances.

Teachers, like many of the professionals listed above, are often exposed to highly demanding circumstances. However, of these 2,800 or so annual allegations, only about 3 per cent get beyond an initial investigative stage and reach substantive allegations. That means about sixty allegations a year, on average, go beyond an initial investigation. I am not being complacent or dismissive about the effect these incidents have either on the victim or the alleged perpetrator, but let's compare this figure to the number of teachers in the country, multiplied by the number of pupils in our schools, and roughly calculate the number of interactions between the two that take place every day. In the UK there are over half a million teachers working in the state sector. Add to this approximately nine million children who go to school every day, and then compute the number of combinations and permutations of social and physical interaction in classrooms, playgrounds, science labs, gymnasia, sports fields, music rooms, art and drama studios, IT suites and wherever else. There are literally tens, if not hundreds, of millions of such interactions every day. There are billions every year. That is the context for the approximately 2,800 initial allegations and fewer than 100 substantive ones.

While I fully acknowledge that the impact of physical and sexual abuse can be devastating for the individual concerned, as a profession, and as a society, we must keep a sense of perspective on the statistics and the likelihood of inappropriate contact occurring in schools. We must not generate an irrational fear about this issue that

10 Department for Education and York Consulting LLP, *Allegations of Abuse Against Teachers and Non-Teaching Staff*. Research Report DFE-RR192 (2012), p. 7. Available at: https://assets.publishing.service.gov.uk/government/uploads/system/uploads/attachment_data/file/361444/DFE-RR192.pdf.

leads pupils to distrust their teachers merely because they are adults in positions of power and authority. Equally importantly, we must not generate a climate of such defensiveness and caution that a teacher's legitimate need for confidence, including physical confidence, around pupils is constrained or, worse still, paralysed.

'Yes, yes, yes – but what happens if, or when, an allegation is made?'

If in the infinitesimally small chance that an allegation is made against you, then you should do the following without delay:

- Ask the school to furnish you with a set of their procedures for dealing with such an incident.
- Contact your trade union. (If you haven't joined a union, you won't be able to access their services retrospectively. My advice is to join one now.)
- Do and say nothing until you have spoken to your trade union representative or the solicitor you have chosen to represent you.

Positive physical contact

Before we further consider the complicating factors around these issues, let's discuss the positive aspects of physical contact with your pupils and the ways in which it can enhance your role and make you a better teacher.

Praise, congratulation and affirmation

Most children – but not all – love getting a high-five, fist-bump, pat on the back, handshake or even occasionally having their hair affectionately ruffled (although, I admit, that is usually boys). Praise, congratulation and affirmation are human needs. Children need this even more than most adults. An important aspect of expressing and satisfying this need in most cultures is through some form of physical gesture – but, of course, be aware that not everyone welcomes certain expressions of praise and congratulation.

Forms of welcome, salutation and greeting can vary enormously and, even irrespective of cultural traditions, not all forms of physical contact are met with alacrity. It is common sense to be respectful of people's personal preferences and their bodies as a private space. However, while it is important to be sensitive, let's not make our starting point a presumption that we should not offer personal affirmations because they might offend. Would a responsible parent praise, congratulate and affirm their child? Of course they would. Then why would you deny it to a child for whom you were responsible?

Show, demonstrate and model

One of the most fundamental teaching skills is showing a child how to do something – how it works – through acts of demonstration. To be pedantic for a moment, there is a technical difference between demonstrating (showing the workings of something) and modelling (showing the product of something) – which is why models walk down catwalks to display the product of a clothes designer and don't demonstrate how the garment was made. Teachers demonstrate and model regularly, although demonstrations are more likely to involve physical contact.

Demonstration is a key tool in your teacher toolbox: the more you use it, the more you will enhance your effectiveness as a teacher. My advice is to use demonstration techniques as often as you can, but it is just plain good manners to ask permission to touch someone, as any respectful person would do in any social or professional situation. Don't impose or intrude into other people's personal space just because you have the authority to do so, but don't assume that it is inappropriate to touch someone either. It isn't, especially when you are doing it to increase the effectiveness of your teaching.

You won't be demonstrating techniques all the time, but there are some serious implications for your teaching if you never use this vital tool. Firstly, it will have implications for your confidence; secondly, it will have implications for the effectiveness of your teaching methods; and, thirdly, it will have implications for the quality of your relationships with the children. In my view, all these implications are likely to be negative. The children may not be able to identify the issue immediately, or be able to articulate it, but they will get a sense of it after spending time in your class. They may feel that they didn't connect with your style of teaching or didn't learn quite as much from you as they did from a previous teacher. Perhaps they were unable to establish a relationship with you as a teacher who was sensitive and responsive to their needs. Any of these outcomes would be a shame – and an unnecessary one.

If you think you will still feel awkward or clumsy using demonstration techniques that might involve physical contact, then simply avoid them. There is no point in forcing yourself to be the kind of person you aren't. Just be aware that you are likely to be a less effective teacher, possibly cutting off important methods of communication and relationship-building with your pupils.

First aid

Discuss and reflect

- You are on playground duty. A child falls and grazes her knee. The teaching assistant (who is a first-aider) is off sick that day. Should you give first aid if you are not first-aid trained?

The vast majority of first aid in schools is pretty trivial – grazed knees, minor bumps on the head,[11] splinters in fingers, minor cuts and bruises – but occasionally some first aid can be fairly intimate. You shouldn't be anxious about this. If a child requires first aid, and you deny it to them because you are nervous about touching them, you could be accused of neglect. Of course, there will be members of staff in school much better equipped to give first aid – people who have a First Aid at Work (FAW) qualification – so call on them when they are available. Even a small primary school will have a few trained first-aiders. You will be able to get on with your teaching while the child is attended to properly.

However, don't think that just because you haven't been first aid trained you can abdicate your responsibility to your duty of care. There are always going to be occasions when the first-aider isn't on hand. You may be out of school with a group of kids, so you will be the one holding the green box. If a child needs first aid, it is your responsibility to give it to them whether or not you have had the training.

Imagine you are a parent and your child came home one day with a cut or graze that had not been attended to. You ask your child what happened and he answers: 'I fell over and cut my leg but my teacher said she couldn't give me first aid because she hadn't been trained.' You would be marching straight up to the school to ask why your child's teacher had failed in their duty of care towards him. Would a person with the legal responsibility to act as a responsible parent apply first aid? Of course they would, so don't be afraid to do so.

11 Always use the AVPU (alert, verbal, pain, unresponsive) scale when assessing minor head injuries – see, for example: https://www.youtube.com/watch?v=03yelv8G16I.

Consolation, comfort and support

Would a responsible parent console, comfort and support their distressed child? Yes, they surely would, so why wouldn't you? The Department for Education's advice on this refers to 'Examples of where touching a pupil might be proper or necessary', such as 'comforting a distressed pupil'.[12] There it is in black and white – from the government, no less.

Discuss and reflect

How would you act in the following scenarios, given your responsibilities to provide a duty of care:

- A child with physical disabilities is struggling to dress before a sports lesson. They are visibly frustrated and becoming distressed. What might you say and do?
- It is very hot and sunny. There is little shade in the playground. A child comes to you with sun cream and asks you to apply it to areas of their back, neck and arms (where they can't reach themselves). What do you do?
- A 9-year-old girl is crying in your class but won't tell you why. You ask her to stay behind at the end of the lesson and ask: 'Why are you crying? What's the matter?' At first the child refuses to tell you, but you press her and she says: 'I think my mum's going to die.' 'Why do you think that?' you ask. 'She's been diagnosed with cancer,' replies the child. She then bursts into tears. What is the appropriate response?
- You are doing playground duty and a boy comes to you in a very distressed state. He has been bullied and excluded from a game by a group of bigger boys. What is your immediate reaction?

Direction and guidance

Your job will necessarily include directing children to do things they are often slow or reluctant to do. Sometimes they need to be ushered – physically guided in or out of classrooms, especially when they are dawdling to the next lesson or are reluctant to go into the playground on a cold winter's day. Of course, I am not suggesting that you

12 Department for Education, *Use of Reasonable Force*, p. 8.

push the kids around. Sensible, rational people know the difference between being reasonably ushered and being pushed. Most kids (thankfully) fall into the sensible and rational category.[13]

Some children, especially young children or those with special needs, might need to have their hand held – for example, to be led into assembly, guided to the dining room, to cross the road or on visits out of school. Many children even desire it for the warmth and security it provides. Try doing playground duty on a cold winter's day and see how many children you have crowded around you, all wanting to hold your hand, link arms and cuddle up to you. Is that inappropriate contact? Of course it isn't.

Discuss and reflect

- What is the difference between appropriate and inappropriate physical contact?

Common sense

When I ask my audiences this question about appropriate and inappropriate physical contact, invariably I am met with total silence. So I ask it again. 'Come on, answer me,' I say. 'Do you know the difference between appropriate and inappropriate touching?' I almost never get a response, so I have to answer the question myself. The answer is a resounding, 'Yes, of course you do!' You know the difference between appropriate and inappropriate physical contact for all the reasons, and with all the caveats, we have discussed above. Don't allow your confidence with children to be chipped away and undermined. Don't allow yourself to be overcome by unwarranted fear and suspicion just because you are doing your job.

On the other hand, if there is any doubt in your mind that you don't know the difference between appropriate and inappropriate physical contact, then you need to reappraise your decision to train as a teacher – immediately. People who need to 'make friends' with the pupils they are responsible for educating are unsuitable to be teachers. People who become emotionally dependent on receiving the approval of their pupils are unsuitable to be teachers. People who misuse their authority to

13 But not all. Some will react to any kind of contact as a way of trying to resist your authority or escalate a harmless steer. Don't allow yourself to be destabilised by children who are deliberately being vexatious. We will discuss de-escalation techniques and using reasonable force to restrain shortly.

psychologically or physically bully or assault pupils are unsuitable to be teachers. People who find children and young people sexually arousing are unsuitable to be teachers. Those who display any signs of behaviour reflecting such desires will normally be very quickly noticed by colleagues and will be peremptorily excised.

However, as a profession, we need to get back to using our common sense. We need to reclaim the notion that the default position for *all* teachers, including men, is that they are trusted and trustworthy around children. Teaching is by its very nature an intimate activity, both psychologically (what can be more intimate than trying to get inside someone's head to motivate and inspire them?) and emotionally (how can you motivate and inspire children unless you have an emotional connection with them?). And, at times, physically too – for all the proper, necessary and appropriate reasons we have discussed above.

Unwanted and unwarranted touching is not only unwelcome and intrusive to our privacy and dignity, but it may even be considered an assault on our person. If you are in any doubt that physical contact with your pupils may be unwelcome or inappropriate (for example, from a cultural perspective), then don't do it. Our pupils trust us. We should never abuse that trust and expect to be able to retrieve it. When teachers are doing their job to the best of their ability, physical contact with children is appropriate, necessary and often desirable. As a profession, we must resist any attempt to make it sound anything other than that. We must not let fear degrade or diminish the effectiveness of what we are trying to do or allow others to suggest sinister motives where none exist, otherwise innocent and appropriate professional behaviour is made toxic. Teachers – especially male teachers – are undermined and deskilled by this fear and have their abilities and natural confidence around children drained. That is wrong.

Checklist

Valid reasons for physical contact are to:

- Praise, congratulate and affirm.
- Show, demonstrate and model.
- Give first aid.
- Console, comfort and support.
- Direct and guide.
- Restrain children (including using reasonable force) to stop fighting.

- In any situation you deem to be an emergency.

Invalid reasons for physical contact are when:

- There is no need to do it.

Discuss and reflect

What are the implications of *avoiding* physical contact when:

- Teaching gymnastics (e.g. denying a child physical support when attempting to balance).
- Teaching drama (e.g. ignoring the opportunity to direct or position pupils moving through a scene).
- Teaching dance (e.g. refusing to demonstrate a dance technique by manipulating a child's arms or legs).
- Coaching football, rugby or tennis (e.g. declining to demonstrate how to tackle safely, form a scrum or hold a racket).
- Teaching science (e.g. watching a pupil struggle to measure chemicals or carry out a dissection).
- Teaching design and technology (e.g. refusing to direct a pupil in the safe and proper use of a hazardous tool such as a knife, saw or screwdriver).
- Teaching music (e.g. wasting opportunities to manipulate a child's arms, hands or fingers on a violin, cello or guitar).
- Supervising young children having lunch who are struggling to use a knife and fork.
- Delaying attention to (or even repudiating) the needs of children who are struggling to dress, apply sunscreen or are wearing soiled clothes.

What do I do if I work in a school with a 'no contact' policy?

If you are working in a school that has adopted an 'avoid' or 'minimise' contact policy, then you must work within that policy and not undermine it. However, the reality is that most people soon forget about it and get on with working normally with children, congratulating, praising, comforting, supporting and demonstrating without even thinking about it. I met a teacher recently who told me that his school had adopted a no contact policy only to abandon it within weeks as 'totally unworkable'.

You may feel the same after working in such a school; that you would thrive more in an environment where safeguarding and duty of care is viewed from a positive perspective. Deliberately going against a school policy because you disagree with it is obviously unprofessional. There will be mechanisms for reviewing school policies – such as staff meetings, governors' committees and policy reviews – where you can put forward your case if you feel strongly about it. Once you get into a position of influence and authority, you may want to change things. So go on – have the ambition to become a head of department, an assistant head or a head teacher, and then you will have a lot more influence.

'I hate working in this school!'

I was with a group of PGCE students at a university recently. We were discussing the topic of no contact policies. One of the students, a woman who had been a teaching assistant in a school with such a policy, made what I thought was a fascinating but very sad comment. After two years of operating the policy, the school was reviewing it at a staff meeting. One member of staff, an experienced teacher who had been at the school for many years, suddenly burst into tears. 'I hate working in this school now,' she said. 'The only time I touch these kids is when I have to restrain them.'

In the last few decades, there has been a radical change in the way schools and teachers approach their professional duty to protect children. Sometimes this has come on the back of changes in the law that arose from tragedies.[14] The protection of children from neglect, harm and abuse is fundamental, urgent and critical, and teachers have a key role to play. However, this should not be confused with the equally fundamental, urgent and crucial need to apply a proper duty of care in all the ways we have discussed.

Restraint using reasonable force

We may not like the idea – and it will go against the grain of everything we are trying to do – but sometimes teachers need to use reasonable force to restrain children. Such occasions include when there is a risk of:

- Children harming themselves.
- Children harming other pupils.
- Children harming you.
- In any emergency, where you might be failing in your duty if you did not intervene.

My advice is that before intervening physically you should, wherever practicable, tell a pupil who is misbehaving to stop and what will happen if they do not. Emphasise that restraint will stop as soon as it ceases to be necessary by saying things like, 'As soon as you calm down, I'll stop holding you.' As distressed as you may feel in such a heightened situation, always try to avoid the impression that you have lost your temper or that you are restraining a child out of your own anger and frustration.

Here is some helpful guidance for when our tempers are cool.

Reasonable force can be used for two main reasons: to *control* pupils or to *restrain* them. The Department for Education guidance states: 'There is a power, not a duty, to use force, so members of staff have discretion whether or not to use it.'[15] However,

14 The death of a young girl named Victoria Climbié in North London in 2000 at the hands of an abusive great-aunt resulted in severe criticism of the inadequate procedures of the protective agencies involved: the police, health, social and education services. This case led to a radical overhaul in child protection and safeguarding procedures that has had far-reaching outcomes. You can read more about this case in: House of Commons Health Committee, *The Victoria Climbié Inquiry Report: Sixth Report of Session 2002–03*. HC 570. Available at: https://publications.parliament.uk/pa/cm200203/cmselect/cmhealth/570/570.pdf.

15 Department for Education, *Use of Reasonable Force*, p. 9.

teachers and other school staff have a duty of care to all pupils and that may include using reasonable force to restrain a pupil attacking another child. Failure to do so might be a dereliction of that duty. It goes on: 'Force is usually used either to control or restrain. This can range from guiding a pupil to safety by the arm through to more extreme circumstances such as breaking up a fight.'[16] The word 'reasonable' in this context means using no more force than is necessary. Furthermore, 'control' can be passive – for example, you could position yourself between two pupils who are attempting to fight (although try not to get walloped yourself!) or you could block the path of a pupil who is trying to exit the classroom. Both are examples of passive control.

Discuss and reflect

- There are a variety of occasions where the law authorises reasonable force to restrain and control a pupil. Make a list of what they might be.

What is reasonable force?

Using reasonable force to restrain a pupil is using the least amount of force necessary in order to secure their safety, the safety of others or the pupil's compliance with an urgent and necessary request. It is reasonable, therefore, to forcibly hold a child's hands or arms if they are trying to hit another child or hit you. Sometimes that reasonable force may require a lot of physical effort. You might have to hold them very tightly to prevent harm to another child or to yourself; angry children will resist you vigorously but you will have to hold on firmly if you are going to prevent slaps and punches being landed.

Reasonable force – however much force is required – is therefore intended to prevent harm, as long as it is no more than what is necessary. In such circumstances, the law will give you the benefit of the doubt and be on your side. Obviously, what is not considered reasonable is that you twist a child's arm behind their back or apply a few 'accidental' slaps and punches of your own to subdue them. Then the law is not on your side. That is assault. Assaulting a pupil is not using reasonable force to restrain or control them. Any form of restraint or force used as a disciplinary measure is unacceptable. The law does not protect you in those circumstances.

16 Department for Education, *Use of Reasonable Force*, p. 4.

Sometimes, though, in the event of restraining a pupil, accidents do happen and unavoidable injuries are the unintentional outcome. We will come to an example of this later, but let's start with one of the most common reasons for needing to use reasonable force to restrain.

Fighting

Occasionally children fight. Sometimes when they do, they quickly lose their temper and before you can get across the classroom to break it up, they are knocking seven bells out of each other. Break it up you must. That is your responsibility under your duty of care. No caring, responsible parent would stand back and let their children fight. The good news is that most kids will respond to a verbal command like: 'Stop it! Stop fighting now!' because one if not both children really don't want to continue – after all, fighting hurts! What has often happened is that they have momentarily lost their cool, so shouting at them to 'Stop fighting!' gives them an opportunity to regain their composure without losing face.

On some occasions, though, they don't stop and you will need to get between them. The act of placing yourself between two children fighting is often enough for them to desist. Most kids know that to continue might mean striking you in order to land a blow on the other child. That is something the vast majority of children won't want to risk, so they may make only half-hearted attempts to hit out. You may now find that such perfunctory blows are easy to block, and within seconds they calm down and you can begin to reason with them.

However, there are times when it isn't so straightforward. If a child continues hitting out – and now they may be hitting you in order to get at the other child – you have got no option but to restrain them, especially if they won't calm down or fail to respond to your repeated verbal exhortations: 'Stop that now! Calm down! Stop!' You may need to intervene physically. It is always a good idea to tell them what you are going to do. You may have time for only one warning if the fight is in full flow, but be guided by the old British Army dictum of: Tell 'em what you're going to do. Then do it. Then tell 'em what you've just done.

In my experience (though I have never been in the army) this procedure is very helpful. You might say something like: 'If you don't stop immediately, I'm going to restrain you.' They don't stop, so you intervene. As you are restraining them, tell them why you have to do it: 'I'm holding on to you to stop you hitting me/yourself/Sam/Sara.' If they don't calm down and you have to continue with the restraint, repeat what you have said with some variation: 'I'll stop holding on to you as soon as you calm down, but I'm not going to let go until you do, because you will hurt yourself/me/Sam/Sara.' Once they have calmed down – and it may take some time – or there has been some resolution of the incident away from the scene, you can finally say calmly: 'I didn't want to have to do that but you gave me no option. I asked you to stop and you didn't. It's my job to make sure you and everyone else is safe around here. I'm sure you understand that.'

It will not be easy, especially in the heat of the moment, but if you can, keep talking to them while you are holding their flailing arms and fists and try to add some calming words. You may need to wrap your arms around theirs bear-hug style. Personally, I always found this technique to be effective with primary-age children as it allowed my body weight and proximity to be a powerful but non-threatening barrier. At the same time, I would speak quietly but firmly into their ear, saying something like: 'Calm down now ... sshhh ... come on, this is not like you ... come on, take control of yourself ... calm yourself ...'

This is all well and good in theory, but fights can happen very quickly and sometimes you will need to act before you can think things through. Some children have difficulty managing their anger or are prone to sudden violent outbursts. It is even more complicated as kids get bigger and stronger. Trying to restrain a physically mature 14-year-old from throwing a desk or chair is a different story from restraining a 5-year-old who is having a tantrum. If the pupils are physically large or a group of them are brawling, then call for assistance immediately – send a child to go and get another member of staff. Don't leave the scene yourself. Try to calm things down using verbal exhortations while you are waiting for help.

Your duty of care does not extend to putting yourself at serious risk of harm or injury. You will need to assess that risk very quickly – and with experience you will – but the size, strength and number of pupils involved are all factors in deciding whether you can make an effective intervention. As I have indicated, even older children will usually respond to the confident-sounding command of a respected teacher to stop, but if they have really lost self-control and they are punching and kicking each other for all they are worth, don't try to get between them. Send for assistance, stay in the vicinity of those fighting and continue to implore them to stop. Be confident and assertive in your tone and body language, even if you don't feel it.[17]

17 Restraint training or positive handling training is available and can give you confidence if you find yourself working in a school where a lot of restraint is going on. If that is the case, ask your head teacher or head of CPD if they can arrange for it to be provided.

Preventing self-harm

Children sometimes need to be restrained from trying to harm themselves. If you see a child jabbing a pencil into their thigh or scratching their wrist with a pair of scissors, you won't casually stroll over and ask: 'May I take that away from you, please?' You will need to act quickly to restrain the child and remove the offending object. Of course, you will try to use calming and non-threatening language and gestures to minimise the trauma of the intervention, but act you must. The child's psychological state may be very vulnerable, but you will need to indicate verbally that you are in control of the situation. Having said that, if there is a child in your class with a history of self-harm, you are likely to be aware of that already and so will be alert to the problem.

With such children, you will need to be cautious when using hazardous tools or potentially harmful objects and supervise their use very closely. Remember that children even in temporary psychological distress or with longer term special needs have as much right as others to access the curriculum, so don't prevent them from using tools. Managing how you do that is just another of the hundred and one things you will have to master.

Removing disruptive children

The law gives teachers the power to remove disruptive children from classrooms, physically if necessary (using reasonable force, which means the minimum amount necessary). However, as we have noted, this is a power, not a duty, and should be used with discretion. Removal is always a last resort. As you will discover, one of the best techniques for managing behaviour is to try to spot problems early and nip them in the bud. Always try to de-escalate tension, although that is easier said than done. Sometimes kids push at boundaries relentlessly and force you into a confrontation where you cannot avoid taking action.

If these measures don't prove effective and a pupil is disrupting your teaching to the extent that it has become intolerable, then you will need to remove them from the lesson. Removals should always be done in accordance with your school's behaviour and discipline policy, so you will need to become familiar with these and work within them. However, it is likely that you will have more experienced support near at hand – quite often, in the room. When that is not the case, your school policy will advise on sending for a more experienced teacher (who may have years of experience of dealing with truculent kids) to come and remove the pupil from your class.

As a trainee or early career teacher it is unlikely that you will be expected to physically remove a child from the classroom. It is rare for a situation to escalate to the point where even an experienced teacher has to physically remove an unwilling pupil from the classroom, although it does happen occasionally. It is not that more experienced teachers have some special superpower or some additional legal authority that you don't, but they do have more experience. They are a teacher that the child will know well and whose moral authority (at that time) may carry more weight with the child than yours. In five or six years' time, you may be the experienced teacher to whom some struggling trainee or early career teacher is sending for help.

You should never feel that deferring to a more experienced or skilful teacher is somehow a climb-down on your part or a humiliating loss of face. The culture of teaching is not like that, or at least it shouldn't be. In my experience, teaching is a highly collegial, team-reliant profession. All good teachers know that we all need help sometimes to achieve the desired outcomes. In this case, you want to put an end to the disruption that is undermining the effectiveness of your teaching. If what it takes as a last resort is to remove the offending pupil from the room, then you have achieved the desired outcome, even if someone else has done it. The rest of the class, and even the disruptive pupil, will ultimately recognise and respect that too.

As a trainee or early career teacher you will – or should – be given lots of support to manage what is often called 'behaviour for learning'. Naturally, you will make mistakes and your mentors should recognise that as part of your learning. However, I repeat: read and get to know your school's policies on behaviour and discipline and work within them. They will tell you how to follow the school's established procedures. These are procedures that the children should also be familiar with, such as the expectation that they will receive a warning or notice of detention, referral procedures to heads of year and so on.

Preventing a pupil from leaving the classroom

The same goes for preventing a pupil from leaving the classroom – follow your school policy. It will almost certainly state that if a child gets so upset or angry that they try to run out of class, don't try to stop them; trying to prevent them may make them even angrier. School premises are secure places, after all, and children can't get far. However, the first thing you should do is to send another pupil to tell a designated or senior teacher what has happened.

For much of the time when I was teaching, schools were much less secure than they are now. In those days, if a child ran out of class with a cloud of red mist swirling before their eyes, before you knew it they would be out of the school gate and across a busy road. Obviously, we have to prevent any chance of that happening. If the children you are responsible for are not within your locus of care, then you need to ensure they are within someone else's.

In my experience, the child will often be found sitting in the toilets, crying or cooling down. The sympathetic and kindly presence of an experienced teaching assistant is often best in situations like these – someone detached and often seen as neutral. If you have someone like this available, send them to look for the child while you continue your teaching. A period of reflection outside your classroom is usually all they need for the upset to vent, especially if a trusted teaching assistant can be the conduit. In any case, read and follow what your school policy says about such situations.

Preventing behaviour that disrupts a school visit or event

The same maxim applies to school visits or events taking place beyond the school grounds: follow the advice set out in your school policies. However, situations beyond the school premises clearly illustrate the reason why the law gives teachers the power to deal with disruptive behaviour, including physical restraint. If a teacher takes a class of thirty kids to a theatre or concert hall and one starts kicking off – disrupting the play or performance – the theatre manager will likely ask: 'Who is the responsible teacher here? Please can you take this child out of the theatre!' It is not their job to do that; it is yours.

In all of these scenarios I am describing the option of last resort. Remember, it is a power, not a duty. The reason the law gives teachers the authority to use reasonable force to restrain or remove disruptive children is that sometimes there is no other option. In such cases, you may be failing in your duty of care if you do not use that power. The law gives us this authority in any situation, but especially in emergencies where we might be failing in our duty of care if we did not intervene.

Checklist for maintaining your safety when using restraint

You are not expected to put yourself at serious risk of injury.

- Assess the age and strength of the pupil(s), especially where there is a group involved and/or where they are physically mature.

- It may not be advisable to intervene at all without the assistance of other adults.
- Send another pupil for help if necessary.

Accidents will happen ...

Once when I was a class teacher, and an experienced one at that, I was taking my class out of school on a local visit. We were trying to cross a busy road in London. I had given the kids the usual briefings about the hazards of being out of school and told them to keep together, walk in twos, watch where they were going and so on.

As we approached a pedestrian crossing, I could see from the corner of my eye that one boy was mucking about playing 'tag' with his mates. In a split second he was jumping back and into the road. Without even thinking, I grabbed him by the arm. There were 32-tonne trucks and double-decker buses thundering past. I was furious, and with a flush of adrenalin rushing through me, I gave him the length of my tongue: 'I told you to behave and watch where you're going! This is a very busy road! Behave yourself or I'll take you back to school!' As with most incidents like this, they are soon forgotten by all concerned. But in this case, not quite.

Next day, in came dad. 'Why has my boy got a bruise on his arm?' To be quite honest, I didn't even know what he was talking about. I hadn't connected his comment with the incident, so it took a minute or two of discussion with the father to realise what had happened. Finally, we both worked it out.

Little Johnny had gone home that evening and his dad had seen a bruise just above the bicep where I had pulled him. Quite understandably, he asks his son: 'How did you get that bruise on your arm?'

Little Johnny then replies: 'Mr Newland pulled me!'

'Why did Mr Newland pull you?'

As innocent as a newborn lamb, Little Johnny shrugs his shoulders and says, 'I dunno.'

'What d'you mean you don't know? Why did your teacher pull you?' asks dad.

'I don't know,' insisted Little Johnny. 'He just pulled me!'

So, dad comes in to school, wanting to know why his son has an unexplained bruise on his arm caused by his teacher. Quite right too. Any responsible caring parent would want to know what has happened.

Now, what would be your response to a parent asking that question?

Firstly, let me tell you what my answer was. The first thing I did was to apologise. I had caused an injury, unintentionally, and I was sorry in the sense that I was expressing regret (for necessarily but accidentally causing it). I have no problem with that. It is different from saying sorry in the sense of expressing remorse (for doing something I wished I hadn't done because I shouldn't have done it in the first place). Regret and remorse are two different aspects of being sorry.

I saw no reason not to apologise to the father as an expression of my regret, so I said: 'I'm really sorry, Mr So-and-So. Obviously, it was an accident and I'm sorry that I've bruised your son. To be honest, I didn't even think about it – I just pulled him from the busy road. He was mucking about, so I had to …' Before I got much further into the explanation the father interrupted me: 'Don't worry, Mr Newland, I get the picture now … No, no … Don't worry about it. I get it … I get it … I see what happened now … He didn't tell me any of that … I understand now …' And off he went.

This particular parent was understanding and supportive, but not all parents are like that. Some will come in and start shouting at you: 'You've assaulted my child! I'm going to report you to the police! I'm going to sue this school! I'm going to get you the sack!' Such a scene might feel intimidating, but it is usually a lot of hot air and anger. If a parent's initial anger is not assuaged by your explanation or does not quickly subside, and they are misguided enough to go to the police or to a solicitor, they will soon be told that you were doing your job to provide a duty of care that satisfies the requirements of the law. In other words, you behaved *in loco parentis*, as a responsible parent would in the circumstances.

However, the fact that questions are asked about such incidents is reasonable too. A child was injured – although accidentally and in the pursuance of keeping him safe. A parent will naturally want to ask questions and receive a justifiable explanation, and so will the head teacher. In a more serious or critical incident, the police and emergency services will ask questions too. People with a legitimate interest will want to know what happened, but that does not make you culpable of wrongdoing or even misjudgement, and you should not feel intimidated when providing a truthful answer.

When responding to a parent (or anyone else) who is questioning you on what happened, you don't have to quote chapter and verse from 'Act of Parliament this' or 'Department for Education Circular that' to justify what you have done. Simply explain calmly and professionally why you acted in the way you did to protect the child from harm. Think about what is reasonable in the circumstances for the purposes of safeguarding and promoting the welfare of the child, and you will be, in almost all conceivable circumstances, within the law and thus given the benefit of the doubt.

Of course, if my anger with that boy had extended beyond a telling off and into grabbing him by the arms and giving him a damn good shake just to drive home my point, and shouting: 'Why can't you behave, you stupid little idiot!' for good measure, then that would not have been reasonable in the circumstances. It would have been assault or at least verbal abuse. The law would not protect me for doing that.

Conversations with parents, such as the one I have described, would normally be dealt with by the head or a senior teacher. However, if you do find yourself having to explain a minor accidental injury to a parent, you now know that your answer should be along the lines of: 'I'm sorry an injury has occurred, but I was fulfilling my duty of care to protect your child from harm. I regret the injury but the alternative could have been much worse had I not acted.' And don't forget to include an apology for the unintended harm caused; saying sorry usually goes a long way to de-escalate anger and upset.

In my case, I was genuinely unaware that I had accidentally injured the boy, but if you think it is possible that a minor injury may have resulted from restraint or contact, then it would be a good idea to pre-empt the situation by:

1. Asking the child if they have been hurt by your action.

2. Reporting what happened to your head of department, DSL or head teacher.

3. Contacting the parents of the child concerned and explaining the incident.

Remember, there need not be any implication of culpability or guilt from explaining what happened, even if the child was unintentionally injured. If you were doing what was reasonable and necessary in the circumstances to prevent harm, then you were fulfilling your duty of care.

Checklist: the golden rules to using physical contact

From years of working in schools with challenging children and capable and sensitive colleagues, I have distilled the following four golden rules for physical contact with children:

1. Know your school policy on behaviour and discipline (and read the Department for Education's guidance document, *Use of Reasonable Force*).
2. Ask yourself: is the physical contact intended to meet the child's needs? If it is, especially if the child welcomes and consents to it, then how can it be wrong?
3. If an educational, physical, emotional or social need has not been identified or is not your clear intent, then you probably don't need to do it and should avoid it.
4. When there has been any kind of emergency where reasonable force was necessary and an injury may have occurred accidentally, report it to those who have an interest (such as your DSL, head of year or head teacher), who will notify the child's parents.

School discipline

Teachers have express legal powers to enforce school discipline as set out in the Education and Inspections Act 2006. This includes penalties for misbehaviour both in school and on the way to and from school. So, if you thought that your position of being *in loco parentis* extended only as far as the school gates, you are wrong. There are caveats, of course, some of which we have already discussed and some we will explore further.

The disciplinary authority of teachers extends to the following:

- The confiscation of inappropriate and prohibited items.
- Detention (after school).
- The power to search (although this is a power invested initially in head teachers).

Once again – these are powers, not duties, so they don't have to be exercised just because you have the authority. Be familiar with and follow your school policies.

Confiscating inappropriate or prohibited items

Teachers have the legal authority to confiscate inappropriate or prohibited items. Individual items are not specified by the Act, so schools have the autonomy and discretion to decide this for themselves. When mobile phones first became widely popular in the late 1990s, most schools banned pupils from bringing them in. Later, when we were all engulfed by the tsunami of mobile phone use and both children and parents began to perceive that normal life was impossible without them, many schools simply gave up trying to regulate their possession. Most managed the issue by confining their use to essential or emergency communication, but it was a hopeless task. These days we all have a mobile phone and it seems that many of us are addicted to them too. However, with an alarming increase in the sharing of indecent images and social media bullying, many schools are once again trying to reintroduce regulation.

Schools don't usually find it necessary to have a published list of prohibited items as most of them are common sense: cigarettes, alcohol, drugs, weapons and so on. Once again, you should follow your school's policy on confiscation, but as a teacher you can confiscate any item that a child is using inappropriately, especially if they are using it dangerously, hazardously or to distract others from your teaching. Even pens and pencils can be used as weapons. It doesn't matter how valuable it is or whether it is someone's private property, you have the authority to take it away from them.

The item will remain the property of the child or their family (unless it belongs to the school) and therefore should be returned to them either at the end of the lesson (if it is a minor infraction) or at the end of the day or week (preferably to their parents). If it is an item that should not have been in a child's possession in the first place, like stolen property, then it does not need to be returned at all. Be guided by your school policy, but don't be afraid to assert your authority where the safety of the pupils (or your own safety) is concerned.

Detention

I am aware that I am sounding like a broken record, but on all matters of discipline and behaviour you should be guided by your school's policy. This is also where you will find out how your school manages detention. However, teachers have the legal authority to detain pupils as punishment for misbehaviour, as set out in Section 92 of the Education and Inspections Act 2006. You may be surprised that it can be done both at the end of the school day and on most weekends throughout the year. (I am sure you are looking forward to the prospect of spending your treasured Saturday mornings supervising detentions at school – but don't worry, it is quite rare!) If you are a primary school teacher, you will almost certainly not hold detentions outside of school hours. In all the primary schools I have ever come across, detentions take place at playtimes and lunchtimes.

There are some constraints on imposing detentions that you should be aware of:

- The pupils concerned must be under 18 years of age. Once they are adults, they can graciously decline your generous offer of detaining them!
- The head teacher must have made the school's detention policy 'generally known', which means that it should be in the school's published behaviour and discipline policy and on the school's website or in the prospectus.
- Officially, detentions must be imposed by a paid member of staff, although as a trainee the power may be delegated to you by a qualified teacher. It is common for a senior teacher like a head of department to say something like, 'You've got a right Charlie in your Year 9 chemistry class this afternoon. If he won't behave himself after your warnings, you can put him on detention and I'll approve it.' Experienced teachers will generally offer you support but, obviously, don't take it for granted.

The Education and Inspections Act 2006 includes little detail about the way schools should impose and manage detentions, so there is a great deal of leeway. The guiding principle is that detentions must be reasonable and proportionate. For example, the Act says nothing about the length of a detention, which is left to schools to determine. It goes without saying that during wintertime, expecting children to go home in the dark after a detention is not a reasonable thing to do. Nor is it reasonable to flatly disregard the religious and cultural calendar. It would be an act of staggering arrogance and disrespect for a school to impose detentions in the face of minority, let alone mainstream, customs or sensitivities. While some older children might be able to get on with homework during a longer detention, once they start stretching to forty-five minutes or an hour, it is legitimate to ask whether this is reasonable or proportionate for a pupil of any age. It is an obvious point, but children must be allowed access to toilet facilities as well as food and drink if it is a lunchtime detention.

You may be surprised that detentions can be imposed without parental consent. While schools do not need a parent's permission to impose a detention, parents do have a legal right to twenty-four hours' notice. However, this is widely flouted by secondary schools all over the country – and for good reason. As you will quickly learn, the best way to deal with disciplinary issues is to get them resolved as soon as possible, so you and the child concerned can move on and put the matter behind you. Many schools now impose fifteen- or twenty-minute detentions on the day – immediately after school – so the issue leading to their detention and the inevitable sense of grievance is not carried over to the next day.

Schools have circumvented the letter of the law by implicitly getting parents to forego their right to twenty-four hours' notice by including a reference to the practice on the school's website or the school brochure or explicitly through a home–school agreement. As with so many things, good communication between the school and parents is key. When a school is effective in regularly communicating its policies to parents, it does not need to inform them of the details of disciplinary procedures on a daily basis.

The power to search

The Education Act 1996 empowers a head teacher to search a pupil.

Discuss and reflect

- Under what circumstances might a head teacher need to search a pupil?
- What conditions and constraints might be imposed on the way it is done?

The first thing to emphasise is that the law gives this power to the head teacher, not every teacher, although it is often delegated to other (usually) senior teachers. It is highly unusual, and in my view poor practice, for it to be delegated to a trainee or early career teacher. However, once you have become an established teacher in the school, certainly as a senior teacher, it is something that you should expect to be delegated to you.

However, a head teacher must have reasonable grounds for suspecting that a pupil is concealing a prohibited item, such as:

- Knives or weapons.
- Alcohol.
- Illegal drugs.
- Stolen items.
- Tobacco or cigarettes.
- Fireworks.
- Pornographic images.

- Any article that the member of staff reasonably suspects has been, or is likely to be, used to commit an offence or to cause personal injury to, or damage to the property of, any person (including the pupil).

Head teachers and authorised staff can also search for any item banned by the school rules which has been identified as an item which may be searched for.

Confiscation

School staff can seize any prohibited item found as a result of a search. They can also seize any item they consider harmful or detrimental to school discipline. Those reasonable grounds might be your suspicion based on an observation or other circumstantial evidence such as the credible report of a reliable pupil. As I have said, the power to search can be delegated by the head to another teacher, but a head cannot *direct* you to carry out a search if you are unwilling to do so. Busy heads will need to delegate many things to their colleagues, often at short notice, so tell your head teacher well beforehand if searching pupils is something you are unwilling to do.

Being subjected to a search is potentially embarrassing and humiliating for everyone concerned, even when it is done for essential safety reasons. We know how undignified it feels to pass through airport security, and yet we all know why it is necessary. Searches should always be done courteously and with due consideration for maintaining respect and dignity – for example, staff carrying out the search should be the same gender as the pupil. If you are the person carrying out the search, always have another member of staff present – also, ideally, the same gender as the pupil. This may not always be possible; in many primary schools, men are in short supply or are non-existent. If you are a female teacher in a small primary school and you need to search a boy for a weapon, for example, you and a colleague will need to get on with it – urgently – even if you do not have a male member of staff available. You cannot let a pupil walk around all day in school if you think he is carrying a knife.

Apart from what I would call 'critical incidents' (like searching for weapons or drugs), you will be involved more regularly in searching for stolen property. Some pupils are foolish enough to bring valuable possessions into school to impress their friends, only to lose them to some unscrupulous classmate. Some pupils steal from each other on a regular basis. Minor theft was the bane of my life with some classes I taught. In primary schools it is usually trivial items, although for the child involved it can be very upsetting and needs to be taken seriously, as time consuming and annoying as it may be.

'Sir! Mandy's taken my new pencil case!'

'Sir! Mandy's taken my new pencil case!'

'How do you know?'

'I've seen her with it. She's showing all her friends in the playground!'

'How do you know the one Mandy has got is yours?' [Here I'm testing 'reasonable grounds for suspicion'.]

'I got it from Wilko's on Saturday, Sir. It's got pink elephants on it. There's only one like it in school and I know it's mine!'

So I go and get Mandy.

'Mandy, have you got Sarah's pencil case?'

'No, Sir!'

'Tell the truth. Have you taken Sarah's pencil case? She says she's seen you with it in the playground.'

'No, Sir, I haven't.'

'Are you telling me the truth?'

'Yes.'

'Mmm … If I were to search your coat, your bag, your tray and your locker, might I find Sarah's pencil case?'

From the look on the child's face, you will probably know whether you need to take the matter any further.

You can search school lockers, classroom trays and other school property. You can also ask pupils to turn out their bags and the pockets of their trousers, skirt, jacket or coat. It is always best to get the pupils to do this themselves, although don't underestimate even a young child's ability to use sleight of hand to conceal something. I clearly remember a 6-year-old using the skills of a full member of the Magic Circle to hide the pound coins he had taken from the school dinner money box.

If you aren't satisfied that the pupil has shown you the full contents of their pockets or the depth of their bag, then insist until you are. Don't be intimidated by any lack of cooperation in the process. If you think they are being obstructive, tell them that you will search their lockers and trays yourself if they won't do it properly – after all, such things are school property. Having an additional member of staff present is not just to ensure that protection is afforded to you and the pupil in case of a false allegation, but also to protect the dignity of all those involved. If a pupil is innocent, you will want to leave them with as little grievance as possible. Once it is over, thank them for their cooperation if they have provided it.

Personally, I believe it works best when you tell the pupil what the allegation is and ask them to voluntarily give the offending item to you. If they don't cooperate or deny the allegation, then in the presence of another member of staff, go through the following procedure:

1. Tell them that you are going to search their belongings, clothes and so on, and how you are going to do it – by getting them to fully turn out their pockets, remove their jacket or blazer, open and empty out their bag and so on.

2. Explain clearly why you are doing it – that you have information or a suspicion that they are concealing a prohibited item.

3. When they (or you) have done it, tell them what has been done – either you have found the offending article or you haven't – and what consequences will follow.

4. Get a colleague to record the whole process on video-phone if you think it is necessary, although this may intensify the sense of grievance. Remember, you are trying to minimise indignity and injustice while fulfilling your responsibilities to keep everyone safe.

If you do not find anything, then you can apologise – in the sense of expressing regret that it was unfortunate but necessary, perhaps saying something like: 'I'm sorry I had to search you, but I had grounds for suspicion that you were concealing a weapon/drugs/stolen property. I have a duty to do something about that to keep everybody in school safe, including you.' After such incidents, I would offer the pupil my hand to shake too. In my experience, it was an offer that was never declined. Such a gesture can help to minimise any sense of unfairness and usually brings the matter to a close.

Clearly, we are not talking about anything approaching an intimate body search. As a teacher, I cannot conceive of any situation where that would be justified, even if you think a child has a knife or drugs in their possession. You should not even pat them down, as you do not have the authority to do so; technically, it would be assault. If you are still not satisfied with the way they have opened their bag or turned out their pockets, then escalate it to the head teacher or a more senior member of staff. If weapons or drugs are involved, the head teacher will have to take the matter to the parents or police if the pupil refuses to cooperate. The police have the authority to carry out bodily searches; you don't.

Remember the British Army maxim I mentioned earlier: tell 'em what you're going to do. Do it. Then tell 'em what you have just done. You can be trained to search pupils; ask the head or whoever is responsible for CPD to provide search training if you are working in a school where this is necessary on a regular basis. It is not an unreasonable request.

'Sir! Jason's got a knife!'

As a head teacher in an East London primary school, there were three occasions when I had to formally search a child for what I would describe as a critical incident: twice for the suspected possession of a knife and once for suspected possession of a Class B drug.

One day a boy came to me and said, 'Sir! Jason [I will call him] has got a knife in school!'

'How do you know?' I asked.

'I've just seen him with it in the boys' toilets. He's waving it about and showing off with it. It's one of those red ones, a Swiss army knife.'

This report was coming from a boy I knew to be a sensible kid and his description was credible, so I thought that gave me reasonable grounds for suspicion to question Jason and carry out a search if necessary.

I went and found Jason, by now in the playground, and said to him: 'Jason, a little bird has just told me that you've brought something into school today that you shouldn't have. Is that right?'

'No,' he said.

'Now, just take your time about your answer, son, because you might not have meant to bring it in and now you're embarrassed. You don't need to be. Have you got a knife in school?'

'No.'

'Someone has told me they've seen you with a knife in the boys' toilets. Tell me the truth. Have you brought a knife into school today?'

'No.'

'Now, as I said, mate, you might not have meant to bring it in. It might have been in your pocket and you've forgotten it was there …'

'No. I told you, I haven't got a knife! I told you that!'

Here is a situation where, as I advised earlier, you will always try to give children options to get out of the tight corner in which they find themselves. Endeavour to de-escalate where you can, and always try to resolve the problem without humiliating the child or risk them losing face. Most kids will take those options when and where they are offered. But some won't. Some will force you into a confrontation. In a situation like this, where a knife is involved, I cannot avoid a confrontation if the child does not accept my offers to de-escalate.

Now I have to say to Jason: 'Well listen, son, I've got reason to believe that you have a knife in school today so I'm going to search you. I'm going to search your pockets, your coat, your bag, your tray and your locker … and if I find that you've got a knife – or anything else that you shouldn't have – I'm going to be very mad at you. So mad, in fact, that I'm going to call your mum and ask her to come and get you and take you home, because I'm going to exclude you from school. Do you understand me?'

I let that sink in for a second. I am not intending to sound unnecessarily confrontational, but it is important that I project a confident and assertive demeanour and be clear about the repercussions of any lack of cooperation.

Then I said: 'So, once again … are you *absolutely sure* that you didn't bring in a red Swiss army knife today *by mistake*?'

Jason looked down furtively. I could tell he was weighing up his options now. After a second or two, he said: 'It's not mine, it's my brother's. I think he put it in my coat pocket and I didn't know it was there …'

'OK. Give it to me …' I said. 'I'll keep it safe until home time. I'll give it to your mum when she comes in and tell her you brought it in by mistake and that you *won't do it again*. Will you?'

He shook his head.

'Because if you do, mate …' I said, stiffening my tone, 'I won't accept the same excuse a second time. But for now, you've got a clean slate. All right?'

He nodded his head. He pulled out the knife from his pocket and gave it to me.

As busy and distracted as you will often be, you cannot ignore a situation in which a child might be in possession of an offensive weapon. If I had received a report that Jason had a knife and my reaction had been to say, 'I'm very busy at the moment, I'll deal with it later' or if I had dismissed the report as unreliable, perhaps coming from a child who had a reputation for telling tales about his classmates, then I have put myself in an untenable position. If Jason had gone on to take out his knife and use it, not only do we have a potentially critical and tragic incident, but now I am really in trouble, because I had been given the relevant information and hadn't responded to it appropriately.

As unpleasant as the notion is, the power to search is there for a reason and must be used when necessary. If your career in teaching lasts half as long as mine did, there will certainly be occasions when you will not be able to avoid using that power, either delegated to you by your head or when you are a head teacher one day yourself. Some of my audiences who are training to be secondary school teachers are not always reassured by the example of how I dealt with Jason. They are handling the behaviour of teenagers, many of whom are regularly carrying knives in the misguided belief they need them for 'protection' and will openly and defiantly refuse to be searched.

What do you do if a pupil refuses to be searched?

Let me just remind you, by way of reassurance, that the searching of pupils will be the responsibility of the head teacher or a senior member of staff, not you – at least, not while you are a trainee or early career teacher. A head teacher or authorised member of senior staff will be bringing their full weight of experience and authority to bear in such situations. If you think one of your pupils is carrying a knife, *do not attempt to carry out a search without your head teacher's authority*. You could, of course, ask the pupil if he or she has a knife in their possession, and if they admit they have, ask them to hand it over – thereby obviating the need to carry out a search. In most cases, though, that would be an unlikely scenario. It may also escalate beyond what you are prepared for or capable of dealing with. You will therefore need to *alert the head or a senior teacher immediately*. As I said earlier, if you have reasonable grounds for suspicion that an offensive weapon is being concealed, you cannot let a pupil walk around school for any length of time once you know about it.

Let's imagine that the head or a delegated senior teacher has arrived and taken over, but the pupil is still refusing to be searched. The head is certainly not going to use force to carry out a search. This is not an example where using reasonable force can be justified. Apart from the fact that it would involve an assault on the pupil, it could also escalate dangerously. No, the head would not try to force the issue physically. They would step up the matter another level by warning the pupil, perhaps saying something along the lines of: 'If you won't hand over the knife/drugs/stolen property voluntarily, and you are refusing to be searched, then I'll have to bring in your parents to take you home' (in the same way I threatened to do with Jason earlier).

There were occasions when, as a head, I had to call parents and ask them to come into school and take their children home following a similar incident. Some parents refused. I remember one mother telling me in no uncertain terms over the phone: 'I can't come into school – I'm at work! You're the head teacher! You deal with it!'

In the case of a pupil suspected of carrying an offensive weapon refusing to be searched, and the parents declining to cooperate, the head would have no alternative but to escalate the matter further, which might involve bringing in the police. Clearly, everyone (especially the police) wants to avoid that. Sadly, however, we are living in times where the likelihood of such incidents is increasing. As I suggested earlier, good management of discipline means always seeking to de-escalate issues where possible. Good experienced heads and senior teachers have a wide range of techniques for taking the steam out of heightened situations. Watch them carefully and learn.

'What if a pupil threatens me with a knife?'

I was asked this question recently by a secondary trainee. My immediate answer was to say: 'Don't worry, that's almost certainly never going to happen.'

That is the problem with raising an issue like this – you end up worrying people more than you intended – so I added: 'In the hypothetically, infinitesimally nanoscopic chance that a pupil might threaten you with a knife, what would *you* do?'

The trainee looked at me totally perplexed. 'I don't know,' he said.

'Come on! You've asked the question. I'm giving you the scenario: a pupil is threatening you with a knife. What do you do?'

'I don't know,' he insisted. 'Tell him to put it down?'

'Yes! That's a start, isn't it? Of course, you try to calm the situation, talk to him or her …' But before I could get much further, he interrupted.

'What if the situation is beyond that? What if they are coming at me, brandishing it?'

'You're worrying too much,' I said.

But the trainee was insistent. He wanted to know what he should do if a pupil actually wielded a knife in his classroom.

'OK, if you insist,' I said, realising that I was going to have to deal with his nightmare scenario. 'Imagine it's really happening. Tell me what you would do *right now* if I came at you brandishing a knife?'

'I honestly don't know!' he said.

I heard someone in the audience say: 'Run!' and everyone laughed.

'Yes!' I said. 'You'd run, wouldn't you? That would be a very sensible thing to do – seriously.' When the laughter subsided, I asked: 'But what if I am standing between you and your escape route? Or you have twenty-nine terrified children screaming and cowering behind you? What do you do then?'

The trainee still had no idea. He shook his head, stupefied. 'I honestly don't know what I'd do,' he said.

Someone else in the audience provided the answer: 'Hit him with a chair!'

'Yes!' I said. 'You'd defend yourself, wouldn't you? So, if a chair is handy, pick it up, hold it in front of you and say: "If you come any closer, I'm going to hit you with this chair!"'

'I can't do that!' he said.

'Why not? I'm threatening you with a knife! You have a right to defend yourself!'

'Really? Am I allowed to hit you with a chair?'

'Yes! Of course you are, if you are defending yourself. If I take no notice and continue coming at you, then you hit me with a chair – hard. At least as hard as you need to in order to disarm or disable me.'

'*Really?* Can I do that?' he asked incredulously.

'Yes! The law gives us all the right to defend ourselves, especially in situations where we think our lives, or the lives of those we are charged with protecting – the children in our class – are in danger. The law allows us to use *reasonable*, even *robust force* if necessary in such situations.'

The trainee was looking at me in sheer disbelief and amazement.

'However,' I went on, 'if you did have to hit me with a chair, and you knocked me prostrate to the ground, sending the knife flying across the classroom floor and out of my reach, then it would not be considered reasonable to come over and continue pummelling my head with the chair. That would obviously be going well beyond using reasonable force to defend yourself. The law does not give you the right to do that.'

Of course, I am not advocating that teachers pick up chairs and threaten pupils, but in an extreme situation where you fear for your life (or the lives of the children it is your duty to protect) then it is common sense – and the law – to defend yourself.[18]

Safeguarding and abuse

Schools in the UK spend a good deal of time training staff and maintaining a high degree of alertness and sensitivity to issues around safeguarding. As a trainee teacher, your course will devote a considerable amount of time to it. As an early career teacher in a school, you will get additional training and be regularly reminded of its importance. The reason? A series of scandals in recent decades brought to the fore the inadequacies of the way that the teaching profession and other social caring professions dealt with vulnerable children. In the case of Victoria Climbié, for example, the failings of all the agencies involved – from her school to the medical profession and from the police to social services – led to a revolution in the way they worked together to better protect children.

The school's DSL is trained and responsible for dealing with all the issues related to abuse, neglect and any necessary onward referrals to relevant agencies. If you have questions or concerns about the well-being of any child, the DSL is the first person to turn to for advice. However, it is worth highlighting some points to underline the legal responsibilities of teachers in this area.

The Children Act 1989 states that: 'A person who … has care of a child, may … do what is reasonable in all the circumstances of the case for the purpose of safeguarding or promoting the child's welfare', which includes understanding the meaning of child

18 You will find more useful information on the Department for Education website: Department for Education, *Searching, Screening and Confiscation: Advice for Headteachers, School Staff and Governing Bodies* (January 2018). Available at: https://www.gov.uk/government/publications/searching-screening-and-confiscation and *Keeping Children Safe in Education (2020): Statutory Guidance for Schools and Colleges* (2020; updated January 2021). Available at: https://www.gov.uk/government/publications/keeping-children-safe-in-education--2.

abuse and recognising the signs.[19] It is therefore your professional and legal responsibility to understand the signs and symptoms of child abuse and respond accordingly. Gone are the days when a child might appear in school with bruises on their face and a young teacher (like me) haphazardly asks the child how they came by them. I was naively placated by answers like: 'I've been fighting with my brother' or 'I fell off my bike.' These days, thankfully, teachers are trained to be alert to the signs of possible physical abuse or neglect and act on them.

However, there may be occasions, even in your early career, when a child comes to you – perhaps because you have already earned their trust and respect – to discuss an issue that is making them unhappy. They may even come to you to disclose a more serious matter.

Discuss and reflect

- A child in your class asks if they can speak to you in private. When you ask what it is about, they say: 'My stepdad comes into my bedroom when I'm in bed at night and touches me under the duvet and I don't like it.' How would you immediately respond to that disclosure?

What to do if a child discloses abuse to you

If a child confides in you, initially just be a good listener. While the disclosure might be distressing, and you know that you will need to inform the DSL as soon as possible, just listen to what the child has to say. If your immediate reaction is to say: 'Hang on a minute while I go and get the designated safeguarding lead teacher, she'll know what to do!' then you are likely to find that by the time you get back or the DSL has arrived, the child doesn't want to speak to anyone any more. Remember that the child may have chosen you because they trust you. Be sensitive and empathetic and give them your full attention.

Similarly, if you reach for a pen and notepad as soon as the child starts to tell you their story, then you might find they say very little else. Making notes about what people are saying, as they are saying it, can be very intimidating. You only have to attend a job interview to experience that feeling. Obviously, you will need to write an account at some point, but leave that until the child has finished speaking – unless there is some

19 See https://www.legislation.gov.uk/ukpga/1989/41/section/3.

crucial detail that you think you will forget otherwise. Alert them sympathetically and tactfully that you would like to make a note of something they have said. Remember: this is not an interrogation. The child is not obliged to provide details, dates, times and so on. You are there merely as the initial conduit. Don't ask the child leading questions. Simply say things like: 'Tell me what happened' or 'Go on, tell me everything you can remember' or 'Is there anything else you'd like to tell me?' (without making it sound as though they have missed something out).

You cannot promise to keep this to yourself, of course, even if the child pleads with you to do so. You will need to consult with the DSL or head teacher immediately after the conversation. But, once again, if you start by saying: 'You do know that I'll have to tell the head teacher about this …' you are likely to bring the conversation to an abrupt end. Choose the moment when you make this clear to the child carefully: 'What you've told me is so important that I need to get advice about what we do next, so I'll need to chat to the designated safeguarding lead (or the head), so we can all work together to stop what is happening.'

Don't take any direct action yourself in relation to the child or the family. Teachers are not responsible for investigating child abuse. The DSL is trained and knowledgeable about the next steps. As soon as the conversation is over, be reassuring to the child and tell them that you are going to help them. Make notes immediately afterwards.[20]

Checklist for safeguarding and disclosure

1. Know who your school's DSL teacher is and your school policy on safeguarding.
2. If you are the recipient of a disclosure, then listen, receive and report:
   - **Listen** to the child. Don't ask leading questions; simply say, 'Tell me what happened …'
   - **Receive.** Don't promise confidentiality. Don't take direct action yourself – teachers are not responsible for investigating child abuse.
   - **Report.** Make some notes as soon as possible, then contact the DSL or head teacher.

20 If you don't feel this area has been adequately covered on your training course or at school, raise it as a point of discussion with your CPD lead or the head. If you want further information, see: HM Government, *Working Together to Safeguard Children: A Guide to Inter-Agency Working to Safeguard and Promote the Welfare of Children* (July 2018). Available at: https://www.gov.uk/government/publications/working-together-to-safeguard-children--2. or go to the website of the National Education Union: https://neu.org.uk/safeguarding.

Anti-discrimination and equalities legislation

In the UK, the Special Educational Needs and Disability Act 2001 makes no distinction between special educational needs (SEN) and disability. All teachers must understand their responsibilities under the SEND Code of Practice[21] to:

- Set suitable learning challenges for all the children in their care.
- Respond to diverse learning needs.
- Overcome barriers to learning and assessment.

Under the Equality Act 2010, there are nine 'protected characteristics':

1. Age
2. Disability
3. Gender reassignment (or trans status)
4. Marriage and civil partnership (in employment only)
5. Pregnancy and maternity
6. Race (and ethnicity)
7. Religion or belief
8. Sex
9. Sexual orientation

Schools, and implicitly teachers, have a general duty to eliminate discrimination, harassment and victimisation, advance equality of opportunity and foster good relations between people who share a protected characteristic and those who don't. Schools also have a specific duty to publish sufficient information to demonstrate compliance with the Act (e.g. record racist and homophobic incidents) and prepare and publish equality objectives (e.g. maintain school policies on equality and anti-bullying).

It is unlawful to discriminate against a pupil on the grounds of race, sex, colour, nationality, ethnicity or national origin. It is also unlawful to discriminate against a pupil on the grounds of sexual orientation, religion, belief or trans status. These are clear-cut legal

21 Department for Education and Department of Health, *Special Educational Needs and Disability Code of Practice: 0 to 25 Years* (January 2015). Available at: https://www.gov.uk/government/publications/send-code-of-practice-0-to-25.

strictures and they are incontestable. Racist or sexist abuse, threats or incitement are similarly indefensible. These protections are also afforded to trainees and new teachers, so if you think you are being unfairly treated while on teaching practice or during your induction period, report the matter to your tutor or mentor, who should take it up with the head teacher. If you think that the issue isn't being dealt with or the head is the source of the treatment, then take the matter up with the school's chair of governors.

Nevertheless, there are some issues of clarification to explore. For example, if we did not intend our actions to be discriminatory, it can be difficult to decide whether they have been so. As far as the Equality Act 2010 is concerned, the outcome is the important issue, irrespective of whether there is intent to discriminate. A victim of alleged discrimination does not need to prove intent; they just need to show that the victim received less favourable treatment. For example, a school's policy might be that children do not wear jewellery in school. This policy might be applied to all children, irrespective of background, and is not intended to discriminate. However, if the outcome is that the policy only affects Sikh children, for example, whose religious tradition is to wear the *kara* (a steel bangle worn around the wrist), then although the intent was general, the outcome was discriminatory (although they may be expected to remove it for PE lessons for reasons of safety).

'Can I have a word?'

A young woman came up to me after one of my sessions wearing an agonised grimace. 'Can I have a word?' she said. She explained that she was a devout Christian and was worried that she would be required to teach things she didn't believe in. I asked her to give me an example. She said she feared that she would be expected to teach children that there are 'at least 120 different genders, and I just don't believe that'.

My answer to her was that neither the Equality Act nor the school expects or requires her to believe that there are upwards of 120 different genders. What the Equality Act and the school will expect is that her teaching tries to eliminate discrimination, harassment and victimisation, and endeavours to advance equality of opportunity and foster good relations between people who might or do believe such a thing and those who might or do not believe it.

'Can you do that?' I asked her.

She thought about it for a moment. Suddenly her face brightened. She began to smile as she realised that her religious faith was entirely compatible with what was being expected of her both by the law and the ethics of her profession.

'Yes, I can do that!' she said.

'Great,' I said. 'Then I'm sure you'll be an excellent teacher.'

Teacher misconduct

The secretary of state for education has the power to act in cases of misconduct through the auspices of the Teaching Regulation Agency. The Education Act 2011 defines misconduct as:

- A relevant criminal conviction.
- Unacceptable professional conduct.
- Conduct likely to bring the profession into disrepute.

If it is alleged that you have committed any of the above breaches, you may find that you are not only at risk of dismissal from your employment but also prohibited from teaching. The Disclosure and Barring Service (in England and Wales) operates to help employers make safer recruitment decisions by checking whether teachers (and those applying to become trainee teachers) have relevant criminal convictions or cautions that might deem them unsuitable to teach children and other vulnerable people.

Discuss and reflect

Which of these offences and situations do you think would result in you being prohibited as a teacher by the Teaching Regulation Agency or disbarred by the Disclosure and Barring Service?

1. A caution for being drunk and disorderly in a public place.
2. Being an alcoholic.
3. A caution for possession of a recreational Class A drug (e.g. ecstasy/MDMA).
4. A conviction for possession of a Class B drug (e.g. cannabis).
5. A conviction for speeding at 100mph on a motorway.

6. A conviction for domestic violence.
7. A sexual relationship with an 18-year-old pupil at your school.
8. A sexual relationship with a 16-year-old pupil not at your school.
9. Active membership of an extreme political party.

We will examine these discussion points in more detail in the pages that follow, but first there are one or two other issues about teacher misconduct that are worth clarifying before we proceed.

Teachers are exempt from the Rehabilitation of Offenders Act 1974, which means that their cautions and convictions are never 'spent'. All cautions and convictions are recorded by the DBS and are disclosed to potential employers on request. In the case of teachers, these disclosures are 'enhanced' – in other words, if you were arrested for a violent offence but not charged due to lack of evidence, the police may have advised the DBS to record the fact you were arrested but not charged as 'relevant information' to determine your suitability as a teacher.

When embarking on a career in teaching you must therefore declare all cautions and convictions on all your application forms, however minor and historic they may be, and do so for jobs that you apply for throughout your career. This does not mean that if you have an existing caution or conviction that your career is over before it has even begun. Nor does it mean that if you get a caution or conviction while you are a teacher it will end your career. The main test of whether you are suitable to become a teacher or remain a teacher is the relevance and seriousness of any offence.

Believe it or not (and there are over half a million teachers in England alone), there are tens of thousands of teachers who have cautions and convictions for all kinds of things – sometimes quite serious offences. They are nevertheless enjoying happy and successful careers, some as head teachers! Indeed, if every teacher who had been issued with a speeding ticket, a drink driving ban or even been busted for cannabis possession had been struck off the teaching register, the UK wouldn't have a sustainable teaching profession. Teachers are people too and while expectations of their probity are rightfully high, they are fallible.

You may think that a teacher who has been convicted for driving at 100mph on a motorway (point 5) has shown reckless behaviour and put other people's lives in danger. I do too, but there may be extenuating circumstances.

'But what if ...?'

Let's say it is the first day of the school holidays and the roads are jammed with holiday traffic. A teacher is running late for their well-earned flight to a sunny holiday destination. As the traffic clears they make up the lost time by speeding down the motorway, touching 100mph at times. Would that make it more forgivable? You may not think so. After all, the law is the law. Driving at 100mph is potentially very dangerous. No exceptions.

But what if the teacher is your own child's? And the teacher is brilliant?

Let's imagine this: your daughter has hated going to school for years. You have had to virtually drag her to the school gates every morning. She has struggled to do her homework and has no aspirations to further her education. This year, though, she got a new teacher and things suddenly changed – her brilliant and inspirational teacher understands her needs. Suddenly, she is leaping out of bed in the morning to get to school, she is doing her homework without the usual hectoring and bribes, and now she has aspirations for university. She even talks interestingly at the dining table about what she is doing at school. You can't believe your luck!

Then one day she comes home in floods of tears. Her brilliant and inspirational teacher has not only been sacked but also prohibited from teaching – prosecuted and convicted for driving on the motorway at 100mph while trying to catch that holiday flight. Your daughter goes back to hating school, refusing to do her homework and has totally lost interest in going to university.

Do you still want to maintain such lofty standards for the teaching profession?

I am not condoning illegality, and nor am I making an exceptional case for why teachers should be allowed a degree of tolerance that we would not extend to other members of society. However, I think the guiding principle of considering the relevance and seriousness of the offence is correct. Is the caution or conviction likely to undermine public confidence either in the teacher as an individual or the teaching profession in general?

If the teacher had been driving at 100mph with a minibus full of children, then that would be an entirely different matter – that is relevant. If the teacher had caused an accident where people had been injured or killed – that is serious. It would also be a different matter if the teacher had been convicted for the same driving offence on a third or fourth occasion, which may suggest that this person is irresponsible by character and habitually reckless in their private life. Tolerance of such behaviour can reach a tipping point where the public (whose interests are represented by regulatory bodies like the Teaching Regulation Agency) may finally lose confidence in the ability of an individual to be responsible and trustworthy with children.

What does it take to get prohibited?

Many of the discussion points in the section above can be usefully dealt with by asking, 'Is the offence (or breach of trust) relevant or serious enough to undermine public confidence in the teaching profession?' As I have outlined, the public (in the form of the Teaching Regulation Agency's professional conduct panels) are guided by this principle. They are also influenced by the ethical commitment that teachers make to 'uphold public trust', as set out in the Teachers' Standards (which we will look at in more detail in Chapter 4). Each case the Teaching Regulation Agency deals with is therefore considered on its own particular circumstances and merits and in the broader ethical context.

Let's take a look at a few of the discussion points.

Point 2: If you were an alcoholic, would you be prohibited from teaching? The answer to that question is no. Alcoholism is a disease and will be dealt with as a health issue, as long as you are seeking support and treatment to manage the condition. Of course, if you were discovered furtively drinking alcohol on the school premises or turned up at school smelling of it, that would be a legitimate disciplinary matter. You cannot expect support from your head or colleagues for that type of behaviour. However, you can expect to be supported by your employer if you have a serious health issue. If you don't feel supported, you should address the issue, perhaps accompanied by a representative from a teaching union (if you are a member of one).

Point 6: Is domestic violence an offence relevant to a teacher's professional standing? The perception of whether intimate partner abuse is relevant or serious enough to undermine public confidence has changed over time. Public perception (in other words, the public's conception of its own morality) is always in a state of flux. There was a time in my own professional life when domestic violence was not taken seriously even by the police, let alone a matter for teacher misconduct. Now, however, there is a growing feeling that a conviction for domestic violence would result in severe disciplinary measures by a professional regulatory body, such as suspension or even prohibition. The basis for this is that a person who could not be trusted to refrain from violence with their partner or spouse might not be trustworthy with the people over whom they have a duty of care – in this case, children.

Point 9: You may think that active membership of an extreme political party is intolerable for a teacher expected to show 'mutual respect' and 'tolerance of those with different faiths and beliefs'.[22] It certainly would be intolerable if that political party also happened to be a banned (in other words, illegal) organisation. But what of parties that are not banned but merely extreme? Britain is a liberal democracy and we should value diversity, including the diversity of political opinion, even when it challenges the mainstream. We cannot expect to agree with everyone else's opinions, even if we do perceive some of them to be extreme. Teachers have the legal right to be members of any political party they wish, as long as it is a lawful one. Teachers, like other citizens, have the democratic right to participate in political activity – rights that they should guard jealously.

The definition of an 'extreme' political party is, of course, subjective.[23] Are the British National Party or the English Defence League, for example, extreme political parties? You might think so. Are the Communist Party of Great Britain or the Socialist Workers Party extreme? What about Greenpeace, Friends of the Earth or Extinction Rebellion? We will explore in Chapter 4 the issues surrounding how teachers' political affiliations in the public realm might affect their reputation in the professional realm, but it is another area where public perception has changed in recent years and will continue to do so.

Point 8: Is it an issue of professional misconduct for a teacher to have a sexual relationship with a 16-year-old pupil who attends a different school? You may be surprised to learn that the answer is no. Perhaps that disgusts you. 'What?' you might declaim. 'An adult – a *teacher* – having sex with a 16-year-old child who is still at school? That's a disgrace!' That is your morality talking – and, of course, you are entitled to your moral position. However, the legal position in the UK is that the age of sexual consent is 16. Whom you choose to have sex with is a private matter: as long as the person is over the age of 16 and the sex is consensual, it is not a matter for the state. You might not like it, but in a liberal free society people have different values about sexual behaviours and preferences, so you will just have to put up with it.[24] When a teacher is having a sexual relationship with a pupil at a different school from the one in which they are teaching, that teacher is not in an accountable position of trust with that pupil; therefore, it is neither a legal nor an ethical issue. Whether it is an issue for you depends on your personal moral stance.

22 Department for Education, *Teachers' Standards: Guidance for School Leaders, School Staff and Governing Bodies* (July 2011; introduction updated June 2013), p. 14. Available at: https://www.gov.uk/government/publications/teachers-standards.

23 The UK government defines extremism as 'vocal or active opposition to fundamental British values': *Prevent Strategy* (June 2011), p. 107. Available at: https://www.gov.uk/government/publications/prevent-strategy-2011.

24 The UK has one of the highest ages of sexual consent in Europe. Only the Republic of Ireland and Cyprus, at 17, have a higher age of consent than the UK. For most of Europe, the age of consent is 15 and in some countries – like Germany, Italy and Austria – it is 14.

Point 7: The issue of a teacher having sex with a pupil who is attending the same school is an entirely different matter, however. This is considered an extremely serious breach of professional trust. A school would almost certainly sack the teacher, even if the pupil was 18 and had the agency of an adult. The teacher is in a position of trust and this has been abused. The school is also obliged to refer the matter to the Teaching Regulation Agency, which would likely result in them being prohibited from teaching. The Sexual Offences Act 2003 made such an offence illegal even if the pupil is over 16 and consenting. As a 16- or 17-year-old, they are still considered vulnerable to people in positions of trust over them. The morality is irrelevant as far as this discussion is concerned because it is both unethical and illegal. Once the pupil reaches the age of adult agency – 18 years old – it is not illegal any more, but it remains an ethical issue and a teacher would likely be sacked and prohibited for it.

However (and to complicate matters even further), there has been a relatively recent transformation of the legal, ethical and moral landscape. In 1999, the then chief inspector of Ofsted, Sir Chris Woodhead, admitted to a relationship he had begun with a 17-year-old girl from the school he had taught at more than two decades earlier. He denied the contested claim that it had become sexual while the pupil was still at the school, but the relationship itself lasted for many years – a fact that, when it came to public attention, neither party said they regretted.

Only four years after this admission, the Sexual Offences Act 2003 came on to the statute book in the wake of the murders of two 10-year-old girls, Holly Wells and Jessica Chapman, in Soham, Cambridgeshire, in August 2002. They were murdered not by a teacher but by a school caretaker, Ian Huntley. The moral outrage, both nationally and internationally, was phenomenal and doubtless influenced the urgency for statutory reform. Moral climates change, occasionally on the back of a horrific incident. When they do, new laws are sometimes the outcome. When the law changes it can impact on ethical codes and professional standards – an area to which we will shortly turn our attention.

Trainees and early career teachers should recognise their particular vulnerability to the infatuations of the pupils they teach. The proximity of age in the case of older pupils attracted to younger teachers is an additional complicating factor, further compounded by the possibility, even the likelihood, of common interests or shared tastes in music, fashion, technology or other aspects of popular youth culture. However, while I feel that young teachers are vulnerable, the law is clear on this issue. Abuse of a teacher's position of trust was enacted (not without some controversy) as a criminal offence in 2000, later incorporated into the Sexual Offences Act 2003 and then into subsequent teaching codes, including the Teachers' Standards in 2011. The Sexual Offences Act 2003 draws lines (arbitrarily) at the ages of 13, 16 and 18:

- Those at ages 16 and 17 are thought to be potentially vulnerable from those who have a responsibility to be in a position of trust over them.

- Those at ages 13, 14 and 15 are protected from sexual activity against them by an adult, although the adult may claim a defence if they had grounds for believing that the child was over 16 at the time.
- There is no defence for sexual activity with a child under 13 and it will be considered rape or sexual assault.

What should I do if I am accused of misconduct of any kind?

My first piece of advice is: don't wait for an allegation of misconduct of any kind (let alone sexual impropriety) to happen before you join a union. If you are not a member of a union, my very strong advice is that you join one now. If you are not a member of a union and you are accused of misconduct, you are very exposed. Unions are not particularly welcoming to people who only need their support after the fact, so do yourself a favour and pay the monthly fee. You will find it a very good insurance policy, especially when the allegations of misconduct (or indeed incompetence) are groundless. (However, unions are keen to point out that protecting their members from charges of misconduct is the least of their use and benefit. Unions have a variety of supporting services, including networks for all kinds of teaching interests and opportunities for CPD.)

If you find yourself in this position and you are a union member, you will need to contact them immediately. If you are working in anything larger than a village school you will probably have a colleague on the school staff who is a union representative. They will guide you through the procedures for responding to any allegation. Many schools have their own protocols, especially since the growth of academies and free schools and the gradual demise of local authorities. Faith schools often have very good, clear processes set out by their affiliated diocesan boards. However, all procedures must include the following:

- At the outset, a teacher accused of a failure in competence, negligence or a disciplinary offence must be furnished with the employers' procedures for dealing with the case.
- At every stage, a teacher has the right to be accompanied by a friend or trade union representative.
- They must make clear what the process entails – stages, hearings, timescales, time limits and possible outcomes.

- The process must include a right of appeal.

One final reminder: if you think there is a possibility that your actions could be misconstrued, always inform the DSL, head of year or deputy head. If they advise you to notify the child's parents, try to view it as a development of your professional self-awareness rather than as an admission of culpability.

The Prevent duty

The Counter-Terrorism and Security Act 2015 places a duty on schools 'to have due regard to the need to prevent people from being drawn into terrorism'.[25] This is known as the 'Prevent duty'. It is intended to help schools think about what they can do to protect children from the risk of radicalisation and suggests how they can access support to do this.

As a trainee or new teacher, you will defer to your DSL if you suspect a pupil is at risk from radicalisation. They will most likely have attended a Workshop to Raise Awareness of Prevent (WRAP) – a training package developed by the UK Home Office. They will know how to take the matter forward, if necessary, or whether to refer the issue to the Channel panel, which will focus on providing support at an early stage to individuals who are identified as being vulnerable to radicalisation. It is important to understand that an individual pupil's engagement with the Channel process is entirely voluntary at all stages.

Having said that, what should we do when a pupil, colleague or even parent comes to us with concerns that one of their friends, neighbours or children is behaving strangely? What do we do when a pupil suddenly starts expressing extreme religious beliefs, shows an unhealthy interest in violent or extreme ideology, or expresses opinions that advocate violent extremism?

25 Department for Education, *The Prevent Duty: Departmental Advice for Schools and Childcare Providers* (June 2015), p. 3. Available at: https://www.gov.uk/government/publications/protecting-children-from-radicalisation-the-prevent-duty.

Notice, Check, Share

Your DSL will provide information (or even in-house training) on a procedure known as Notice, Check, Share. This will train you and your colleagues to:

- Be alert and *notice* changes in behaviour that might lead you to suspect a child is being groomed for extremism.
- *Check* yourself – that your initial impressions make sense and have not been taken out of context or imagined – and check with colleagues (or even with parents) that unusual behaviour is also noticed by them.
- *Share* your concerns with the DSL (who may, in turn, check within a wider context of concern and share it with others more formally).

Many people have been critical of the Prevent duty because they believe that it unduly targets and victimises the Muslim community. Some, including politicians like Baroness Sayeeda Warsi and Manchester Mayor Andy Burnham, have even branded it as 'toxic'.[26] Some teacher unions have rejected it as a cack-handed, blunt instrument that puts teachers in the invidious position of snooping on their pupils. However, it is clear that teachers do have a role in safeguarding their pupils' welfare, so their role in relation to Prevent is no different than if their pupils were in danger of being drawn into sexual exploitation, drugs or gangs.

For example, if you saw a 14-year-old female pupil from your school behaving inappropriately with a group of mini-cab drivers on the high street, or apparently accepting an invitation to get into the car of an older man whom you suspect is not a relative, would you not think that was a matter of legitimate concern? I hope you would. If a pupil told you that a fellow pupil had brought a knife into school or had illegal drugs in their possession, would you not think that was a matter on which to take immediate direct action? I hope so, because it is your legal, ethical (and, in my view, moral) duty to do so. I also hope you would not think that to notice something untoward was 'targeting' a community or 'snooping' on the private life of a pupil or their family. You wouldn't think that if you noticed a child coming into school with bruises on their face or with soiled clothes or if a child was regularly complaining of hunger. We don't regard noticing signs of physical or sexual abuse as targeting or snooping, so we shouldn't have a different attitude if children are at risk from other forms of danger.

26 See, for example: BBC News, Baroness Warsi: Prevent Scheme Should Be Paused (26 March 2017). Available at: https://www.bbc.co.uk/news/av/uk-39399011; and Frances Perraudin, Andy Burnham Calls for 'Toxic' Prevent Strategy To Be Scrapped, *The Guardian* (9 June 2016). Available at: https://www.theguardian.com/politics/2016/jun/09/andy-burnham-calls-for-toxic-prevent-strategy-to-be-scrapped.

If you see or hear something that causes you concern, you should obviously confirm that what you saw or heard has some substance and was not a misinterpretation or misunderstanding. You might want to check with the pupil – for example, by asking them to repeat or clarify a statement or explain a behaviour. This is not to suggest that alternative opinions, views and beliefs, even ones that are radically different from the mainstream, should not be examined or challenged. They should, but you might also want to speak with a colleague who knows the pupil or their family better than you do. You may want to check with their friends or with their parents that what you have seen or heard is not untoward or that you have not got the wrong end of the stick.

If your concerns are not allayed, then you will want to share your concerns with the DSL more formally. They will be able to provide additional information or a more nuanced assessment of what you have seen or heard. They may be able to place the matter in a wider context about which you were unaware (perhaps without going into much detail) or they may take it forward themselves (not necessarily sharing it with you for legitimate personal or confidential reasons).

To notice, check and share is not to target, victimise or snoop. It is the professional role of a responsible teacher to apply their duty of care.

Discuss and reflect

Based on the Notice, Check, Share procedure, what would you do if:

- A pupil says that his brother attends rallies of the English Defence League.
- A pupil whose family you know to be members of the Islamic Deobandi sect shares leaflets with fellow pupils condemning the Ahmadi sect.
- You see a pupil sharing leaflets published by the Animal Liberation Front.
- You overhear a pupil in class saying to her friends that she has viewed videos of suicide bombings on the internet.
- You see a pupil reading a book titled, *Britain First: Let's Take Our Country Back.*
- A group of pupils refuse to observe the two-minute silence at a school assembly marking a recent terrorist atrocity or the Armistice Day commemorations.

Chapter 4

THE TEACHER AND ETHICS – THE TEACHER YOU NEED TO BE

What are ethics?

Put at its most simple, ethics are the principles by which a person's behaviour is judged while conducting an activity. Modern philosophers often use the words 'ethics' and 'morality' interchangeably; although ethics are associated with principles of morality, I am going to focus on ethics as the behaviour and practices that are thought of as right (or wrong) in the public and professional realm. While the distinctions are often fine and debatable, I am going to paint with a broad brush for the purposes of the issues I will raise in relation to teaching.[1]

The difference between ethical and moral standards is essentially connected with the reasons people use to justify them. For example, if I disapprove of same-sex relationships and condemn those who enter into them without a supporting justification for that belief, then that is a moral standard but it is not an ethical one. If I disapprove of same-sex relationships but I do not condemn those who enter into them because I recognise that there is no supporting justification for that belief, then that is a moral standard supported by an ethical one. I can have any moral standards I like in my personal value system, but they are not necessarily ethical.

In contrast, I may adopt vegetarianism as a personal standard and make no attempt to convert others; even though I may be distressed by others eating meat, I do not condemn them for it. I am therefore a moral vegetarian. Or, I may use my vegetarianism as a platform to rebuke and admonish meat-eaters and advocate regulation and restriction on the basis of rational, justificatory beliefs – for example, to argue that there is evidence that eating meat is cruel to animals, wasteful of natural resources and environmentally damaging. In that case, I am an ethical vegetarian.[2]

Obviously, I am going to focus here on the professional ethics of teaching as opposed to a teacher's individual personal morality. I will concentrate on the ethics of what teachers do and why they do it, how and why they make choices from the dilemmas

1 We will explore the concept of morality in teaching in more detail in Chapter 5, but for the purposes of this book I am referring to morality as a set of personal values and individual behavioural standards in relation to things like welfare, justice, compassion, honesty, respect and fairness.

2 See Hand, *A Theory of Moral Education*, pp. 22–28.

they face, how things like professional codes of conduct guide their behaviours, practices and choices, and, ultimately, how this contributes to the formation of an ethical if not a moral character.

Discuss and reflect

In Dallas, Texas, a scheme in schools paid 8-year-old children US$2 for each book they read. Another offered high school students US$50 for achieving an A grade and $35 for a B.

- Discuss the issues related to such a scheme.
- Were they ethical? Were they moral?

While I recognise the connection between ethics and morality (you will see many overlaps in the following pages), for the purposes of this book I am advancing the idea that teaching involves technical activity as both an endeavour of knowledge and a moral enterprise, and that these are distinct but essentially inseparable concepts.

There are three major philosophical traditions based on how we act:

1. Deontology. Actions based on the rules of obligation and duty – of what you must do and what you are not permitted to do. The Ten Commandments are an example of deontological ethics.
2. Utilitarianism. Actions that take cognisance of the consequences of the action – doing what is necessary to create the greatest good for the greatest number of people. This notion was developed by the English Enlightenment philosopher Jeremy Bentham.
3. Agency. Actions that focus on the agent of the action rather than the action itself – which will prompt questions like: 'What sort of person should I be?' and 'How should I live my life?'

Virtue ethics[3]

The problem with most ethical theories, and certainly the ones described on the previous page, is that it takes time to reflect upon them. When we are confronted with an ethical quandary like: 'How do I know right from wrong?' or 'How do I know what to do in this situation?' we cannot spend time discussing this with Plato, Socrates or Aristotle to find the right answer. As teachers, we will often find ourselves in situations that require immediate and sometimes critical responses.

Soldiers on the battlefield are an (admittedly vivid) illustration of this problem. While the British Army are expected to adhere to the Geneva Convention and the (deontological) rule-based ethics of soldiering, the 'rule book' is a very large volume and includes literally thousands of pages on the rules of engagement. Soldiers don't have time to reflect on these rules when they are suddenly confronted with a perilous situation. (For example, a man surrounded by sheep in a village notorious for its allegiance to the Taliban. Is this a shepherd innocently herding his sheep? Is this a decoy for a Taliban ambush? Is this a suicide bomber with an explosive vest strapped to his body?) Ethical judgements are required in the blink of an eye or the soldier, and perhaps his comrades too, may be in immediate danger of losing their lives.

Teachers are required to make immediate judgements too, and although they aren't usually life or death, they will sometimes be critical – for example, admonishing children, restraining them (perhaps using force) and making disciplinary judgements based on incomplete knowledge. In the real world, ethical theories cannot be given leisurely consideration, so what can we rely on?

Virtue ethics has gained popularity in recent decades. It concerns itself less with actions and deeds, and more with what kind of person carries out an action and why. In other words, was the person of good character? Was their motive to be noble or virtuous? The British Army tries to train its soldiers to be of good character, so that when they are confronted with a life-or-death split-second decision, like the one described above, they draw more on temperament, disposition and attributes of who they are. This is because rule-based deontological ethical theories cannot adequately serve them at critical moments.

In virtue ethics, therefore, virtuous character – what Aristotle called 'practical wisdom'[4] – can be trained. Aristotle gave examples from crafts like carpentry. How do you become a good carpenter? Through the practise of good carpentry: by being challenged to acquire new skills, overcome more difficult tasks, correct mistakes, achieve a

3 Virtue theory was developed by the Cambridge philosopher Elizabeth Anscombe in the late 1950s.

4 Aristotle believed that flourishing in life was achieved by developing a virtuous character – what he called *eudaimonia*.

high standard and enhance your reputation. You do not become a carpenter by not practising carpentry or by exhibiting poor and shoddy workmanship and thinking, 'Oh, that will do.' You must practise the good habits, not the bad ones – as anybody learning a musical instrument will know. Likewise, if you want to become a good teacher, you must practise it and focus on the good habits.

Character develops with challenging experiences that force us to make difficult choices. Over time, we get better at it. Character also develops through practice; what is regularly practised becomes intuitive. At the heart of virtue ethics is the question: 'Am I basically a good person trying to make the right decision?' The problem comes when a bad outcome results from a good intention and the action then has to be justified. A soldier might kill a shepherd because he thought the lives of his comrades were in danger, only to find the man was indeed an innocent shepherd.

Teachers are confronted with similar situations – for example, they might physically injure a child when using force to break up a fight. Virtue ethics therefore concentrates on the ethical *agent* rather than whether the *action* itself was right or wrong; the morality of the action is demonstrated by the virtue of the character of the person carrying them out. In virtue ethics, you behave in a way whether the rules say so or not, whether the rules endorse you or not, or whether you feel it or not. You have trained, prepared and rehearsed the virtues of good character – at times you may even have pretended – but you keep on demonstrating those virtues because good character emerges from that practice. 'Fake it until you make it' is the modern idiom for an ancient ethical tradition.

Of course, rules still apply. We still need an ethical code to guide us.[5] We still need defined legal and professional responsibilities to which we are accountable. We still need school policies on discipline and behaviour. But we also need good character and a practical wisdom.

Artificial intelligence – the ethics of educating for consciousness

In the twenty-first century, how should teachers be teaching? What should teachers be teaching? As a classroom teacher, I was involved in constant debate about whether the three Rs (reading, writing and arithmetic) were still relevant. You are more likely to be involved in heated discussions about whether the four Cs (critical thinking, communication, collaboration and creativity) should now take curriculum's centre stage. These are serious matters, ones that teachers themselves – many of whom were

5 We will examine teaching's ethical code, the Teachers' Standards (in England), shortly.

fashioned in 'old-world' educational models – may lack the skills or the intellectual or mental flexibility to deploy. Most teenagers already know more about IT than their teachers. That trend is only likely to gather pace. Without an ethical framework provided by a professional class of people like teachers, what is to stop the technology of educational tools controlling the pupils? The evidence for such risks is already abundant. Look at the way we all, never mind young people, walk the streets like zombies glued to the screens of our mobile phones.

The likelihood that artificial intelligence (AI) will develop human-like consciousness is still some decades, if not generations, away. However, new technology is changing everything we thought we knew about the way humans behave; the structure of groups and their identity, the nature of politics and economics, the idea of national cultures and the concept of the nation state are all in flux.[6] New technology is even challenging our views on the way the architecture of our brain is constructed. The internet is also making it increasingly difficult for us to distinguish between truth and falsity, yet it disseminates hatred and paranoia faster and more effectively than anything previously invented.

The questions AI raises for becoming a teacher and the character of a teacher are many and varied. For instance, if we could educate our children better at home, should we do it? This is a question that more people are asking, particularly in the United States where a significant proportion of children are home educated, and since the COVID-19 pandemic when children all over the world were homeschooled for months.

If we could educate children better through AI, should we do it? If Alexa and Siri can read a story to a child more efficiently or more empathetically than a teacher – or, indeed, a parent – should they? If AI can teach calculus more efficiently than a human, then why not have it dispense discipline and punishment as well? Why not have AI educate children about sex, relationships, gender and religious and racial tolerance? These are questions that will be asked more and more in the coming years, as technology becomes more intuitive. They are not just practical or pragmatic questions; they are ethical and moral ones too.

Some industries are highly vulnerable to AI and automation, and for good reason. Apart from increased efficiency, AI provides opportunities to perform menial and routine tasks that few people enjoy doing. As a greater proportion of the population grows older, the care industry will increase in size. Many of us are progressively coming to rely on Alexa and Siri to line up music, make a drink, heat up a meal or tell the washing machine to wash our clothes. AI can already compose music, paint and sculpt works of art, but it still won't be able to summon innate creativity and inspiration in

6 We will explore these issues more in the appendices when we look in detail at fundamental British values, multiculturalism and spiritual, moral, social and cultural (SMSC) education.

the first place or simulate the human intimacy of having dinner with company – these still require flesh, blood and consciousness – at least for the foreseeable future. While AI can provide efficient and even intelligent solutions to human problems, it is still a very long way from feeling pain, joy, love or anger.

Alan Turing, the genius of early computer design and wartime hero of the Enigma code-breaking endeavour, described the threshold when computers would be considered 'intelligent' as the point at which they could carry on an extended conversation with a human being. If that is true, teachers are still far ahead of computers in providing both *techne* (the skills and knowledge of education) and *phronesis* the (practical wisdom and character that is the outcome of an education).[7] Machines are still a very long way from bonding, trusting, emotional understanding, modulating tone, eye contact, body language and sharing vulnerabilities – all of which take place a thousand times a day when a teacher and a pupil are in face-to-face contact with each other. Our ethical and moral senses are exponentially exercised by teacher-to-child encounters and engagements.

AI replicates what social media is doing to the quality of our social interaction: it distances us across time and space and it outsources the personal responsibility that comes with physical presence. When that happens, morality is unlearned and our ethical compass is disorientated.[8] The danger of too much AI in teaching is therefore both an ethical and a moral issue. Even if AI could be creative to the extent that humans are, would we – should we – want it? If an AI teacher could teach larger classes, answer more questions, correct more mistakes, demonstrate a wider range of techniques, mark more exercise books and do all the other technical things that human teachers do, would we – should we – want that? As teachers, we are not yet closely confronted by the ethical questions presented by AI, but it will come – and when it does we should be prepared for the questions it will raise, particularly those where the teacher's duty of care – that is, *in loco parentis* – serves the child's basic needs.

Of course, there are aspects of teaching that are menial and routine. Handing them over to AI would create more time and release creative energy for busy teachers to respond sensitively to the individual needs and moods of their pupils. There isn't much of an ethical issue there. But what about the impact it might have on teacher–pupil relationships? Sometimes, we have to accept that removing the emotional complexity of human interaction can have value too. What will happen to teaching and teachers when non-conscious but highly intelligent algorithms know us better than we perhaps know ourselves? And what about teaching efficacy? What will happen when we can design systems that teach more efficiently, more accurately, more effectively and

7 For more on Aristotle's distinctions about education, see Jonathan Barnes, *Aristotle: A Very Short Introduction* (Oxford: Oxford University Press, 2000).

8 See Jonathan Sacks, *Morality: Restoring the Common Good in Divided Times* (London: Hodder & Stoughton, 2020), pp. 57–59.

perhaps more judiciously than teachers? Who will design, own and control these systems? Whose values will they represent? How will we feel if our own child is taught by an algorithm that we don't understand? While these questions are still some decades away, we need to start making compelling arguments for why human teachers should retain a controlling agency over algorithmic systems, especially when these systems are trained by and reflect human biases.

We might not agree about the sources of disparity and inequity now, but in the future, AI systems will likely provide us with detailed and incontrovertible evidence about the ways in which individuals and groups are unfairly treated, particularly in the allocation of resources. Such evidence will throw up enormously challenging ethical issues. This will be true in teaching as much as in any other profession. It is also likely to reinforce already entrenched biases. The corollary of this is that we will also be morally accountable for the moral good we fail to do when AI provides us with the tools and data to achieve so much good. We must be engaged – and, as teachers, we must engage children – in real-world ethical and moral decision-making.[9]

Discuss and reflect

- Is human work essential to human dignity?
- If so, is being taught by a human essential to dignity?

The logical consequence of technology is that it aims to achieve more with less effort. The spade was invented because it could dig better than your hands, the tractor was invented because it could dig better than a spade, and so on. Technology therefore has the potential to enhance the effectiveness and efficiency of human activity, including teaching. Teachers once chalked diagrams on blackboards to illustrate chemical reactions or the periodic table; now they can use electronic whiteboards to model and demonstrate compounds using video and animations.

Technology doesn't just increase efficiency; it can make things obsolescent too. When humans began to ride horses, they could travel further with less effort. When humans invented the wheeled carriage, it enhanced the efficiency of the horse. But when humans invented the motor vehicle, both the horse and carriage quickly became redundant for transporting people and goods.[10] Could the imminent exponential advances in AI and super-intelligent tools transform the efficiency of teaching and make teachers themselves obsolete?

9 See Harari, *21 Lessons for the 21st Century*, ch. 2.
10 See Harari, *21 Lessons for the 21st Century*, ch. 2.

If we get to the stage where the knowledge and skills encapsulated in the thirteen years of a school curriculum could be downloaded into a child's brain in an instant, what would be the continuing value of a schooled education? If and when such a situation comes to pass, what will teachers actually do every day? What will their value be in the economic marketplace? Who will they be in the eyes of the children, parents and the community they serve? What will be the ethical basis of teaching? What will be its moral purpose?

Discuss and reflect

- If we could control or improve children's behaviour through AI, should we? If not, why not?
- In *The Brothers Karamazov*, Dostoyevsky asks the question: if you could create a paradise by torturing just one innocent child, would you do it? Would you want to be part of that 'paradise'?
- If you knew that you could solve all discipline problems in schools by reintroducing corporal punishment (like caning), where even the deterrent effect might suffice, would you approve of it?

The ethical teacher

What constitutes an ethical teacher? In order to be ethical, you have to examine that which is inherently wrong and identify those things that promote harm, such as deceit, manipulation, deprivation, neglect, fraud, intimidation or blatant use of others for your own selfish ends. An ethical teacher is therefore someone who attempts to counter such wrongs and operates by the principles of:

- Beneficence – doing that which promotes human welfare and flourishing and actively tries to prevent harm.
- Non-maleficence – doing that which does no harm.
- Tolerance – doing that which requires us to tolerate the intolerable (in itself a problematic clash of virtue, which we will come back to later in this chapter).

The daily ethical dilemmas of teaching – homework, marking and report writing

When I was a pupil at school, I was never interested in what my teachers wrote in the margins. I always went straight to the summative marks out of ten at the bottom. I suspected the children I taught had the same attitude. As a class teacher, I had very mixed views about the virtues of detailed marking and feedback, particularly of homework tasks. Apart from the time and energy it took (ultimately away from other activities I thought were more beneficial), it never seemed to me that the children found the formative aspect of writing helpful, or ever took much notice of encouraging comments or detailed corrections on the page. For years I agonised about whether my time would be better spent doing other things. It was a constant dilemma: should I attend assiduously to individual homework tasks when I couldn't observe the process or know who was helping them? Or should I spend more time in class giving them direct feedback on the things I could see them doing? Of course, you might respond: 'You should do both.' If you are a super-teacher, go ahead. I was just a fallible human being with a limited amount of time and energy.

When I was a head teacher, I came across some software that provided scores of attainment descriptions spanning every curriculum subject. I thought I had found the holy grail. I edited them (as they were a bit American in tone and style) and made them available to my staff in advance of the report-writing season at the end of the summer term. Every year, my colleagues had complained that they were fed up of writing the same old things, so they leapt at them. The descriptions offered various graded accounts of attainment that, to be honest, we hadn't even thought of.

As the weeks went by, they began telling me that the software was improving their report writing and saving them hours of time. As the head teacher, of course, I had to read every report before it went out to parents. Although there were some repetitions, I was pleased that the reports were much better written than in previous years. They were more descriptive, more objective and more accurate of each child's attainment. The saving of staff time was also a massive bonus.

The parents didn't agree. As soon as they got wind of teachers using software-based pro formas to describe their unique and very special little darlings, they complained in droves. Some accused us of doing what was 'convenient' just to 'save time' rather than come up with 'original' descriptions of their individual child's attainment. We abandoned the practice the next year. Looking back, I regret not having had the professional confidence to face down those objections.

Taking the mickey or having a sense of humour?

I worked with a colleague who was a brilliant mimic and could have had a career in stand-up comedy. He mimicked pupils, he mimicked parents and he mimicked his fellow colleagues, including me, relentlessly. It was never done in an unkind way, although he managed to capture the absurd in all of us – often in a brutally truthful way. At breaktimes and lunchtimes, his impressions produced gales of laughter in the staffroom. He provided a much-needed safety valve for highly pressured, hard-working and often stressed teachers. However, his mimicry would have almost certainly caused severe embarrassment (and probably official complaints) had it been witnessed by those who couldn't be relied on to see the funny side. Was his behaviour unethical?

Being political or showing passion?

I was a classroom teacher in Hackney in the 1980s when some of the most contentious issues of modern British history were being hotly, and sometimes violently, played out: the miners' strike, the Falklands War, the poll tax, inner-city riots. I have been guilty of politicking and grandstanding on occasion – holding my impressionable young pupils hostage to my passionately held views about the wickedness of racism and social injustice or the evils of apartheid in South Africa. Were these expressions of personal belief unethical? Could they 'exploit pupils' vulnerability' or 'lead them to break the law' (as Part Two of the Teachers' Standards warn against)?[11]

Discuss and reflect

- Are there any issues (either educational or political) that challenge your ethical position as a teacher? For example, what would be your response if pupils at your school wanted to demonstrate in school time about issues such as:

11 Department for Education, *Teachers' Standards*, p. 14.

- The climate emergency.
- The rights of trans and gender-fluid pupils in the school.
- Black Lives Matter.
- Reducing the voting age to 16.
- Period poverty (i.e. menstrual hygiene).

- Would you support or condone their actions if they included non-violent civil disobedience?

In teaching, discouragement is demoralising and sarcasm is a killer. I am often struck by the compelling testimony of people who are convinced that their lives were damaged by the crushing words of a teacher's dispiriting pessimism. Words matter. They can deeply affect the way we feel and respond, particularly when uttered by those we regard as 'significant others'. We expect teachers to be encouraging, supportive, constructive and even motivational.

I think we would rightly have concerns about colleagues who were regularly sarcastic or unrelenting in their cynicism towards pupils. Few of us would tolerate colleagues who insulted the children, let alone were abusive towards them, even with extreme provocation. Clearly, such behaviour is unethical, unprofessional and unacceptable. But what about teachers who say things that might be regarded as merely negative? What about those who simply don't make the appropriate response or give the kind of encouragement that a child (or their parent) thinks they deserve? Is that unprofessional too?

'You say I can't do that? You just watch me!'

When I was at school studying for my A levels, a teacher told me, in front of the whole class: 'You will never get the A levels to get into university.' That remark impacted on me so deeply that I remember the incident as if it were yesterday. I can recall the teacher's exact words, her tone and facial expression. I even remember what she was wearing. Such was the significance of that moment it is burnished on my memory nearly fifty years later. How did it affect me? How did I react? I sat there and thought to myself: 'You say I won't get into university? Won't I? Well, that's what you think! I'll show you!'

> And I did. I look back on that incident not as a humiliating put-down by a cruel and discouraging teacher (whom I may have frustrated and angered by my constant interruptions and Scouse-lippiness), but as perhaps the greatest motivating comment I had ever received in my life. Even now, when I hear someone telling me: 'You can't do that!' it provokes me to say to myself: 'Oh, yes I can. You just watch me!'

I am not advocating that you use scathing put-downs in your repertoire of motivational techniques; that would be unethical. However, it is a paradox for teachers that the adversity they sometimes create through criticism or low expectation can bring out, perhaps unwittingly, virtuous character traits that ultimately enable some young people to achieve their potential. For some, adversity is more motivating than endless expressions of encouragement, constant positivity and unimpeded enablement. Shakespeare knew about this. In *As You Like It* he wrote: 'Sweet are the uses of adversity;/Which like the toad, ugly and venomous,/Wears yet a precious jewel in his head.'[12] So did Benjamin Disraeli, who said: 'there is no education like adversity'.[13] Being ethical is not straightforward. It will involve interpretations and contradictions. What one teacher may regard as treating children equally requires differentiated input to achieve an equitable outcome; another teacher may see that as an unacceptable deviation from impartiality and equal treatment for all.

There will be similar dilemmas. For example, can you be an ethical teacher in an unethical school? Would you accept a job in a school that employs an 'avoid physical contact' policy (discussed in Chapter 3) if you thought it wasn't in the best interests of the children or constrained your ability to apply an appropriate level of care? Would you prepare emotionally vulnerable children for GCSEs if, in your judgement, their mental well-being was at risk?

A teacher's ethical character is reflected daily in their attitude, demeanour, expression and behaviour. For example, the effort you make to provide all pupils with the opportunity to answer questions is not just a demonstration of your teaching competence but also of your fairness. Your effort to return marking and feedback swiftly and diligently is not just a demonstration of your efficiency but also of your ethical agency. If the extent to which you discipline a disruptive child is tempered by your concern for their family background, your professional judgement is arguably not compromised but enhanced by the virtue of compassion. As a teacher, you will be dealing on a daily basis with ethical quandaries like these, weighing competing virtues one against the other. The knowledge you acquire and the judgements you make in doing so are

12 William Shakespeare, *As You Like It*, Act II, sc. I, ll. 12–14.

13 Benjamin Disraeli, *Endymion* (London: Longmans & Green, 1880), ch. 61. Available at: https://www.gutenberg.org/ebooks/7926.

situated within a virtue-based professional ethic. The good news is that all this weighing of competing virtues and consideration of ethical dilemmas will make you a better and more characterful teacher.

What would you do if …?

You are an enthusiastic, talented and hard-working new teacher. You have good skills and good professional values. You love the job and despite the long days and short weekends you are as keen as mustard. You are a non-judgemental 'live and let live' kind of person, well liked by your colleagues. They have even elected you teacher-governor and the union rep. OK, you have made a few minor mistakes here and there but your hard work makes up for it. Anyway, you know the difference between right and wrong. You certainly know what should be done with a dentist who was embezzling thousands from the NHS, or a nurse who was snorting cocaine while working on an intensive care unit, or a doctor who has sex with a patient – chuck 'em out! It is easy to make moral judgements, especially from a distance, isn't it? You can stand back and be the arbiter of other people's unprofessional behaviour.

What would you do if a colleague (who has become a good friend) tells you in the strictest confidence that she has started a relationship with another early career teacher in the school. 'So what?' you say. 'Most people meet their partners at work, don't they?' Actually, I didn't get that quite right – she tells you that the colleague she has started a relationship with is not another new teacher but a member of the senior leadership team. Take a second to think about this … In fact, that isn't the whole truth either. The person she has been sleeping with (for the last three months) is the deputy head teacher, who is married. Oh, and another thing, his wife also teaches at the school. What would you say to your friend then? Would you do anything about it?

One day you discover a large number of empty alcohol (spirit) bottles in a school store cupboard. Mystified, you go to the head teacher and tell her. She closes her office door and asks you to sit down. She tells you they belong to her. She pleads for your discretion and admits that she has been drinking heavily to cope with the stress of the impending Ofsted inspection. Also, she is trying to look after her elderly mother who is terminally ill and needs constant care at home. How would you respond?

After school you walk into a room you thought was empty. A well-respected, experienced senior colleague (who also happens to be your mentor) is sitting alone accessing an adult porn website. He apologises for the embarrassment but says it is his own computer – and anyway, it is after school. You catch a glance at the screen. It is hardcore pornography featuring women dressed as teenage school girls. What do you say?

You are good with figures and spreadsheets, so as a teacher-governor you have been appointed to the governors' finance committee. You are confused by discrepancies in some unreconciled accounts. You talk to the head teacher about it. She breaks down and admits that she has used school money to pay for additional palliative care for her mother, who died recently. The discrepancies in the accounts are not the result of her withdrawing money but paying the money back into the school account. The sums involved are tens of thousands of pounds. She insists that she has now repaid every penny she 'borrowed'. What would you do?

(I suggest apply for another job because that is one hell of a school you are working in!)

Seriously, consider what you would think, say and do in all of these very unprofessional but also very human situations. I suspect that if (and when) we actually find ourselves in the midst of an ethical dilemma, our responses aren't as straightforward as we might like to think.

One more thing. Just in case you think that all these scenarios are fictitious and totally inconceivable, and you will never find yourself in such a messy situation, these are all authentic disciplinary cases from the former professional regulatory body in England.[14]

Trust and accountability

Every profession needs to be trusted. Trust is a valuable social commodity that should not be squandered. In the last thirty years, there has been a revolution in accountability to address the assumed crisis of trust in professional and public life, but it is very uncertain whether this has enhanced trust in professions or undermined it even further. As professional people, we have huge responsibilities and potential influence over the lives of others, so it is unquestionably right that we should be called on to explain ourselves. The issue is whether the methods by which we do it are conducive to adding value and wisdom to what we do. Are these methods, in fact, obstructive

14 The General Teaching Council for England (GTC) which was in existence between 2000 and 2012.

and a hindrance? Might they even be harmful to our purpose? Has the managerialism that has been superimposed on the activities of professionals burdened them to the point of crippling their performance?

As professionals, we must be actively involved in questioning whether the reporting methods distort or clarify the aims, practice and purpose of our professionalism, and actively investigate and consider whether other methods would serve our purpose better. There are only twenty-four hours in a day, so the more time we spend recording and analysing the spurious data and units of measurement we have accumulated, the less time we have to perform the central tasks of the service we have been trained for and for which we are charged and trusted to deliver.

For example, does the public really need to know which police officer has recorded the most offences or solved the most crimes in a particular town or borough? Do patients need to know who is the most skilful surgeon in a given hospital? Do parents need to know which teacher has got the most pupils through a particular exam? In my view, no. What the public and our clients really need to know is that we are good at our jobs, and when we are underperforming, that there will be active remediation and, where necessary, disciplinary measures to remove those unfit to practise.

It is undeniable that perverse incentives have emerged in many professions as a result of over-zealous performance measurement. For the police service, some crimes are easier to solve than others. For doctors and nurses, some diseases and ailments are easier to cure or alleviate than others. For teachers, some subjects are easier to teach (and easier to achieve higher grades in) and thereby boost a school's appearance of high performance.

Would we expect an ethical police service to put more effort into recording speeding offences than violent crime? Would we expect an ethical medical profession to spend more time alleviating the common cold than cancer or Alzheimer's disease? Would we expect an ethical teaching profession to put forward more pupils for examination in media studies, sociology or psychology than for physics, maths or chemistry? The answer is, of course, no, and yet there is plenty of evidence that this has been the case in one way or another over the last two to three decades.[15]

I constantly repeat the adage that new teachers should be able to feel free to learn from their mistakes. However, I know full well that the current culture of accountability makes it almost impossible for teachers and schools to live with honest failure, not least because failure comes with so much scope for blame and retribution, making it difficult, if not impossible, to learn from our mistakes.

15 See Onora O'Neill, *The Reith Lectures: A Question of Trust* [radio series], BBC Radio 4 (2002). Available at: https://www.bbc.co.uk/programmes/p00ghvd8.

Trust, like hope, looks to the future, but trust cannot be established in schools or in civic society if we overemphasise rights and neglect an understanding of and commitment to our duties and responsibilities. This applies to teachers and pupils. Teachers must point out to children – on all those difficult and taxing occasions when children demand their rights – that they must recognise their duties and responsibilities to others first. Indeed, encouraging children to claim rights for others is an effective way for them to understand this and will help them to become more active and informed citizens.

Many professions must earn trust from their clients, but one of the extraordinary things about teaching is that parents and pupils assume trust in their relationship with teachers. However, the nature of trust is complex and varied. A parent may trust a particular teacher to teach their child arithmetic but not calculus or to teach reading but not past participles in the future perfect tense. Over-architectured accountability might provide parents with more information about schools, more comparisons between them and more opportunities to complain about them, but it can also build a culture of suspicion, low morale and cynicism.

Part of our professional duty and responsibility must be to argue for intelligent forms of accountability that allow for the good governance of our schools and our profession, not standardised measures that are designed for a one-size-fits-all approach. We must be willingly called to account, but in substantive, narrative and qualitative ways as much as (or more than) quantitative ways. We must commit ourselves to a culture of public service and an acceptance that not all things can be measured. We should argue, perhaps especially in teaching, that some of the things we are trying to achieve are, by their nature, subjective.

Transparency is another fashionable idea in the current accountability culture, but it is not necessarily appropriate in all professions and certainly not in all contexts. A doctor being publicly transparent with patient records or teachers being publicly transparent with pupil records would constitute gross ethical misconduct and would result in catastrophic loss of trust. A lack of transparency, even secrecy, is not necessarily damaging to trust; and neither is making honest mistakes, especially when they are accompanied with an apology expressing regret.

Intentional deception is damaging to trust, however. The intention to deceive is rightly considered a deeply ethical and moral issue, especially in a profession like teaching where one of the core principles of education is the search for truth. But an overbearing accountability culture can create a huge pressure to deceive: teachers who falsify exam answers because they are convinced their pupils would know the answer to the questions if it weren't for their exam nerves; teachers who give their pupils inside information or prior knowledge about exam questions; teachers who exaggerate or fabricate their own curriculum vitae, knowing that some claims simply cannot be checked; head teachers who write glowing references about colleagues merely to get rid of them or minimise conflicts of interest when employing others. Pupils are not exempt either. How many of us can be confident that when we set pupils research tasks they do not plagiarise from others or wantonly copy from the internet?

On the other hand, demands for universal transparency can also result in forms of deception that undermine trust. If you know that everything you write, record or say about a child will be recorded and that you will be accountable for it, you are likely to say less, massage the truth or say something so bland and inoffensive that it is utterly banal.

Teachers are trusted as few other professions are. Why? Firstly, because we are members of a respected profession with a legacy bequeathed to us from previous generations that we must not taint. Secondly, we are trusted because the relationships we establish are consequent on activities diligently and conscientiously carried out. The information and data we provide can be verified and inspected. Doing these things well builds trust. If people can't inspect and check what we do, they won't trust us – at least not implicitly or over the long term.

Trust is undermined by coercion and deception – choices that are open to vulnerable teachers – where an accountability culture provides the logic to do so. The challenges that teachers must regularly contend with are tests of our trustworthiness and, ultimately, our character.

Collegial loyalty

There is a long-standing tradition that teachers do not criticise each other, at least not in public. The established convention is that we do not interfere with or expose each other's weak practice, even when some of those practices might involve an element of minor negligence. We tend to leave the exposition of minor infractions to the eagle eyes of the senior leadership team or Ofsted inspectors. I am not referring to illegal acts – like physical or sexual abuse, assault or sexual grooming – but things that most of us have been guilty of at one time or another, like inadequate planning and preparation of lessons, haphazard or improvised teaching, or disrespectful and bullying language towards pupils in a fit of annoyance. In all the years I was working in schools and in my observations since, loyalty, solidarity and collegiality were deeply established characteristics of the teaching profession – and for good reason too.

Discuss and reflect

- What are the grounds for criticising a colleague?
- How should criticism be managed and conducted? Should it ever be done informally, peer to peer, or should it be left to those with management and leadership responsibilities?

Collegial harmony is an important professional value to nurture and maintain. Not at any cost, obviously, but it is a precious commodity, especially when teachers are working hard and under significant physical and emotional pressure. The support and understanding of our colleagues may be the single element that sustains an otherwise intolerable workload. Even in the most collegial of environments we are still individuals. There is always a danger that we can feel compelled to conform and obey the perceived and sometimes arbitrary judgements of a majority, particularly when that majority might be led by a forceful and charismatic head teacher.

I came across a school a few years ago where the head teacher – very popular with staff and parents – suddenly announced that she wanted to introduce a school dress code for teachers. This wasn't about the men wearing stylish shirts and ties or the women wearing smart blouses and pencil skirts. No, the head teacher thought it would be a great idea for all the teachers and support staff to wear sweatshirts in the school colours with the school's crest and its mission logo emblazoned on the front – identical to the children's school uniform. In this case, I think the head teacher was swept up by a sudden enthusiasm for team-building which wasn't shared to the same extent by her staff. But no one would question such an assumption if they worked for an airline or even a trendy retail tech company – and uniforms are usually very popular with parents and children – so why not teachers?

Discuss and reflect

- Many places of employment have uniforms for their staff. Should schools?
- What about the wearing of visible religious symbols? Should teachers be free to wear religious symbols?

Tyrannical group mores can weaken moral and ethical principles. Certain aspects of union membership, for example, can – in extreme circumstances – threaten ethical principles. The pressure that is sometimes brought to bear on colleagues unwilling to join strike action can be immense and the resulting damage to collegial cohesion can be irreparable. I was involved in supporting 'work to rule' action in the 1980s, when my colleagues and I (those who were members of teacher unions) withdrew our commitment to providing voluntary and extracurricular activities. This was part of a long-running dispute with employers over pay.

Looking back, I wonder if my professionalism was enhanced by the action I felt forced to take at the time. I now think it did significant long-term damage to the children's interests, especially to things like team sports and extracurricular activities, such as concert and theatre attendances. It also damaged relationships with colleagues, although in most cases they repaired over time. Teachers of every generation are faced with similar ethical dilemmas over issues they perceive to be fundamental to their values.

Discuss and reflect

- You and your colleagues have identified a small group of vulnerable Year 11 (16-year-old) pupils whose mental and psychological well-being you think has become fragile. In school, they are easily and increasingly brought to tears, and they display nervous anxiety even in the least demanding of situations. Their parents have (in some cases) reported loss of sleep, poor appetite and even bed-wetting. You and your colleagues feel that the pressure of approaching GCSE exams will only exacerbate their condition. What options are open to you?

Harassment

Although teachers may be highly educated, mature, experienced and in possession of status and authority, they are sometimes ethically compromised in their relationships with pupils. Ostensibly, teachers hold the reins of power, but in the reality of complex teacher–pupil dynamics teachers can be the victims of occasional, even brutal, harassment in ways that embarrass, humiliate and degrade. In most cases, the victims are usually female teachers and the perpetrators are usually (although by no means always) boys.

The most dramatic example I experienced as a head was when a brilliant teacher in her late twenties decided to move from teaching children in Key Stage 2 (7–11-year-olds) to the school's reception class (4–5-year-olds) for her own professional development. Within weeks she was struggling to manage, not because of the teaching style or the curriculum content, at which she excelled, but because a group of very tight-knit boys were undermining her confidence and authority by relentless gender-related and sexualised taunts. Even the involvement of parents and my threats of temporary exclusion failed to break up their close little cabal. By the end of the year she was both disillusioned and exhausted. These boys were just 5 years old.

Unethical professional behaviour is often related to status, but not always. Even senior managers can be the victims of sexual and racial harassment by teachers who are nominally junior. Of course, there are many dimensions to sexual harassment – pupil to pupil, pupil to teacher and vice versa, teacher to teacher, teacher to parent and vice versa. We cannot deal with the detailed complexities of all these permutations here, but there are some overarching principles to draw out. As far as pupil-to-pupil flirting and sexual harassment is concerned, I will leave that for a discussion elsewhere (it is more relevant as a school discipline issue). Flirtatious behaviour and sexual harassment by a teacher towards a pupil is clearly a serious matter. It should be seen in the context of the abuse of trust and in terms of the ethical and legal ramifications we explored in the previous chapter.

However, there are some complex issues to be considered even in relation to this case in point. For example, it can be difficult to distinguish flirtatious banter from sexual harassment (which is classified as unwanted behaviour of a sexual nature), particularly as it can be easily denied. Some people argue that flirtatious banter should be dealt with as an internal disciplinary issue, while others suggest that more mature senior staff member should counsel younger teachers found culpable of ill-judged behaviour, especially when it involves a teacher whose age is relatively close to their pupils. In more serious cases (or recidivist occurrences where sexual harassment is clearly evident), resignation or dismissal might well be required. Some people contend that the involvement of the police or the courts only exacerbates the trauma suffered by the pupil and undermines their individual agency as a young person.

There is also the duty of care that teachers have a right to expect to receive. Young and impressionable teachers in their early twenties, recently out of university and still acquiring their professional persona, may be prone to making silly mistakes. Should the foolhardy, rash or imprudent behaviour of a young and possibly immature teacher result in life-long criminalisation or prohibition from teaching?

As far as pupil-to-teacher sexual harassment is concerned, newly qualified, trainee and supply teachers can be particularly vulnerable to the flirtatious, intimidating and sexualised behaviour of adolescents. In 2004, a 14-year-old girl was suspended from an English secondary school for exposing her breasts to a trainee English teacher whom she had persistently sexually harassed. Young male teachers, particularly in primary schools (where men are a relative rarity), can be the relentless targets of flirtatious and sexualised attention of female parents and, believe it or not, pubescent pupils.[16]

The public attitude to tolerating relationships between pupils and teachers has changed markedly over the decades in which I have been teaching. I say this to illustrate how values change, not as self-indulgent reminiscence. Up until the mid-1990s, there were many cases of teachers and pupils who became romantically engaged at school and later married – a situation that would seem shocking and intolerable now. Commenting on the transformation of ethical values and public morality, one woman wrote to the *TES* in 2004 to say: 'There is a distinction to be made between the dangers of teachers exploiting young pupils and a genuine relationship between an 18-year-old pupil and a 26-year-old teacher.' Of her own relationship with a teacher, she adds: 'We are about to celebrate our Ruby wedding anniversary'.[17] These days there would be very little tolerance for such a romantic interpretation. Times have changed, and so have values.

The general principle we are applying here is that a professional person should not be having a personal relationship of any kind with a client where it might compromise or conflict with the individual or general interests of that client or the client group to which they belong. In the case of teachers, the principle could equally apply to parents as well as pupils. Engaging in a relationship with a parent is considered a breach of professional trust and a teacher can expect to be disciplined both internally by their employer (with likely dismissal) and probable disciplinary action by the Teaching Regulation Agency (possibly being prohibited from teaching).

Discuss and reflect

Are there ethical implications to the following:

- A teacher having a relationship with more than one colleague.
- A teacher having a relationship with a parent or school governor.

16 On another tangent, male teachers are much more likely to be threatened with physical aggression from male parents than their female counterparts.

17 *TES*, Lost Age of the Discreet Dalliance (30 January 2004). Available at: https://www.tes.com/news/lost-age-discreet-dalliance.

Racial harassment

Racial harassment has been illegal for many decades but, sadly, that does not mean it has been eradicated. I worked at a university in London that prided itself on recruiting up to 40 per cent of its teacher trainees from black, Asian[18] and minority ethnic backgrounds, reflecting the actual demography of London. This was in the early to mid-1990s. The university attained this astonishing achievement through imaginative advertising campaigns and courses structured to attract people with multilingual strengths and diverse cultural backgrounds.

The students were invariably highly motivated, but some of their experiences on school placements left me dismayed. For example, black and Asian students would occasionally suffer veiled racial harassment and disguised insults at the hands of children and parents. Sometimes the response of school leadership teams to such incidents was less than robust, leaving the trainees unable to protest yet feeling humiliated and undermined. On other occasions, black and Asian trainees complained that school mentors were judging them to a different standard than their white counterparts.

This was exceptional and far from the norm even in the 1990s, but it would be naive to think that we are entirely free of such harassment today. I don't have the space in this book to interrogate the statistics relating to the recruitment of black and ethnic minority students to teacher training courses or the recruitment of ethnic minority teachers generally, but I am still troubled by the relatively low levels of ethnic minority teachers in the teaching profession.

In 2019, according to the UK government's 'School Teacher Workforce' document, 87.2 per cent of teachers were White British or White Irish. About 8 per cent of teachers were from Asian, Black or Mixed Ethnic heritage. Of these, just under 20,000 were of South Asian origin (Bangladeshi, Indian, Pakistani or Mixed Asian) – that is, about 4.4 per cent of the teacher workforce compared to about 7.5 per cent of the working age population (based on the 2011 Census). Only 800 were of Chinese origin – 0.2 per cent of the teacher workforce compared to 0.9 per cent of the working age population. About 10,600 teachers in the UK are Black (those of African origin about 4,200, of Caribbean origin about 4,900 and the remainder of about 1,500 of Black Other) – that is about 2.3 per cent of the teacher workforce yet they comprise 3.6 per cent of the working age population. There is an additional 1.4 per cent (about 6,400) who identify as Mixed Heritage.[19] We could go on to break down the figures even further or look at

18 In the context of the UK, the term Asian usually refers to people with a South Asian – that is, Indian, Pakistani or Bangladeshi – heritage.

19 HM Government, School Teacher Workforce (18 February 2021). Available at: https://www.ethnicity-facts-figures.service.gov.uk/workforce-and-business/workforce-diversity/school-teacher-workforce/latest#main-facts-and-figures.

the comparison between the percentage of ethnic minority teachers in relation to the percentage of ethnic minority school-age pupils, but I think you get the drift. There is a lack of ethnic minority teachers in the UK given their presence within the general population and particularly within the school population.

I speak to audiences at universities in the UK's largest and most diverse cities. Walking through campuses, I see students of all ethnic backgrounds and at some universities they even sometimes appear to be the majority. When I enter the auditorium to speak to those training to be teachers, however, I often see only a handful of ethnic minority faces among the hundreds sat in front of me. This problem is not isolated to classroom teachers. For example, UK government figures confirm that the number of ethnic minority teachers in management positions shrinks further as seniority increases.[20] Why is this? Are ethnic minority teachers not being promoted as they progress through the profession? Are they leaving teaching in greater numbers than their white counterparts? Other professions – including medicine, nursing and law – all have a better record of recruiting and retaining people from ethnic minority backgrounds. More research in this area is clearly required. The issues around the recruitment, retention and progress of ethnic minority trainees and teachers are both ethical and moral. (There's a good topic for your MA or PhD thesis!)

Discuss and reflect

- Should we be more concerned with outcomes rather than fairness? Does it matter what the ethnic backgrounds of teachers are if everyone has an equal opportunity to enter the teaching profession and progress within it?
- Would it matter if over 90 per cent of teachers were black or Asian? Or if the majority of white children went through their entire school career never having been taught by a white teacher?
- According to the 2011 Census, there are about 400,000 people of Chinese heritage living in England and Wales, yet only 800 of them are teachers. Do disparities like that matter? Why?

20 HM Government, School Teacher Workforce.

Ethical codes of conduct and practice

All established professions have professional codes of conduct and practice. Although they may be revised to take account of modern norms and societal expectations, they are a traditional feature and marker of professionalism. As we have seen, such codes not only affirm the values of the profession to its practitioners, but they are also an expression of the profession's values to its clients and the general public. In effect, they declare: 'This is what we do, this is who we are and this is what we believe in.' Given that, they play a very important part in the espousal of a professional ethic.

Codes of conduct are also used to hold a profession to account, so they are the reference point for disciplinary matters of competence and behaviour. They are used to judge whether a member of a profession has failed to live up to the published standards or even sought to undermine them by bringing the profession into disrepute. Although codes are a useful starting point for clients and the general public, a layperson is obviously not technically capable of judging a qualified professional on the finer points of competence. That is not to say they cannot make a justified complaint about competence or the lack of it. A dental patient may feel they have received a standard of service below that which they have a right to expect, but they cannot make a technical judgement about the dentist's competence in the way that peers and fellow practitioners can.

What clients and the general public have a more direct right to judge is the conduct of a professional person – for example, whether your doctor has broken the bond of patient confidentiality or your solicitor has missed a court deadline so you are unable to pursue a claim. Until the advent of the general teaching councils, teachers in England, Wales and Northern Ireland operated without any national code (although some local authorities had them and Scotland has had a professional body since the mid-1960s). The Teachers' Standards (which came in as England's professional code in 2011) replaced the GTC's Code of Conduct and Practice.[21] Traditionally, though, the collective wisdom and values of the teaching profession in most of the UK was largely implicit and highly subjective. Local authorities variably dealt with such matters. Typical of what might happen thirty years ago was that a local authority and/or trade union official (if allegations of incompetence ever got as far as a formal procedure) would quietly advise the alleged miscreant to resign and move on to another job elsewhere. Incompetence cases that led to dismissal were virtually unheard of, certainly in my experience of teaching throughout the 1980s and 1990s.

21 General Teaching Council for England, *Code of Conduct and Practice for Registered Teachers: Setting Minimum Standards for the Regulation of the Profession* (2004). Available at: https://dera.ioe.ac.uk/8257/3/conduct_code_practice_for_teachers.pdf.

What is the purpose of a code of ethics?

Firstly, codes of ethics serve public and professional interests by making explicit the values of the profession. Secondly, they exist to inspire confidence in the profession – to itself and its members. They are also intended to inspire confidence in the public – about the profession's mission and the standards maintained by its practitioners. Professional ethics cannot be imposed by written codes alone. They must become part of an internalised individual and collective consciousness of care, competence and commitment. They cannot be merely codes of professional etiquette but must powerfully link to, in our case, what teachers do and why they do it.

Conforming to a code without being committed to its values and ideals is a sham. That is not to say that professional people should not question codes or raise issues about their content. Teachers do this all the time with elements of the Teachers' Standards (which we will turn to shortly), but ethical codes should be broad statements about principles. They should describe:

- Idealism – what ideally (even romantically) do teachers want to achieve?
- Beneficence – what good are teachers trying to do?
- Non-maleficence – what harm are teachers trying to prevent or minimise?

In 1995, the Universities' Council for the Education of Teachers published a set of ethical principles that they proposed were fundamental to teaching.[22] They said that teachers must:

- Have intellectual integrity.
- Have vocational integrity.
- Show moral courage.
- Exercise altruism.
- Exercise impartiality.
- Exercise human insight.
- Assume the responsibility of influence.
- Exercise humility.
- Exercise collegiality.

22 The list appears in James Arthur, Kristján Kristjánsson, Tom Harrison, Wouter Sanderse and Daniel Wright, *Teaching Character and Virtue in Schools* (Abingdon and New York: Routledge, 2017), p. 10.

- Exercise partnership.
- Exercise vigilance with regard to professional responsibilities and aspirations.

There are a number of references to integrity in this earlier blueprint for a teachers' code. I would go further and interpret some of the references to integrity as references to truth. Truth is the intellectual equivalent of a trustworthy public space. Science knows this, and so does medicine and law. Education should too. A respect for truth and integrity is essential if pupils are to trust us and respect our authority. But, as the above list suggests, we must exercise humility too.[23]

The Teachers' Standards in England

The Teachers' Standards set out in two parts – the technical requirements (Part One) and the ethical and personal attributes (Part Two) – what is expected of teachers working in schools in England.[24] In summary, they require teachers to do the following.

Part One: Teaching

- Set high expectations which inspire, motivate and challenge pupils.
- Promote good progress and outcomes by pupils.
- Demonstrate good subject and curriculum knowledge.
- Plan and teach well structured lessons.
- Adapt teaching to respond to the strengths and needs of all pupils.
- Make accurate and productive use of assessment.
- Manage behaviour effectively to ensure a good and safe learning environment.
- Fulfil wider professional responsibilities.

---

23 Humility also has enormous implications for the education of civic virtues and values, which we will explore in Chapter 5.

24 The Teachers' Standards were introduced in September 2012 by the Department for Education to replace the GTC's Code of Conduct and Practice and the Training and Development Agency for Schools' Standards for Teachers. The equivalent codes of standards and practice for teachers in Scotland, Wales and Northern Ireland are set out in Appendix G, and those for the United States, Canada, South Africa, Australia and Aotearoa New Zealand in Appendix H.

Part Two: Personal and professional conduct

A teacher is expected to demonstrate consistently high standards of personal and professional conduct. The following statements define the behaviour and attitudes which set the required standard for conduct throughout a teacher's career.

- Teachers uphold public trust in the profession and maintain high standards of ethics and behaviour, within and outside school, by:
  - treating pupils with dignity, building relationships rooted in mutual respect, and at all times observing proper boundaries appropriate to a teacher's professional position.
  - having regard for the need to safeguard pupils' well-being, in accordance with statutory provisions.
  - showing tolerance of and respect for the rights of others.
  - not undermining fundamental British values, including democracy, the rule of law, individual liberty and mutual respect, and tolerance of those with different faiths and beliefs.
  - ensuring that personal beliefs are not expressed in ways which exploit pupils' vulnerability or might lead them to break the law.
- Teachers must have proper and professional regard for the ethos, policies and practices of the school in which they teach, and maintain high standards in their own attendance and punctuality.
- Teachers must have an understanding of, and always act within, the statutory frameworks which set out their professional duties and responsibilities.[25]

Discuss and reflect

- What is helpful about having an ethical code such as the Teachers' Standards? Identify two or three reasons why such a code might be helpful to you as a new teacher.
- Identify any real or potential issues with the wording in either Part One or Part Two.

25 Department for Education, *Teachers' Standards: Overview* (2011). Available at: https://www.gov.uk/government/publications/teachers-standards.

What is helpful about having a code?

As a trainee teacher, you may be in the early days of a course in which everything seems bewildering, even overwhelming at times. If you are training to be a teacher at a university via an undergraduate course, there will be a relentless tide of information to absorb, knowledge to gain and skills to acquire. If you are doing a postgraduate certificate (PGCE) or diploma (PGDE) the course will be very intense, utterly consuming your time for the best part of a year. If you are embarking on an employment-based route into teaching (the SCITT route or School Direct in England), you will be working in a school before you know it – in the thick of planning and preparation, teaching your first lessons and getting familiar with a plethora of school policies and practices. Whatever route you have chosen, it may seem that you can't see the wood for the trees. Any objective view of teaching as a profession you might have had can soon be lost by the intense, close-up subjectivity of classroom and school life.

The Teachers' Standards provide some perspective, but it is important to remember that the standards have a subjectivity of their own. They have been written in a particular time and place, and therefore reflect a specific set of professional as well as political values in England in the early twenty-first century. A code written for the teaching profession in a society like the United States (let alone one with a very different set of social and cultural values, such as Saudi Arabia) might (and does) look quite different.[26]

While Part One of the Teachers' Standards is a simplified version of what teachers do, it at least describes the extent of a teacher's technical role in a way that can be easily digested. I hope you will find it useful in framing what will be expected of you, not just as a trainee but also as a qualified teacher. These are the teaching profession's minimum standards of technical competence stated as plainly as possible and, as such, are accessible not just to every teacher but also to members of the public, parents and most pupils.

As a new teacher, you will be reminded by your tutors and mentors that taking on a professional mentality includes reflecting on what you did in class that day and whether you could have done it differently or better, what you will change about the way you do things tomorrow and so on. Being reflective is an axiom of being professional. Codes such as the Teachers' Standards are a starting point for this process of reflection. They help you to look at your own emerging competence and identify places where you are making progress and areas where you may need to put more

26 See, for example, the Association of American Educators' Code of Ethics for Educators at https://www.aaeteachers.org/index.php/about-us/aae-code-of-ethics; or Huda M. Al-Hothali, Ethics of the Teaching Profession Among Secondary School Teachers from School Leaders' Perspective in Riyadh, *International Education Studies* 11(9) (2018): 47–63. Available at: http://www.ccsenet.org/journal/index.php/ies/article/view/76845.

effort. By using the Teachers' Standards and other performance and assessment criteria,[27] you will very quickly begin to feel confident about your strengths and how to build on them.

There will always be areas that you will need to develop; I felt that even after decades in teaching. Having an established set of minimum expectations of competence is a necessary reminder that it is our responsibility to work on remediating weaknesses as well as playing to our strengths. You will rarely feel that you are keeping all your plates spinning at the same time. Even after years in the job, there were times when I felt that I had more than my fair share of children with challenging and complex needs in my class. That is when 'managing behaviour effectively to ensure a good and safe learning environment' would be uppermost in my mind. While it didn't entirely distract me from the need to 'plan and teach well structured lessons' or 'adapt my teaching to respond to the strengths and needs of all pupils', I sometimes felt that 'building relationships rooted in mutual respect' was an ethic that came under intense pressure!

At the time, I didn't have the advantage of having an explicit code like the Teachers' Standards to refer to, but I am convinced it would have been a helpful reminder to me in trying to maintain an ethical and professional perspective. The process of reflecting on how you have tried to juggle competing interests makes you realise that teaching requires judgement and that the outcome is the development of a practical wisdom – the character of being a teacher. (More on that in Chapter 6.) When you are feeling it is all too much, my advice is not to worry about keeping all the plates spinning at the same speed; just try not to let them crash to the floor. You are in the process of learning, after all, and your tutors and mentors understand that. Having criteria that you are both working towards is both useful and judicious. Focus on the positives, try to enjoy it and don't fret. Believe me – you will get better at spinning plates!

The Teachers' Standards are intended to be a list of objective criteria for describing competence; however, they are also very subjective in the way they can be interpreted. For example, statements like 'plan and teach well structured lessons' and 'make accurate and productive use of assessment' can be explained in one way by one tutor or mentor and in an entirely different way by another. You will only need to go through two Ofsted inspections to understand how one team will interpret the Ofsted Framework very differently to the next.

27 For example: Ofsted, *Education Inspection Framework* (May 2019). Available at: https://www.gov.uk/government/publications/education-inspection-framework; Department for Education, *ITT Core Content Framework* (November 2019). Available at: https://www.gov.uk/government/publications/initial-teacher-training-itt-core-content-framework; or Department for Education, *Early Career Framework* (March 2021). Available at: https://www.gov.uk/government/publications/induction-for-early-career-teachers-england.

I taught in places like Hackney and Tottenham for many years – relatively deprived areas of London with ethnically diverse populations. The way to 'manage behaviour effectively to ensure a good and safe learning environment' in these areas may differ from the way it might be done in the more leafy middle-class suburbs of outer London. Similarly, the challenges of adapting your teaching 'to respond to the strengths and needs of all pupils' in rural and remote areas of the UK is likely to be very different from those in dense inner-city conurbations. This is not to suggest that these challenges are easy anywhere – they aren't. Every child in every class, in every school, in every village, town or city presents diverse and often wide-ranging complexities, but 'managing behaviour effectively' and 'adapting to strengths and needs' is often very context-specific.

The difficulty inherent in any document like the Teachers' Standards is the perennial, indeed philosophical, struggle between objectivity and subjectivity. The more we try to keep things simple, the more we risk generalising. The more we add detail, the more we risk ending up with a tome akin to the Holy Bible. While many might feel that the Teachers' Standards are an inadequate representation of the values of a noble profession, we might have some sympathy for those trying to write such an all-encompassing canon.

Finally, a helpful aspect of having a nationally recognised list of criteria is that wherever you go to work – whether it is Liverpool or London, Cornwall or Cumbria, Newcastle or Nottingham – you will be working to the same set of minimum standards. The professional expectations required of you are – or should be – commonly interpreted and consistently applied, not by fine levels of definition, of course, but in broad terms. The culture of individual schools varies enormously, but a code provides a prevailing and predictable doctrine. Although the Teachers' Standards relate to England, the other nations of the UK have very similar professional codes (set out in Appendix G) as do other largely English-speaking countries with technically similar but culturally contrasting education systems.[28]

Discuss and reflect

- Does teaching have universal values?
- Can you think of any part of the world where teachers might have a different set of ethical values? Why might that be?

28 You can compare summaries of the codes of standards and practice for teachers in the United States, Canada, South Africa, Australia and Aotearoa New Zealand in Appendix H.

Part Two of the Teachers' Standards

Part Two addresses the personal attributes that teachers are expected to embody and display. The two parts of the Teachers' Standards remind me of the distinction that Aristotle made when he referred to *techne* and *phronesis*. In other words, the practice (of wisdom) on the one hand and the (practical) wisdom that accrues from learning to make judgements on the other. Part Two is clearly a set of ethical expectations that are situated as much in the public realm as in the professional one. There are a number of references to personal as well as professional behaviours – for example:

- A teacher is expected to demonstrate consistently high standards of personal and professional conduct.
- Teachers uphold public trust in the profession and maintain high standards of ethics and behaviour, within and outside school.
- Ensuring that personal beliefs are not expressed in ways which exploit pupils' vulnerability.[29]

Most of the trainees and students I speak to find this section is beneficial in helping them to know what is expected of them personally in the wider context of their professional lives. For many, though, references to the 'personal' raise some highly contentious concerns.

Is it anyone else's business what you do in your private life? This question goes to the heart of living in a liberal society. As long as what you do is not illegal, why should your personal behaviour be under public scrutiny both in and outside of school? After all, you are not a teacher twenty-four hours a day. Why should you feel judged when you are innocently doing your shopping after school, having a drink in the pub at the weekend or sharing your embarrassing holiday photos online?

While teachers are expected to be role models, and in my view quite rightly, they should resist unwarranted intrusions into their private life. Employers have a legitimate right to comment on and make judgements about professional competence and conduct. Parents and pupils are entitled to remark on professional conduct. Neither, however, have a right to make the same comments or judgements about how you manage and conduct your personal life, as long as what you do is not illegal – although, as we will see, the line demarcating the two is not always clear for teachers.

29 Department for Education, *Teachers' Standards*, p. 14.

Fundamental British values

I have done literally hundreds of lectures and presentations in recent years and met thousands of trainees. In every single session without exception, at least one person has raised an issue with the statement from Part Two which reads that teachers should 'not undermin[e] fundamental British values, including democracy, the rule of law, individual liberty and mutual respect, and tolerance of those with different faiths and beliefs'. Some people get quite exercised about this point. When I ask them to expand on why the statement is so contentious for them, a typical response is: 'Why did they have to add the word "British"? Values like these are universal – they're not exclusively British.' Of course, part of my job is to test and interrogate their thinking, so I do. I will often respond by saying something like: 'But the statement does not say that these values are *exclusively* British.'

Some people will retort, 'Then why even use the word "British"?' or 'The phrase implies ownership and exceptionalism.' So I respond: 'Well, the Teachers' Standards apply to those teaching in England, which is part of Britain. Are we not talking about the values that are expected to bind us together, to protect us as a society?' Some people then say: 'Yes, but these are universal values found in most societies – they are values held by people in most countries of the world.' I respond: 'Do we really think these values are found across the world? Are they really universal?' And so it goes on and a debate is soon in full flow. I try not to get too distracted by diverse perceptions of British politics with all its recent complications (devolution, Brexit, etc.) or British history with all its trappings (imperialism, colonialism, etc.) when we are trying to discuss the pros and cons of a professional code, but where I can, I make the point that even an apparently neutral set of seemingly objective criteria for describing the role of a teacher have deep political and cultural implications.

'I know what fundamental British values are – and I'm from Italy!'

I was leading a session with thirty-five PGCE trainees at a school-based training centre. At the point at which we were discussing Part Two of the Teachers' Standards, a trainee – an English guy – said: 'What are British values anyway? I haven't got a clue! Does anybody know what they are?' He looked around. There was silence. Nobody seemed to have a response.

Then another student, a woman, said: 'I know what British values are.'

'Do you?' I said.

'Yes,' she said quite confidently. 'And I'm from Italy!'

We all laughed.

'How do you know what British values are?' I asked her.

'If you come from a foreign country to live in another place like I have – I've lived in the UK for six years now – it's easy to see what the values of that country are,' she said. 'Values are more apparent to outsiders than insiders. They are invisible to those who were born and brought up here, but they are obvious to foreigners. You guys,' she said, looking at her colleagues, 'are just like goldfish in a bowl. You are swimming around and immersed in all these values, but you don't see them like I do as an outsider. If you go and live in Italy, you'll soon see the difference.'

'Give us an example,' I suggested.

She laughed. 'Men!' she replied in a tone of mock exasperation. 'Italian men are very different to British men – around children, around women, around their families – both in public and in private. You immediately know if you're in the company of a British or an Italian man. Surely, the way an entire gender behaves is a reflection of a society's values?'

I thought it was a really interesting observation but she hadn't finished – far from it. 'Another one is British humour,' she said. 'Everybody all over the world knows how crazy and quirky British humour is. The British are famous for it. I grew up in Italy watching episodes of *Monty Python*, *Dad's Army*, *Fawlty Towers*, *Only Fools and Horses* – all on Italian TV. These self-mocking comedies are typically British. You laugh at your pomposity, your snobbery, your social class consciousness …'

Then she said something profound: 'What a society chooses to laugh at is a reflection of its values.'

A fascinating and brilliant comment that I thought was acutely observed and deeply philosophical. But she still hadn't finished: 'Then there are jobs. If you go for a job in Italy, and you have a relative working in the company, you will tell them: "Hey, my uncle works here!" and you'll expect it to make a difference as to whether you get the job or not. When I went for a clerical job at the Isle of Wight Council I had to sign a "conflict of interest" declaration that I had no relatives working in the organisation! We have a different sense of family culture in Italy. In Italy, nepotism is still widely accepted in ways that it isn't in Britain. All these things are reflections of the values of British society. But you don't see it the way I do!'

I thanked her for her fascinating contribution and went back to the English guy who had started the discussion. He shrugged. 'Look, I know what you mean,' I said to him. 'British values are very difficult to define, aren't they? They're complex and diverse – like all values anywhere. Everyone has a different interpretation of what they are, let alone what they should be. Just because British values are complex and difficult to define doesn't mean they don't exist. I think British values do exist, but they're not easy to describe in a simple way.'

Then I challenged them all: 'If you as a teacher were to say to me as a parent, "I don't know what British values are," I might answer you by saying: "Well, don't you think you should find out? You're about to teach my children! And they're part of your teaching standards!"'

Would that be an unreasonable thing for a parent to say to a teacher?

Of course, the Italian trainee was right about the difficulty of defining British values in general terms. We live in a diverse and pluralist society and everyone will have a different take on what it means to be British. After all, we don't live in some Orwellian nightmare where everyone has to think, speak and behave in the same way.[30] Every single one of us will have a different interpretation of British identity and culture. You don't even have to go to the four national regions of the UK – England, Wales, Scotland and Northern Ireland – to find that out. Just drive around any part of the country and you will come across huge diversity every few miles: different accents, grammar and vocabulary; local ales and pies one place, unique beers and pasties in another; sandstone houses in one town, granite in the next; thatched cottages in one village, millstone grit in another. Go to the northern and western edges of Britain and you will be among people speaking the native languages of these islands, living in mountainous landscapes with rugged coastlines or on tiny isles.

Britain has one of the most varied landscapes and most diverse societies in the world, even before you get to the more ancient peoples and cultures of its various regions. Add to that the influences of groups that have migrated in recent decades and you have a society that is rich and multicultural. However, it is still bound together by values that are fundamental not only to its identity but also to the way it survives and thrives – its safety, security and flourishing. The way these values are defined, interpreted and demonstrated by the British is unique. Not exceptional or necessarily better, but undeniably unique. In my view then, as complex and challenging as it is,

30 Although, if you want a fine articulation of English civic patriotism, read the works of George Orwell.

discussion about the nature and character of fundamental British values is extremely important. It is particularly important to people about to subscribe to an ethical code like the Teachers' Standards.[31]

My personal fundamental British value

If you want to know one of my fundamental British values, it is this: fish and chips on a Friday night. If you think that is a joke, it isn't. The subject is a matter of heated debate every Friday in our household. I want to go and get supper from the local fish and chip shop and bring them home to eat with the family around the dinner table: cod and chips with mushy peas, salt and vinegar and tartar sauce. I would do that every Friday night if my wife would let me. She thinks I am mad; she just doesn't understand.

Why do I want to eat fish and chips every Friday night? Well, partly it is because it takes me back to my working-class childhood in Liverpool. I would go out on Friday evenings with my mum or dad to get the fish and chips, bring them back and eat them around the kitchen table with the family. The kettle was on; the plates, knives and forks were set; the white-sliced bread would be buttered and stacked. We would spread out the newspaper wrapping and divide up the fish and chips between us. The whole activity brings back vivid and fond memories of family life. Those recollections connect me to my past, my working-class roots and my background as a Liverpudlian.

Fish and chips is an icon of Britishness, isn't it? Everybody around the world knows that we eat fish and chips from a newspaper wrapping (supposedly!). It is the archetypal British meal (although my award-winning local fish and chip shop has been run by a Greek family for forty years). Whether or not this is British (evidence suggests that it was a meal introduced to England by Ashkenazi Jews in the nineteenth century, while others insist it originates from Portuguese fishermen sharing *bacalhau e batatas* with their English counterparts) to me is irrelevant. I just love eating fish and chips on Friday evenings because it is part of who I am.

I wouldn't necessarily expect you to share my view of British identity and culture (although, of course, you might). We all have a different way of connecting with our past, expressing our customs and culture and sharing our background. We certainly have different ways of thinking about ourselves as British, or not as the case may be. I am not expecting that you should seriously think that eating fish and chips on a Friday is somehow a fundamental British value, even though for me it is.

31 In Appendices A and B, I extend and illustrate this discussion in much greater detail.

Perhaps as a nation, let alone as a teaching profession, we are generally uncomfortable when talking about anything 'British' and especially something as loaded as 'British values'. In my experience, people in most other countries (including teachers) are entirely unselfconscious about discussing and celebrating what they perceive as their national values. I have never heard an American, for example, question the practice of their schoolchildren starting each day by reciting the Pledge of Allegiance. In France, every school child knows that the fundamental values of the French Republic are *liberté, egalité, fraternité* and the revolutionary history that brought them about.

But ask the average British teenager what the Magna Carta is or the significance of the 1689 Bill of Rights and you are likely to get blank stares. We are much more circumspect and suspicious about displays of national values, especially if there is the slightest whiff of nationalism about them. If the Department for Education were to suggest that British schools began the day singing the national anthem or pledging allegiance to the Crown, I think British teachers might start a revolution of their own (even if they were monarchists and patriotic); doing something like that is just not British!

Of course, the fundamental British values referred to in the Teachers' Standards are of a completely different order to singing 'God Save the Queen' in assembly every morning or believing in clichés about British identity, like adopting a stiff upper lip, cheering for the underdog, starting every conversation with the weather or the propensity for queuing. Obviously, this is not about attempting to make a definitive list of stereotypical customs or behaviours that people should adopt or identify with as British. It would be absurd to think, for example, that you have to be a supporter of the monarchy to demonstrate loyalty. It would be equally absurd to think that queuing is a uniquely British phenomenon.

Any attempt at defining a national identity must contend with a highly complex nexus of customs, language, laws and culture. While I genuinely think that traditional customs (like eating fish and chips on Fridays) do play an important part in cultural and national identity, because they are in a real sense an expression of your personal values, these are not examples of the fundamental British values under discussion in the Teachers' Standards. While you may take issue with the word 'British' and you may think it raises issues about the political context in which the standards were conceived, I am focusing on the values that are fundamental to protecting rights, freedoms and the flourishing of human existence. For a teacher, that is not a tangential concern but a fundamentally ethical matter.

'What's so good about democracy anyway?'

In some of my sessions with trainees, if we have time, we will discuss the merits of the fundamental British values set out in the Teachers' Standards.[32]

For example, I have heard people say: 'What's so special about democracy in this country, anyway? Look at our electoral system. In the 2015 general election, UKIP [a right-wing party that campaigned for Britain's exit from the European Union] got almost four million votes but only one MP got elected. The Scottish National Party [campaigning for Scotland's independence from the UK] only got around one-and-a-half million votes but ended up with fifty-six MPs! Where's the democracy in that?'

Another student at a different session made a similar point: 'Where's the rule of law in this country? How many bankers were sent to prison for their role in the financial crash of 2008? And yet we're sending poor, working-class people to prison every week for benefit cheating [making false financial claims to social services]. Where's the justice in that?'

These are good points. Our first-past-the-post electoral system has many anomalies, but then so do all electoral systems. None of them are without anomalies. The same is true with our justice system. It too throws up inconsistencies and injustices, some of which are very serious. Just because we have anomalies in our electoral system doesn't mean we don't have a democracy. Just because we have injustices in our legal system doesn't mean we don't have a rule of law. I think we have both, but I readily accept they are not perfect. The same goes for the other values of individual liberty, mutual respect and tolerance. We can always find fault, but that doesn't mean we shouldn't recognise progress when and where it has been made.

If a teacher were to say to me: 'Actually, I don't believe in democracy' or 'I don't believe in the rule of law,' then I might respond by asking a very direct question: 'What do you believe in, then?' If the teacher were to reply: 'I believe in authoritarianism – that seems to be an effective system of government in many countries' or, 'I believe in dictatorship – that works really well in some places' or, 'Violence – history has shown us that violence can be an effective agent for political change', then my response would be: 'OK. You can hold those views in your personal life if you want to, that's a tolerance of your personal beliefs that I'm prepared to extend to you. But I don't want you promoting those values to my child, thank you very much, especially not as their teacher. I don't want my child being taught by someone who is not prepared to defend democracy and promote the rule of law, especially when those values come under attack. And, come to think of it, I don't want anyone's child to be taught by someone who will not

32 For more detail see Appendix A.

defend democracy, the rule of law, individual liberty, mutual respect and tolerance for people with different faiths and beliefs.' I don't think that is an unreasonable thing for a parent to expect of a teacher.

Discuss and reflect

- Should teachers be free to discuss their personal values with pupils, especially if they diverge from fundamental British values?

Why is all this stuff about values so important?

The reason I am spending so much time discussing values, and why I think I think it is so important, is because the moral development of children is an ethical issue for teachers and always has been.[33] Teachers have been the purveyors of every civilised society's core value system since time immemorial. Values are the meat and drink of ethical principles. They form and sustain what we hold to be worthy and valuable. Sometimes we are cognisant of their importance; at other times we take our values for granted, only realising their significance when they come under attack or, worse, when they are lost altogether.

These challenges are not philosophical or theoretical. They are real. They can be severe and testing. And they will happen to you in your classroom. I am not talking about the kind of severe and testing challenge that might come from a right-wing extremist, the kind of person who might stab and shoot a politician on the streets of Birstall, West Yorkshire (as happened to Jo Cox MP in June 2016), or that might come from jihadists who strap suicide vests to their bodies and walk into pop concerts to murder children (as happened with Salman Abedi at the Manchester Arena in May 2017). Traumatic and shocking though these incidents are, we would be extremely unlucky to be the victim of such an event or even to witness one. No, I am talking about the severe and testing challenges that will come from the children we teach.

Sadly, in school playgrounds and classrooms across the country there are regular examples of children who abuse, threaten and incite hatred against each other. Not just petty name-calling, but children saying things like: 'Don't touch me, you poof!' 'All Muslims are terrorists!' 'You're a dirty slag!' 'My mum's told me not to play with black kids!' or, just as common in my experience, 'My mum's told me not to play with white

33 See Hand, *A Theory of Moral Education*, p. 88.

kids.' When these acts of abuse, threat and incitement happen, we are challenged to act in defence of the fundamental values that are not just part of our professional code but fundamental to our flourishing and survival.

'Sir, I don't want to read *The Diary of Anne Frank* any more'

Years ago, when I was a class teacher – decades before the Teachers' Standards were even thought of – I was teaching the Second World War as part of the history curriculum with my class of 10- and 11-year-olds. I had organised some interesting activities to help the children understand more about that era and the privations of war on the civilian population. We prepared meals made from rations, we dressed up and role-played in 1940s clothes, we listened to the music of the period and heard the testimonies of elderly people who had been sent away from home as child evacuees.

I also read daily extracts from *The Diary of Anne Frank* – the story of a Jewish girl whose family had gone into hiding from the Nazis in an attic above a warehouse in Amsterdam where her father ran a business. The children were fascinated and absorbed. After about two weeks, one girl (I am going to call her Sarah) came up to me and said: 'Sir, I don't want to read *The Diary of Anne Frank* any more.' 'Why not, love?' I asked. 'I don't like Jews,' she replied.

Discuss and reflect

- What would you say to a child in your class who said something like that?
- How would you respond, both immediately and in the longer term, while trying to maintain dignity and respect for all the children in your class, including the girl herself?[34]

You may be interested to know how I responded to this incident. I tried not to show how disturbed I was by her comment, but it came as quite a shock, especially from a little girl who had previously shown not the slightest antipathy towards her classmates of any other ethnic background, of which there were many. There was even a girl of mixed-Jewish heritage in the class who was best friends with Sarah, so it all came as a rude awakening.

34 I deal with how to respond to challenging situations like this in greater detail in Appendix E.

Incidents like this will happen to you too. Sometimes they are shocking and surprising, and come from children you would least expect. They might happen at the most inopportune moment when you are too busy to deal with them satisfactorily. You can't simply drop everything to tackle a distracting and potentially inflammatory issue, but respond to these incidents we must. You may be so stunned that you don't know what to say and may need time to think. The remark may be so odious that you are even left speechless. Postponing your response until you have collected your thoughts and composure is a perfectly legitimate thing to do. As long as the child in question, and if appropriate the rest of the class, know that you will definitely deal with it at some point, that is fine.

If you do have time to respond at that particular moment, what might you say and do? The first thing is to challenge the opinion or attitude by asking: 'Why?' However offended or cross you may feel, the tone you use is absolutely crucial in maintaining the child's engagement. If you say: 'Why do you say that?' in a way that sounds defensive or annoyed, then you will probably alienate them and the child may simply walk away and bring an end to any meaningful conversation.

I challenged Sarah in as kindly a tone as I could muster: 'Why do you say that, love?' You have probably guessed what her answer was already. She replied: 'My dad says *The Diary of Anne Frank* is a lot of Jewish propaganda.' If the issue wasn't complicated enough already, now I have got her dad in the picture too.

Incidents like this are never easy. I can assure you that you will make lots of mistakes in the way you deal with them, but deal with them we must. If you were to brush off her remark and say something like: 'Oh, don't be silly. Go and get on with your work' or 'We don't have time to discuss this now – we're too busy,' then you have failed to address a critical issue.

Clearly, there is a conflict going on in the mind of a child who says something like this. She will know from the culture of the school (and society at large) that it is a highly controversial, offensive and potentially inflammatory remark. The fact that she is prepared to share it with you is a mark of two important things: firstly, she wants to resolve the conflict within herself and, secondly, she trusts you enough to bring it to you for guidance.

So, failing to address her comment is an abdication of your ethical duty, not only to the individual child but also to the rest of the class, some of whom may have overheard her and may be sitting there waiting to see what you are going to do about it. They know intuitively – although they may not be able to articulate this – that if you fail to challenge an instance of prejudice or bigotry, you might not challenge other offences of which they may be the victim next time. The children deserve to know where you stand.

If you are too shocked or too busy to address it at that moment, especially as a young and inexperienced teacher, then say something like: 'Look, I can't deal with this right now as we're too busy. But I want to talk to you about it later after class, OK?' Giving the child some time to reflect will also allow her to manage any discomfort induced by the face-to-face challenge, necessary though this was. Teachers may be understandably reluctant to unsettle pupils by impugning their parents' attitudes and values, but children should not be shielded from the disorienting effects of educational challenge. We must not leave children like Sarah in thrall to ethical and moral standards that lack rational justification.[35] That would be unethical in itself.

It may be sensible to discuss the matter in private away from the danger of other children inflaming the situation. Like any incident that has the potential for wider repercussions, whether disciplinary or pastoral, other children don't need to know how you address a problem, but they do need to know that it has been addressed. Take your time, collect your thoughts and regain your composure, even take advice, but come back to it and deal with it. You are still likely to make mistakes. That is what learning from experience is all about. Challenging expressions of bigotry while trying to maintain a child's dignity is an example of the application of competing virtues, which will turn you into a teacher of character and practical wisdom. The important thing is not to be a coward and shy away from exploring what lurks behind expressions of intolerance and bigotry.

But I didn't want to say anything that would add to the emotional conflict Sarah was clearly experiencing, so I said: 'Look, love, I'm not going to come between you and your dad. Your dad loves you and you love your dad. If taking *The Diary of Anne Frank* home is causing a problem then you don't have to take it home. Just leave it here in class at the end of the day.' I paused here to indicate that I was prepared to take her difficulty into account and then added firmly: 'But in class we *are* going to read *The Diary of Anne Frank*, and the reason we are going to read it is because we are studying the Second World War. This book is a true story about the war but it is also about a young girl, not much older than you, who suffered terribly for no other reason than because of who she was. There are lessons we can all learn from this book. So, in class we are going to read *The Diary of Anne Frank*.'

This was me – as a teacher – defending fundamental values when they came under attack. Similar challenges will face you too. Whether you think such fundamental values are British or universal, it doesn't matter. If you are not prepared to defend them, then, in my view, you are abdicating your ethical responsibility as a teacher. As my old Irish maths teacher used to say: 'You go ahead and make as many mistakes as you like. God will love you for trying. But He hates a coward.'

---

35 See Hand, *A Theory of Moral Education*, p. 90.

Chapter 5

THE TEACHER AND MORALITY – THE TEACHER YOU OUGHT TO BE

What is morality?

Morality comes from the Latin root *mores* – meaning 'the customs and conventions of behaviour within a group'. Ethics comes from the Greek *ethos* – meaning the 'character of a community'. Morality is therefore about behaviour *within* a group, while ethics is about the behavioural characteristic *of* the group – similar but distinct. The ancient Greeks thought that good moral order – or *kalon* – could be created by music and the arts; an appreciation of an aesthetic outer beauty and a moral inner beauty. Their legacy is with us every day in schools when we teach music, art, literature and poetry, in the belief that an appreciation of these things contributes to self-improvement.

Morality in its most general form is about doing the right thing because we ought to – not just for me as an individual but ultimately for us all. It relates to the principles we live by as individuals but that also lift us above the pursuit of self-interest. It is a personal expression and demonstration of the values and virtues that bind us together as a society. Morality is about promoting responsibility for the common good, based on the idea that some things are wrong even though they may be legal; they may also be wrong even when others, including a majority, are doing them. Concepts like duty, obligation, responsibility and honour may have come to seem unfashionable, even antiquated, in Western societies in recent decades where social non-conformity has become a more popular and dominant discourse. Nevertheless, it is difficult to refute that these concepts are fundamental aspects of human relations.

Discuss and reflect

- Is the ancient Greek belief in *kalon* – where good moral order emerges from an appreciation of aesthetic outer beauty and moral inner beauty – justified?
- Do you think the arts and music inspire us to be better human beings?
- What are the dangers of taking this idea too far?

Morality comprises of a list of moral promises we make to one another on the basis of trust and social bonding. It fosters the belief between people that we do not need to be constantly on our guard against exploitation, deceit, betrayal or violence. The stronger the bonds of community, the more powerful the forces of trust.[1] Morally, humans are promise-making, covenantal creatures. At some point in our lives, we will almost certainly make (or intend to make) fundamental promises – to a spouse, partner or family; to a vocation or a profession; to a philosophy or faith; or to a community. Ultimately, we judge our lives on how well we fulfil these undertakings. Take them out of the equation and, morally speaking, we have demeaned ourselves.[2]

Morality is what enables us to get on with each other when society's other forms of regulation (like economics and politics) are insufficient or fail completely. Take, for example, what happened as the COVID-19 global pandemic took hold in the spring of 2020; people in the UK (and elsewhere) responded immediately with offers of help to the vulnerable: to do shopping, fetch prescriptions and reduce their isolation. People demanded that supermarkets take action to prevent panic buying, impose rationed supplies and reserve times to ensure that key workers and the vulnerable could shop. These were moral responses. People were inserting their personal values into the public realm, promoting common virtues and values, common rules and responsibilities, common codes and customs, and even constraints in the face of instances of weak social responsibility or the inadequacy of economics and politics to cope.

Similarly, during the Second World War the dominant morality in both the UK and the US was drawn from a group-oriented communalism that asserted something like: 'An existential threat exists, so we must all pull together.' To a greater or lesser extent it happened. Even into the 1950s that moral culture pertained. Then, in the 1960s, a decreasing sense of deference to authority and class status, coupled with a social and sexual revolution on the back of rising wealth, heralded the emergence of a morality based much more on individualism. By the turn of the twenty-first century, many felt that individualism had come to dominate our common morality – economic individualism from the political right and social individualism from the political left. Now, in the 2020s, there is a growing crisis of social solidarity, especially among young people.[3] More of us feel lonely and depressed. Fewer of us feel that we have meaning in our lives. We have less trust in our traditional social institutions (like parliamentary politics, the justice system or faith communities) and in our leaders and authority figures (like politicians, the police, judges and the clergy) than was the case fifty or sixty years ago.[4]

1 See Sacks, *Morality: Restoring the Common Good*, pp. 12–13.
2 For more on the idea of a covenant, see Sacks, *Morality: Restoring the Common Good*, p. 64.
3 See David Brooks, *The Road to Character* (London: Penguin, 2016), ch. 1
4 See Jonathan Sacks, *Morality in the 21st Century: Robert Putnam* [radio programme], BBC Radio 4 (3 September 2018). Available at: https://www.bbc.co.uk/programmes/p06k4t86.

Discuss and reflect

Recent research reports that, on average, teenagers spend between seven and nine hours a day looking at a screen – on the internet, texting, gaming, video chat and watching TV – often simultaneously.[5]

- Are there moral implications to social behaviours like this?
- Should schools and teachers respond to this phenomenon? Why? How?

We should not despair. A series of studies on the attitudes of the generation of people born between 1990 and the early 2000s reveal they are much more aware of and motivated to act on environmental issues, much more tolerant of various forms of diversity and much more intolerant of financial and political corruption.[6] While young people are obviously amenable to a theoretical moral *education* in school, they discover real moral *purpose* through direct experiences that test their courage, judgement and integrity – again in schools, but also at home and in their communities.[7]

I recently met a teenager in East London who had been inspired by a teacher at his school to do something about knife crime in his community. He felt so strongly about it that he first went on a protest march and then joined other campaigners and volunteered to mentor young people tempted to carry knives. If you could influence the life of only one of your pupils in such a way, would your professional life have been valuable? The answer to that is, of course, a resounding yes. You don't have to be a Christian to recognise the moral truth of the parable of the shepherd who left his flock to find one lost lamb and return it to the fold. It is a moral maxim whose truth is universal.

Whether or not we are religious or believe God exists, as human beings we feel that some things, some actions and some people are inherently noble and elevated. Others – like people who carry and use knives to pursue and settle gang feuds – have become base and degraded. This is not to be moralistic, high-minded or judgemental; I am the least qualified person to sermonise on personal morality. This is merely to illustrate how society, not just in this country but across cultures and over time, has judged the

5 See Sacks, *Morality: Restoring the Common Good*, p. 51.
6 Cited by the economist Noreena Hertz in her interview with Jonathan Sacks: *Morality in the 21st Century: Noreena Hertz* [podcast], BBC Radio 4 (3 September 2018). Available at: https://www.bbc.co.uk/programmes/p06k3v6v.
7 An area we will explore more when discussing spiritual, moral, social and cultural education in Appendix C.

kinds of behaviour we ought and ought not to demonstrate towards one another. Indeed, recent research by anthropologists from Oxford University studied sixty cultures around the world and found seven common moral principles:[8]

1. Help your family.
2. Help your group.
3. Return favours.
4. Be brave.
5. Respect superiors.
6. Divide resources fairly.
7. Respect other people's property.

Neuroscientists tell us that our brains have evolved to be constantly asking the question: 'What comes next? In the next moment? In the next day? In the next year?' We react to this question first for reasons of survival and later for reasons of deliberation and analysis, by developing instincts and intuitions. Experiments have shown that a lot of our moral decision-making is made on the basis of gut feelings first and then rationalisation. They also show that this kind of moral decision-making can be trained.[9] If we can train ourselves to react ethically to morally ambiguous situations, this has important implications for the teaching of virtues in schools.[10] I will not be lecturing you on your personal values, but this book is a call for teachers to more fully recognise and articulate the moral purpose of their professional role.

8 Oliver S. Curry, Daniel A. Mullins and Harvey Whitehouse, Is It Good to Cooperate? Testing the Theory of Morality-as-Cooperation in 60 Societies, *Current Anthropology* 60(1) (2019): 47. Available at: https://doi.org/10.1086/701478.

9 See Sacks, *Morality: Restoring the Common Good*, p. 311; see also the section on virtue ethics in Chapter 4.

10 See Melvyn Bragg, *A History of Ideas: How Can I Tell Right from Wrong?* [radio programme], BBC Radio 4 (12 November 2018). Available at: https://www.bbc.co.uk/programmes/b04prhq3.

Discuss and reflect

David Brooks and Rabbi Lord Jonathan Sacks speak of covenants (promises of responsibility) and commitment, as opposed to contracts (relationships based on legal agreement).

- Which promises of responsibility have you made in your life?
- To whom or what have you made the strongest promise? Why?

Moral foundations

While we all may want to become better people and avoid judgemental moralising of one another, we must also be wary of the moral relativism that could leave us in an amoral vacuum. When we tell ourselves that every individual is deserving of self-esteem this unavoidably relegates emotions like guilt, shame, contrition and remorse. There are and must be some fundamental moral foundations upon which every society depends.[11] Evolutionary anthropologists and behavioural psychologists have tried to describe some. Indeed, these moral foundations are so ubiquitous they are often referred to collectively as 'human nature'. They include:

- **Care.** Care of our vulnerable offspring has sensitised human beings to signs of suffering and cruelty; we naturally want to care for those who are victims of it.
- **Fairness.** We have evolved to reap the rewards and benefits of cooperation without exploitation; we have come to feel a sense of reciprocal altruism of what is good and just, making us want to shun or punish those who cheat or commit crimes against us.
- **Loyalty.** We have developed social bonds as a result of forming and maintaining groups, tribes and teams, which has made us sensitive to trusting and rewarding those who are loyal to us, and to ostracise, hurt or even kill those who are treacherous to our group.

11 See Jonathan Haidt, *The Righteous Mind: Why Good People are Divided by Politics and Religion* (London: Penguin, 2002), esp. ch. 7. The book has much to say to teachers who want to understand the moral implications of teaching.

- **Authority.** We have evolved relationships that reflect social hierarchies, which has made us sensitive to rank and status; we display appropriate respectful behaviours in relation to those who take responsibility or risks on our behalf (like the police or the military).
- **Sanctity.** We have evolved an extreme biological sensitivity to pathogens and parasites – leading us to invest extreme and sometimes irrational value (both positive and negative) in symbols, objects and rituals that we believe keep us healthy, safe and bind us together.

To give some illustrations of this, we treat certain things as though they were sacred: objects like flags, historic documents and religious symbols; places like historic battlefields and religious shrines; people like heroes and saints; and principles like equality, human rights and liberty. Whatever their origin, the psychology of our belief in sanctity binds us together into moral communities. When someone from another group desecrates one of these sacred pillars supporting our real, imagined or perceived community, the reaction is often swift, collective and highly emotional – and sometimes punitive in the extreme.[12]

These moral foundations have implications for the way we conceive of political morality. Liberal-left morality is largely based on the foundations of care and fairness that underpin the wider notion of justice. Indeed, the liberal left often reject the other foundations – loyalty, authority and sanctity – as bordering on the immoral, if not entirely so. For example, they are more likely to characterise authority as legitimising oppression rather than as a way of legitimising leadership; they are more likely to characterise loyalty in reference to exclusionary behaviours like racism and nationalism rather than as a way of binding people together; and they are more likely to characterise sanctity as religious mumbo-jumbo that legitimises the repression of women or the promotion of homophobia rather than as something that gives due respect or veneration to symbols of national or patriotic identity (like the flag), national emblems or collective historical memories. To put it simply, those on the political right have a wider perception and acceptance of the psychology of moral foundations and how this appeals to the greatest number of people. Those on the political left tend to rely on fewer moral foundations and narrower interpretations of them, and therefore appeal to fewer people.[13] Believe it or not, all this rather heavyweight philosophical stuff has important implications for teaching too.

12 See Harari, *21 Lessons for the 21st Century*, ch. 5.

13 Some political analysts conclude that this is the reason why the Conservative Party wins more elections than the Labour Party in the UK and why the Republicans win more than the Democrats in the United States.

Moral foundations and teaching

Teachers are leaders. Anyone who has ever reflected on the nature of leadership is struck not so much by why leaders are motivated to be leaders, but why people are prepared to follow them. Leaders must construct a moral matrix of cultural, social and political values for their followers. In *The Righteous Mind*, Jonathan Haidt describes five moral foundations: care (and its obverse harm), fairness (and cheating), loyalty (and betrayal), authority (and subversion) and sanctity (and degradation). These are the principles on which all societies – large or small – must rely. They are observable and necessary in any group, like a tribe, clan or society, and across time and cultural context. They are observable and necessary in schools too.

Obviously, care is a virtue that morally we would wish to bestow on all those who need it and who are willing to reciprocate it. If someone repays our care with indifference or, worse, harm, then this has implications for the way we subscribe to and demonstrate other moral foundations. For example, we would certainly find it difficult to show loyalty to someone who knowingly or recklessly aroused our distrust or did us harm; it would be interpreted, quite rightly, as unfair or even as a betrayal of our real friends who had maintained their allegiance to us. It might even lead those friends to believe that we did not really care for them in the first place (think here of the bickering and bullying that goes on in every playground).

We are normally willing to show respect and loyalty to someone with legitimate authority (like a teacher or police officer), but not if they are unfair, duplicitous or use their position to cheat or confer unjustified favour. Similarly, we would find it difficult to return loyalty to or respect the authority of someone who degraded and defiled the things we sanctify, like our sacred religious texts or the symbols, memorials and statues of those we venerate (but think here also of the way that teenage boys in particular will use obscenities to disrespect each other's mothers).

Haidt's moral foundations are also elements of our personal identity. The people we can rely on for care, fairness and loyalty are the same people we will come to love. Those whose authority we respect and whose symbols we are willing to revere are those to whom we give licence to lead us: our family, our community, our society, our nation and even our school.

When I trained teachers at a university in London, I would remind them that the children they taught probably would not remember the details of the wonderful literacy, numeracy or science lessons they had spent hours preparing, but they would never forget the teacher who gave them the opportunity to play for and represent their school or the pride they felt when they first pulled on the football or hockey team's shirt bearing the school's colours and badge. Care, fairness, loyalty, authority and sanctity are all encapsulated in such moments.

If we consider the moral foundations that underpin the virtues that teachers are charged with purveying, we quickly realise that some are fostered and promoted more than others – for example, care, fairness and authority are values regularly emphasised by teachers in their everyday work. These foundations relate to the virtues that we teach explicitly. However, we must take care that we do not neglect or even ignore other values, such as loyalty and sanctity. This may have important implications for the way we promote (or fail to promote) a range of spiritual, moral, social and cultural activities in schools.[14] It may also have very specific implications for the way we teach certain subjects, like history, literature, religious education, politics, sociology and citizenship.

Society needs cohesion. We don't construct social cohesion by rational argument but by the concrete engagement of young people in the processes of building social and moral capital. The conservative right believe that people need external constraints in order to thrive socially, like laws, institutions, customs, traditions, nations and religions.[15] They believe these are necessary for us to behave well and cooperate (although, of course, many on the conservative right also believe that we need fewer external constraints to thrive economically). They assert that these constraints contribute to the health and integrity of social and moral capital. While the conservative right see themselves as doing a better job of preserving moral capital, they often fail to notice the social victims created by those processes and the sometimes untrammelled powers of vested interests.

The liberal left, on the other hand, tend to believe that people are inherently good and will thrive the more these constraints are removed. They want to bring about freedom and equal opportunity, and they are often impatient to bring about this process. This can lead to overreach when attitudinal change has not been fully embedded, which may unintentionally reduce the stock of social capital and thereby inadvertently reduce the stock of moral capital too.

Whether teachers see themselves on the conservative right or the liberal left, they must understand (and help children to understand) the nature of power and how it is different from authority. Power is fundamentally an assault on human dignity and a denial of freedom; it is dangerous to both those who discharge it and those who must submit to it. It should not be used to impose truth, only to preserve peace. In contrast, authority is legitimate; it is the jurisdiction to make decisions, direct others and sometimes even use power to enforce obedience for the common good. A teacher's authority is not given merely in order for them to police behaviour in schools. It is invested in them as a moral authority as much as a legal one.

14 SMSC education is explored in more detail in Appendix C.

15 Here I am referring to those who are intellectually conservative, not members of the UK Conservative Party or Republicans in the United States.

The distinction between power and authority should not be understood only from a legal, political and historical perspective, but also from a philosophical and theological one. The limitations of authority – of what we can and cannot do – stem from the tenets of the Abrahamic religious faiths. Under this way of thinking, a locus of limitation enhances human potential because it forces us to seek more. The idea originates from Jewish mysticism: that God limits Himself to make space for us.[16] Teachers do this too, in the way that we limit our authority in order to allow children to take ever-increasing levels of responsibility.

Schools simply cannot work as totalitarian labour camps. The teaching of games and sport illustrates this: the rules of sport impose limits in order to seek potential and enable possibility. The commands teachers give as demonstrations of their authority must, therefore, be both task-oriented and rational, appropriate for directing and scaffolding a given situation. If commands are merely status oriented, then authority will quickly degenerate into the mere exercise of power. Teachers must learn to be in authority without being authoritarian.[17]

Moral schools

A good school creates a culture that binds people into groups, creating a sense of altruism among its members and relegating the egotism of the self. While our genes impel us to be selfish, communities teach us to be selfless. Schools are providers of the higher levels of Maslow's hierarchy of human needs. They offer a sense of belonging to a community rooted in strong and rewarding relationships, the esteem of valuing and being valued, and the fulfilment derived from personal achievement – in other words, a meaningful life. What could be a greater source of inspiration for a teacher than to help young people strive for a meaningful life? Morality – like Aristotle's notion of doing the right thing, at the right time, in the right way, in the right measure[18] – is about knowing when it is right to be competitive and when it is right to be cooperative; when 'we' is more important than 'I'. Schools are forums that teach us about the morality of what makes a society, concretised in the immediate neighbourhoods and cultures they serve. Schools create communities, and communities create moral people.

Schools as moral communities develop and sustain enduring social relationships, promote and encourage civic values, and act as a bulwark against individualism and forms of identity politics that are accelerated by social media networks. However,

16 See Sacks, *Morality: Restoring the Common Good*, ch. 21.

17 See Peters, *Ethics and Education*, p. 264.

18 Aristotle, *The Nicomachean Ethics*, tr. David Ross (New York: Oxford University Press, 2009), Book II, Chapter 4.

while strong and cohesive school communities can be crucial drivers in fostering the development of virtues, they can also be vulnerable to inward-looking narrowness, complacency and prejudice.[19] As we have learned from examples of parents with 'conservative' religious values in places like Birmingham protesting against the 'liberal' values of schools,[20] what the spokespeople of a section of the community believes to be good is not necessarily for the common good, and nor are they necessarily speaking for anyone but themselves.

We will return to the practical ways that schools engender morality through the development of civic values in Appendix C, but there are four specific virtues that teachers must develop in themselves and their pupils in order to achieve this aim:

1. **Moral virtues** – these help us to respond in ethically sound ways to any situation. They include courage, self-discipline and compassion.
2. **Performance virtues** – qualities that enable us to manage our lives effectively, such as determination, confidence and teamwork.
3. **Civic virtues** – those things necessary to promote the common good, like public service, good citizenship and volunteering.
4. **Intellectual virtues** – rational principles that guide right action and correct thinking, such as autonomy, reasoning and perseverance in order to analyse, interpret and evaluate the pursuit of knowledge.[21]

Discuss and reflect

- Can schools and teachers determine a moral path for their pupils?
- Can a moral path be defined or is it arbitrary, culturally specific and context dependent?
- Should we leave children to discover their own moral path?

19 See Arthur et al., *Teaching Character and Virtue in Schools*, p. 57.

20 In 2014, Parkfield Community School in Birmingham devised a teaching project called 'No Outsiders' based around fundamental British values and the Equality Act 2010. It touched on same-sex relationships and transgender issues. The project was successfully piloted at Parkfield and later adopted by other primary schools across the country. In January 2019, a parent from the school started a petition, claiming that it contradicted the Islamic faith. This led to protests outside schools in Birmingham which lasted for months and resulted in children being removed from classes and head teachers being threatened.

21 See Arthur et al., *Teaching Character and Virtue in Schools*, pp. 10–11.

Morality and multiculturalism

In an effort to determine moral paths of one sort or another, schools often find themselves in a moral bind. I allude to a number of instances of this kind of dilemma in this book, but one stark example has been the promotion of multiculturalism in schools as a moral and societal virtue. Let me make it clear: I was a fully paid-up member of the 'multiculturalism is a good thing' faction for the best part of my career. As a teacher, I thought multiculturalism meant nothing more than a generalised respect for other peoples, cultures and religions. I assumed uncritically that multiculturalism promoted integration and acceptance.

Where people took issue with these assumptions, their views were often dismissed as intolerant or bigoted. This discourse has dominated not only schools but also much of wider society and public policy for the last three or four decades. However, in the pursuit of valuing the backgrounds of all children, teachers like me confused valuing *all children* with valuing *all values*, especially where those values were cross-referenced with culture. As I will repeat throughout this book without apology, teachers must demonstrate and model respect for *all people* in general and *all children* in particular. However, teachers do not have to respect and value *all ideas*. Respect for others is not the same thing as a willingness to integrate. We do not have a moral right to withhold respect from another human being, but we do have a right not to integrate with wider society if we choose not to do so. However, we must accept that negative repercussions may ensue from an unwillingness to integrate.

Over the past fifty years, the discourse of moral relativism has dictated that there are no moral absolutes in life, no right and wrong – only choices. To argue that one way of life is better than another is now regarded as partisan and prejudiced. This outlook has clouded our judgement around values and, particularly in education, promoted an uncritical view of multiculturalism.

What evolved within the multiculturalism movement, in my view, was a patchwork of incomplete and incoherent ideas, both within schools and in wider society. By applying the multicultural agenda, the political arena became a system of competing interests with ethnic and religious groups vying with each other for resources. More broadly, multiculturalism promoted a non-integrative dualism: a society that lacked a unified identity. In schools, this translated into a patronising and muddled tokenism purveyed by untrained and ill-informed teachers haphazardly teaching a made-up syllabus with poor quality materials. Confused and ill-educated children were the hapless victims of a well-intentioned but ill-thought-through experiment. Teachers, especially those in inner-city areas, believed this was an urgent moral issue (as I did). Were we naive and uncritical about the eventual outcome? I now think that we were.

If, as a profession, we continue to be uncritical about the cultural values of either wider society or its subcultures, we are failing to set and maintain standards which will ensure that our rights and liberties will flourish. If, as well-meaning teachers, we insist that every culture is equally entitled to respect regardless of whether its cultural values lead to, for example, neglecting the elderly, sexualising children, robbing the young of their freedom to independent play, mutilating the genitals of minors, objectifying women or denying equal opportunities, then we are failing as a society. We are also failing as a teaching profession, charged as we are with imparting society's most fundamental and superlative values. In my view, we are in danger of making the same mistakes with tokenistic teaching of fundamental British values, 'identity politics' and intersectionality as we did with multiculturalism. I believe that we should teach fundamental British values, but we should understand and be knowledgeable about the ethical and moral reasons for doing so. We will return to this area, much more positively, in Appendix A.

Contrasting moral compasses

I am now of an age when I can contrast the moral purpose of my parents' generation with that of my own. My father joined the RAF in 1939 aged 17 and went off to war. My mother was a teenager during the war years, helping my grandmother with the responsibilities of raising twelve siblings and spending many nights crouched in the cellar of their terraced house listening to the drone of the Luftwaffe bombing the nearby Liverpool docks. They didn't really have expectations from life but found themselves being questioned by life – sometimes on a daily basis. While this may not have been an intellectual questioning, it was certainly a moral one.

The German philosopher Friedrich Nietzsche said: 'He who has a why to live for can bear almost any how.'[22] The Second World War gave that generation of young people a why. My generation, by contrast – growing up in the 1960s and 1970s – had a very different experience of a guiding moral compass; one characterised more by the desire for self-fulfilment than by the imperative to survive through self-sacrifice. However, at the time of writing, the COVID-19 pandemic is wreaking havoc in the UK and I am observing a heartening revival of the public morality with which my parents were familiar. Doctors and nurses of all ages, but noticeably many in their twenties and thirties, are working long hours in the most hazardous of conditions, caring for the desperately ill and putting their own young lives at serious risk.

22 Quoted in Viktor E. Frankl, *Man's Search for Meaning*, tr. Ilse Lasch (London: Random House, 2004 [1959]), p. 84.

Care workers (particularly of the elderly in nursing homes), delivery drivers, supermarket and shop assistants, pharmacists, refuse collectors, postal delivery workers and many others in essential roles have found themselves being questioned by life in ways they could not have imagined only a few months earlier. Teachers have also been in the frontline of those enabling others to work by keeping schools open for the children of key workers. A new generation has unexpectedly discovered the difference between expectations from life and being questioned by life, as my parents' generation did.

The development of moral character

When I was a young teacher going to job interviews, I would prepare myself for the question (still asked by some): 'What is your philosophy of education?' or the one asked almost as often: 'What is the purpose of education?' I used to say something along the lines that it was 'to engender a sense of wonder' or 'to turn children into lifelong learners'. I still stand by those answers, and no doubt you may have offered them too. But if I were asked that question now, my answer would be different. After forty years in teaching and education, I think the purpose of what we do as teachers is to develop character.

There is a dynamic symbiotic relationship between teacher and pupil when it comes to the development of character. Imparting values to pupils involves continual contests and challenges, some of which are successful and others less so, but these challenges come back as life-enhancing personal and professional lessons, not otherwise easily learned. As a teacher, therefore, you will find teaching to be a 'struggle'. That is not a bad thing. You may be fortunate enough to avoid many of life's fundamental challenges – chronic ill health, family dissolution, relationship breakdown – but a well-lived, purposeful life is one where you throw yourself into struggle and test your moral courage. Teaching thirty challenging kids can provide that struggle: facing down moral opposition when it inevitably arises, reacting with a range of virtuous responses and, ultimately (hopefully), finding the satisfaction and happiness that arrives with having chosen a profession that develops character in yourself and in young people. It will be a struggle. Relish it.[23]

Some people say that teaching is a 'vocational' profession. What they mean, in line with modern connotations of the word, is that it involves training and the practical application of skills as well as academic knowledge. The word vocation comes from the Latin *vocare,* meaning 'a calling'. It is derived from the religious notion of 'a calling to serve

23 For more on the Kantian notion of struggle as virtue, see Roger Scruton, *Kant: A Very Short Introduction* (Oxford: Oxford University Press, 2001).

God', as a priest might. The word also connotes the sense of purpose that others, such as doctors and nurses, might feel about their role in society: it is not just a job, it is a mission.

A person with a deep sense of vocation is not dependent on constant positive reinforcement; they may even feel extended periods of dissatisfaction or frustration. Try to train yourself to recognise something positive from each day – there will always be something – but don't be so naive as to think that you will come home every day during your career with a warm glow of achievement. There is a bigger picture. For the majority of children, an appreciation of their education will come as a reflection later in life when it is probably too late to tell you.

A colleague of mine in teacher training once told me: 'Children won't remember what you taught them, but they'll remember how you made them feel.'[24] Most of the really fundamental human achievements occur over a generation or longer, not in the timeline of a day, month, year or even a school career. We must satisfy ourselves that we are playing our part in a historical process that will transcend our lifetimes.

When people dream of their future lives and careers, they envisage things that they think will make them happy, like a satisfying job with a good salary. But when people look back on the events of their life, they don't usually point to things like that; they talk about the ordeals and struggles that forged their character.[25] How do teachers form character in themselves and in the children they teach? It isn't a question I asked myself much in my career as a teacher, but I wish I had. When I did consider it, fleetingly, I thought it was all about developing the children's personalities, enabling them to express themselves and fulfilling their self-actualisation.

It is a question that people in other professions often ask of new recruits. Take the military, for example. They know that character is essential to being a good soldier. More to the point, they know that character can be trained. For members of the armed forces, that process can happen from the outside in. It is through the exercise of drill that a person becomes self-regulating. It is through the regular expression of courtesy that a person becomes polite. It is through the gradual resistance to fear that a soldier develops courage. They believe that the act precedes the virtue.[26]

If you go into teaching thinking that children will become better people through mere education alone, then you are mistaken. Prejudice, bigotry and racism are characteristics of the well-educated as well as the poorly educated. What is needed is for the good to stand against the bad and for the right to stand against the wrong. We must

24 The original quote is by Carl W. Buehner (but often misattributed to Maya Angelou). It reads: 'They may forget what you said – but they will never forget how you made them feel.' Quoted in Richard L. Evans, *Richard Evans' Quote Book* (Salt Lake City, UT: Publishers Press, 1971), p. 244.

25 See Brooks, *The Road to Character*, ch. 4.

26 See also the section on virtue ethics in Chapter 4.

provide young people with the opportunity to exercise a range of virtues, so that when their moral character is tested, they respond with an increasing sense of intuition. We can put some faith in education, sure, otherwise we wouldn't believe in its possibilities. But the faith we put in the historical process of education and the human goodness it produces must be matched by a willingness to recognise the wrong in human nature. Evil must be met with the relentless opposition of virtue.

Teachers draw inspiration from history, such as the non-violent civil rights movements led by Dr Martin Luther King and Mahatma Gandhi or the dignity shown by Nelson Mandela in the face of state-sponsored prejudice and oppression. King and Gandhi saw evil and responded with the revolutionary idea that they could coerce people to do good things even against their will. Indeed, that is exactly what schooling is about. It trains, even forces, young people to accept and do good things for themselves and others, even when it is something they resist or do not want to do of their own volition.

Teaching is not merely about passing on skills, knowledge and information, or even creating opportunities and experiences that enable individual growth and self-actualisation. Teaching exists to develop children's moral values – of knowing the difference between good and bad, right and wrong. Teaching exists to enrich children's understanding of how to choose between those two opposing elements. Teaching exists to develop knowledge and courage about when to stand against that which is wrong.

The morality of disciplining children

Apart from imparting skills and knowledge, schools are places where moral induction and instruction take place. This is also part of the process of education – *ducare* – the process of 'leading out'. Schools are places where moral definition is in a constant state of flux. The language that teachers use and the actions they take involves demonstrating and modelling moral values. Whether we realise it or not, we are deeply engaged in Aristotle's 'reasoning about values' (*techne*) and 'reasoning from values' (*phronesis*).

As we have seen, teachers must act like good responsible parents. This includes disciplining children and, yes, the law allows punishment for misdeeds and morality requires it. Punishment is not by definition a violent act, and nor is it an angry act of revenge wielded by those with physical or legal power over the weak. It is a combination of attentive interventions. In our case, that means accepting the moral responsibility to constrain children's damaging behaviour.[27]

27 See Peterson, *12 Rules for Life*, ch. 1.

As a new teacher, you will inevitably make mistakes when learning to discipline children. The advice and wisdom of more experienced colleagues and the guidance of school procedures will help you to avoid repeated errors, but you will make mistakes. When you do, you might apologise when that is appropriate. Apologising is a good and moral thing to do. Your pupils will respect you for it.

It is important not to abdicate your responsibility for pointing out the difference between what is right and wrong. If you surrender your duty to correct bad behaviour, you may win a disingenuous smirk from a habitually misbehaving child, but you will both know, deep down, that you have been manipulated. The recalcitrant child will expect to be able to misbehave again – only next time they will make it even more difficult for you. From a weakened position, you will be trying to recover a situation from where they resist your efforts to impose outside order on their inner chaos.

The application of disciplinary measures by teachers on children is a good example of the struggle I was referring to earlier. It isn't easy to confront misbehaviour. In fact, it is often easier to turn a blind eye to it or dishonestly allow a child to manipulate you when you should have squared up to their naked bad behaviour. If you do stand against it – and you should – and apply virtuous principles when doing so, you will build character in yourself and the children. But it is a test – one that you cannot shirk without abdicating your moral responsibility.

Moral values and the law

Moral values are not the same as the law. Values can be personal, communal and even universal, but that doesn't mean we necessarily make laws out of them. Justifying moral values sometimes involves establishing a hierarchy of competence – a set of preferences based on principles rather than whim or prejudice. Some teachers feel uncomfortable about establishing hierarchies, although, of course, we must do it; testing children in examinations is one such example. This is not to say that schools should be places where the ranking of children's abilities is all they think about, but instigating, establishing and expressing moral values is an inescapable duty.[28]

In Western, liberal-democratic societies, the state does not use punitive laws to dictate moral conduct; instead, the role of law is primarily to protect the vulnerable from harm. In the UK, the state avoids using the codes of criminal law to proscribe private morality when it does no harm to others. That hasn't always been the case. Take the experience of homosexuality, for example. During most of my teaching career being an openly

28 See Peterson, *12 Rules for Life*, ch. 2.

gay teacher was considered a moral as well as an ethical issue (and for the generation before me it was a legal issue too). Now, sexuality is protected by anti-discrimination legislation.

Values change. But whose values determine what is considered right and wrong? In societies dominated by authoritarian dictatorships we know the answer to that question. In countries that have evolved centuries-old philosophical and religious wisdoms – gleaned and distilled from reflection, debate, experience and, perhaps most important of all, struggle – decisions about the way we want to live are determined democratically and peacefully.

Objectively, morality in the public realm is a pre-eminent set of values based around matters of human welfare, justice, compassion, honesty, respect and fairness. The vast majority of world cultures hold these same values in high regard. However, in moral terms not all opinions are considered as 'good' as one another, and nor should they be. While in recent decades Western society has been characterised by greater social tolerance, the dominant public morality can still be disapproving of conduct outside the mainstream.

There aren't many parts of the UK where the values of teachers and the values of the host community are at serious variance, although there are some instances. There is a widespread social tolerance for single parenting, divorce and minority lifestyles (such as gay and lesbian relationships), even if the majority does not share that particular lifestyle. But new challenges to tolerance are emerging constantly and teachers may find themselves teaching in communities where attitudes towards transgender people, particular codes of dress or new immigrant groups might be less tolerant than the wider norm.

Discuss and reflect

- When events like the Birmingham LGBT school protests take place, whose values should prevail? The school's or the parents'?

Two and a half millennia ago, Socrates pointed out that doctors are not answerable to their patients. They should not do what their patient wants but what is medically desirable to 'cure the body'. As for teachers, they are not answerable to what pupils or parents want, but (to paraphrase Socrates) what is desirable to feed the soul and banish ignorance and delusion.

Is morality a private matter?

Should teachers be accountable for what they do in their private lives? Where is the boundary between what is legitimately in the public domain and what is a matter of private concern? It is an obvious truism that what may be acceptable in private is not necessarily acceptable in public, but if you are working in a profession that deals with educating and promoting moral values to children, then matters such as sexuality and sexual relationships, for example, may require a complex range of judgements. These issues are challenging for teachers in ways that are quite distinct from those posed to members of other professions.

Discuss and reflect

For a teacher, are the following issues moral?

- Flaws in personality, such as being:
  - Hypocritical.
  - Lazy.
  - Self-righteous.
  - Superstitious.
  - Unpredictable.
  - Zealous.
- Engaging in morally contentious conduct, such as:
  - Appearing in adult sex films.
  - Hunting animals for sport.
  - Compulsive gambling.

Being a teacher and modelling lingerie

Teaching and lingerie modelling may seem an incongruous juxtaposition, but after one of my talks a young woman completing her teacher training course approached me for my advice. She had been modelling lingerie in her spare time and had made a good deal of money doing so, which was helping her to pay for her course. Now that she was about to graduate (and she had been offered a permanent teaching job) she was worried that her new school colleagues might view her lucrative sideline differently to the way she did. One university tutor had already advised her that modelling lingerie 'wasn't compatible with a career in teaching'. However, she was reluctant to give up an activity that she not only enjoyed but which also afforded her significant additional income. Added to that, it took little time or effort away from her main focus, which was her new teaching career.

- What would be your advice to a new teacher who was modelling lingerie?

Now that we have come this far, you should have a sense of the differences between the legal, ethical and moral distinctions that the Romans worked so helpfully to bequeath to Western philosophy. It may be helpful when considering the lingerie model's predicament (and a series of other questions to follow) to think about whether the legal, ethical and moral implications are entirely separate or if they overlap.

If your advice to this young woman is that she should stop modelling and remove traces of her past career from the internet (if that is even possible), then you will probably fall within the majority mainstream opinion. Although I have no data on this, my anecdotal experience is that the teaching profession has become remarkably cautious and defensive – dare I say, conservative – in relation to issues of reputation management. The perceived good standing of schools is jealously guarded by head teachers and governing bodies, who are often fearful of the possibility of a scandal. The advice of teacher union representatives usually endorses this defensiveness. It is understandable – the stakes are very high.

My advice to this young woman was to ask whether she thought what she was doing was illegal, unethical or immoral. When I asked, 'Is modelling lingerie illegal?' she answered, of course, no. (By the way, I did ask tactfully whether what she was doing could be perceived as pornographic, and she answered no to that too. Not that I am making a judgement about pornography, but it might have involved an alternative set of questions.) She had to think for a moment about the second question, 'Is it unethical?' but she concluded that she couldn't see how it had any ethical implications given that she spent no more time modelling lingerie than she would on a sports activity or any other hobby outside of school in her own spare time. Finally, I asked: 'Is it immoral?' 'Not to *me*,' she said immediately. And there is the rub. Not to *her*. However, it is conceivable that it might be regarded as immoral to others. She quickly realised that a teacher appearing in lingerie, half-naked so to speak, on a website that pupils and parents might access could be considered immoral to some people. Justifiable or not, it might risk personal ridicule and potential reputational management issues that her colleagues and the school might not welcome.

There is no hard and fast advice in situations like this, but I did ask her two further questions. Firstly, would she be embarrassed if colleagues, governors, parents or pupils saw the images? She answered confidently that she would not. Secondly, would she be prepared to face down the possible innuendo, gossip and snide jokes that might ensue? She had to think about that, but then concluded, yes, she would. In conclusion, I offered her one single piece of advice: 'Go to your head teacher and tell him or her that you have a "hobby" as a lingerie model, that you enjoy it and want to continue, and that you are convinced that it won't interfere with your preparedness or commitment as a teacher. See what the reaction is. If your head is prepared to support you, it seems that the moral values of the school are aligned with your own. If they are unwilling to support you, then my advice is to find another school to work in as soon as is practical – one where your values about your preferred lifestyle are compatible with the moral values of the school.' It is not an easy choice to make. Standing by your principles sometimes requires sacrifice and struggle.

Educating by example

As highly esteemed as many other professions are, not even doctors, lawyers and nurses need to be quite so concerned with (excuse the pun) modelling moral behaviours to their clients in the same exemplary way as teachers. Teachers are expected to educate by example. As soon as anyone begins their teacher training, and particularly when they begin their first teaching practice, they become sensitive to how they model their personal values. Not only are they suddenly on show, but they are also under scrutiny in ways that were not hitherto the case.

For example, as a trainee or early career teacher you may find yourself in a supermarket one evening doing your weekly shop. Suddenly a child from your class appears from behind the tins of baked beans with a parent in tow. The child is excited to greet you. She introduces you to her mum or dad: 'This is my teacher!' Now, for the first time in your life, you become acutely aware of having two bottles of red wine, a bottle of vodka, a two-litre bottle of cola, a family-sized pack of potato crisps, half a dozen microwavable ready meals and a multi-pack of frozen margherita pizzas piled up in your trolley.

A few years ago, I was leading a session with a group of PGCE trainees in a school-based training centre in Swindon. Towards the end of the session, one student commented: 'Now that I'm training to be a teacher, I've got to be careful about what I do in my private life.'

'Really?' I asked. 'Why?'

'Well,' he laughed. 'I did a degree in Bristol and it's a great city for pubs. I used to be out every weekend,' he said, gesturing a drinking motion with his right arm. 'If I had the money, I'd be out week nights as well. Sometimes I'd come home legless and totally off my face! I can't do that now. I'm on teaching practice in a small town and I can't let the parents see me stagger home from a pub at closing time. Once, I even saw my Year 12s (16–17-year-old pupils) in the local pub!'

Another student chipped in: 'Yeah, but you can still drink and enjoy yourself. You're not a teacher every minute of every day. You've got to let off a bit of steam and keep a balance in your life.' (In my view, that is very good advice – I endorse it.) 'Just go and socialise miles away from where you work,' he continued, 'where nobody knows you. Keep your private life *private*.' (That is also very good advice – I wholeheartedly endorse it too.)

Interestingly, he then went on to say: 'If you want to drink, that's up to you, isn't it? As long as you don't go into school drunk or go in hung-over on a Monday morning. If you're a good teacher, what you do in your private life is nobody else's business.' He paused, then it got even more interesting: 'I'm not a drinker myself,' he said, enticingly, 'but I like to smoke a bit of weed at weekends. So what?' he shrugged as people laughed. 'I do that behind closed doors. Nobody knows about it. I'm not harming anyone. I'm not taking drugs into school and selling them to the kids, am I? I'm just smoking a bit of weed. I don't see why it has anything to do with anyone else.'

Right away, another trainee challenged him. 'Of course it has!' she said.

'Why? How?' he responded.

'It's illegal!' she said. 'Didn't you know that smoking weed is illegal?'

But the guy wasn't going to be patronised. 'What? Have you never done *anything* wrong?' he asked her. 'Never? Have you *never* parked on a double yellow line, *never* jumped an amber light, *never* driven down the motorway at 80 or 90 miles an hour, *never* paid your car mechanic in cash to avoid the VAT?' (I must admit that I felt slightly uncomfortable myself when he gave that particular example!)

It's a fascinating challenge isn't it? This young man was effectively saying: 'If I'm a good teacher, what I do in my private life is none of your business, thank you very much!'

Discuss and reflect

If you are a good teacher, does it matter if you:

1. Regularly get drunk in pubs or clubs at weekends.
2. Use recreational drugs in the privacy of your own home.
3. Regularly exceed the speed limit.
4. Download or stream adult pornography using your home computer.
5. Engage in flirtatious or sexualised banter with colleagues.
6. Use social media platforms to network with pupils on educational matters outside of school hours.
7. Become active in an extreme political party.

Spend some time thinking about these issues and, if you can, discuss them in a small group.

Discussions around these questions in my sessions always results in lively debate. Why? Because the new teachers I am meeting are beginning to grapple with the application of virtue – the dilemmas that are inevitably involved in managing competing moral principles to make the right decision: to do the right thing, in the right way, at the right time, in the right measure. Perhaps, unwittingly, they are also using their judgement to interpret the legal, ethical and moral implications of these behaviours. That is only natural – we are predisposed to defend our own moral conduct. Not only do I welcome the frank discussions that ensue, but I also challenge some of the participants' assumptions, often playing devil's advocate. Let's consider some of the issues raised above.

Social media

A typical response to question 6, on using social media platforms to network with pupils on educational matters outside of school hours, is an outright no. Very few trainees, if any, would condone this. By the time my session appears in the programme, most trainees have already had lectures on e-safety and how to protect children from online grooming and social media bullying. Their tutors, quite rightly, have drilled them about keeping their own social media profiles discreet, so when this question is presented to them, their immediate reaction is usually to say: 'No way! I would never accept a friend request from any pupil on a social media platform!'

I endorse all the advice that tutors and mentors give trainees about maintaining discretion in their own social media use, but there are some interesting points to consider even with this scenario. The first and obvious one is that you should not seek inappropriate relationships with your pupils either offline or online. Instagram, Snapchat, Twitter and Facebook are all social platforms. You do not primarily have a social relationship with your pupils; you have a professional one. However, schools are utilising social media platforms to engage pupils, parents and the wider community, often very effectively – for example, schools have long used Facebook groups to organise orchestras, sports teams, clubs and parent forums. Of course, these groups are managed by the school's official IT infrastructure and have strict protocols.

However, there are exceptions. I met a teacher a few years ago who was a peripatetic dance teacher working with over eighty pupils. She had to organise rehearsals and performances across five different schools. She couldn't use a single school intranet, but with the permission of the schools involved and the children's parents, she set up a Facebook Dance Group of which she was the designated administrator. Nobody could access the pages without her permission and nobody could post blogs or tag photographs without her approval, so she was able to organise her dance groups simply and efficiently. That seemed to me a very effective and professional use of a social media platform. There are risks, of course, but this teacher managed those risks very well.

My point is not that you should be seeking opportunities to engage your pupils on social media platforms, but neither should you regard social media as some kind of untouchable evil that immediately compromises your ethical position as a teacher. It doesn't.

Getting drunk and speeding

Many trainees at my sessions reveal how relaxed they are about questions 1 and 3: 'regularly getting drunk in pubs or clubs at weekends' and 'regularly exceeding the speed limit'. A typical reaction to both of these is: 'Most people do it, don't they?' I sometimes test this proposition with the wider audience. Occasionally, I will ask for a show of hands. I am often very surprised at how many people declare themselves not just infrequent drinkers but completely teetotal. Many trainees are far from tolerant of speeding as well, even on motorways. Indeed, some point out the risks to life and limb from people who speed.

Remember the male trainee in Swindon who admitted to smoking cannabis? He was mocked by a female colleague for not realising the legal implications of what he was doing. In a later exchange in the same session, the female trainee admitted to speeding on motorways, adding in a rather blasé tone: 'Everyone breaks the speed limit, don't they?' The dope-smoker saw his opportunity and pounced: '*I* don't!' he said. 'And what I do – smoking a bit of weed at home – doesn't harm anyone. But what you do – speeding in your car – puts other people's lives at risk!' Exchanges like this illustrate that our personal morality is sometimes at variance with the law. We cannot always assume what other people do with any confidence or accuracy, and nor should we use it as a guide to our own moral standards.

Viewing adult pornography

Whose business is it if you are 'downloading (or streaming) adult pornography on a home computer' (question 4)? The answer is simple: it is no one else's business. If you enjoy viewing adult pornography on your home computer, that is a private matter. Adult pornography is legal. There are no ethical implications – unless, of course, you were stupid enough to take your own laptop into school and allow pupils, by intent or neglect, to view material you had downloaded. That would be a legitimate disciplinary issue.

To see this issue from another angle (and to contrast the ethical with the moral), let's imagine that you somehow discovered that your child's teacher was regularly viewing adult pornography at home. You might feel annoyance, dismay or even disgust. You are entitled to your feelings and your moral stance, but you are not entitled to impose your personal morality on others. As that trainee in Swindon advised: 'Keep your private life *private*.'

Flirtatious and sexualised banter

Is there anything wrong with 'engaging in flirtatious or sexualised banter with colleagues' (question 5)? My audiences are usually young people in their twenties and thirties. In spite of the growth of dating apps, a recent survey for the BBC judged that about 40 per cent of young people still prefer to meet their romantic partners through friends, family and in the workplace.[29] Mixed-gender workplaces have traditionally

29 Daniel Rosney and Roisin Hastie, Dating Apps: Tinder, Chappy and Bumble 'Least Preferred' Way to Meet People, *BBC Newsbeat* (3 August 2018). Available at: https://www.bbc.co.uk/news/newsbeat-45007017.

been places where banter – sometimes flirtatious and sexualised – has been a common feature of social interaction. However, in recent years, and especially since the rise of the #MeToo (anti-sexual harassment) movement, what was once thought 'innocent' or 'humorous' is being either discouraged or contractually prohibited. Some organisations actually try to ban romantic relationships between employees because of the potential for productivity issues and conflicts of interest.

Having said that, and to play devil's advocate once again, how are you ever going to signal attraction to a prospective romantic partner if you never engage in a bit of banter with someone to whom you are attracted? Many people would say that banter and joking make the drudgery of work life more tolerable. When my audiences discuss this there are always a range of attitudes on the subject. Some will say: 'Teaching is an intense and busy job with little time to socialise. The workplace is where people have time to meet, get to know each other, decide who to like (and dislike), trust and bond with.' Others will qualify that by saying: 'Obviously, you don't flirt in front of the children' or 'I wouldn't do it in the staffroom if it embarrassed my colleagues.' By contrast, others will challenge the idea entirely: 'No, no, no! In a professional environment you should be professional. You just don't do that kind of thing. It isn't appropriate in the workplace!' 'Why not?' someone else might respond. 'It isn't unprofessional to banter with colleagues as long as you don't take it too far. If it's discreet and reciprocal – and you're not harassing anyone – then it's harmless.' Some will remain unconvinced: 'Where's the dividing line between sexual banter and sexual harassment?' And so the debate goes on.

Consensual, flirtatious and even sexualised banter is not illegal, although sexual harassment clearly is. Whatever your moral stance on the matter, you will need to make an ethical judgement about where the dividing line is, as some of these trainees were evidently beginning to do. I am not going to give you a lecture on the topic (especially as I engaged in it myself as a young man and had relationships that began in the workplace) because these are fine judgements indeed. But they are judgements that you are trusted to make as a professional person. One of the reasons why people are prepared to call you a professional is that they trust your judgement.

Political extremism

The issues relating to teachers and politics are complex. Question 7 raises one such difficulty: 'becoming active in an extreme political party'. Some trainees feel very strongly about this. They are convinced that this type of activity is incompatible with statements in the Teachers' Standards requiring teachers to show 'respect for the rights of others' and 'tolerance of those with different faiths and beliefs'.[30] Some people are convinced that a teacher cannot possibly show respect for all pupils, whatever their ethnic or religious background, if outside of school they support parties that (in the view of some) are bigoted or racist.

I will challenge this view: 'Don't you think you can leave your political views at the school gate and operate solely by professional, ethical standards?' Some students vehemently believe that extremism is a circle that cannot be squared. On one occasion a trainee said to me: 'If you support an extremist party, especially if you are active in a party that espouses racist and intolerant views, then you cannot possibly leave those attitudes at the school gate and be a different person just because you are a teacher.' Another added: 'Attitudes and beliefs are part of you. If you think that immigrants and foreigners should not be living in the UK, you can't possibly treat the children of immigrants and foreigners equally with British children.'

I extend the challenge to that assumption too: 'If that is the case, is it impossible for a teacher to leave other deeply held convictions – such as their religious faith – at the school gate and come into school and operate by professional standards? Do you think that a devout Christian, for example, cannot teach children of other faiths without wanting to convert them? Or that a devout Muslim would discriminate against children from avowedly atheist families? Or that they would want to secretly proselytise and try to convert them to their faith?'

Discuss and reflect

- Do you think that you can leave your deeply held political convictions or your devout religious beliefs at the school gate?
- Can your practice as a teacher be governed entirely by professional, ethical standards?

30 Department for Education, *Teachers' Standards*, p. 14.

When discussing this issue, some inevitably ask what is meant by an 'extreme' political party? This is an important question. Many people will be guided by the government's definition of extremism, which is 'vocal or active opposition to fundamental British values'.[31] Ultimately, however, individuals determine their own definition. For some, it will include only banned or illegal groups (such as far-right, ultra-nationalist, neo-Nazi or anti-immigrant groups like National Action, or jihadist and militant Islamic networks like Al-Muhajiroun). These groups advocate or engage in violence or incitement to violence, which is why they have been made illegal. Other people will see extremism in groups that are legal but on the political fringes – for example, extremist groups like the Socialist Workers Party or the English Defence League or Islamist groups like Hizb-ut-Tahrir. For some people, single issue groups will fall within their definition of extreme, such as animal rights, climate action or anti-globalisation groups.

While some may feel that extremism is in the eye of the beholder, we should remember that in a democratic country like Britain, even extreme views should be tolerated (if not necessarily accepted) – as long as they do not abuse, threaten or incite violence. The question for you as a teacher is whether your political involvement could compromise you ethically. Of course, you have a perfect right to engage in political activity – to join, campaign, become active and even stand as a candidate for any legal political party you wish. That is your democratic right, and you should protect that right jealously from the interference of anyone who might seek to constrain or remove it by virtue of your profession. However, once you enter the public realm on the basis of your political views (by standing for election, for example), then people will have the right to make a judgement about you. The more people know about your private life, the more they will judge it from their own moral and subjective viewpoint, over which you have no control.

'Who are you going to vote for, Mr Newland?'

During election times, children are likely to ask you which way you are going to vote. I made a decision never to answer this question.

'Mind your own business,' I would say.

'Oh, go on, Sir. Tell us!'

31 Department for Education, *The Prevent Duty*, p. 5.

'No.'

'Why won't you tell us?' they would ask.

'For the very important reason that it's a private matter. In fact, it's secret too, for reasons you'll understand more when you grow up.'

Then, depending on the age and maturity of the kids (remember, I taught mainly in primary schools), I would sometimes do better than that. I would add: 'Actually, you know when we have elections for school council? You cast your vote in secret, don't you? That's so nobody can see who you've voted for, so nobody can put pressure on you or bully you to vote for a particular person. You are free to vote for the person of your choice. That's why we call it a "secret ballot". When you grow up and vote in general elections you will realise even more why it's important that you don't have to tell people who you voted for – not if you don't want to. And I don't want to tell you, so there!'

Of course, it is not only inappropriate but also unethical for teachers to try to persuade their pupils of the moral rightness of their particular politics, however passionate and heartfelt they may feel about it. Some teachers will hold fervent views about certain moral issues, such as climate change. The way to demonstrate that urgency is to educate pupils about the scientific evidence that climate change is happening and what its effects are and will be; then the moral case makes itself. This is not a matter of objectivity versus subjectivity; art, music and history are all subjects dominated by subjective values and judgements. It is our job to educate children about the moral dimensions of an issue and provide them with the tools to analyse, interpret and criticise. It is not our job to enlist them as supporters or admirers of our own partisan causes.

'We can't have racist teachers teaching in a borough like this!'

When I worked at the General Teaching Council for England, we often visited employers (usually local authorities) who were seeking advice about taking forward disciplinary cases of teachers in their employ. One day, my colleague and I were asked to attend a meeting at a local authority in the Midlands to discuss the fate of a teacher who had been suspended by his school for standing as a candidate for the British National Party (a far-right, anti-immigrant grouping) in elections for the European Parliament.

As the meeting began, my colleague asked a senior member of the local authority to explain the issues involved in the case. The answer was curt: 'What do you think the issues are!' the council officer said. 'We obviously can't have a teacher standing for the BNP in a multiracial, multi-ethnic borough like this!'

'Is this a case of misconduct, then?' my colleague asked. 'Are there allegations that he has shown prejudicial attitudes and behaviour towards pupils, colleagues or parents?'

'Good Lord, no!' replied the official. 'He's worked in the borough for nearly twenty years and has excellent relationships with everyone – pupils, colleagues and parents – from all ethnic backgrounds. We're all totally shocked at this! Nobody even dreamt he held such views, let alone that he was prepared to stand as a candidate for the BNP. We can't believe it!'

'So, if it's not a misconduct case,' enquired my colleague, 'is it a competence case? Has he somehow failed in his performance as a teacher?'

'No, no, he's brilliant! He teaches maths and physics at A level. He has a fantastic record as a teacher – he gets amazing results. Quite outstanding.'

My colleague and I looked at each other, then after a moment he tactfully informed the local authority officer: 'If there is no issue about this teacher's conduct, and there is no issue about his competence, then I'm sorry to tell you ... there is no issue at all. We are not in the business of telling teachers what they must think or believe or how they must behave as citizens in a democratic society.' There was a look of shock and consternation from across the table. 'I'm no apologist for the BNP,' my colleague added, 'but they are a lawful political party in this country. Unless this teacher has shown prejudicial attitudes and behaviour towards pupils, colleagues or parents – and you've said there is no evidence of this – or unless he's failing as a teacher – which you've said he isn't – then there is no case to answer. He is free to engage as a citizen in democratic political processes as he sees fit.'

While this teacher had enjoyed an unblemished reputation as a 'brilliant maths and physics teacher' who had 'excellent relationships with everyone' for nearly twenty years, the problem is that he has taken his private morality – in this case, his political convictions – into the public realm. While he is fully entitled to do this in a free and democratic society, it is also a space where we, the public – parents, pupils and colleagues – are entitled to judge that morality. The consequence may be that he now finds it much more difficult for people to separate what they know of his competence (and ethical position) and what they now know of his politics (and moral position). They will also judge what they perceive to be his character. Once again, as the trainee in Swindon said: 'Keep your private life *private*.'

Tolerance

The concept of tolerance has become so contentious in the modern era that it is essential to consider aspects of it in a variety of educational contexts. Tolerance is referred to explicitly in the Teachers' Standards, so let's begin by examining its moral dimensions.

Tolerance is a virtue. One understanding of it is based on the awareness that conflict is an ever present and inevitable feature of the human condition.[32] This doesn't mean that violence is inevitable, but it does mean that fundamental and conflicting differences of belief are. Opinions and beliefs are not usually good neighbours. If you believe that everything will be hunky-dory if we are just nicer to each other – celebrating diversity, valuing everyone's culture, making sure nobody is left out and so on – then there is no need for tolerance. If you think that all moral values point in the same direction, then it follows that you don't need to moderate your behaviour. You can simply march in the direction of your chosen truth – and the devil take anyone who gets in your way.

Tolerance is what happens when our values are challenged and tested, when our beliefs and convictions don't fit neatly together like a completed jigsaw. We need tolerance in a world where politics is a competition between opposing interests, where philosophy is a struggle between competing half-truths, where human characters are battlegrounds of valuable but sometimes incompatible traits.

A tolerant person has the capacity to contain difference and opposition. A tolerant person can start out with tension and division but achieve proportion and moderation. A tolerant person can accommodate what sociologists call 'cognitive dissonance' – they can hold fundamentally opposing views in their head at the same time, not necessarily feeling the need to subscribe to either. A tolerant person can balance their desire for security with their desire for risk. They can also balance their desire for liberty

32 See Harari, *21 Lessons for the 21st Century*, ch. 11.

with their need for restraint. Above all, a tolerant person knows there is no easy resolution to the fundamental tensions between opposing values. Indeed, there may not be any resolution at all.

These dilemmas are played out almost every day in our classrooms: giving a child the freedom to play and express themselves risks encouraging them to indulge in unruly behaviour. Limiting their licence to be unruly necessarily limits their freedom. There is no easy trade-off between these two competing values, but the virtue of tolerance enables us to accommodate them.

During discussions on this issue with trainees, I will often refer to the Teachers' Standards and remind them what it says about tolerance as part of an ethical code. Teachers must show 'tolerance of and respect for the rights of others' and not undermine 'fundamental British values, including democracy, the rule of law, individual liberty and mutual respect, and tolerance of those with different faiths and beliefs.'[33] I am struck how regularly trainees respond by associating the word tolerance with negative connotations. They will often say things like: 'The word tolerance sounds as though we have to put up with something.' Others will say: 'Why can't we be more positive? Wouldn't it be much better if the Teachers' Standards said *celebrate* different faiths and beliefs, not just *tolerate* them?'

This provides another opportunity for me to play devil's advocate. So, I reply: 'OK, let's imagine we can celebrate all faiths and all beliefs. That would be nice, wouldn't it? But what if you *don't* agree with my beliefs? What if you abhor them and feel you must actively oppose them? What if you find my beliefs fundamentally incompatible with your own? Are you sure you want to celebrate my beliefs now?' I follow it up with a concrete example: 'If you're an atheist and I'm a devout Christian, you might say to me: "Religion is a fairy tale. Can't you see that? It's a delusion. Try reading Richard Dawkins or Sam Harris. Be rational! Get into the twenty-first century!"'

While that is quite an insulting thing to say, you nevertheless have a right to say it, especially in a liberal, democratic society where free speech is valued. You are not abusing me, you are not threatening me and you are not inciting violence against me. You are just expressing your belief in quite a strident (and potentially offensive) way – but in a way that you are entitled to do. In a democracy, I have to tolerate your belief and I have to tolerate your expression of it – indeed, I have a duty to tolerate it even though, as a devout Christian, I might be deeply offended by it.

As an atheist, you will not want to celebrate my devout Christianity. My religious faith is incompatible with your atheism. As a devout Christian, I might say to you in turn: 'I think abortion is not only wrong, I think it's murder.' Now, that is the kind of remark you don't have to be a woman to find offensive; it is one that most people will find

33 Department for Education, *Teachers' Standards*, p. 14.

objectionable. But I have a right to say it. I am not abusing you (or women), I am not threatening you (or women) and I am not inciting violence against you (or anyone else). I am merely expressing a deeply held but controversial and contentious opinion. You have a duty to tolerate my opinions and beliefs, even if you would rather not embrace them or celebrate them.

We must not acquiesce to the mistaken belief that we have a right *not* to be offended. Indeed, if it means we don't challenge ideas because we are oversensitive to causing offence or we veto the right of others to make remarks that might offend, then we are abandoning academic freedom and the search for truth. According to the former Chief Rabbi Jonathan Sacks, refusing to challenge offensive remarks or ideas is 'the intellectual betrayal of our time' and an attempt to 'outsource our moral conscience by delegating our moral responsibility', raising intellectual and moral expectations that cannot be met but which will be exploited by extremists. By the far-right – who will tell us we can return to a golden era that never existed; by the far-left – who will tell us we can find a utopia that will never exist; by religious extremists – who will promise a paradise for those willing to kill others; or by aggressive secularists – who will tell us that peace will come when we get rid of religion.[34]

We must tolerate the free speech of others, even when it deeply offends us. What we don't have to tolerate is abuse, threats or incitement to violence. That is beyond the bounds of acceptable speech even in a liberal democracy. We have made it illegal (many decades since), based on a philosophical precept established hundreds of years ago that free speech does not extend to the right to shout 'Fire!' in a crowded theatre.[35]

The children in our schools can easily be taught the difference between offensive speech on the one hand, and abuse, threats and incitement on the other. I know because I have done it. I would say to the children in my classes, some as young as 7 or 8 years old, whose behaviour or language towards each other was sometimes unacceptable: 'You can say things I don't agree with, you can say things I don't really want to hear, and I won't tell you off for saying them. You can even say things I really disagree with, and I won't forbid you to say them. But you cannot say things that abuse, threaten or incite violence or hatred against your classmates. That is wrong. I won't allow you to do that, not in my class or in this school. And do you know what else? You're not even allowed to do that outside of school either, because it's against the law.'

I stand up for tolerance as a teacher and as a citizen. It is not a negative or a cynical concept. Tolerance is a deeply positive moral virtue. We should be proud to stand up for tolerance, even when it makes our blood boil to listen to foolish or ignorant people

34 See Jonathan Sacks, *Morality in the 21st Century* [radio series], BBC Radio 4 (2018). Available at: https://www.bbc.co.uk/programmes/b0bh7jkp.

35 This phrase originates from the opinion of US Supreme Court Justice Oliver Wendell Holmes Jr who, in 1919, used it to illustrate the limits of free speech in Schenck v. United States.

expressing opinions and beliefs we find abhorrent. If we think we have a better belief, then we must come up with a better argument to challenge or replace it. That is what we should be demonstrating and modelling as teachers and what we should be teaching our children to do too.

What I have been trying to show through these discussions and anecdotes are some of the ways you will be challenged, not just by ethical (professional) but also moral (personal) dilemmas. Some of them illustrate the philosophical difficulty of trying to distinguish between the two, but as I mentioned earlier, you will find that some issues are inextricable. The Teachers' Standards are not a prescription for how to be a good teacher, although they are useful as a set of ethical guidelines. They throw up as many issues as they attempt to resolve – and so they should.

Ethical codes declare moral values because they are proclaiming what 'ought to be', and so will be seen by some as inherently political, hierarchical or as having cultural bias. All such texts, however sacred, need to be seen in a given context in order to interpret them. Try to view the dilemmas and challenges that present themselves positively. They are an opportunity for you to learn, develop and, as Aristotle put it, acquire *phronesis* – the practical wisdom that will ultimately make you a teacher of good character.

'What would Jesus think of your behaviour?'

I was leading a SCITT session with trainees at a large and respected Roman Catholic secondary school in London. One trainee in the group said he was very challenged by the statement in the Teachers' Standards that teachers should 'ensure that personal beliefs are not expressed in ways which exploit pupils' vulnerability or might lead them to break the law'. When I asked him to explain why, he said: 'Look, this is a great school and I'm not complaining about anything – the kids are lovely, the staff are brilliant and I'm getting a great training here. But it's a Catholic school … and, well … I'm an atheist.'

'Go on,' I said.

'There are some things that some of the teachers say here that bother me.'

Now I was curious. 'Like what?'

'Well, there is a senior teacher here, he's wonderful – he's so good with the kids that we end up sending all the naughty ones to him because he deals with them so brilliantly. But sometimes, when he's telling them off, he'll say to them: "Now, what would Jesus think of your behaviour?" I know why he's saying that – he's a devout Catholic, it's a Catholic school and parents send their kids here because it has a Catholic ethos. But as an atheist, I'm very uncomfortable with that kind of language. I think he may be expressing personal beliefs in ways that might exploit the vulnerability of those young kids.'

I thought this was a fascinating remark, so I asked him how he dealt with his dilemma.

'I don't say anything to the teacher himself,' the trainee assured me. 'I don't challenge him when he says it. I wouldn't do that. I know he's a devout Catholic, I know he means well and, anyway, challenging him in front of the kids would be unprofessional. I wouldn't want to undermine him or the ethos of the school.'

Discuss and reflect

- Should teachers in faith schools invoke religious authority to try to influence and correct children's behaviour?

This trainee's experience is an excellent illustration of how your moral as well as ethical values will be challenged. Here is a new teacher who, on the one hand, has his own set of personal, moral values as an atheist; and on the other hand, is being asked to integrate a set of professional (ethical) values with his personal values (morality) as an atheist. He is discovering some tensions when he tries to integrate the two.

The ethics and morality of faith schools

You may find yourself working in a faith school, even though you have no committed religious belief of your own. About 25 per cent of all schools in the UK are categorised as faith schools. In England alone, just under 30 per cent of all primary schools and nearly 20 per cent of secondary schools are faith based.[36] There is an even higher proportion in the independent sector. The faiths are mostly denominations of Christianity – the Church of England and the Roman Catholic Church predominate – but there are also a small number of Jewish, Muslim, Sikh and Hindu state schools.

36 Robert Long and Shadi Danechi, *Faith Schools in England: FAQs*. Briefing Paper Number 06972 (20 December 2019) (London: House of Commons Library), p. 21. Available at: https://commonslibrary.parliament.uk/research-briefings/sn06972.

The reason why faith schools feature prominently in the UK system is down to our religious, political and education history. Church schools that provided for the poor go back as far as pre-Reformation times and continue right up to the twenty-first century. To illustrate this, the school where I was head teacher in Hackney was a Church of England primary school whose trust deeds dated back to early Victorian times (well before 1870) when the state first introduced free, compulsory education in England. The deeds stated that the mission of the school was to be a 'community school' (note: a community school, not a Christian school) and to provide 'an education to the poor of Hackney' (no mention of a Christian education or a Church of England education) but 'an education within a Christian ethos', specifically to 'the poor of Hackney'. The governors of the school consequently oversaw the provision of an education within a Christian ethos to the children who lived closest to the school, irrespective of their religious affiliation. The school's admission criteria prioritised those who lived in closest proximity. Effectively, the school's purpose was to serve the local community – fulfilling the mission set out by its Victorian trustees, including those families who were (in my time as head teacher) Christians, Jews, Hindus, Muslims and of no religious faith at all. Indeed, the latter were often in the majority.

If we were restarting the education system in the UK from scratch, would we make faith schools be such a significant part of the state system? I am not sure we would. It is an anomaly of our history that we do. Arguably, though, like many unique British anomalies (arguably including the monarchy and the House of Lords), it seems to work. Faith schools often perform very highly and are extremely popular with parents. But is that a legitimate justification for having them? Are there legal, ethical and moral issues related to having faith schools in the UK state system? In my view, yes, there are – far too many to consider in this book. However, they are worth exploring elsewhere and I urge you to do it. I am a supporter of faith schools for a variety of reasons (which we need not waste time discussing here), but debating these issues has the advantage of honing our legal, ethical and moral sensibilities. To paraphrase the great Victorian philosopher and ethical theorist John Stuart Mill: he who does not know his opponent's side of the case does not truly know his own.

It is unlikely that your moral and ethical values will be contested on a daily basis, although challenges will come regularly. I can't imagine, for example, that you will look at Part One of the Teachers' Standards and think that this general description of what teachers do represents much of a challenge to your personal values. Part One is a very broad-brush list of statements describing the minimum technical standards expected of a teacher. As we have seen, these provide a useful starting point and future reference for scoping the job.

However, when you look at statements in Part Two like: 'demonstrate consistently high standards of personal and professional conduct', or 'maintain high standards of ethics and behaviour, within and outside school' or 'ensuring that personal beliefs are not expressed in ways which exploit pupils' vulnerability',[37] then you might find some tensions emerging. You may need to discuss these with your colleagues before you can fully assimilate your personal moral values with your professional ethical values, as the atheist trainee in the Catholic school was being challenged to do.

Sexuality

Believe it or not, the mere presence of gay teachers in schools was thought to be a moral and an ethical issue until relatively recently. The 1980s saw a heightened awareness of many political and social issues, and sexuality was one of them. The Local Government Act 1988 included a clause, known infamously as 'Section 28', which stipulated that local authorities (which at the time had almost entire control of the state school system) 'shall not intentionally promote homosexuality or publish material with the intention of promoting homosexuality' or 'promote the teaching in any maintained [state] school of the acceptability of homosexuality as a pretended family relationship'. The Act was not repealed in Scotland until 2000 (by the Ethical Standards in Public Life Act – one of the first acts of the new Scottish Parliament) and as late as 2003 in the rest of the UK. Now, sexuality is a protected characteristic under anti-discrimination legislation.[38]

However, you will find that children are not always the best respecters of social etiquette or personal boundaries.

'Mr Newland, are you gay?'

One day, a group of girls came up to me while I was doing playground duty and asked me whether I was gay. I could see that it was a serious question, so I decided to answer it in kind.

'I might be ...' I said (at which their eyes lit up). 'Then again, I might not ... ' (at which, their eyes dimmed). 'I'm not saying!' I said, tapping the tip of my nose to indicate that it was none of their business.

'Oh, go on, Sir, tell us – we won't tell anyone!'

37 Department for Education, *Teachers' Standards*, p. 14.
38 For more on this, see the section on the Equality Act 2010 in Chapter 3.

'I don't care if you do tell anyone,' I said. 'I'm not telling *you*. It's none of your business.'

'*I* said you were gay!' said one of them quite decidedly, as if she was declaring a scientific discovery. 'You are gay, aren't you, Sir?'

'I've told you: I might be … I might not … *I'm not saying!*' I replied, tapping the tip of my nose again. 'It's a private matter.'

They ran off giggling.

I have met some secondary teachers who have said that, on occasion, they have discussed their sexuality both with individual (teenage) pupils and with a whole class. Their justification was that they could see some children were struggling with aspects of their sexuality and thought it would be a way of reassuring them that they were not alone. Others discussed it with classes to illustrate experiences of homophobia and to demonstrate their moral opposition to bigotry. That is a choice you could make if you thought it appropriate. I would respect that. Over the years, many of my colleagues have spoken compellingly about how a personal account or a tale of frailty or fallibility has helped to make a connection with a hard-to-reach child. To be a role model, they argued, teachers should show their vulnerabilities: that they are human, that they can get angry and make mistakes. Children can relate to that, I agree. But it is a fine balance.

Teachers should not share their private lives with their pupils in order to ingratiate themselves. Teachers who gossip, boast or share intimate details about their personal lives are likely to confuse the issue and are unlikely to gain long-term respect from their pupils. Don't try to be cool – you are their teacher, not their friend. As a young and inexperienced teacher this may be your first significant mistake. Being friendly with pupils is one thing; needing to make friends with pupils is quite another. Any teacher who feels the need to make friends with their pupils is unsuited to the role. They are quite possibly dangerous to children too. The more pupils and parents know about your private life, the more you give them an opportunity to judge it. Some people may manipulate or exploit that knowledge. They won't be judging you from a professional perspective, because they don't have one; they aren't teachers. They will be judging you from a personal or moral perspective. They are entitled to that viewpoint, but it may be very different from yours.

Sometimes you will make mistakes out of the best of intentions. You will push at boundaries in order to make a connection with a hard-to-reach child – one of those apparent 'misfits' who seems incapable of achieving even the smallest task or establishing the most fleeting of friendships. You may try too hard to keep an unbiddable pupil onside. Don't worry too much about making mistakes, as long as you learn from them.

'Mr Newland, would you like to come to my birthday party on Sunday?'

I had only been a teacher for a couple of years when a 6-year-old girl from my class of Year 2s (I will call her Tanya) ran up to me with a couple of friends in tow while I was doing playground duty.

'Mr Newland! Mr Newland! Would you like to come to my birthday party on Sunday?' she said excitedly, looking up at me with eyes full of hope.

'Oh, thank you very much, Tanya,' I replied with faux enthusiasm. 'What a lovely invitation. That's very kind …' She and her friends ran off before the conversation got any further. I thought no more about it. If you are a primary school teacher you will get invitations like this almost every day of the week.

Next day, however, in came a handwritten note from Tanya's mum: 'Tanya's birthday party is at 4 o'clock on Sunday. If you're not busy, you're very welcome!' At first I thought, Oh blimey! That's the last the thing I want to do on my weekend. But then I mused: I am a new, idealistic teacher. I want the kids, the parents and the community to see me as approachable, amenable and committed – prepared to go the extra mile for them. I resolved that it wouldn't hurt for me to go along for half an hour and show my face.

On the Saturday, it occurred to me not to turn up to a child's birthday party empty-handed. I decided to take Tanya a book as a birthday gift, so I went to my local bookshop. As I was browsing, an elderly woman started chatting to me. She turned out to be a retired teacher and asked me about the book I had chosen.

'That's for a pupil of yours?' she asked with raised eyebrows.

'Yes,' I said.

'And you're going to her birthday party?'

'Yes,' I shrugged, innocently.

She gently wagged her finger: 'Don't do it.'

'Why not?' I asked. 'What's wrong with a bit of jelly and blancmange for half an hour?'

'You're crossing a boundary,' she warned. 'You're not their friend, you're their teacher.'

Oh no! I thought. What I am going to do now? I had already told the child I was going. I worried about it overnight, but I did go there the next day – a sprawling housing estate in East London. I remember quite clearly knocking at Tanya's house – a glass-panelled front door and net curtains draped behind it. I could soon see Tanya running up the hallway. She opened the door in her party dress all excited to see me.

'I'm awfully sorry, love! I can't stop,' I said before she could say a word. 'Here's a little reading book for your birthday. Have a lovely party. I'll see you in school tomorrow!' And off I went.

I have reflected on this incident many times over the years and concluded that I was glad I took the elderly woman's advice. If I had have gone to that party – 'crossed a boundary' as she put it – doubtless there would have been other 6-year-old children from my class present. They might have seen me and thought: why didn't he come to my birthday party? There may have been other parents there too. Some of them might have thought: I wonder what his relationship is with Tanya's mother that he comes round here at 4 o'clock on a Sunday afternoon? It is impossible to manage other people's thoughts. I am thankful that I chose to be cautious, especially as a young and inexperienced teacher.

That is not to say that I didn't make different judgements later in my career when I was a more mature and experienced teacher, because I did – especially as a head teacher. On a number of occasions, I went to birthdays, barbecues, christenings, weddings and funerals. I gave the eulogy at two funerals. As a teacher, people see you as a very important member of the community, especially as a head – a position I hope you will all go on to take up one day. They will invite you to important family occasions because they want to acknowledge and recognise your contribution to their child's life. To be honest, most times you will make up an excuse and gracefully decline the offer, but sometimes there will be circumstances where you will judge it fitting and appropriate to accept. Indeed, I felt it an honour to be invited to a wedding and an even greater honour to be asked to give a eulogy. But it is often a fine judgement that you, as a professional person, are trusted to make.

I didn't accept that invitation because I wanted to make friends with 6-year-olds. I accepted it out of the best of intentions. I wanted to motivate the child. At that stage in my career, it was probably a mistake. But I don't regret making mistakes – they are character forming.

Keeping a balance in your life

The last three decades have seen a very mixed picture as far as teacher recruitment is concerned. Throughout the 1980s and well into the late 1990s, it was very difficult to recruit teachers to inner-city areas. That changed for a while, particularly after the New Labour government in 1997 made teaching a more attractive graduate career, but, sadly, the optimism didn't last. While there are still some issues around recruitment, a much bigger concern now is retention. After five years in the job, the churn rate of teachers is enormous – sometimes reaching 25 or even 30 per cent.[39] The reasons often relate to a sense of being overwhelmed: by workload, by stress and the relentless pressure to perform at full pelt, and by the fear of an accountability system that is judgemental and unforgiving rather than diagnostic and developmental. Many complain about how the job takes over their lives in ways they resent, impacting on their family and social life and damaging their emotional and psychological well-being. I counsel new teachers to find ways to protect their social and personal lives. I advise them – as I advise you – to get into routines around the time they leave school at the end of the working day, the time they go to bed during the school week, and about eating moderate amounts of healthy, nutritious food and drinking non-excessive levels of alcohol.

Don't think that staying up all hours of the night to finish your planning and preparation will make you heroic to your colleagues or your pupils – it won't. If you collapse from exhaustion because you haven't had a good night's sleep for weeks on end, your mentor, head of department or head teacher may shower you with faint praise or dutiful words of sympathy, and then get on the phone to an agency and have a supply teacher substituting you before you can say 'Jack Robinson'. No one is indispensable. Learn to plan and work efficiently during the time you devote to working and jealously protect the time you set aside for nurturing relationships with family and friends. Keep up your hobbies and sporting pastimes; they will relax and distract you from the pressures of work.

Yes, you will need to work hard, especially for the first few years while you are learning to imbibe practices that will eventually become routine and second nature. Yes, you will need to work some part of your weekend to feel prepared and confident and to minimise those feelings of utter dread on a Sunday night when the working week looms. But any idea that you must devote your whole life to teaching like some Trappist monk is a dangerous delusion, and one you will live to regret. It may also result in you feeling bitterness and resentment towards your school, your colleagues and the pupils you teach. Your health and well-being is a moral issue too.

39 Catherine Lough, Third of Teachers Leaving the Profession Within Five Years, *TES* (25 June 2020). Available at: https://www.tes.com/news/recruitment-third-teachers-leaving-profession-within-5-years.

If you are feeling overwhelmed by the planning, preparation or paperwork required by your job, talk to your mentor, head of department or head teacher. They will (hopefully) be sympathetic, and if you are lucky, they will have the resources and the capacity to relieve some of the pressures on you. But you may need to be calmly and professionally assertive. If they do not offer practical support that enables you to better manage your workload, they are failing you. Remember: although they may be under pressure themselves, the last thing they want is to lose a good teacher. It is in everyone's interests that you are supported to manage your workload and stress levels. If your school managers don't come up with concrete solutions, then be prepared to make some sensible proposals of your own. Talk to friends and colleagues in the staffroom about what help you need. Talk to your union representative if you are a member of one. It doesn't have to turn into a grievance case. Unions are there to help and advise. Don't suffer alone.

Sometimes, the threats to your work–life balance can come from unexpected quarters. For example, if you happen to live within the locality of the school where you work, it is perfectly reasonable to enjoy a few drinks in the local pub, even on a Sunday evening or a mid-week school night. Don't become paranoid by the prospect of parents seeing you while you are socialising. Be confident that you are not answerable to them for your lifestyle. As long as you are not doing anything illegal, you are at liberty to do whatever you want. Of course, that won't stop some people from trying to intrude on your private life and impose their morality on you. Some will. If a parent approaches you in a pub – as happened to me once – and starts to enquire about how their child is getting on in school, quickly indicate that the conversation should continue somewhere more suitable. I very politely suggested that they should make an appointment to come into school so we could discuss the matter in more detail. The pub was obviously not the right place to discuss such a thing. It was also entirely inappropriate for me as this was in my private life and social time. I was not on duty twenty-four hours a day and I was not going to make myself available just because a parent thought they could grab a moment convenient to them. Occasionally, parents need a respectful reminder.

'I saw you in the Rose and Crown on Saturday night!'

When I was a young teacher, I was in the playground one Monday morning waiting for the kids to line up. The father of a child in my class (I will call him Mr Robinson) approached me. 'I saw you in the Rose and Crown [a pub within a mile of the school] on Saturday night!' he said with a smirk. Oh my days, I thought. I knew what he was referring to: I had been with a group of friends to celebrate one of them getting a new job. We ended up having quite a lot to drink, and although we weren't misbehaving, we did end up being rather loud, boisterous and celebratory. (OK, we were drunk!)

'Oh no! Did you see me?' I replied rather sheepishly, laughing it off.

'Yeah, I did!' he said. 'You looked like you were having a good time!' with an ironic tone.

'We were,' I explained. 'It was a friend's celebration. He'd got a new job ... Yeah, it was a good night!'

'It looked like it,' he said, sounding disapproving. 'I don't know how you can come into school to teach after a night like that,' he said, shaking his head.

'Well, I must admit I had a bit of a hangover yesterday, but I'm fine today, thank you.' But he wasn't going to let it go.

'Huh! I hope you're not starting with a lesson telling the kids how to behave in public?'

At that point, I realised I needed to confront the underlying issue he was addressing – and confusing. 'Excuse me, Mr Robinson,' I said politely. 'Has your child ever seen me drink alcohol? The answer to that is no. Have I ever been drunk in school? No. Have I ever advocated drinking alcohol to your child or anyone in school? No. So, what you saw on Saturday night was my private life and, with the greatest respect to you, what I do in my private life is none of your business.'

Sometimes you might need to say something like this to people who confuse their moral standards with your ethical ones. Be prepared to defend your lifestyle, your morality and especially your right to a private life. If you can't defend it, then maybe you should consider changing it.

Occasionally, parents make moral judgements believing that they necessarily have ethical implications. I accept that I was in a public place and a parent saw me behaving in a way that he disapproved of. He has a right to judge me from his own moral standards. That is his privilege. But it is not his privilege to make it an ethical – that is, a professional – judgement about me. I have a moral right to expect that my private life will not be violated, even in a public place. If that were not the case, the notion of privacy would be turned on its head. You have a right to privacy even in public. For example, the idea that someone could legitimately gossip about you from an overheard conversation in a coffee bar would be immoral in itself. If someone were to film my private conversations in a restaurant on their mobile phone and then broadcast it on YouTube or Facebook that would be outrageous to any right-thinking person.

However, as celebrities and other famous people know very well, we have no legal right to privacy in a public place, which is why paparazzi can lawfully take pictures of famous people drunkenly emerging from nightclubs or relaxing half-naked on beaches. We still consider these as private activities, even though they take place in public. Legally, we can't prevent someone intruding into our private life when we are in a public place. Morally, we know that our privacy has been violated.

It is very important that young teachers resist the notion that their *public-private* behaviour suddenly has to become saint-like. You are entering a demanding job and you will need to have a healthy social life. If you don't, you may find yourself burned out after four or five years – overwhelmed by the workload and the burden of responsibility. What is and should be under scrutiny is your *public-professional* behaviour – that is, the behaviour that parents and others have a legitimate right to expect to be commendable and exemplary. However, you should be cognisant of any behaviour in public that might potentially undermine your position as a teacher or damage the reputation of the school, both of which you have a professional duty to regard.

The moral agency of a teacher is based on two things: firstly, the exacting ethical standards that teachers must live up to and, secondly, being a moral educator and exemplar. Teaching cannot be separated from its moral purpose. It is fundamentally an ethical and a moral activity, not just a technical one. It is both an endeavour to disseminate knowledge and an enterprise to instil morality.

This is not to contradict what I have said above. In the UK and other Western liberal democracies, we recognise an individual's right to have a private life in which they are not morally accountable to others. You may wish to abdicate this right or willingly have it constrained by an employment contract. When working at a religiously conservative school, the governors may take a very dim view of drinking alcohol or having a sexually promiscuous lifestyle (if this has become common knowledge). Remember that the Teachers' Standards requires teachers to 'uphold public trust in the profession and maintain high standards of ethics and behaviour, within and outside school'. If you sign a contract with an employer that includes a phrase like: 'You must not behave in ways that brings the school into disrepute', then you are complying with the school's moral standards as well as their ethical ones. That may suit some people. You must decide whether or not it suits you.

The moral implications of everyday classroom practice

Almost everything a teacher does has moral implications. As a profession, teaching is perhaps unique in that its practitioners usually engage with their clients in groups rather than as individuals. This presents an additional challenge to perceived notions of fairness, especially when fairness is sometimes defined as not treating everyone the same.[40] In the assessment of pupils' work, for example, can an A for effort be the same as an A for a criterion-referenced achievement? Awards that are emotionally or subjectively informed are one thing, whereas ability measured against objectively defined norms are quite another.

The age-old practice of requiring pupils to raise their hands in class to answer questions may seem like an obvious technique. From a management and organisational point of view, it establishes order and turn-taking, it facilitates discussion and listening, it promotes a disciplined classroom and it gives the teacher an opportunity to assess aspects of comprehension. From a moral point of view, it also regulates turn-taking and promotes fairness, mutual respect, self-control and patience.[41] However, in the hands of a thoughtless and insensitive teacher, it may well generate an atmosphere of competition, favouritism and prejudice.

It is very hard for any teacher, let alone a new or inexperienced one, to be unaffected by the behaviour of those children who are more vocal or more confident or those not yet versed in 'polite' discourse and manners. Misbehaving pupils usually get more attention, negative though that may be. Needy pupils get more attention, indulgent though that may be. Pupils with special needs who are integrated into mainstream classes get more attention, professionally justified though that may be. Such judgements are not always apparent to all observers. This leads to uncomfortable decisions, which every teacher must make, about how much attention well-behaved, self-motivated mainstream pupils get when a teacher's focus is being pulled, directed or targeted elsewhere. The answer is usually less.

40 See the section on moral foundations at the beginning of this chapter.

41 See Campbell, *The Ethical Teacher*, ch. 3.

The morality of managing children's behaviour

Managing challenging behaviour is, of course, a moral issue. We recognise moral development in children (as well as in colleagues) when they begin to display a diminishing preference for moral indifference or a willingness to refrain from certain behaviours through fear of the consequences. Or, even better, when children begin to demonstrate self-control, when they feel shame for having acted badly or when they feel virtuous for having acted well. All behaviour is interpreted subjectively, though, and quite rightly.

The school rules apply to everybody; that is the 'equality' part of the equation. But every teacher knows those rules are applied differentially in order to achieve an appropriate and morally just outcome for the individual; that is the 'equity' side of it. You will handle some children with kid gloves, giving them a degree of leeway that you would not afford to others. With other children, you will get to know that any deviation from their norm requires you to come down on them like a tonne of bricks. It may be for the very same infringement that you let go with others. However, you have developed a different set of expectations for that particular child, which they know intuitively themselves, so their transgression needs to be nipped in the bud.

This is not unfair. It is your professional judgement made with an awareness of the ethical issues you have taken into account. One virtue is in tension with another, but you have an ethical justification for differential treatment. The outcome, hopefully, is moral development for the child and a greater practical wisdom on your part. As Aristotle observed in one of history's great maxims on morality (although I cruelly paraphrase him): as much injustice may come from treating unequals equally, as from treating equals unequally.[42]

42 'Now, it is the common opinion, that justice is a certain equality; and in this point all the philosophers are agreed when they treat of morals: for they say what is just, and to whom; and that equals ought to receive equal: but we should know how we are to determine what things are equal and what unequal; and in this there is some difficulty': Aristotle, *Politics: A Treatise on Government*, tr. William Ellis (London: J.M. Dent & Sons, 1912), Book III, Ch. 8. Available at: http://www.gutenberg.org/ebooks/6762.

R-E-S-P-E-C-T

Aretha Franklin was right when she said she needed 'a little respect'. Children need it, teachers need it, we all need it. Teachers are constantly trying to instil respect in pupils, both the self-respect that comes with being a morally strong person as well as the respect that we must all show other people. We cannot expect it from others unless it is demonstrably mutual. It goes without saying, therefore, that teachers must be exemplary role models, generously demonstrating respectful language and behaviour towards pupils. This does not mean that teachers cannot get annoyed or even angry at times. It is difficult to model respect when you are on the receiving end of ridicule, mockery or contempt.

Don't think that you have to tolerate disrespect from pupils; indeed, you must not. You should correct pupils' disrespectful language and behaviour whenever it occurs. Failure to do so is an abdication of your moral responsibility. Of course, you will need to pick your moment – some battles won't be won on the battlefield of your choosing. Confronting a pupil's disrespect when he or she is still pumped up with anger or false bravado may not be the best time to get them to reflect on their behaviour, especially if they are in front of a group of their peers. Sometimes, of course, the level of disrespect shown can be so outrageous – such as foul language or obnoxious behaviour – that it needs to be dealt with there and then. Pick your battles wisely.

In recent years, respect seems to be an example of a word (like 'tolerance' discussed earlier) where connotations have shifted. In popular culture, especially rap lyrics and social media memes, respect has become a much more abstract concept; it is used more frequently as a weapon of intimidation than as a mark of recognition or validation. As teachers, we need to be alert to the tables being turned on our moral standards. We must resist the reinterpretation of concepts such as respect when this undermines the true meaning of appreciation, admiration and esteem. When it is being deployed to harass, menace or subjugate, this needs to be challenged.

I disagree with those who say: 'You must earn the respect of pupils before you can expect it in return.' I think this is a profoundly misguided notion. Respect is a given. It is a basic human right as well as a fundamental value – and all the more powerful when it is proffered reciprocally. I try to show respect to everyone even in the most challenging of emotional circumstances. I expect it from everyone too – including angry, disaffected and alienated pupils and parents. When children get angry they will display disrespectful language and behaviour, but, as suggested earlier, you must make it your business to correct it. You must educate them to understand that it is legitimate to feel emotions like anger, disaffection and alienation, but these must be separated from expressions of disrespect.

Obviously, you should try to avoid emotional escalation, but correcting a pupil's impudence, impertinence or rudeness does not mean you are being disrespectful to them, even if you show annoyance or anger in your tone of voice when doing so. Be clear: teachers have authority, which is based on the important idea they are special people who have been given the right to decide what is correct and to apply and enforce rules widely thought to be in the common interest. While pupils have equal moral standing with you, they do not have equal authority. You have more authority than they do as a necessary part of your role. You have specialist skills and knowledge that they don't. You have qualifications that they don't. You accept responsibilities that they do not have to shoulder. Your role requires you to exert the authority invested in you by law, for which you are accountable to other appropriate persons and authorities – but not to your pupils. You are morally accountable to your pupils but you are not legally or ethically accountable to them.

This is not to say that you are never accountable to your pupils. Of course, you are – quite often as it happens. Every time they walk into the classroom and ask: 'What are we going to do today, Miss?' or 'Sir, you've forgotten to mark my homework,' you are answerable to them. Every time a parent comes in and asks: 'Can you tell me how my child is getting on with their reading, please?' or 'My child doesn't want to come to school. Is there something going on that I don't know about?' you are answerable to them. This is not the same as being accountable to appropriate persons and authorities for your competence and performance, in the way you are to your manager (such as your head of department or head teacher), your employer (the school governors or the local authority) or the government agency tasked to inspect the quality of your teaching (Ofsted).

Challenge your pupils whenever they fail to show respect to you as a human being. Challenge them when they fail to show respect to you as a teacher too. Challenge them when they fail to show respect to others. Don't think you have to earn respect – you don't. Respect is a fundamental value and a basic human right. Mutual respect is a fundamental duty we have towards each other. Don't let the word be used as a weapon against you.

The curriculum as morality

Curriculum choices are ethical decisions that have moral implications. These become apparent every time there is a debate about, for example, what literary texts should be studied in the English literature curriculum or what history we should teach or leave out. Should the novels, plays or textbooks children read reflect a national canon or an international perspective? Should there be a balance of playwrights and historians, female and male, white and minority ethnic? Should we include texts that reflect wide cultural diversity? Should they deal with contentious and controversial topics? Should they include Nabokov's *Lolita* or Shakespeare's *The Merchant of Venice*?

It is not just subjects like English literature or history that must grapple with moral dilemmas. Imagine a science department that offered intelligent design as part of its curriculum. Imagine a history department that included Holocaust denial as a legitimate form of historical analysis. I am not saying that schools shouldn't educate their pupils about controversial topics under any circumstances. But the context in which such teaching takes place – the age, maturity and intellectual capacity of the pupils, the levels of analysis and criticism – are all relevant factors with ethical and moral implications.

I met a teacher recently who said she was uncomfortable about teaching *Romeo and Juliet* to a pupil whose recent mental health had led her to consider committing suicide. I also met another young woman, a conservative Muslim, who found teaching the same play to be both a liberating and an enlightening experience for the teenage girls she taught at her school, as some of them were grappling with the issues raised by arranged and forced marriages in their community.

I greatly value mutual respect, tolerance and free speech as fundamental values (with the caveats I have pointed out about abuse, threats and incitement). However, I am not advocating moral relativism where everyone is assumed to have a justifiable moral standpoint by virtue of having a different opinion. Once again, we do not have to respect ideas. We have to respect people.

Moral dilemmas in teaching – either curriculum subjects or pastoral matters – present themselves in three different ways: (1) as situations where two or more courses of moral action (virtues) are in conflict with each other and each has the potential to be good, (2) as situations where you are compelled to choose between equally undesirable alternatives, or (3) as situations where whatever avenue you choose, your actions will involve doing what is partly wrong in order to do what is generally right.

Discuss and reflect

Use the three points above to assess what moral considerations might apply in trying to resolve these pastoral dilemmas:

- You see a Year 12 (17-year-old) pupil on the bus. You can see from where you are sitting that he/she is viewing pornography on a mobile phone.

- Parents with conservative religious beliefs ask for a private meeting with you. They tell you that they forbid you to discuss homosexuality in the presence of their Year 11 (16-year-old) son/daughter.
- Two colleagues appear in the staffroom on Monday morning. One is wearing a lapel badge for Extinction Rebellion and the other has one that says: 'Choose Life'.

When navigating delicate areas, and distinguishing the moral from the ethical, you might find it useful to ask yourself the following questions:

- What are the consequences, both short and long term, for me and others in allowing morally or ethically ambiguous action?
- Do the benefits of the action outweigh the possible harmful effects?
- Are all the relevant parties being consistent with their own past actions and beliefs?
- Are they responding to the needs of others as human beings with feelings?[43]

Morality requires us to subscribe to moral standards and believe them to be justified. Not all moral standards can be justified, especially those that cannot be supported by evidence or facts. I am an advocate of pluralism, where diverse moral positions are voiced, positions are laid bare, challenged and interrogated, and strengths and weaknesses are duly exposed. I am not an advocate of moral relativism. Rational processes that test moral standards serve the purpose of both proponents and opponents: arguments are scrutinised and honed and the intellectual blade is kept sharp. Of course, teaching based on evidence and fact is in a separate category to teaching based on opinions and speculative theories. Teachers do not have to consider the moral implications of teaching facts – there aren't any. Facts are amoral. Facts are often uncomfortable but they are verifiably true.

43 For more on this see Campbell, *The Ethical Teacher* and Carr, *Professionalism and Ethics in Teaching*.

Dress codes and other bodily adornments – a moral issue?

Today, most teachers, especially in secondary schools, look like they are off to work in the offices of a corporate law firm. Now, if a teacher turned up to school looking like I did – a leftover from the Summer of Love or a reject from a now-defunct conscripted Central European army – they would be told in no uncertain terms to go home and change. New and inexperienced teachers might not consider what they wear to be an issue. However, a colleague of mine puts her sage advice to trainees about dress code very succinctly: 'If you can see up it, down it or through it – change it!'

'You're not going out dressed like that, are you?'

Is there a teenager in the land who has never been asked that question by their parents? My own parents asked it of me regularly in the 1970s when I was deluded enough to think that dressing like a hippie looked cool. By the 1980s, when the height of fashion was army surplus clothing, I thought that sourcing my clothes from trendy market stalls in Camden Town was the thing to do. Then came the 1990s and I dressed like a yuppy: smart white Oxford-style shirts with open collars, sharply pressed charcoal grey trousers held up by flashy red braces. I wore what was fashionable, and nobody questioned my right to do so.

Little more than a decade ago, a teacher wearing a tattoo – even a non-visible one – would have been considered a social deviant. Now it seems that almost everyone under the age of 30 has a tattoo. I have had many discussions with my audiences about this topic and invariably they insist that having a tattoo or a body piercing, even when they are visible on the face and neck, has no ethical or moral implications. However, most people readily accept that if an employer were to object or request for it to be covered, they would try to oblige.

When I have challenged trainees about their view on tattoos, I have had some interesting responses. For example, I have asked them to consider how they might feel if their own teenage child came home wanting a tattoo or a piercing. Most dismissed the question as having no moral issue for them. Occasionally, I test the proposition further by suggesting there may be an overlapping ethical dimension:

- Imagine … you are charged with a serious criminal offence. You are about to appear in court in front of a jury. The barrister representing you appears wearing tattoos and face piercings. Are you comfortable that this person will be your advocate?

- Imagine … you are lying on a hospital bed waiting for an urgent and critical procedure. The surgeon tasked to perform it arrives to brief you about the operation. She is sporting a sweatshirt, jogging bottoms and trainers. Has her appearance affected your confidence in her?

At one of my lectures an audience member challenged me by asking if I would put a question on tattoos to an audience of Maoris or Pacific Islanders in a country like New Zealand. I thought that was a brilliant response. But perhaps that is the point: unless you live in New Zealand or the Pacific Islands (or anywhere else where tattoos are a well-respected tradition), then wearing body art is a potential ethical issue. Why? Because it might have an impact on the trust engendered in the people around you, particularly when issues of trust are critical, like being the patient of a surgeon, the client of a barrister or the pupil of a teacher.

If you have given your clients a reason to question that implicit trust on the grounds that you are willing to flout cultural norms, such as appropriate codes of dress or appearance, then you may have given them reason to doubt other matters on which that trust depends. What else, from their point of view, are you prepared to flout? Propriety? Equity? Confidentiality? In a liberal democracy, you have the freedom to dress as you wish, but you must be prepared to shoulder the consequences of your choices, which may include having to work much harder to regain trust that has been jeopardised or lost.

Sexual relationships

In many jobs where people work long hours in an intense or highly charged atmosphere, group social activities are often an overspill from work life. This can be highly desirable socially and beneficial to business interests – it builds *esprit de corps* and work satisfaction. It is inevitable that some social contact will develop into personal and sexual relationships. You might think that sex is a private matter and that your manager (a head teacher in your case) or employer (in the form of school governors) has no remit to exert any constraints, moral or otherwise, on your romantic relationships.

As I advised earlier: read your employment contract. It may say something along the lines of 'do not bring the school into disrepute', where the definition of disrepute may be very much in the hands of the employer. Also find out if the school has its own code of conduct – as many do – which might include something about sexual relationships with colleagues, governors and parents.

Discuss and reflect

As an exercise in distinguishing moral (private) from ethical (professional) considerations, discuss the implications of a teacher having a sexual relationship with:

- A teaching colleague of the same rank.
- A colleague in the senior leadership team.
- A colleague who is married.
- A school governor.
- A parent of a child not in your class.
- A parent of a child who is no longer attending the school.

Whatever your moral position on these scenarios, aim to explore whether your ethical position is, in fact, a cover for a conservative or even reactionary moral stance. For example, the ethical implications of having a relationship with the parent of a child you teach are obvious. However, they should not necessarily be conflated with the effects of having a relationship with a parent whose child you do not teach or who has since left the school. In a free society that values personal and individual liberty, ethical considerations should weigh differently from moral ones. Notions of 'professionalism' should not always trump the accidental possibilities of two people simply being attracted to each other and falling in love. The reality of life as it is actually lived sometimes intrudes on objective or ethical judgements – messy and inconsistent as they often are – and this can easily make us look like moral hypocrites, frauds and fools.

Chapter 6

BECOMING A TEACHER OF CHARACTER

Aristotle thought of character as 'the crown of the virtues' because it requires the development and acquisition of other virtues for it to emerge.[1] For him, magnanimity and the knowledge of honour – with all its links to how we nurture and protect our reputation – was evidence that a person had developed character. It is to these ideas that this final chapter is devoted.

However, as I am attempting to establish a number of important understandings for you as a new teacher in this book – particularly with the emergence of character – I want to reiterate what they are before proceeding.

Firstly, I want to help you develop confidence in the crucial area of accepting and exercising legal responsibility and authority. Doing so is a testing process – one that develops character – because it requires you not only to work within the law (which hopefully you will be naturally predisposed to do), but also to assume and interpret the legal duties and leadership roles required by the distinctive professional position of a teacher.

Secondly, I want to help you commit to an ethic that will underpin your professional identity. That is another test of your developing character, because imbibing an ethical code requires you to integrate two sets of idiosyncratic values: your personal values must fuse and harmonise with your professional values.

Thirdly, I want to help you discern and appreciate the nature of your own moral agency as a teacher. Making choices in life about what ought and ought not to be is not unique to teaching, but now your moral agency has the added dimension of civic power, authority and influence within a wider community – and that will challenge you in very particular ways that will mould aspects of your character.

Finally, and perhaps most importantly, I have been making the argument that the legal, ethical and moral trials you contend with when becoming a teacher represent a remarkable character-forming process – unique to the teaching profession. It is a rare undertaking, both for you and the pupils you teach, because the character you form in yourself and the character you form in your pupils is a reflection of your professional ethic and your moral purpose as a teacher.

1 Aristotle, *The Nicomachean Ethics*, Book IV, Ch. 3, 1124a.

What is character?

In order to thrive and grow as individuals, it is necessary for us all to strive for a worthwhile life both for ourselves and for others. We must do the same if we are to flourish as teachers. We must first seek a state of flourishing for ourselves and then, in doing so, achieve it for the children we teach. This may seem like a circular tautology but it is not. Think of the air steward's safety procedure direction: you need to put on your own oxygen mask before attempting to help others.

The desire to prosper is synonymous with the purpose of seeking a meaningful life and is fundamental to human existence. This is not about just trying to be 'happy', but about developing your character and fulfilling your potential, and for that to have impact on others – a state of being that Aristotle called *eudaimonia*. This classical idea has regained credence and even political traction in the UK in recent years, where even the Office for National Statistics now measures 'well-being'. Many schools are now dedicated to the notion of explicitly teaching character.[2]

Character development is the emergence of personal traits which produce emotions and inform motivations that guide our conduct. It is not a paternalistic nurturing of conservative or reactionary values. It is not, nor should it be, a form of indoctrination or religious inculcation, although many of the moral foundations of character development derive from religious doctrine. Character development in teachers and the character education in children, while distinct, are both attempts to develop a set of universally acknowledged virtues and values that enable individuals to act in the right way and, ultimately, to do so autonomously and reflectively. This facility grows out of character-building experiences that are testing, onerous, gruelling, stretching, energising and inspiring.

My proposition, therefore, is that character can be formed by regular exposure to ideas and incidents that force us to make choices about doing the right thing, in the right way, at the right time, in the right measure. As I have tried to illustrate throughout this book (and will explore further in the appendices), searching and exacting experiences can be framed within a wide range of educative settings including exposure to demanding sport; the challenging but inspiring way that science, art, mathematics, music, literature and other areas of the curriculum are taught; and the manner in which school life and the school community itself is structured as a microcosm of civic society. All of these things develop character.[3]

2 All the main political parties in the UK are now committed to the teaching of character education in schools. Some school academy trusts have been established on the basis of teaching it, such as the University of Birmingham School in the West Midlands.

3 We cannot consider curriculum subjects in any extended detail in this book, but the matter of the extracurricular development of character is a topic we will return to, particularly in Appendix C on spiritual, moral, social and cultural education.

Direct and indirect ways of developing character

Over 2,000 years ago, Plato posed a relevant question for us: can virtue be taught? He knew that the question goes to the heart of what teachers are trying to do in developing character: to educate with what is taught and inculcate with what is caught. To form moral standards as part of character development, teachers teach and children learn using direct and indirect methods.

Direct methods include:

- Prescription – being told things that we cannot or ought not do. For professional people: the imposition of an ethical code of conduct, like the Teachers' Standards. For children: things like school rules and behaviour policies.
- Rewards for compliance – receiving honour and recognition, such as a verbal compliment, a pat on the back, a badge or even just extra playtime (recess) for being 'good'.
- Punishment for non-compliance – the corollary of the above: getting told off for being 'naughty'. For professional people: being reprimanded for dereliction of duty or non-compliance with standards, being suspended or dismissed from a job, being removed and struck off from a professional register. For children: being put on detention or excluded from school.

Indirect methods include:

- Modelling compliance – watching role models behave in exemplary ways.
- Modelling appropriate reactions – for teachers: ensuring that inappropriate professional conduct is disciplined; for children: ensuring that they see us praising good behaviour and admonishing bullies.

Through these direct and indirect methods, we – and the children – learn the habits that will help us subscribe and commit to moral standards that contribute to building character. To take this a step further, our role must cultivate:

- Moral commitment through moral enquiry and formation.
- An ability to discern justified moral standards and recognise where there are grounds for 'reasonable disagreement'.

- The ability to discern unjustified moral standards and discourage allegiance to them.[4]

However, if we allow ourselves – and the children – to commit to moral standards when they are not justified, or if we pretend that some moral standards do not have grounds for reasonable disagreement when they do, this is an abandonment of our own moral rationale. For an example of the first: if we encourage or allow children to believe in Holocaust denial – an idea that has no moral justification – then we have abandoned our moral rationale and our rationality. Historical evidence has proved it beyond reasonable disagreement. For an example of the second: if we encourage or allow children to think that there are no grounds for reasonable disagreement about the existence of the patriarchy or systemic racism, this is also a renunciation of our moral rationale and our rationality because, however compelling the arguments might be on one side or the other, there are clearly grounds for reasonable disagreement. To allow or encourage a disaggregation of rationale in teaching would be an attempt to indoctrinate children and to do their cognitive development real harm. Children, as well as adults, regularly ask the question 'why', especially when they are being asked to commit to or believe in something. We will need to be ready with a moral justification in our answers.

Some people have argued on the basis of research that teenagers go through a period of moral relativism as part of their growing up when they are constantly questioning received values.[5] Aristotelian-based character education has the potential to counter this opposition because it is universally applicable and not based on religious principles or paternalistic secular values (like nationalism). This is valuable in highly diverse and multicultural societies in Western Europe, North America, India, Australia and New Zealand and other nations where social cohesion may come under greater strain and potential threat.

'I love my son, Mr Newland! I love my son!'

One day when I was a head teacher, my deputy came into my office looking very upset. 'Can you deal with Richard, please, because I can't any more,' she said as the tears began to flow. I knew this was serious because she was not only the best teacher in the school but also the most experienced. If she couldn't manage the misbehaviour of a child in the school – and she invariably did so with genuine compassion and understanding – then no one could.

4 See Hand, *A Theory of Moral Education*, p. 77.

5 See Arthur et al., *Teaching Character and Virtue in Schools*, pp. 46–47.

Once she had composed herself she told me how, for some reason, Richard, a 9-year-old, could not be reasoned with. Throughout the whole day he had continually, by turns, interrupted her, contradicted her, ignored her, tormented her and sworn at her. She had spent part of lunchtime speaking to him sympathetically and trying to get to the bottom of the problem, but to no avail. He had continued in this vain throughout the afternoon, culminating in a salvo of four-lettered abuse and humiliation that contained most of the compendium of misogynist invective. I won't repeat the words he used, but I can guarantee that the most hardened trooper would have been shocked at the vocabulary and imagery.

I went outside and brought Richard into my office. I asked him whether he had used those words. He stood silent and sulky, refusing even to deny it. I asked him to apologise to his teacher. His continued silence was complemented only by an expression of insolence. I had no hesitation in deciding that I was going to exclude him and asked my school secretary to call his parents. At this point, Richard looked not only shocked but also terrified.

After leaving a message for his parents, I was surprised when his mother rang back to say that they would not wait for the end of the school day. She insisted that his father would leave work and take Richard home immediately. Richard's father was a banker in the City and held a very senior position in one of the country's best-known banks. The family was from West Africa and deeply religious. I knew his father had taken this very personally. I told Richard that his father would be coming in to take him home, at which point he burst into tears and began shaking.

When his father arrived, Richard started to cry again and begged his father's forgiveness. He silenced him instantly with a single command. I apologised to him for disturbing his work but he dismissed that immediately, apologising to me and asking for my forgiveness. At this point, he didn't even know what words his son had used, which, of course, I had to convey after a short explanatory preamble.

He turned to his son and told him, quite calmly at first, to get on to his knees and beg forgiveness, which Richard did. His father then told him to prostrate himself on the floor and do so again with a more remorseful tone. At this point, I felt uncomfortable and said this was not necessary, but his father insisted. When the boy seemed slow to do so, his father began beating him to the floor, shouting for his son to 'Beg! Beg! Beg forgiveness!' I could see that he was crying. I attempted to intervene, but he pushed me back with an outstretched arm, continuing to land strikes on his son's head, back and arms as he lay face down on the floor and shouting 'Beg! Beg! Beg forgiveness!' his voice breaking with emotion. Even now, I feel moved recalling the man's sense of deep shame and humiliation that he felt his son had brought on his family.

When I insisted that he stop beating his son or I would have no alternative but to call the police, he turned to me and shouted: 'You English people, you don't understand! You think I don't love my son? I love my son, Mr Newland!' the tears now welling up in his eyes. 'I love my son! That is why, when he does wrong, he must feel pain. Then he will learn the difference between right and wrong. When he is good, we love and reward him. When he does wrong, he must feel the pain that doing wrong brings with it. Where I come from, that is our way! But you English people, you don't understand that and you think that because I hit my son, I don't love him! I love my son, Mr Newland! I love my son!' At which point he totally broke down and wept, and I must admit that I nearly did too.

Discuss and reflect

Under certain circumstances, referred to as 'reasonable punishment', it is legal for a parent to smack their child in England, Wales and Northern Ireland (but not in Scotland).

- Are there grounds for reasonable disagreement in justifying the smacking of children?
- Are there grounds for reasonable disagreement with people who have fundamentally different values from your own, or should principles never be compromised?
- Is the ability to compromise a matter of character?

Values, virtues and character

Aristotle believed that in applying values and virtues to ethical and moral decisions, we often find challenging dilemmas and contradictions inherent within them. Consequently, there will be an element of intellectual and character-developing 'struggle' in synthesising our ethical and moral choices. Ultimately, this process leads to practical wisdom or *phronesis* – a development of character that can be evaluated from a moral point of view.

Character development is amenable to reasoning and coaching, so it can be taught and caught. It can be taught in the classroom with a syllabus and an accompanying awareness of appropriate descriptive vocabulary. Teachers must therefore cultivate the civic skills of reasoning, persuasive argument and rhetoric. Arguably, much more powerful is the way character can be caught. Principally this can be done by good teachers and good schools immersing children in a wide range of challenging social, moral, spiritual, cultural and sporting experiences that build character on a regular daily and weekly basis (see more in Appendix C).

However, there are many such values and virtues to be encouraged. How are we to distinguish those that are fundamental?

Plato's cardinal virtues

Plato described what are now often referred to by philosophers as the 'cardinal virtues': courage, moderation (or temperance), justice and wisdom. He wrote: 'For wisdom is chief and leader of the divine class of goods, and next follows temperance; and from the union of these two with courage springs justice, and fourth in the scale of virtue is courage.'[6]

Courage

When confronted by danger we become alert and tense in readiness to react, but rather than merely reacting, a virtuous person is self-possessed and takes command of his or her unruly responses. Some dangers (like physical threats) appear suddenly and precipitously; while others (like illness or bigotry) emerge or creep up on us. Courage involves summoning up the proper balance of tension and confidence. Too

6 Plato, *Laws*, tr. Benjamin Jowett (1871), Book I. Available at: https://www.gutenberg.org/files/1750/1750-h/1750-h.htm.

much courage can result in a rash response; too little can result in cowardice. There are going to be countless occasions in your career when finding the right balance of courage to confront threats will be necessary.[7]

Moderation

In a consumer-dominated world, we are so bombarded with advertising that it is often hard to moderate our craving for food, luxuries and exciting adventures. Insatiable desires that go unchecked can easily result in unhappiness and ill health. Learning to lead a life of balance between self-indulgence (too much) and self-denial (too little) is crucial for us all. It is also particularly relevant to the lifestyle of teachers, who try (and sometimes fail) to moderate the pressures of imposed (or self-imposed) workload, perfectionism or unchecked ambition, which may result in either arrogance or a gradual resentment and bitterness towards colleagues and children. Moderating our responses to children is a crucial virtue, especially when they say things we find provocative or insulting, or when they display moral standards that we are impelled to correct urgently.

Justice

Justice is the virtue that disposes us to give others what is due to them. Aristotle writes that justice for human beings is different than for other animals, for 'he alone has perception of good and evil, of just and unjust'.[8] This is a crucial virtue for teachers when dealing with conflict and its outcomes – defending and enforcing fairness, even-handedness, resolution and punishment. It is also crucial in the demonstration of wider civic virtues – like the defence of liberty, equality and tolerance – when they come under attack from children.

Wisdom

Like Plato, Aristotle considered wisdom to be the most important of the cardinal virtues because a person who can act in the right way, at the right time, in the right measure has mastered the ability to see, judge and act. *Phronesis* not only bestows an understanding of general civic knowledge and good judgement but also an ability to apply what is appropriate to each situation, challenging though each specific incident

7 You may wish to reflect on the story of Sarah, the little girl who told me she 'didn't like Jews' (in Chapter 4) and then consider the section in Appendix E on responding to challenging remarks.

8 Aristotle, *Politics*, Book I, Ch. II.

may be. Cicero initially translated *phronesis* as 'providential' (meaning foresight) which was further interpreted as 'prudential' (meaning prudence) and refers to the ability to appreciate the uniqueness and complexity of any given situation, and yet have appropriate awareness of the long-term risks and implications of your actions.

Wisdom is a virtue you will need to acquire when coping with individual pupils. When we deal with children lacking in prudence, we may categorise them as short-sighted, wasteful, negligent or thoughtless. We may also recognise children who are intelligent, but who distort that intelligence for personal gain through cunning, fraudulence, deceit or intolerance. That is not to say that those of us charged with the responsibility of being wise (like teachers) cannot be angry too – we can – but we must make emotion an ally of reason and thereby display passion.[9]

Thomas Aquinas (*c.*1225–1274) took the classification of virtuous character traits a stage further and added four social virtues that, in my view, are essential to the character of a good teacher: gentleness, truthfulness, wit and friendliness.

Gentleness

A gentle person finds the right balance between being hot-headed, prone to overreaction or perceiving slights on the one hand, and lacking spirit, being overly submissive, docile or meek, on the other. A gentle person – or a gentle teacher – can still get vexed, but about the right things, in the right way, at the right time, in the right measure.

Truthfulness

We need truthfulness in our relationships and in society or else the essential integrity and purpose of community breaks down. Truthfulness is a fundamental virtue for teachers because we are involved in the pursuit of knowledge and facts. Integrity as a teacher involves modelling forms of truthfulness, candour and authenticity, as well as the accuracy, validity, excellence and goodness inherent in the subject matter we are responsible for teaching. It is fascinating (at least to me) that we take part of our understanding of the virtue of truthfulness from the ancient Greek theatre, where they characterised the excess and deficiency of truthfulness in their depiction of two comic characters: *alazṓn*, the chubby boaster who pretends to be greater than he is, and

9 For more on the cardinal virtues, see Gregory R. Beabout, *Ethics: The Art of Character* (Glastonbury: Wooden Books, 2016), pp. 22–27.

eirôn, the wiry bean-pole who is understated and self-deprecating. The comedy of their excess on the one hand and deficiency on the other enables us to focus on the essential truthfulness which emerges from the drama.[10]

Wit

Everyone loves a witty teacher, especially when that teacher reflects the joke back on her or himself. Everyone hates a teacher who makes children the butt of tactless or wounding sarcasm or who cannot see the funny side of a child making harmless fun – sometimes at their expense. Aristotle summed up wit as a character virtue:

Those who carry humour to excess are thought to be vulgar buffoons, striving after humour at all costs, and aiming rather at raising a laugh than at saying what is becoming and at avoiding pain to the object of their fun; while those who can neither make a joke themselves nor put up with those who do are thought to be boorish and unpolished. But those who joke in a tasteful way are called ready-witted.[11]

Friendliness

Friendliness is a disposition that treats strangers as potential friends. It can show itself as extroversion or introversion. If friendliness is deficient, you may be found contentious or quarrelsome; if it is excessive, you may be seen as annoying, fawning or sycophantic. Teachers must be wary of excessive friendliness with their pupils for the reasons we have discussed. However, an appropriate and balanced level of friendliness represents a teacher demonstrating and modelling good character.

Friendships – in teaching and in life

Friendships are indispensable to human flourishing and to the development of character. As a teacher, you need to make good friends among your colleagues and, what is more, keep them. Your professional life will be immeasurably

10 This tradition of truth emerging through comedy from characters like *alazṓn* and *eirôn* has continued down through the ages to our own time, depicted by the likes of Laurel and Hardy, Abbot and Costello, Morecambe and Wise, French and Saunders and many others.

11 Aristotle, *The Nicomachean Ethics*, Book IV, Ch. 8, 1128a.

enriched and your character fortified by the friends you make and hold onto as a teacher. I have alluded elsewhere to the analogies of teaching with other professions – like acting and soldiering – where the experiences we undergo are deeply character-forming and consequently create very special friendships that abide on the basis of remarkable mutual understandings.

As a teacher, you will provide opportunities both in and outside of the classroom to enable children to make friends – and keep them. In his writings, Aristotle devoted more time to this virtue than to all the others, defining friendship as 'reciprocated goodwill'.[12] But like all virtues, it needs to be nourished in the right way, at the right time, in the right measure. Some friendships are utilitarian, in that they are about reciprocated goodwill for the purpose of a business partnership or a contract. Other friendships are for the sheer pleasure that it provides – sharing the delights of another's company, enjoying a hobby or pastime, or playing sport together.

A complete friendship, however, is one where people are attracted to each other's excellence, celebrating their friend's best features and desiring what is best for their well-being. Such friendships are always tested and stressed – that is what makes them complete – but they endure. Life as a teacher will offer you the opportunity for enduring friendships; treasure them and recognise their role in developing your character.

Categories of virtue

As I hope this book is now beginning to show, the most powerful acquisition that ultimately emerges from the building blocks of values and virtues is character itself, and this is where the role model status of teachers is brought into sharpest focus. Character is not something children are born with. It is a complex set of virtues that are acquired through the iteration of values – demonstrated, modelled and shaped by teachers and others (such as parents). Virtues are the qualities that help us to meet the challenges and struggles of life. They are not skills as such – they are universal values that help us all flourish – but they are made up of components of ability that help us to:

- See or identify the right thing to do at any given time.
- Feel the right emotions at the appropriate time.

12 Aristotle, *The Nicomachean Ethics*, Book VIII, Ch. 3, 1156a.

- Be motivated to do the right thing at the appropriate time.
- Do the right thing, in the right measure, at the appropriate time.

Virtues can be categorised as moral (e.g. courage, integrity, justice), performance (e.g. resilience, teamwork, leadership), civic (e.g. citizenship, civility, patriotism) and intellectual (e.g. curiosity, reasoning, analysis).[13] When these four virtues are brought together through the experiences to which we are exposed in life, work and school, they jostle for position and order. As they do so, a dialectical process of intellectual and emotional struggle for selection or dominance begins to distil as the emergence of 'good sense' and, ultimately, the formation of our character: the ability to do the right thing, at the right time, in the right way, in the right measure.

This process is especially critical when values and interests collide or come into conflict. For example, to act with virtue requires an individual to recognise the need for honesty. But the application of honesty may require some voluntary regulation or moderation if and when there is a conflict with other virtues, such as being kind, sensitive or sympathetic to another person's feelings or circumstances. We referred to examples of this kind earlier in the book when discussing how teachers differentiate their warnings, reprimands and punishments to children not only on the basis of equity but also sensitivity. This is an example of applying competing virtues in moderation. When my wife is getting ready to go out for the evening and asks me: 'How do I look?' my answer is always: 'You look lovely!' That is not because I don't want to be honest with my wife (although, of course, she usually does look lovely) but because I want to moderate the virtue of (complete) honesty with the virtue of kindness. (I can see I am digging a hole for myself here, so let's move swiftly on!)

In a professional context, the application, regulation or moderation of one virtue in relation to another becomes not just a matter of good sense but of practical wisdom – in other words, professional judgement imbued with a moral imperative. Professional people like teachers must become arbiters for the application of rules, consequences and virtues. The tensions in this balancing act will perhaps be most evident when people, perhaps like you, are training to be members of a profession or are in the early years of its induction.

According to recent research at Birmingham University's Jubilee Centre for Character and Virtues, student teachers and early career teachers describe their motivations to teach in virtue-based terms, such as wanting to be kind, honest, fair, creative and so on, and even to retain a sense of humour towards their pupils. But when they describe their own learning needs as new teachers, they will be much more pragmatic and are

13 For more on this, see Arthur et al., *Teaching Character and Virtue in Schools*, pp. 10–16. See also Appendix D for discussion activities on virtues and values that you can do with colleagues and children.

more likely to focus on the requirements necessary to meet the Teachers' Standards.[14] They depict their needs much more in terms of performance virtues, such as the need to persevere or to be conscientious, meticulous or resilient. While we may encourage our pupils to learn from their mistakes, our tolerance for making mistakes as a way of learning from them in our own professional practice is sadly not a virtue we necessarily encourage. However, a willingness to admit and learn from errors is in itself a healthy, realistic and eminently ethical attitude.

Humility

Pope Gregory the Great (*c.*540–604) saw humility as a key virtue. In my view, it is fundamental to being a good teacher, especially when you get into positions of senior responsibility. Every teacher at whatever level must demonstrate and model to pupils a balanced sense of perspective, both of their own individual achievements and their true importance to society. However, on the one hand they must avoid arrogance, conceit and pride, but on the other, not be overly timid and reserved.

Aristotle called this ability to balance humility *megalopsychia* – a greatness of soul – which has also been translated as magnanimity. Teachers should therefore, like the elders to whom Aristotle referred, carry themselves with a moderate but a proper sense of grandeur and gravitas. In modern times, the connotation of humility has taken on the meaning of treating others with respect and not exploiting power relations just because we have authority. The current Pope Francis has also commented on this virtue: 'Humility, far from being opposed to magnanimity, serves to temper it, because humility makes us recognise great gifts … in others.'[15]

14 James Arthur, Kristján Kristjánsson, Sandra Cooke, Emma Brown and David Carr, *The Good Teacher: Understanding Virtues in Practice. Research Report* (Birmingham: University of Birmingham Press and Jubilee Centre for Character and Virtues, 2015), pp. 16–26. Available at: https://www.jubileecentre.ac.uk/1568/projects/virtues-in-the-professions/the-good-teacher.

15 Quoted in Beabout, *Ethics: The Art of Character*, p. 31.

The character of a role model

I have tried to impress upon you many times throughout this book that society bestows on teachers a very special role. They are creators of an ethos – what the Greeks defined as 'the spirit of culture and community' manifested by 'honourable aspirations and attitudes'.[16] But teachers are also created by ethos. Your practice as a professional person, especially when it is with full cognisance of the responsibilities and characteristics I have described in these pages, means that ethos is a reciprocal and correlative process – you are both defined by it and you go on to be a definer of it.

When a pupil emulates you – as they will – they are not just admiring you or even copying your behaviour – as they will. They are actually engaging in a process of recognising and evaluating what character traits are present in you, which is the foundation of being a role model. But let's go back for a moment and explore the roots of this. When we are children and young people, we dream of achieving things in our future lives that we think will make us happy, like a satisfying career with a good salary or having lots of exciting experiences like travelling the world or becoming famous for something notable.

As we grow older (and I know this from personal experience) and look back as mature adults on what formed our lives, we will almost certainly not point to financial or even career success as formative experiences. We will point to the ordeals and struggles that forged our character. We hear this time and again from individuals who have achieved wealth and fame – like Oprah Winfrey, Sir Richard Branson, Bill Gates, J. K. Rowling, Lord (Alan) Sugar and Tina Turner. Their life stories (although I am not holding them up as moral exemplars) point to adversity – the struggle – that shaped their values and character, rather than the mere achievement of fame and fortune.

Something similar is also true in what people think and say about us once we are gone. We will almost certainly be remembered not for how good we were at our jobs, important though that may have been, but more for the kind of person we were – our character strengths. We may have been a carpenter or hairdresser, an accountant or fund manager, we may have efficiently managed hundreds of staff in an office or factory or performed brilliantly as a virtuoso barrister winning momentous test cases in the highest courts of the land, but successes such as these are what the American philosopher David Brooks calls 'résumé virtues' (as in, those virtues you would highlight in your curriculum vitae). They only go so far.

16 For some highly accessible material on Greek philosophy, see the BBC Radio 4 podcast series, *A History of Ideas*, particularly (in this case), *Philosopher Angie Hobbs on Beauty and Morality* (24 August 2018). Available at: https://www.bbc.co.uk/programmes/b04pc7w4.

By contrast, the things people think and say about us after we are dead – what Brooks calls 'eulogy virtues' – describe our character; that we were honest, faithful, true, modest, courageous, sympathetic, humane or capable of selfless love towards others. We all want to be known for the eulogy virtues, but our educational system generally prepares us much better for the résumé ones. We coach our children much more on how to build a good and successful career than how to build a good and resilient character. They are not mutually exclusive, of course, but we should ask ourselves how much time and effort we put into one side of the equation than the other.

As educationalists and mentors, our conversations with pupils are generally much more of the politicised kind rather than the moral. For example, we will confidently engage children in the importance of questions like: how to stand up for your rights; how to be confident about your identity; how to build your self-esteem; how to be proud of your history and background, your ethnicity and culture, your sexuality and so on, but much less about how to build meaningful relationships with one another: how to put ourselves in another's shoes; how to forgive; how to develop the qualities of mercy; how to love. These are all topics and conversations that are much less common between teachers and pupils, yet our human nature yearns for them.[17]

Successful people (like the ones listed on page 222) will often attribute their success to someone significant who redirected them or gave them a leg-up at a crucial point in their lives. It is remarkable how often that person turns out to be their teacher.[18] Likewise, if you read autobiographies of the rich, the famous and the high-achieving in professional, artistic and sporting fields, a teacher is frequently cited as the source of their inspiration, confidence or transformation. If you were to end your career knowing that you had transformed just one person's life for the better, never mind becoming successful or renowned, that in itself would be a legacy of which to be proud. As a teacher, you are in a role where you have the potential to have that influence every day with scores, if not hundreds, of young people.

'What did you do before you became a teacher?'

Me: What did you do before you became a teacher?

Trainee: I was an investment banker.

17 For more on the résumé and eulogy virtues, read David Brooks' fascinating book, *The Road to Character.*

18 See the heart-rending but utterly inspiring two-minute YouTube video of the former Arsenal and England footballer Ian Wright being reunited with his old primary school teacher, Sidney Pigden: https://www.youtube.com/watch?v=omPdemwaNzQ.

Me: Oh, really? Where?

Trainee: In the City. Merrill – the investment bankers.

Me: Oh, wow. That's quite a change!

Trainee: Yeah, a huge change. I had a very big salary … even bigger bonuses … flying to New York business class every couple of weeks … five-star hotels … all that.

Me: So what brought you to teaching maths in a secondary school in Plaistow? [A relatively poor part of East London.]

Trainee: I was sitting in a meeting one day at head office staring through the window. Outside I could see all these amazing skyscrapers – the Shard, the Gherkin, the Cheesegrater – and the dome of St Paul's Cathedral, and I thought: 'If I were to die tomorrow, what would anyone be able to say about me at my funeral?' I couldn't think of anything really. Nothing at all, except maybe that I was good at making money for people who were already very rich. I realised that nobody would be able to say a single good thing about me. That's when I thought: 'I'm going to be a teacher.'

Me: Any regrets?

Trainee: No, not for a single second.

This woman realised that a worthwhile life was much less about material happiness and much more about achieving something meaningful. Such a realisation comes through struggle – and as she readily acknowledged, most of her friends and family could not understand why she wanted to give up a huge salary and a privileged, even luxurious, lifestyle. She had to face down their incredulity and constant questioning. She often doubted herself too: first when she handed in her resignation letter to her disbelieving boss, then when she faced her first classroom full of noisy kids, and then again when they appeared not to give a toss about her meticulously planned and well-crafted lessons. But she continued to struggle. She needed to find out what was fundamentally worthwhile about her life.

I hope you will be fortunate enough to avoid too many misfortunes in your life – especially grievous ones – but a well-lived and purposeful life involves confronting adversity and testing your moral courage. As a teacher, you will often find that the job is a struggle. That is a good thing. It builds you and your character.

Struggling with opposition

In a classroom of challenging children, you will need to contend with their robust and sometimes resisting personalities. You will need to face down their sometimes persistent moral opposition and find the confidence and dignity to rise above their occasional ridicule. You are not going to be a good role model, let alone a good teacher, if you think that all you have to do is to be nice to children to win them over. There will be many occasions when you will have to confront problems. If a pupil is behaving in a destructive way, you cannot attain peace with them by appeasing them. Immediately, you will need to confront them with moral boundaries within which they cannot harm themselves or others. In the long term, you will need to attend to the underlying issues that are producing such destructive behaviours, some of which will be daunting, but you must act.

When children are in a classroom together, they have to contend not just with you but also with one another. They have to engage in the arts and skills of argument and persuasion that inform thinking and change minds – their own as well as others'. In other words, they have to tolerate one another, a virtue learned principally from your modelling and demonstration.[19] By contrast, the so-called discussions they see on the internet allow for the total abdication of responsibility for engaging in those arts and skills, resulting in coarse, ugly and offensive discourse that degrades and erodes human respect.

We need to teach children to move away from the shaming subculture that is so prevalent online and in the playground. In my view, this phenomenon has evolved out of 'honour culture' (which still holds sway in many parts of the world) where reacting vehemently and sometimes violently to a perceived insult, however slight, is part and parcel of maintaining dignity. It was very much part of British culture at one time too; you only have to read Shakespeare's plays for ample evidence of this. Duelling with swords and firearms were methods of resolving honour disputes before it finally fell out of favour in the mid-nineteenth century (even though it was made illegal much earlier).

Instead of honour culture we have to encourage greater subscription to 'dignity culture', where children and young people are encouraged not to take things personally but to develop the skills of rational argument and debate – character forming in itself. As we discussed earlier, we must discourage the idea that to offend someone with words is equivalent to inflicting physical harm, nor even, necessarily, an insult. If we grant feelings, especially highly sensitive feelings, an unassailable position in moral arguments then we quickly become irrational. We cannot have a rational argument when fuelled by emotion.

19 See Appendix A for more on tolerance as a fundamental value.

We must also teach children to challenge a range of associated phenomena that blunt their rational minds. Behaviours like:

- 'I know what you think!' – when we infer too much from what is assumed or crudely characterised to be another person's beliefs.
- Dog whistle politics – when someone can be accused of doing something morally unjustifiable, not based on evidence but on unsound assumptions about their beliefs.
- Catastrophising – believing that political or social issues can be given incontrovertible weight by invoking impending doom or disaster, unless we think or act in a particular way (*our* way).
- Labelling – when stereotypes take precedence over individuality. (This is not to say that stereotypes don't have a function – they do, often as a shorthand in discussion – but they should not be adopted as a modus operandi for thinking.)
- Dichotomising – when people are viewed only as being with us or against us, and we are forced into one camp or another with either the victim or the oppressor.[20]

We must alert children to the dangers of using moral blackmail to embolden irrational arguments.[21] Instead, we must give them confidence and social skills to talk to people with whom they don't agree – once again, a character-forming undertaking. We must train children to use sharper intellectual and rhetorical tools based on rationalism, not emotion. If we don't, we are allowing totalitarian thinking to occupy the intellectual and moral vacuum we have negligently produced. Schools and classrooms should be forums for encouraging an ethos of 'we' and not 'I'. Being a role model for this is a complex and contentious moral process, but a deeply worthwhile and formative one both for children and teachers. Struggle is a good thing. Relish it.

Moral heroes of great character

The idea that the dead watch over us occurs in many cultures. It suggests that it is beneficial to have moral and ethical heroes – that is, role models. We should let our heroes watch over us by having pictures of them on our walls, learning about

20 For more on this see Sacks, *Morality: Restoring the Common Good*, pp. 180–183.

21 See Appendix C for how a school debating society is a powerful way for developing the skills of making rational arguments.

what they gave to us and what they gave up for us, acquainting ourselves with their character and heroic deeds, their virtues as well as their vices.

When I go into schools, I delight in seeing classrooms dedicated to moral heroes like Dr Martin Luther King, Mother Teresa, Nelson Mandela and Sir Winston Churchill. I am reminded of the heroic stances they took, but I do not want to see these individuals (or anyone else) promoted to a personality cult. They were human beings with great character as well as significant flaws. Children need to know that Dr Martin Luther King was a philanderer, that Mother Teresa was criticised for financial impropriety and 'deathbed baptisms', that Nelson Mandela advocated violence to achieve his political goals and that Sir Winston Churchill made disparaging remarks about people of colour.

The humble backgrounds of people like Grace Darling, Anne Frank, Rosa Parks and Malala Yousafzai remind us that great moral heroism can also emerge from ordinary people who are not seeking fame or even public recognition – yet we are still given a sense of the greatness of character to which we can all aspire.

Discuss and reflect

- Make a list of your heroes and heroines – your role models – both alive and dead.
- Are they heroic because of their moral and ethical stance or because of their character traits?

'Today I walked in the footsteps of Anne Frank'

Give your pupils the chance to experience what some historians call 'historical ecstasy' – the opportunity to stand in the place where great people made speeches, rendered sacrifices, stood, fought and even died. Let them have the opportunity to be motivated and roused.

I once took a group of children to Amsterdam to visit the Anne Frank House after a term of reading her diary. During the visit, one child wrote in her journal: 'Today, as I climbed the stairs to the attic where Anne Frank had to hide from the Nazis, I felt I was walking in her footsteps.' We visited the housing estate in an Amsterdam suburb where Anne grew up and went to school before going into hiding. It was built in the 1930s to house German-Jewish refugees fleeing from the persecution of the Nazis.

It was a neighbourhood that these children from Hackney could easily identify with – high-density apartment blocks, convenience stores, off-licences selling cheap liquor, betting shops, launderettes and graffiti on the walls. Even the nearby school Anne had attended looked similar to theirs. One boy looked up at the apartment block where she lived and said: 'Anne Frank was really just like us, wasn't she, Sir?' Our lives can be moved and affected by the narrative of a person whom we feel we can relate to or emulate. That is called inspiration.

How schools build character

Teachers create social networks in schools that build virtues and, ultimately, character in children. At school, children get an education, they get protection, they get exercise and they get fed (if they stay to eat a school lunch), but they get so much more than these mere practical benefits. They also get social, emotional, psychological, physical and mental health benefits, from the one-to-one contact with peers and the group contact they have with significant others, such as teachers. These connections have a moral as well as an educational value.

It is not just about the immediate social networks either. They (and we) also derive benefit from being a bystander. A vivid analogy for this is the neighbourhoods where we live. Those of us who know our neighbours are likely to feel a much greater sense of community than those who don't. When we feel a sense of community, we know (from research as well as anecdote) that there are, for example, lower rates of crime because people are consciously and unconsciously looking out for each other. Likewise, when children go to school they have access to social networks that are both explicit and implicit. When a school builds social bonds and has a strong sense of community, bullying and fighting are rare.

If we are integrated into a wide range of social networks in our neighbourhoods (especially ones that reach out into the community, like sporting clubs, volunteering and civic institutions), we form bonds with other people, not just friendships but also tentative connections with those we don't know well, which is good for our personal health and well-being. We also make and strengthen the bonds of community, which is good for the social capital of society.

In recent decades, sociologists and economists have given much greater credence to the idea of social capital. While no society has eliminated the negative consequences of economic and financial inequity, the effects of wealth inequality are nowhere near as important as the inequality of social and cultural capital. A child who is born into a poor family in a community with high levels of social capital and strong social networks is infinitely better off than a child born to rich parents with weak levels of social capital and diffuse social networks.[22] A good example of this is partaking in team sports that develop social networks which, as we have seen, have character-building as well as social value. Playing a team sport like football, rugby, cricket or netball not only develops cardiovascular fitness and promotes good physical and mental health but also has obvious social value – it gets people together to have fun, share experiences and bond.

The social networks that schools nurture and promote have similar social capital benefits for participants. Furthermore, these networks provide social capital for 'bystanders'. When a community, like a school, does things together – like providing platforms for team sports or cultural events or actively building links with civic institutions – this generates associated social networks beyond the initial activity. Playing one sport can and does lead to playing another. Some people then go on to join a drama group or perform music in a band or orchestra, or dance and sing together for fun or performance, or take part in a myriad of other activities where they commune. This benefits even those who do not take part. It brings together parents who support their children, who then commune to support the school in other ways.

Everyone – participants and bystanders – feels the benefit of the social capital that has been created. They feel greater trust in their fellows – their fellow parents, their child's school and the community at large. They feel committed to their community and they identify with it. These regular social interactions produce behaviours that are interdependent: we behave well towards others because we want people to behave well towards us. This is one of the fundamental bases of moral and character-building behaviour – the idea that because we will meet again in the future, we need to build trust between us now.[23]

22 For more on this, see Robert Putnam, *Bowling Alone: The Collapse and Revival of American Community* (New York: Simon & Schuster, 2001).
23 This phenomenon is strongly evident in game theory, where it is called 'the shadow of the future'.

Gratitude as a character value

There is an apocryphal story of former US President John F. Kennedy visiting the NASA Space Center prior to the launch of one of the missions that ultimately led to the first successful moon landing. The president stopped and asked a man holding a broom what his job was. The man answered: 'Mr President, I'm helping to put a man on the moon.' Whether this story is true or merely a neat PR line, it is good to remember that everybody working in an organisation is involved in its mission to succeed, however apparently menial their role.

Try teaching in a dirty classroom where the cleaners have been slapdash or sloppy. Try getting children to concentrate when they are hungry because the kitchen staff have failed to provide appetising and nutritious food. Try teaching in a cold or poorly maintained school because the school janitor is feckless and unreliable.

Make sure you thank the members of staff who do their jobs diligently, who are there to support you and who add social capital to the community of the school. Make sure you train the kids to do the same. And yes, I mean *train* them. The training and practice of virtuous behaviour builds character in a child's personality.

If, as teachers, we neglect to promote social networks (through things like team sport or choirs), we are denying children much more than merely the opportunity to get some exercise or entertainment or the opportunity to learn how to form a rugby scrum or maintain a choral note. We are denying them the soft skills that will equip them for life as much as any exam qualifications will. Perhaps, most of all, we are restricting their social mobility because, when children do not interact with each other in teams and networks, they lack the social capital that equips them to be socially and (ultimately) economically mobile. A lack of social capital therefore results in the loss of social mobility, and this, astonishingly, is increasingly being lost in the UK and many other Western societies, where the greater emphasis on individualism in the last forty years has resulted in less, not more, social mobility.

When schools promote social networks, they build character and promote social mobility. When they don't, they exacerbate social inequality. When schools fail to provide networking opportunities, middle class parents will (almost always) succeed in compensating their children, by paying for them to join or attend the extracurricular activities that they know build character and strengthen social capital – football, rugby, cricket, hockey, tennis, sailing and rowing clubs, music, languages, acting, ballet lessons and so on. Schools therefore generate a 'we' not an 'I' society. Every generation of teachers, like every generation of young people, is at the forefront of fashioning a new 'we' – a re-evaluation and reconstruction of values. It is a 'we' that combats the appeal of individualism, that promotes social responsibility, that abjures exclusive tribalism and fragmented cultural identity, and that is socially inclusive, culturally and creatively heterogeneous and tolerant of challenge and diversity.

How, might you ask, with everything else teachers are expected to do, can we build character in our pupils, and in ourselves, which in turn builds social networks, restocks social capital and helps to build a new 'we' for this generation and the ones to come?

Spiritual, moral, social and cultural education[24]

A spiritual, moral, social and cultural education has been the friendly ghost of every education system since time immemorial, although, of course, it has rarely ever been called that. Ill-defined and implicit, it has comprised the elements of a fully rounded education that have been at the heart of every good school since Aristotle was a boy at Plato's Academy. A spiritual, moral, social and cultural education is not, in itself, a discrete subject, but it has been an overarching characteristic of all good academies, gymnasia and schools since people began thinking seriously about what a good education is – and that is thousands of years.

In the UK, a spiritual, moral, social and cultural education has been an explicit feature of the national curriculum since 1988. It is an attempt to provide a framework for teaching virtues and values. I think it is fair to say that most teachers' awareness of this area is often fairly low, focused as they are on subjects. Although that is not to say that spiritual, moral, social and cultural education doesn't go on in schools; it most certainly does – regularly, creatively and often extremely imaginatively.

What is lacking in most schools is an awareness of how this might consciously and systematically contribute to, firstly, the building of character and, secondly, a wider sense of civic patriotism – which, in my view, is essential for constructing modern identity. Some might (and do) say that the strength of a good spiritual, moral, social and cultural education is that it is not conscious or systematic, and that its power lies within its implicit, inherent and inferred nature. I largely agree with that (and it ties in with the idea that most of the really valuable things in education are caught rather than taught), but I think we are living in an age when the teaching of civic virtues and values through spiritual, moral, social and cultural education also needs a higher profile and a greater priority, not least because the identity of our modern society is in an extraordinary state of flux. If that means making some things more explicit, so be it.

24 See Appendix C for a list of activities and best practice for spiritual, moral, social and cultural education.

The Department for Education's guidance (for England) sets out a list of character-building requirements that a spiritual, moral, social and cultural education should provide. It should:

- enable students to develop their self-knowledge, self-esteem and self-confidence;
- enable students to distinguish right from wrong and to respect the civil and criminal law of England;
- encourage students to accept responsibility for their behaviour, show initiative, and to understand how they can contribute positively to the lives of those living and working in the locality of the school and to society more widely;
- enable students to acquire a broad general knowledge of and respect for public institutions and services in England;
- further tolerance and harmony between different cultural traditions by enabling students to acquire an appreciation for and respect for their own and other cultures;
- encourage respect for other people; and
- encourage respect for democracy and support for participation in the democratic processes, including respect for the basis on which the law is made and applied in England.[25]

What is to be applauded about the Department for Education and the relatively liberal way we manage our education system in the UK, is that each school is allowed to interpret teaching in this area in whatever way they think is appropriate to their local needs, taking into account the socio-economic circumstances, culture and background of their particular intake of pupils.[26]

For example, 'contributing positively to the lives of those living and working in the locality of the school' will naturally take on a slightly different form in a school located in an urban industrial setting compared to one in a rural farming community. For the most part, this requirement is an entreaty to provide an educational environment where the building of character through the teaching of values and virtues relating to spirituality, morality, society and culture is given the space to be nurtured and

25 Department for Education, *Promoting Fundamental British Values as Part of SMSC in Schools: Departmental Advice for Maintained Schools* (November 2014), p. 5. Available at: https://www.gov.uk/government/publications/promoting-fundamental-british-values-through-smsc.

26 See also the separate legislation requiring schools in England and Wales to provide acts of 'collective worship … of a broadly Christian character' from which parents have a right to exempt their children: see School Standards and Framework Act 1998. Available at: https://www.legislation.gov.uk/ukpga/1998/31/schedule/20.

inculcated. As we have seen, this is done not as a curriculum subject but as part of an implicit education based on the civic values considered fundamental to the flourishing of children in a diverse and plural but cohesive society.

Discuss and reflect

- What activities does your school currently offer that provides a spiritual, moral, social and cultural education?
- Does your school teach character, values or civic patriotism in any explicit way? If so, how?
- Are these, in your view, better caught than taught?

In Appendix C you will find many examples of activities, some of which you may be familiar with from your own school. I offer them for two reasons: firstly, as examples that contribute to the teaching of not just character but also a conscious explicit notion of civic patriotism and, secondly, in the hope that you, as a new teacher, will be inspired and take responsibility for initiating some activities in your own school when the time arises.

'How's school going, Ben?'

A friend of mine sent his son to a posh independent secondary school. Whenever I saw the lad I asked him: 'How's school going, Ben?' He regaled me with an account – more like an inventory – of all the extracurricular activities he was doing: fencing, debating, theatre critic, editor of the school magazine and volunteering at a wetlands reserve. I often wondered when he got time to do any academic work. He went on to get a first class degree from Cambridge. I think the two things are entirely related. Colleagues I visit at an outstanding state secondary school in the Midlands are equally convinced on this point – that a wide-ranging and challenging extracurricular menu is directly linked to building character, resilience and, ultimately, academic success.

The character of identity and belonging

Human beings are a social and cultural species that seek bonds that bind them to others like themselves. It is an established characteristic of human social psychology that we seek out like-minded people who confirm rather than challenge our own conceptions of self.[27] As children mature and become less egocentric and more cognisant of wider society, they begin to ask less: 'What's in it for me?' and more: 'What's in it for my group?' As social creatures, we all desire and seek ways to give collective expression to shared histories, culture and community. Children, like everybody else, are hungry for a public life of larger meaning – one where they can share their play, pastimes, adventures, food, customs and values with their fellows. That is why schools can be such great places for children to flourish.

When children are denied constructive opportunities to have a public life, either by neglect or by design, or when their public life is so uninviting to the exploration and expression of morally robust and ethically rooted civic identities, they will lash out with strident or even vengeful forms of behaviour – gang violence, sectarianism, factionalism and xenophobic nationalism. Human beings, and perhaps especially children, cannot tolerate for long conceptions of self that are devoid or detached from a healthy, morally vigorous sense of history, tradition and culture.[28] The domains of families, communities, religious congregations, voluntary associations, local charities, neighbourhood groups and the like are places where we relate to each other on the basis of kinship, friendship and reciprocity, and where social and moral bonds build strong civil society. Astonishingly, none of this requires the power of the state (although, as a democratic socialist, I believe much of it can be nurtured and encouraged by the state).

In the four decades of my career, I have seen how Britain has become a hugely enriched, diverse and immeasurably more tolerant society. It is also one of the pre-eminent multi-ethnic and multicultural societies in the world, achieving exemplary levels of tolerance and integration.[29] For example, in 2020, Ipsos MORI found that only 3 per cent of people in the UK thought that 'to be truly British you have to be White' and that 89 per cent would be 'happy for their child to marry someone from another ethnic group'. These attitudinal trends have been accelerating in the last two decades.[30]

27 Sadly, this is also why many bullied children seek out the company of bullies: they confirm the low opinion they have of themselves. See Arthur et al., *Teaching Character and Virtue in Schools*, p. 36.

28 For more on this, listen to Jonathan Sacks, *Morality in the 21st Century*.

29 See Commission on Race and Ethnic Disparities, *The Report* (March 2021). Available at: https://www.gov.uk/government/organisations/commission-on-race-and-ethnic-disparities.

30 Kully Kaur-Ballagan, Attitudes to Race and Inequality in Great Britain, *Ipsos MORI* (15 June 2020). Available at: https://www.ipsos.com/ipsos-mori/en-uk/attitudes-race-and-inequality-great-britain.

However, entrenched forms of social class and ethnic inequality and immobility persist. While teachers have been instrumental in shaping some of the successes (and the failures) of our multicultural society, I have particular misgivings about the way my generation of (largely liberal, left-leaning) teachers abdicated their commitment to articulate important aspects of a professional ethic that was required to run alongside that well-meaning endeavour.

One aspect of this omission is the lack of a coherent vision for promoting engagement with civic values and issues of national identity. British identity is currently in a highly complex state of flux, not least because of the devolutionary assemblies in Scotland, Wales and Northern Ireland and the associated independence and nationalist movements in various parts of the UK. The decision of the UK to leave the European Union in 2016 has added to the complexity of issues around what it means to be British (and perhaps especially English). Indeed, the very notion of identifying as English seems to be in deep crisis. This vagueness and equivocation has left a woeful vacuum in terms of developing ideas that promote civic virtue, values and national identity – gaps that have been exploited by the far right, the far left and other extreme groups, some associated with only a very narrow concept of identity.

I wholeheartedly welcome and embrace the complexity that comes with diversity in a multicultural society,[31] but I find dismaying the apparent ambivalence and confusion that surrounds the teaching of fundamental British values. As we saw in Chapter 4, many trainees openly resist the legitimacy of the notion, arguing that the phrase itself implies some kind of British exceptionalism and even a kind of exclusive nationalism. While I respect their right to such views, I disagree. However, I also recognise that the widespread discomfort with the term reflects a complex ambivalence towards British history and our national identity – an ambivalence that, should it continue to grow and entrench, will result in us failing the children we teach, especially those from minority ethnic or cultural backgrounds that originate outside the UK. All the children we teach deserve a cogent and vivid sense of our shared belonging. They need to develop a rounded personal, social and cultural identity in order to flourish. It is a human need to explore our identity in personal and idiosyncratic ways, as well as sourcing and extending our roots to realms beyond our ken.

We are social creatures, so we need to make connections with the local, the regional, the national and the international. Children also need to explore what social class, gender and ethnicity mean in relation to their own personal identity. Identity is a multilayered and multidimensional fabric which defines 'what I am' as well as 'what I am not'. Understanding the structure and characteristics of identity requires knowledge – and deep levels of knowledge at that, not just inarticulate attitudes or incoherent

31 I discuss the pros and cons of multiculturalism as opposed to a multicultural society in greater detail in Appendix B.

feelings, as legitimate as they may be – of what it means to be ourselves, of what it means to be British or not, to be English or not, to be Scottish or not, to be Welsh or not, to be any other identity or not.

Children must be given opportunities to explore how identities both complement as well as exclude, merge as well as overlay, cohere as well as demarcate. Above all, they must feel agency over a process that is challenging but can also be exciting and inspiring and character-forming. Indeed, it echoes the process Aristotle refers to in the development of character – the forging of identity through dialectic – which brings into contention ideas that are sometimes oppositional and sometimes congruent. It is also a process that, although fraught with disputatious but hopefully rational dialogue, ultimately results in a synthesis of something new. These are all relevant and urgent issues that demand exploration in twenty-first century schools and classrooms. Why? Because we all, especially children, need to feel that we belong.

Just because the issues surrounding definitions of 'Britishness' or 'British values' are complex, it does not mean we should try to deny that Britishness or British values exist. It does. They do. The complexity of the issue is daunting, but we must not abdicate our professional responsibility to address it. As teachers, we need to constantly generate opportunities for children to explore their sense of belonging and identity. Failing to do so is negligence. Into the spaces left by our negligence others will appear – extremists who do not have a moral or ethical sense of civic values or a morally robust commitment to developing resilient character in our children. They will occupy the vacuum we have left and exploit it ruthlessly. History has countless examples of their tyranny.

I am not advocating that teaching children should be in any sense nationalistic. I reject bombastic, exclusive and phobic notions of national identity as inept and immoral. Indeed, that is not education; it is more akin to indoctrination. I cringe when I visit schools and see displays on corridor walls supposedly illustrating British values that are no more than banners for the words 'democracy', 'tolerance' or 'respect' – as if by displaying the words the children will understand the concepts and subscribe to the ideas and values behind them. Posters of Big Ben, the Houses of Parliament or the Royal Family can appear more like advertisements for British tourism than an exploration of the institutions at the heart of the British constitution.

We must not descend into crass tokenism (although, I did myself on many occasions as a young teacher). What children need are opportunities to explore the ethos around the language, laws, customs and culture that underpin shared national values. Being British (or even being English, Welsh, Scottish or Northern Irish) should mean more than merely living in a geographical area. Our language and history and everything that goes with it – community, culture, conventions and codes – make us different, distinct and particular from others, even when we are close neighbours and friends to other countries. However, to conceive an identity on the basis of othering others is, in my view, immoral.

What I advocate and support is not a form of othering nationalism but civic patriotism. In contrast to nationalistic patriotism, it is a unified identity of plural characters – like the bands of a rainbow – which is why the rainbow is such an appropriate symbol for a diverse but unified society. It shows how the bands of colour are integral through their relationship to one another. The colours retain their individual character but the rainbow is a plural entity where the relationship of one characteristic – following on but emerging from the previous one – is integral to the whole.[32]

The mission at the heart of what schools are trying to do is to build a core of morally robust civic purpose in both pupils and teachers, which will cultivate virtues and develop character based on the foundations of the fundamental values we all share. This, then, is a civic patriotism to which we can all belong. Civic patriotism is a virtue. The socialist George Orwell thought so, and so do I.[33]

Finally ...

I hope the idea of 'becoming a teacher' is beginning to makes sense to you. You will become a teacher when the practical wisdom you have gained through the experiences of challenge and struggle enables you to weigh moral, performance, civic and intellectual virtues against each other. You will then know, in most circumstances, what to do – in the right way and in the right measure. By contending with this process you will acquire good sense. It may take several years to develop this to any satisfactory degree, but stick at it. Aristotle had to work out the virtues that informed practical wisdom and good sense for himself. With the help you will get from your professional peers – friends, colleagues and mentors – it is time for you to do the same.

You are on the threshold of becoming a teacher and dealing with the struggles, dilemmas and mistakes that will inevitably unfold. Don't think you have to be a 'perfect' teacher to be a good one – you don't. You don't have to live up to the impossibly high performance standards that some people think is a way to raise the bar. Goalposts that are always being moved are not measures of worth, but a kind of tyranny. Don't think you have to be saintly either. Don't try to be a teacher who never allows herself a mistake or an error of ethical or moral judgement. Don't think you are heroic if you stay

32 The emergence of the rainbow in the UK (and elsewhere) as a national symbol of hope and unity during the COVID-19 pandemic was both gratifying and fascinating. It was representative mainly of the NHS – another important symbol of British diversity, hope and unity.

33 See Appendix A for more on civic patriotism.

up all hours of the night planning and preparing lessons that you don't have the energy to teach in the morning. Don't endlessly beat yourself up just because you have lost your composure, raised your voice or even shouted once in a while. Don't think you are a total failure because the lesson you planned so laboriously is greeted with a funereal response from the first minute you begin to teach it.

You don't have to be a brilliantly inspirational teacher every single day of every school year. Just be the best teacher you can be. Although it is crucial to be a professional in all the ways we have discussed throughout this book, the most powerful and significant way you can impact on a child's life is to model the character you want to see emerge from them. That is your moral and ethical duty, and it requires a huge amount of character. You are about to get no end of a lesson which will do you no end of good. Go ahead – become a good teacher and you will see that you are a teacher of character too.

Epilogue:

'WHEN I RETIRE, I WANT TO HAVE SOME MEMORIES!'

So said Tim (or something very similar) in an episode of Ricky Gervais' now classic comedy series *The Office*. Tim was the lovable character (played by Martin Freeman) who tells the hapless and annoying Gareth (played by Mackenzie Crook) – who is 'assistant to the manager, not assistant manager' – that he wants to leave his job, go back to university and do something important with his life. Teaching is very hard work and I can't promise that every day will be inspiring, but when you do retire (and that may be a very long way off) you can look forward to memories that people like Gareth can only crave.

In 1979, I was studying the Victorians with my class of 10-year-olds. We decided to put on a Victorian Music Hall for the Christmas show. I was the master of ceremonies and donned a tuxedo, white dress shirt with butterfly collar, dicky-bow and handlebar moustache for the part. Colleagues and children sang and danced to a packed house for three consecutive nights. Everyone laughed.

Twenty years later, I employed two young black guys who could sing and play gospel music on the piano. Within six weeks, they had trained sixty children to be a gospel choir. They performed a concert in the church across the road from the school. Their beautifully harmonic voices nearly lifted the roof. Tears streamed down my face.

Four years earlier, I was sitting on a Tube train being intently stared at by a young man wearing a hoodie. He got up and stood over me: 'You're Mr Newland, innit?' I nodded. 'Darren?' He nodded. The train stopped. The doors opened. He sniffed. 'It was good, ya know,' he said as he got off.

One day in 1986, I was teaching maths to a group of 9-year-olds struggling with long multiplication. In the middle of the session, a little boy with a speech impediment started tugging forcefully at my shirt. I turned to see what was the matter. He was nodding his head vigorously. His eyes and face beaming. 'I get it now! I get it now!' he gasped with delight.

Seventeen years later, I receive an email. It read: 'I've googled "Mr Newland" and found this email address. Are you the Mr Newland who used to teach me between 1980 and 1982? You were my best teacher.'

Fourteen years earlier, I am in the Lake District with thirty kids doing adventure sports and orienteering. One girl, who has never been out of Hackney, gets lost in the countryside but finds her way back to base by asking a farmer for a lift on his tractor. Another who has never seen a real-life horse before falls off one but jumps straight back on it. And a boy wakes me up in the middle of the night to tell me: 'Sir! I've just seen the stars!'

One day in 1984, a 7-year-old boy with learning difficulties is painting. It is home time and I ask him to pack up his stuff. He says: 'Can I stay here forever? I want to paint for the rest of my life!' Twenty-eight years later, he invites me to his one-man show at a posh West London gallery.

Two years before that, on a visit to a local museum with a Year 6 class, a girl sees an old photograph and recognises a railway arch that is near the school. It turns out to be the place where the first British pilot built and flew the first British-made aeroplane. We visit the site. It is derelict. We campaign to have the place restored and recognised. There is a blue plaque there now marking 'the first all-British powered flight by Alliott Verdon Roe'.

Five years later, an 11-year-old girl in my class refuses to speak a word to me for three days solid. I give up asking her what is the matter. At the end of the week, I find a note tucked under the windshield wiper of my car: It reads: 'Sorry about this week. I started. Being a woman.' A couple of years ago, the same person contacted me to say: 'I've been living in Australia but I'm home at the moment to see my mum. Can we meet for coffee? I've got a little boy now and I want him to meet my teacher.'

I can't promise that every day of your teaching career will produce significant moments. Not many jobs demand from you what teaching will, but when you do retire you will have many memories like this.

Gareth won't, but you will. That I can promise.

APPENDICES

This section gives you the opportunity to reflect in greater detail on a number of topics, particularly fundamental British values and other complex but urgent issues for new teachers. Although I readdress aspects of themes that have occurred in various parts of the book, this is not careless repetition. I am providing additional detail and dimension to a number of important discussions, enabling you to absorb and reflect in greater depth and equip yourself with important justificatory arguments with which you will need to be armed in the coming years.

Appendix A

FUNDAMENTAL BRITISH VALUES AND CIVIC PATRIOTISM

Fundamental values

There are no value-free societies or value-free people. Consequently, there are no value-free schools. While we may keep our attitudes and views discreet, there are no value-free teachers either. Questions that are key to this discussion are: what values must pertain within our schools for them to be universally valid, robust and incontestable? Which of these will our pupils readily subscribe and commit to when they become full citizens? As we explored in Chapter 4, I am referring to those values so fundamental that without them society simply cannot flourish. It may be able to function, but not without the state exerting considerable power to interfere, regulate and suppress.

For example, I am writing this at a time when American and British cities are experiencing widespread demonstrations as a result of an incident in which a black man, George Floyd, died while being arrested for a relatively minor offence at the hands of a white Minneapolis police officer. If we feel that such an incident is symptomatic of a norm – that the rule of law, individual liberty and mutual respect is not paid to one section of society to the same degree as to other sections of it – then, in order for society to continue to function, the state must exert a repressive and sometimes even oppressive power. But society cannot flourish under such circumstances, not when some sections of it feel either regularly or institutionally disadvantaged, discriminated against or oppressed. Society cannot flourish until fundamental values apply justly and equitably for all. People will tolerate mistakes and anomalies; they will not tolerate injustice that appears to be systemic.

We cannot subscribe and commit to more than a few of these fundamental values. Once we start to include values that are important to us, but not necessarily to everyone else, then we get diversity. As rich and bounteous as this may be from a cultural or social point of view, diversity requires that we must also exercise the virtue of tolerance in order to accommodate it. When we have a very wide range of diversity, particularly of political beliefs and social attitudes, before we know it we are asking ourselves whether we can tolerate things that test or even undermine what we assumed was foundational, like democracy or the rule of law.

Most people agree that we should willingly subscribe and commit to such fundamental values. The *quid pro quo* is that we are all equal citizens – recipients of the benefits and protections that such values confer. Fundamental values, whether British or not, are those without which we cannot feel safe and secure, without which we cannot cohere and unite, without which we cannot prosper. (Not even financially. Although an elite might for a time, a society cannot flourish when the disparity between rich and poor threatens its cohesion.) In the absence of fundamental values, society simply fails.

Let's now examine each fundamental British value – democracy, the rule of law, individual liberty, and mutual respect and tolerance of those with different faiths and beliefs – in more detail.[1]

Democracy

The success and quality of democracy relies on a willingness to engage in public life where there is a consensus on the fundamental principles of reason. Children, without necessarily understanding, will imitate and live their lives on the basis of how they observe significant others (like teachers) demonstrate and model values. Education is the process that initiates children into reasoning. Education develops the intellectual tools for logically and methodically solving problems. Education underpins our actions both ethically and morally. Education recognises that the imitation of an action precedes the acquisition of a virtue. As the eminent educational philosopher R. S. Peters said: 'The palace of reason is entered by the courtyard of habit.'[2] A democratic society, like our own, is not an arena of unlimited personal choices, and nor is it a morally neutral domain. It is one in which we initiate and induct participants through reason.

However inadequate we may feel our current democratic institutions to be or how poorly they function compared to other democratic societies, it is nevertheless our arena for making promises to our fellow citizens. This is a philosophical way of saying that we agree to make decisions and do things without fighting and killing each other; or, rather, we promise to make changes by accommodating compromises peacefully through our elected representatives. The political culture of any democratic society will have opposing, even incompatible, religious and philosophical positions. This does not mean they are unreasonable. Indeed, 'reasonable disagreements' – a willingness to agree to disagree – are an essential part of the diversity of a liberal democracy. This brings us back to the importance of children learning about and practising free

1 See Department for Education, *Promoting Fundamental British Values as Part of SMSC in Schools*, p. 5.

2 Peters, *Ethics and Education*, p. 314.

speech and understanding its vital qualities as a foundation stone in their lives, both in school and in wider society, including the idea that some views will be irreconcilable.

Why is free speech so important? For the following reasons:

- It is necessary for self-expression.
- It necessary for me to describe myself and what it means to be me.
- It is essential for the listener as well as the speaker in any conversation.
- Without it, I don't know where you are coming from.
- It is necessary for me to be able to evaluate and judge arguments and propositions (like school rules or government policies).
- It helps us all to seek truth and search for knowledge.[3]

The future of democracy is undermined and eroded if people – perhaps, especially, young people – do not feel they can speak their minds. Democracy cannot function at all unless people – perhaps, especially, young people – can learn to express deep and fundamental disagreements honestly and reasonably. Their 'locus of control' – a behaviourist idea that expresses a sense of personal agency – depends on learning these things, and so, ultimately, does their health and flourishing.

We discussed some general threats to free speech in Chapter 5, where such things as a dominant discourse or a fashionable political trend can inhibit and constrain it, but there are also some concrete and specific threats to free speech that we need to educate children to guard against. They include:

- **The assassin's veto.** This is the threat of violence calculated to curb free expression: 'If you say *that*, I will kill you!' (The fatwa of the Ayatollah Khomeini against the novelist Salman Rushdie in 1989, the threats by the Mafia towards Italian journalists over many decades, the murders of investigative journalists Veronica Guerin in Ireland in 1996 and Daphne Caruana Galizia in Malta in 2017 by organised criminal gangs, and the murder of the *Charlie Hebdo* journalists by jihadists in Paris in 2015 are all examples of this kind of attack on free speech.)
- **The heckler's veto.** This is the disruption of meetings or events by demonstrators because they disagree with what is being said by the invited speaker or performer. (For example, Sikh protestors preventing the performance of the play *Behzti* in Birmingham in 2004 because it featured sexual abuse in a

3 For more on free speech, listen to Timothy Garton Ash's five essays on the subject: *Free Speech* [radio series], BBC Radio 4 (2016). Available at: https://www.bbc.co.uk/programmes/b077ndw5.

gurdwara, and radical feminists, LGBTQ activists and conservative Muslim protestors preventing speakers being heard at UK universities by shouting them down.)

- **The offensiveness veto.** This is where people prevent others from speaking – 'You can't say *that*!' – because they are offended by what is being or might be said. This is particularly effective when the person demonstrating claims to be speaking on behalf of a 'victimised other' or preventing the expression of hate speech or the perpetration of harm to others.

- **No-platforming.** This is where (usually well-known) speakers are dis-invited or blocked from public engagements because of their controversial views. It may have an inhibiting impact on the less famous who might self-censor to avoid confrontation. It also denies other people the opportunity to assess the arguments for themselves. (Examples of this are the feminists Julie Bindel and Germaine Greer who have been regularly no-platformed at UK universities, and the Canadian academic Jordan Peterson who has also been no-platformed at British, US and Canadian universities, because of their views on transgender issues.)

As teachers, we have a responsibility to educate children to counter such threats by giving them the opportunity to acquire a language and vocabulary to do so, through forums like school debating societies (see Appendix C) but also by educating them to accept the moral principles that:

- We neither make threats nor submit to intimidation.

- We accept no taboos against truth and knowledge; truth can only be tested by alternative arguments that prove to be false.

- Free speech should be limited only when it causes palpable and demonstrable harm (e.g. threats, abuse, incitement), not when harm is conflated with offence.

- No verbal insult, however extreme, is ever equivalent to physical violence.

- People have a right to hear extreme views, not be protected from them.

- While we have a right to offend, we do not have a duty to offend.

- Privacy is a precondition of free speech, and once privacy has been violated it cannot be restored.

- We have a right to decide 'what I share with you' and 'what you share with me' (except in legitimate areas of public interest, like criminality).

Discuss and reflect

- Would you tolerate pupils at your school heckling, disrupting, vetoing or no-platforming an invited guest?

The rule of law

The evolution of the rule of law – the idea that all people, even monarchs and presidents, are subject to the constraints set out by legal codes and processes – goes back so far that no one can reliably trace its roots. Even Aristotle referred to the idea. Here in the UK, we look to the Magna Carta as the first really significant moment when an absolute ruler, in the form of the Plantagenet King John, was forced to relinquish power to the English barons and submit to sixty-three clauses of law by signing, or rather sealing, the 'great charter' on the banks of the River Thames at Runnymede in June 1215.

Of course, our ideas around the rule of law have taken a number of evolutionary turns since then, and while that event might not have been the 'birth certificate of freedom' as we know it today, most historians and lawyers see it as the 'death certificate of despotism'.[4] What we have today is a much more extensive and sophisticated system of legal constraints to protect our rights and property. A key point to understanding the rule of law is not the rights that are guaranteed by the concept, but the constraints it imposes on those who might wish to do us harm.

When we impose rules in school, children should be taught and encouraged to understand and accept that those limitations and constraints on behaviour have not been conceived to grant them rights but to prevent them harm. Limitation and constraint therefore enable further and greater freedom to flourish. Handled sensitively and appropriately, even 4-year-old children entering kindergarten for the first time can begin to grasp this concept.

For example, consider how limitation enables possibility in sports and games. The rules of a sport impose order on chaos. The great thing about learning this concept through playing sport is that children don't need to be taught it, they just need to participate. They learn the rules as they go along. Caught not taught. It is a lesson for life: play by the rules and the possibilities are endless. Break the rules and there are

4 Simon Schama, *A History of Britain. Vol. 1: At the Edge of the World? 3000 BC–AD 1603* (London: Bodley Head, 2009), p. 142.

consequences and penalties. We need to make sure that children play the kind of sport that imposes limitations, not just games that allow their limitless imaginations to burgeon. The metaphor of a rule of law in sport is therefore a fundamental value for children to acquire.

Let's take another example for contrast. What goes by the name of 'freedom' in some arenas of social media is actually about shaming, trolling, abusing and revenge porn – some aspects of which have reached epidemic proportions. Social media platforms that permit such practices are not promoting freedom in a moral sense, but are in fact enabling social regression and undermining our notions of the rule of law. They normalise toxic social behaviour. They give credence to public dishonouring of individuals without a fair trial. They erode due process and rule out pleas of mitigation. They marginalise any possibility of redemption or forgiveness. Conversely, established judicial processes in society are not processes of shaming or revenge; they uphold the right to due process, justice, punishment and redemption. We must give children the tools to analyse how social media platforms undermine their rights, protections and responsibilities to one another through the lack of constraint they permit.[5]

Whether laws should reflect moral principles is redefined with each passing generation. For example, sexual activity with children was prevalent in Victorian times. Incest was not even a crime until 1907. Now it is unthinkable that we could have ever tolerated either. Until recent decades, adults having consensual sex with teenagers approaching the age of 16 was, although illegal, widely tolerated. Now, even an 18- or 19-year-old is likely to be added to the sex offenders register for such an offence. Death by dangerous driving received relatively lenient sentencing until the 1980s. Now you might expect to get the equivalent of a life sentence for a serious case.

Legality and morality are not always on the same hymn sheet: adultery, euthanasia, abortion and surrogacy are all examples where they do not perfectly overlay. Social values towards issues like homosexuality and same-sex marriage may also diverge from what the law has only recently prohibited. What pertains in a multicultural society like ours is an increasingly diverse range of values which force us to question whether there can ever be a universal rule of law.

5 For more on this see Sacks, *Morality: Restoring the Common Good*, ch. 15.

Discuss and reflect

In his 'Letter from a Birmingham Jail', Dr Martin Luther King quoted St Thomas Aquinas:'An unjust law is a human law that is not rooted in eternal law and natural law. Any law that uplifts human personality is just. Any law that degrades human personality is unjust.'[6]

- Do the rules in your school reflect moral principles – of what ought and ought not to be, of what is just and unjust? If not, why not?
- Do they focus on rights and liberties or constraints and limitations?

Individual liberty

The source of our understanding of concepts like liberty and rights derives essentially from the respective revolutions in England, France and the United States over the centuries. From Magna Carta in 1215 (for most historians a landmark event that initiated limits to the power of the monarch), through to the Glorious Revolution in England in 1688 (consolidating those limits on monarchical power and defining the role of a constitutional monarchy for the modern age), on to the Declaration of Independence in 1776 (which set out the liberties of the individual to 'pursue happiness') and then the French Revolution in 1789 (which sent shock waves across Europe, establishing, eventually, rights and freedoms for the common man).

The Anglo-American model of liberty and rights was distilled and passed on to us principally from the philosophical traditions of people like John Locke and Thomas Jefferson (and also the moral philosopher Adam Smith). Their view was that society was the development of a 'covenant' which attempted to bring together individuals and civil society in the form of families, communities and voluntary associations to produce a 'common good' that protects us from the overbearing influence of the state.[7] Locke was particularly influential in promoting the idea that individual liberty could transcend the authority of the state and that 'natural rights' to life, liberty and property should be protected. The French Revolution, by contrast, established a different understanding of liberty and rights, which was distilled from the philosophical

6 Martin Luther King Jr, Letter from a Birmingham Jail (16 April 1963), *Center for Africana Studies – University of Pennsylvania*. Available at: https://www.africa.upenn.edu/Articles_Gen/Letter_Birmingham.html.

7 For more on the idea of a covenant, see the beginning of Chapter 5; and Sacks, *Morality: Restoring the Common Good*, ch. 23.

tradition of people like Jean-Jacques Rousseau. Under this way of thinking, rights are delivered by the state and the idea of civil society is regarded as untrustworthy and potentially dangerous to an individual's rights and liberties to do what they please as long as they do not harm others.

The Anglo-American model, with its emphasis on civil society, gives more importance to forming 'moral communities' where we care about our neighbours through civic action – considered vital to the health of democracy. Of course, the UK, the United States and France have evolved to broaden their philosophical and political traditions and moved away from these narrow interpretations. However, their DNA is still very evident. While the state can deliver much in terms of health, welfare, education, defence and the rule of law, it cannot deliver the civil society that grows from active citizenship, voluntary work and face-to-face care that constitutes a good society.[8]

For teachers trying to better understand the characteristics and complexity of individual liberty as part of fundamental British values, exploring the ideas of a covenant can be a very useful tool of analogy. A covenant embodies the idea of people coming together in mutually beneficial ways which are collaborative, cooperative and transformative of our identity – like the relationship we have with a significant other, such as a close friend, marriage partner or even a teacher. A covenantal relationship with a community means that we volunteer to do things for the common good, irrespective of whether we are recognised or benefit financially. Covenantal relationships in communities promote civic virtues and values, and they build relationships between individuals, groups and civic institutions.

By contrast, a contract is a transaction based on what benefits the interests of those who enter into it. It is therefore framed within a competitive market-driven environment and is encapsulated in the idea: 'I'll provide something for you if, and only if, you pay me or if you do something for me in return,'[9] or the more sinister: 'I'll do something for you if you vote for me.' Teachers are very important role models for demonstrating covenantal relationships,[10] and schools are very important institutional models for demonstrating covenantal relationships within communities. What has this got to do with individual liberty as a fundamental value? What has it got to do with the understandings children must acquire about individual liberty at their own personal level? The answer takes us back to constraints.

If children grow up thinking that individual liberty is the absence of constraint – in other words, the freedom to do what they want, when they want, where they want – then they will only be confused and overwhelmed by the choice that this so-called

8 Sacks, *Morality: Restoring the Common Good*, pp. 124–128.

9 Sacks says more about the distinction between covenants and contracts in Sacks, *Morality: Restoring the Common Good*, p. 64.

10 By contrast, we don't have a covenantal relationship with, for example, a yoga teacher or even a maths or language tutor – we have a contractual relationship.

freedom offers – which is not really a choice at all. As teachers, we must not acquiesce to the view of equating or conflating choice with individual liberty. We must not allow children to mistake individual liberty for unrestrained freedom. In doing so, we do them a huge disservice, compounding their intellectual ignorance and allowing greater doubt and uncertainty to fester in their personal development. They will grow up perplexed by their inability to discriminate rationally, they will be equivocal about commitment to others and, perhaps most pervasive of all, they will be paralysed by the fear of missing out – always thinking that the next choice will be better than the last.

Our teaching has to show children that real individual liberty includes the capacity to choose constraints – the right constraints. As Aristotle said: choose the right thing, in the right way, at the right time, in the right measure. Children might better understand these down-to-earth constraints: choosing to practise playing the piano in order to achieve the freedom of playing it fluently; choosing the discipline of regular swimming training in order to achieve the privilege of being selected for the team and competing with others; choosing not to overeat in order to achieve the liberty of physical agility and robust health.

However, there is a delicate balance between the individual and the liberty parts of this equation. We pass on our genes as individuals but we survive socially and psychologically in groups. We want to be respected as an individual but we also want to be recognised as a member of a group – and that group may be a team, tribe, social class or nation. But when we allow our individual selves to be totally subsumed into the identity of a group collective, we are in danger of becoming fascist.

I am very wary about bandying about words like 'fascist', so let's define it. The meaning derives from the Latin word *fascis* – or a bundle of rods. The symbolism is important. A single rod can be broken – snapped in half over your knee. Try to do that with a bundle – it is impossible. That is why fascism privileges the rights and liberties of the group collective over the rights and liberties of the individual. Fascists believe they must act as a group, never tolerating the human spirit or agency of individual liberty that dares to break free from the bundle of the collective will. George Orwell – unapologetic and articulate about his English patriotism – understood how easily notions of exclusive nationalism transmute into fascism, which is why both *Animal Farm* and *Nineteen Eighty-Four* remain classics of English literature to this day, because they teach us how to think about individual liberty in a completely new way.

Discuss and reflect

- What constraints enable individual liberty in your school and in your life?

Mutual respect

The American philosopher Stephen Darwall distinguishes between two kinds of respect: 'recognition respect' which focuses on the fundamental respect for the person which is due to all by virtue of their basic human rights, and 'appraisal respect' which allows us to appraise the rationality or the veracity of an idea.[11] In making this distinction, Darwall claims that respect is not a single, unified absolute. We do not necessarily have to respect ideas, but we ought to respect people. Some with a devout religious faith challenge this, arguing these two types of respect are a single concept and cannot be separated. Their view can be summarised by the claim: 'I cannot be separated from my faith, so in respecting me you must also respect my religion.'

If this is true, it means that we cannot challenge religious assertions and, therefore, people of faith can lay claim to a vast no-go area that rational argument cannot access. This is clearly absurd. However, as we noted earlier, we all have a responsibility not to show gratuitous disrespect, even to ideas that people might hold very dear. If we are reckless in this regard there are consequences, which might include reactions like anger or violence. Attacking ideas in a way that carelessly confuses or conflates them with the people who hold them is in itself disrespectful. Don't be afraid of challenging ideas, but demonstrably show respect to people even when you find their ideas ridiculous or abhorrent.

'I cannot leave my Christianity at the school gate'

I once had a devout Christian in one of my sessions. He said: 'My Christianity is part and parcel of who I am. I cannot leave my Christianity at the school gate.' While I sympathise with that sentiment, I challenge it, at least in part. I am not asking a teacher to leave behind their faith or forget they are a Christian. I am asking that they do not come into school with the idea they are a 'Christian teacher', but rather see themselves as 'a teacher who happens to be Christian'. That distinction is ethically very important.

Is offending others disrespectful? The question of whether we should give offence is a moral question; however, it should be kept separate from the issue of people taking offence. The fact that someone might be offended by a remark does not mean that

11 This is discussed in Timothy Garton Ash, *Free Speech: Respect Me, Respect My Religion* [radio programme], BBC Radio 4 (13 April 2016). Available at: https://www.bbc.co.uk/programmes/b076zxyt.

offence was intended. The question of people's feelings is key. Morally, we should be sensitive to others' feelings and should not gratuitously seek to offend or wantonly disregard the hurt someone else has felt, even if no harm was intended.

The immorality of disrespect is not the same as bad manners. Sometimes the offensiveness of certain people can be genuinely put down to bad manners without the intention of harm. There are times when honesty demands that offence is given and may be taken. Occasionally, justice cannot be served without it. Other things being equal, the giving of offence is not to be avoided at all costs, only in general.[12]

Former generations were brought up with the adage: 'Sticks and stones will break my bones, but names will never hurt me.' Today, this would be to risk denying the hurt and pain someone might feel at being offended. Some people claim that making offensive remarks causes real mental and psychological harm that is comparable to physical harm. This cannot be objectively quantified, so there is a huge and heated debate about the issue. This has given rise to the emergence of ominous phenomena such as safe spaces, trigger warnings, micro-aggressions and no-platforming – all of which are intended to limit the expression of opinions that might offend and cause psychological harm. The fact that trends like these seem to be increasingly common in universities (of all places) is a paradox, and led the former Chief Rabbi Jonathan Sacks to describe the phenomena as 'the great intellectual betrayal of our time'.[13]

It is an obvious truism that not all harm is serious. Some harms are mild and some are severe. Wagging a finger is not the same as poking someone in the shoulder; poking someone in the shoulder is not the same as punching them in the face. Saying: 'Jews like to stick together' is not the same as saying: 'Jews predominate in the banks and the media', which is not the same as saying: 'Jews are part of an international conspiracy to dominate the world.'

What is a hate crime?

You may be surprised to learn that it is not a crime to say hateful things unless you abuse, threaten or incite violence. Sometimes the dividing line is very fine, which makes life difficult for the police when they are assessing allegations, and for victims on the receiving end of victimisation and intimidation.

12 See Hand, *A Theory of Moral Education*, p. 92.

13 Jonathan Sacks, The Danger of Outsourcing Morality [speech delivered on being awarded the Templeton Prize] (27 May 2016). Available at: https://rabbisacks.org/danger-outsourcing-morality-read-rabbi-sacks-speech-accepting-templeton-prize.

A physical assault is clearly a crime, but if it is motivated by hostility towards a particular ethnic or religious group then it may also be a breach of Section 29 of the Crime and Disorder Act 1988 and classified as 'racially or religiously aggravated assault'.[14] This gives a judge a wider scope of sentencing options for those who have been found guilty of such a crime. Motivated and aggravated crimes of this nature have been tagged as 'hate crimes', although the phrase itself does not appear in legislation.

Discuss and reflect

- Should your punishment of children be differentiated if there is evidence (or you suspect) that playground bullying is racially or religiously motivated?

However mild or severe the harms – and you may not think any of my previous examples are mild – the cumulative effect of constantly repeated mild harms can take a heavy psychological toll. Furthermore, gratuitously offensive conduct can and does cause real problems – for example, it can easily result in the erosion of trust, cooperation and outbreaks of physical violence.[15] It seems obvious to any fair-minded person that everyone should be able to have their say. In Jewish tradition, for example, there can be no justice in which all sides have not had a fair hearing: 'Who is wise? One who learns from every man.[16] We all know something, after all. Even a little knowledge may be the germ of truth that enlightens another's greater knowledge. What is more, it is important for two opposing views to be aired, not just because one might be true and the other false, but because one might offer a different perspective on reality – not contradictory but complementary. When people are regularly or systematically denied a platform to make their argument, violence is usually the outcome.[17]

As we have seen in relation to the rule of law and individual liberty, we must inform children that mutual respect is under serious threat from social media platforms. Firstly, because the way the algorithms work mean they overwhelmingly present to us like-minded people (many of whom may not even be people but bots), creating an echo chamber of self-confirming views. This is what sociologists call 'confirmation bias', where we think our views are shared by most other people and are therefore right.

14 See https://www.legislation.gov.uk/ukpga/1998/37/section/29.
15 See Hand, *A Theory of Moral Education*, p. 95.
16 Stated by Simeon ben Zoma in *Ethics of the Fathers* [*Pirkei Avot*], 4:1, a collection of Jewish laws, aphorisms and guides to ethical behaviour dating from the first century CE.
17 See Sacks, *Morality: Restoring the Common Good*, pp. 228–229.

Secondly, if we only converse and associate with those who share our views, there is a tendency for those views to become more and more extreme. Thirdly, the anonymity allowed on social media exacerbates a tendency to drop our inhibitions and say things we would not say where the social responsibility of a face-to-face encounter would require mutual respect. If children are growing up believing that others should 'like' the banal pictures of their cat, their breakfast or them staring vacuously into a mirror, they should not be surprised when some people decide not to 'like' them, but in fact to 'hate' them for their self-absorption and self-obsession.

Discuss and reflect

- How can we promote mutual respect when social media participants are anonymous, invisible, asynchronous (can post and exchange not in real time), unregulated and impersonal (can post and exchange without face-to-face contact)?[18]

It is very important that, as teachers, we cultivate civic skills in schools. This includes how to challenge others on the basis of mutual respect; how to argue with others on the basis of rationality and evidence (and not emotion); how to persuade others based on the skills of rhetoric and eloquent language; and how to address others without resorting to slurs, smears and defamation. These are skills that need to be taught; they are too critical to allow them merely to be caught.

Tolerance for people with different faiths and beliefs

Much of our modern thinking about tolerance – or toleration, as it was known – is an inheritance from John Locke, an English philosopher, physician and influential Enlightenment thinker who lived through the turbulence of the civil and religious wars that engulfed England and the rest of Britain during the late seventeenth century. During a period of exile in Holland, he wrote his famous *Letter Concerning Toleration* (published in 1689) in which he set out his belief that the state had no authority to impose doctrine or coerce individuals; that religious beliefs were voluntary and no one could think on our behalf; and that the state could not banish sectarianism but this evil would be eliminated only by reason and toleration of different religious beliefs which would allow the individual conscience to roam free and unhindered. He

18 See Sacks, *Morality: Restoring the Common Good*, pp. 224–225.

believed that to discriminate on the grounds of religion was as silly as discrimination on the grounds of eye or hair colour. He also challenged the notion, revolutionary in his day, that religious diversity equalled sedition. His thinking is attributed to our modern ideas around identity, defining as he did the self as conscious of both pleasure and pain and largely self-concerned.

However, while acknowledging Locke's legacy and influence on tolerance, liberalism and Enlightenment ideas, I want to discuss how exercising tolerance for people of different faiths and beliefs is also an excellent example of the Aristotelian idea of the application of competing virtues. Being tolerant of someone else's faith or beliefs is easy when they do not offend us. Should we tolerate Hindus celebrating Diwali, Sikhs Vaisakhi, Muslims Eid, Jews Passover and Christians Easter? Of course we should (as long as nobody breaks any laws), even if we are devout atheists. Should we tolerate the demonstrations of those protesting against globalisation, climate change, rape culture, fathers' rights or the visits of odious foreign leaders, or in support of Extinction Rebellion or Black Lives Matter? Of course we should (as long as the protestors do not commit or incite violence), even if we are outraged by their views. We may not want to celebrate or participate ourselves, but we could have no morally robust argument for not tolerating them.

In some cases, however, we are not talking about an obvious good versus an obvious evil, but a particular good versus another kind of good. For example, it is good that people want to celebrate a religious festival and it is good that other people will tolerate that. But what about tolerating something that we think is wrong or evil? For example, I have a number of friends who are radical atheists – they fundamentally reject religion and think that it causes real psychological and social harm. However, they are prepared to accept that there can be a reasonable disagreement over that view because the harm cannot be verifiably quantified as a direct outcome of religious beliefs; therefore, they are willing to tolerate people who practise a religion. That is tolerance. But not everyone demonstrates such a virtuous approach to the faith or beliefs of others: try practising Christianity in Saudi Arabia, or any kind of religion at all in North Korea, and see how far you get.

Over the last thirty years, here in the UK and in many other Western countries, we have stood together under the banners not only of 'tolerance' but also of 'diversity' and 'inclusion' – almost assuming that these things are more or less the same virtues. Diversity and inclusion – they are good things, aren't they? Well, let's test this proposition. Sometimes there is a genuine conflict between the interests of diversity and inclusion on the one hand, and the interests of tolerance – in the form of free speech – on the other. In recent times, a growing number of people have not only confused these concepts, but assert that when they conflict, diversity and inclusion should always win out over tolerance.

For example, if we ask the question:'Should we tolerate the free speech of racists?' the answer, from a diversity and inclusion point of view, is almost certainly no. It is considered at the very least offensive and at worst abusive, threatening or inciting. But in a democratic liberal society which values free speech the answer has to be yes. This has become a difficult position to defend, but even from a classical liberal point of view allowing the expression of racist opinions does not mean that racists are permitted to use language that abuses, threatens or incites violence. The law, let alone reasonable disagreement, has set such discourse beyond its limits.

Of course, any morally robust person will find the claims of a racist deeply offensive – but do you want to be protected from extreme views or do you want to have the right to hear them, judge for yourself and challenge them? Hearing the claims of a racist means that unsavoury views are exposed to the examination, deconstruction and judgement of the wider public. It also furnishes the possibility that the racist may reflect on his views and reconsider his position. It is absurd to think that racists will cease to hold racist views simply because they have not been allowed to express them. If forced to do so, they will take their views underground or onto anonymous internet platforms where they cannot be interrogated or challenged and where their fallacious claims will not be exposed.

To call for diversity and inclusion across society is a noble endeavour, especially if it is also an appeal for unity in a common cause. However, if the call for unity is to oppose a common enemy, then that needs to be considered with much greater care. The epithets 'fascist' and 'Nazi' are now used so widely that they encompass anyone (from either the political left or right) who is either an opponent of diversity and inclusion or is a 'liberal' and sits outside that of a particular group. This is the psychology of puritanism, which we see played out in a number of conservative and orthodox religious practices where deviation from strict norms of behaviour, language and ritual are considered taboo. It is also a politics of purity, where dissent from equally strict norms of behaviour, language and practice are enforced by moral panics and ideological re-education and punished by witch-hunts and purges.

Another contemporary example where the concept of tolerance has been confused and distorted is the clash over 'safe spaces'. The idea of a safe space was conceived by groups who feel vulnerable or protective of others they perceive to be vulnerable by virtue of their ethnicity, race, gender, sexuality or whatever. The urge to protect others is virtuous. The idea to provide a forum – a safe space – for people to speak or listen freely is also virtuous. Of course, it isn't a forum to say whatever you like, and nor is it a forum for preventing anyone from challenging what is said. If either of these is true, we have a clash of the Aristotelian notion of competing virtues, in which one virtue is trying to trump the other and virtue itself does not win.

If the expression of a reasonable disagreement is merely contrary to the prevailing view, or if the victim sees the reasonable disagreement as intimidation or an intolerable offence, then the space neither allows free speech and nor is it safe – for anyone, not even the supposed victims. Are we to be protected from other people's opinions? Are we not fit to judge for ourselves any harm that may accrue from the expression of a point of view? To say: 'I cannot allow you in the same space as me because I find your presence or your opinion offensive to the point of causing psychological harm' is to contribute to a process of ghettoisation.

In parts of nineteenth-century Europe, Orthodox Jews were not allowed to walk the streets on Sundays because their presence offended the sensibilities of Christians going to church. A safe space for Christians therefore created a ghetto for Jews. Why does all this matter to teachers and teaching? The damaging phenomenon of a safe space is promoting a ghetto mentality and is thriving on social media platforms. This is a threat to the pupils and students in our schools and universities. A safe space where you can only talk to the like-minded is impoverishing both to the public discourse of our communities and to our individual intellect.[19]

Are British values different?

We might ask what the difference is between British values and American or European values. After all, these values emerged from the European Enlightenment of the seventeenth and eighteenth centuries and have converged in the present day with attempts to transcend culture and context and come up with a comprehensive set of universal values, as encompassed in documents like the United Nations' Universal Declaration of Human Rights and the Convention on the Rights of the Child. It is a valid question. All Western values are indeed very similar, but similarity is not necessarily affinity.

Of the many examples we could unpack, let's look at just two. Firstly, let's contrast the characteristics of the British democratic system with those of the United States. Both are well-established, vibrant, liberal democracies with a deep respect for the rule of law. Yet here in the UK we don't have a written constitution. There is a long and complicated debate about the pros and cons of written versus unwritten constitutions, but I would argue that if we were writing a constitution in the UK today, I don't think we would include, for example, the amendment which gives people the right to keep and bear arms. While I am aware that the Second Amendment to the United States Constitution should be seen in the historical context of reliance on civil militias at that

19 See Sacks, *Morality: Restoring the Common Good*, ch. 11.

time, we have only to imagine what would happen if a president or a Congress attempted to remove it now. I think the United States would descend once again into bloody civil war.

Next, let's compare fundamental British values with those of our European neighbours. Once again, Western European democracies are well-established, vibrant and liberal with a deep respect for the rights and liberties of the individual based on mutual respect and tolerance. That said, contrast the British view of Muslim women wearing face veils (for example, the niqab or burka) with that taken by our French, Belgian, Dutch, Danish, German and Austrian neighbours – all of whom have brought in various levels of prohibition. The debates in these countries have taken different perspectives on religious freedom, female equality, secular traditions and even fears of terrorism (which may or may not be justified). Although Prime Minister Boris Johnson has made disparaging remarks about women who wear the burka, he did so in the context of defending the right of women to wear whatever they want.[20] I am not defending Johnson or any of these positions on the rights of gun owners or the wearing of face veils; I am merely pointing out that it is a fallacy to believe that fundamental British values are not different to the fundamental values of other countries, even those closest to us in terms of political, social and cultural history.

The way each country interprets its values, particularly those it considers fundamental, is distinctive; indeed it is more than that – it is unique. It is unique to be British, as it is unique to be English, Scottish, Welsh or Irish; as it is unique to be French, Belgian, Dutch, German, Australian, Indian, Canadian, American or any other national identity. Failure to recognise the uniqueness of these distinct interpretations of values in the context of national identity is a palpable failure to recognise what is an essential truth about us all. It is not an eternal truth, however. Identities change, but they do so in the context of a time and a place – which brings us to history.

History and British values

I am not a specialist history teacher but I have enjoyed teaching history to primary school children for many years. One of the issues history teachers contend with is whether the teaching of history can avoid thematic approaches, even worse teaching it by 'episodes'. The great risk of teaching the history of any period, epoch or civilisation, let alone that of a people or nation, is how little can be accommodated within the

20 Boris Johnson, Denmark Has Got It Wrong. Yes, the Burka is Oppressive and Ridiculous – But That's Still No Reason To Ban It, *The Telegraph* (5 August 2018).

scheme of work of a school year or phase of education. Themes and episodes consequently deal with little or nothing about the context of what went on before or after the period or the events being taught. And, of course, context is everything.

In British schools, for example, children may be taught 'the Romans', 'the Vikings', 'the Stuarts', 'the Victorians' or 'the Second World War'. Important and fascinating though these are – and deeply relevant to how we have got to where the British are now – they are taught as stand-alone topics. This approach to teaching history does not provide children with the broad sweep of the narrative and fails to fulfil the essential requirements of what Simon Schama has called 'the three Cs' – 'comprehensive chronological continuity'. Additionally, in recent times, history teachers have opted to try and get children to understand history through empathy – an approach that Schama and other historians have heavily criticised. 'If empathy means weepily identifying with victims,' Schama says, 'it can be sentimental mush. The ability to put oneself in someone's shoes requires a lot of knowledge.'[21]

The teaching of the British Empire is an excellent example that illustrates the difficulties to which Schama is wisely alerting us. The British Empire was the largest empire the world has ever seen and so, understandably, it has shaped our national story, our character and our population over centuries. The legacies of its wealth moulded the character of our cities and countryside. Many of the grandest and most famous of our urban public buildings and country houses were built with money derived from the Georgian and Victorian entrepreneurs who dominated world trade – including the slave trade – for almost three centuries. Our national literature, our national culture and our national heroes – both historically and contemporaneously – are products of the British Empire. Since decolonisation, however, our perception of the British Empire has been clouded by a mixture of guilt, shame, embarrassment and denial – all very unhelpful emotions for assessing our historical legacy and moving forward as an integrated multicultural, multiracial society.

Yet, the ebb and flow of world history is characterised by empires. The British Empire is merely one episode – albeit the largest to date – in that epochal tidal flow. Whether the British Empire, in comparison to other empires, could be described as relatively benevolent is neither here nor there; the history of both its horrors and its perceived moral purpose is complicated by the particular histories and values of its time and its place. People who believe the British Empire was 'bad' will have undeniable facts to support their view. People who think the British Empire was 'good' will also have undeniable facts to support their view. Both views are necessarily simplistic and reductionist in order to serve the needs of those who want to promote their version of history. However, the moral complexity of the British Empire is a very rich amalgam for those who wish to study it seriously. As challenging as this undoubtedly is, these

21 Schama quoted in Hugh Williams, *Fifty Things You Need to Know About British History* (London: Collins, 2008), p. xiii.

complicated motives and outcomes should be better known by us all, so that we can understand and appreciate the consequences evident in the values and identity of contemporary British society. We cannot be fully and authentically British unless we fully embrace that complexity.

Some historians argue that we must 're-remember'[22] Britain's imperial past, face up to our collective guilt and more fully acknowledge those aspects of it that were shameful. Such arguments have their merit, rooted as they are in a desire to promote social justice, but they are fraught with dangers, especially when it comes to balancing that desire for social justice with the need to reveal 'the truth'. Take, for example, re-remembering the chain of historical events that led to British rule in India and later, the British Raj. We need to come to terms with the fact that, on the one hand, hundreds of millions of people and a myriad of ancient and immeasurably rich cultures were plundered for naked commercial gain for over 200 years; while on the other, this could only be achieved because rivalries between corrupt local dynasties could be exploited and manipulated by a handful of British officials and a tiny military garrison. The full story of the British in India is not just one of external domination but of internal collaboration and collusion.

Similarly complex is Britain's role in the Atlantic slave trade – an episode of British history that I think should have a much higher profile in our national collective consciousness. Re-remembering the horrors of the full story is potentially painful, and needs skilled and sensitive teaching along the lines Schama advocates. However, we should all know better that the wealth of cities such as London, Edinburgh, Bristol and Liverpool derived in large part from the profits of the Atlantic slave trade – and that 'trade' involved staggeringly brutal and barbaric levels of terrorism to subdue its victims. We must also re-remember that it too could not have been achieved without consorting with and exploiting long-established networks run by African slave traders acting as 'middle men', who used one ethnic group to enslave another (often as 'trophies' of tribal wars), sourcing their victims from networks that predated European slavery and reached deep into North, West and Central African hinterlands.

Another dimension for teachers addressing this urgent and necessary aspect of our history is that researching ancestral slave history may reveal forebears who were not only enslaved Africans but also European slave owners. While this research will commonly expose widespread sexual exploitation and rape as a commonplace, it may also reveal the progeny of legitimate relationships and marriage.[23] As teachers, we need to

22 A term coined by the American novelist Toni Morrison to assert the need to re-remember the history of slavery in the United States. See Catherine Hall, Britain's Massive Debt to Slavery, *The Guardian* (27 February). Available at: https://www.theguardian.com/commentisfree/2013/feb/27/britain-debt-slavery-made-public.

23 This is a common occurrence for those researching their ancestry and was poignantly illustrated by the British actress Naomie Harris in the series, *Who Do You Think You Are?* [TV programme], BBC One (29 July 2019). Available at: https://www.bbc.co.uk/programmes/m00077q4.

be sensitive not only to the potentially painful and shame-inducing effects of teaching history, but also to the fundamental purpose of teaching – which is not simply to promote the values of social and racial justice but also to seek truth.

The history of the British Empire has produced complicated outcomes – some that can be judged morally worthy as well as some genocidal horrors. It involved genuine cultural exchange as well as cultural appropriation; economic, scientific, medical and infrastructural development as well as slavery, exploitation and brutality. It developed the values of communication, reciprocity, mutual admiration and intermarriage as well as exclusionary racism, bigotry and sexual exploitation. In India, for example, the British Empire ultimately conferred a rule of law and a legal system based on English common law and property rights with an independent judiciary, a world renowned army and independent civil service, a geological and geographical survey which has revealed great natural resources, a flourishing free press and world-class public schools and universities, free market capitalism, the world's largest fully functioning democracy and the English language as a unifying form of communication.

The English language emerged from the British Empire as the world's first global language, which has been reciprocally enriched by the assimilation of vocabulary from those nations with which it has cohabited. Indeed, the British Empire has not only shaped the modern world but the modern society that Britain is today – pre-eminently multicultural, multi-ethnic and, arguably, the most creative and culturally diverse on the planet, with high levels of ethnic intermarriage.[24] It is important that we avoid any simplistic views of the British Empire as 'all bad'; that is a view for ideologues who want to make political statements, not for teachers – and especially not for teachers of history who are trying to purvey the fundamental educational and moral value of seeking historical truth.

As teachers, we must not be in the business of rewriting history; that is the tendency of those with totalitarian inclinations. And nor must we gloss over it. Oliver Cromwell is a historical character who captures both the complexity and the honesty that we must try to encompass in representing our collective past. He was both a revolutionary anti-monarchist and a tyrant, but when he commissioned his portrait to be painted by Samuel Cooper, he instructed the artist to depict him 'warts and all'.

While initiatives like Black History Month have served a purpose in the past (and I taught it every October throughout the 1980s and 1990s), I think they are now an anachronism. For reasons I have already alluded (and develop in Appendix B), Black History Month seems to be a feature of that now misguided notion of multiculturalism, where identity is seen more as a collection of strands rather than as a distinctive part of an integral whole. I became increasingly troubled that it was a tokenistic

24 In 2011, an Office for National Statistics survey revealed that 10 per cent of all long-term relationships in the UK were interethnic. Of all people in the UK in interethnic relationships, just under half included someone who was White British.

gesture and did nothing to banish a growing mentality that contributed to the ghettoising of aspects of the curriculum, rather than integrating them.[25] The history that is most relevant to British school children is the history we all share.

As a young teacher, I was very enthusiastic about 'redefining the curriculum' to make it more relevant to the children I taught. If that is one of your concerns, go ahead. I applaud you and encourage you to do so. Questions about redefining values confront every generation of teachers afresh. But if 'decolonising the curriculum' becomes your passion, make sure you don't end up ghettoising it in the process. We must be critical of the quality of resources and teaching materials that claim to offer an alternative viewpoint, especially if they promote a particular political agenda or a narrow view of history. Just because we may lack the knowledge or the confidence to teach something like 'black history' does not mean we should use the first thing that comes to hand.

Of course, we may want to go on and study the history of black people or other cultures and countries in more depth and detail; that is all well and good. I did it myself at university. But while children are at school in the UK, it is important that they know the principal events and characters that have shaped British history – the myths and legends that both celebrate it and depict it, warts and all. In the case of black British children (although the principle stands for any ethnic group), their history is principally 'British history', not 'black history'. This is true for all children irrespective of their ethnicity.

Black British history is and should be an integral part of mainstream British history and our national collective consciousness, not a subset of it that is targeted at black and ethnic minority children because we think their self-esteem depends on it. Nor should it be targeted at white children because we think it will educate them about racial justice or ameliorate their 'white privilege'. We must also be careful not to embrace what some have called 'the soft bigotry of low expectations'. We must seek to create equality of opportunity, relentlessly expose discrimination and, where possible, rectify its effects. In doing so, however, we must not unwittingly foster an irredeemable sense of alienation or grievance in a section of our population for whom this country – their country – is the only one they are likely to live in and be a citizen of. We all want to belong.

Black British history should rightfully be part of the nation's collective memory. Given that it will include the history of slavery, it will necessarily require a measure of truth and reconciliation as part of the process. The stories of its victims, villains and heroes

25 It was after reading Dr Martin Luther King's 'Letter from a Birmingham Jail' that I began to question the idea of a Black History Month. I could not reconcile the idea with the aspirations for racial integration he spoke of: 'All segregation … [is] unjust because segregation distorts the soul and damages the personality. It gives the segregator a false sense of superiority and the segregated a false sense of inferiority.'

must be fully told and recognised. It is fascinating to me that black people have been part of British history from the earliest historical records. Their stories, contributions and tribulations are known – to all those who wish to avail themselves of the knowledge – through the lives of soldiers, traders, authors, enslaved servants, courtiers, campaigners, princes and kings who came to Britain from the time of the Roman occupation in AD 43 through to the courts of the Tudors, the Stuarts, the Georgians, the Victorians and into the twenty-first century.

Names and events like, Ukawsaw Gronniosaw (James Albert), Olaudah Equiano (Gustavus Vassa), Dido Belle, Ottobah Cugoano (John Stuart), James Somerset, Lord Mansfield and the slave ship *Zong*, Francis Barber and Samuel Johnson, Jonathan Strong and Granville Sharp, Bill Richmond, Zachary Macaulay and the Sierra Leone colony, the West Africa Squadron, Sarah Forbes Bonetta and Queen Victoria, Ira Aldridge, Mary Seacole, William Wilberforce and the abolition movement, Mary Prince, Samuel Coleridge-Taylor, Frederick Douglass, the Lancashire Cotton Famine, the service of Commonwealth soldiers in both world wars, Learie Constantine and the Lancashire (cricket) League, Harold Moody and the League of Coloured Peoples, Paul Robeson, Black GIs in England, Claudia Jones, the Bristol Bus Boycott, the *Empire Windrush*, the Notting Hill riots, the Notting Hill Carnival, Johnson Beharry – and, of course many, many more. And that doesn't include Asians, other ethnic minorities and people of colour like Dadabhai Naoroji, Mancherjee Bhownaggree and Noor Inayat Khan, and nor does it include more contemporary history. Their lives and stories are not *black* history, they are an integral part of *British* history.

This brings us back to notions of how 'Britishness' (and perhaps particularly 'Englishness') has been historically constructed. All identity (not just historical notions of a British ethnic identity) is forged as much by what it is not as by what it is. How do you know you are a Scot? By your language, customs and culture and (throughout history) knowing that you are *not English*! How do you know you are British? By your language, customs and culture and (throughout history) by knowing you were *not a French or Spanish Catholic* or *not a Lutheran German* and so on. In other words, by identifying and defining yourself with and by distinctive characteristics, but also in contrast to an 'other'.

Some historians argue that the other has had a significant influence in shaping British (along with other European) identities, especially in the latter part of the nineteenth century when nationalism was at its height. This included the particular dimension of the 'racial other' – where, in the case of the British, they began to see themselves as 'not Indian' or 'not African' (and most recently for some 'not European'). Other historians maintain that antithetical attitudes towards Islam and Africans as the other have been present in European historical consciousness since antiquity.[26] Whatever the truth, there can be no moral justification for a national identity that defines itself on the basis of a distinction to a racial other.

The way any society remembers and teaches its history is a reflection of its values. Any re-remembering of British history – and, in particular, the British Empire – must embrace all its complexity and not fall foul of historical revisionists and apologists on the one hand, or politically correct versions which claim that 'only white people did terrible things to black people' on the other. Teaching history – even contentious history – can, should and, indeed, must create a positive sense of belonging and identity for children of all ethnic backgrounds. Although the process is fraught with risk, we should teach children about the British Empire with confidence and honesty, not with guilt, shame, embarrassment or denial – as long as we all are prepared to share fundamental values by honestly examining the past while forging a confident future together. Teachers are the perfect people to model and demonstrate this challenge to the rest of society.

Civic patriotism

As we have noted, historians usually define nations by the commonality of language, laws, customs and culture, all of which are imbued with values. If the British do have a language, laws, customs and culture that could be described as common, then the consequence of such a view is that British values are characteristic of them. Of course, there can never be a definitive list of British values, any more than there can be a definitive list of what makes up morality, ethics or character. Signing up to fundamental British values is not a box-ticking exercise, but a collective commitment to a range of civic values and virtues. The crucial question for me about so-called British values is this: what are the rallying points around which we can all gather?

In a society as diverse and multicultural as ours, the answer must be that we come together and stand together as British, with a set of values we can all subscribe to irrespective of origin or background. As difficult as these are to isolate or define, we can coalesce around what Simon Schama has called 'the idea of being British'.[27] This has been a very powerful idea for hundreds of years. The value of that idea, let alone the practice of values and virtues that surround it, should not be degraded or lost, or we shall find that we are all the poorer.

26 For more on this discussion, listen to Melvyn Bragg, *In Our Time: The British Empire's Legacy* [radio programme], BBC Radio 4 (31 December 1998). Available at: https://www.bbc.co.uk/programmes/p005459p.

27 Simon Schama, *A History of Britain. Vol. 3: The Fate of the Empire 1776–2000* (London: Bodley Head, 2009), p. 516.

Any community or society that seeks to grow, cohere and bond needs to weave its stories of old and new together. All successful communities throughout history have done this whether they are tribes, religions or nation states. Myths and legends are what unite us. Throughout history, scholars with privileged access to the powerful have struggled with the dilemma of whether to serve power or truth. Christian priests, Confucian mandarins and communist ideologues have all grappled with the moral quandary of whether to elevate the myths that unite people over the truth that might lead to a better understanding. Teachers must do this too.

How does a fascist or a communist evaluate a work of art, a play, a film or a symphony? By asking himself: does it serve the group collective – the party, the nation or the workers' interest? If it does not, then it is a bad work of art. If it does, then it is a good one. For a fascist or a communist, it is as simple as that. How does a fascist or a communist decide what teachers should teach and what children should learn in school? He uses the same yardstick: whatever serves the interests of the group collective, not the individual, is what matters. To them, truth does not matter.[28]

Liberal-democratic societies that extol the virtues of fundamental values and the search for truth are not like this. They balance the myths of a national identity with the truth of its evidential history. This is a complex matter. While common language, laws, customs and culture are usually the defining characteristics of a nation, the complexity of the issues around national identity is highly dynamic and multifaceted. For example, nations do not necessarily convert into states – just look at the nations of the aboriginal peoples in North America or Australia. Possession of a common language or a common religion is not always the conclusive criterion for nationhood either – just take Indians or Slavs. Likewise, a common history – take Arabs, Jews, Kurds or Armenians.

However, national identity is not an invalid concept because it happened to be an outcome of a trauma, like invasion, colonisation, enslavement, domination, war or even civil war. Indeed, such events are often the catalyst for an emergent national identity, as has been the case for most North and South American nations and most modern European ones too, like Belgium, Spain, Italy and Germany. National identity cannot be dismissed merely because it is multifaceted, multidimensional or, as we have noted above, because it defies categorisation.

Daniel Defoe, the author of *Robinson Crusoe*, wrote as long ago as 1706 that British history was (as paraphrased by Simon Schama) 'a history of happy mongrelism and had been all the better for it'[29] – a description that could just as well be applied to British demography, which has both an ancient and a modern history, comprised as it is of Gaels, Welsh, Norse, Picts, Scotti, Northumbrians, Angles, Romans, Saxons, Vikings, Normans, Moors, Friesians, Huguenots, Flemings, Jews, Irish, Italians, Caribbeans, South

28 See Harari, *21 Lessons for the 21st Century*, ch. 3.
29 Simon Schama, *A History of Britain. Vol. 2: The British Wars 1603–1776* (London: Bodley Head, 2009), p. 275.

Asians, Sub-Saharan Africans and many more. Our historic emperors, earls, lords, lairds, kings and queens have therefore included Gaels from the Celtic fringes who spoke Gaelic, Romans from Italy who spoke Latin, Vikings from Scandinavia who spoke Norse, Normans from France who spoke French (who, in turn, had been Norsemen from Scandinavia and had earlier invaded Northern France), Tudors who were partly Welsh and partly Spanish, Stuarts who were Scottish and Dutch, Hanoverians from Prussia (Germany) who spoke German – that is a thousand years of 'British' history that does not include an 'English' dynasty. While this is all very interesting from a historical point of view, and an entertaining illustration of where we have come from, it is not really relevant to the discussion about where our national identity is today or where we are going with it.

It is crucial that, as teachers, we construct a professional identity that is ethical, positive and forward-looking. Teachers should be confident about their role in helping young people to forge a modern identity that continuously shares its customs, evolves its language, revises its laws and reconstitutes its culture. Without schools that foster shared meanings, shared understandings and shared values, children will feel alienated and grow up to live in a society where their identity will flounder. If a child who has been born and brought up in the UK says: 'I'm not British, I'm Pakistani' or 'I'm not British, I'm Jamaican' or 'I'm not British, I'm Somali' (as some did during my time in schools), that is not a healthy view. Of course, anyone might rightfully say: 'I'm Pakistani-British' or 'I'm British-Pakistani' or 'I'm British of Pakistani background', proudly reflecting their dual heritage and identity. But a child who has been born and brought up in the UK who says: 'I'm not British' is not reflecting the healthy condition of a diverse society, but a divided and neurotic psychology dangerously vulnerable to division and exploitation.

I believe strongly that children growing up in this country should see themselves as British. Why? Because, as we saw earlier, like all clans and tribes throughout history and throughout the world, human beings have a deep psychological need to belong – to create myths and legends that forge bonds of affiliation, integration, loyalty and, perhaps most importantly, identity. Myths and legends are not lies, but nor are they historical truths. They are foundational stories that convey a society's concept of itself forward to the next generation.

I reject nationalism which sees itself as superior, exceptional or exclusive, although I do believe that national identities are ingrained psychologically as much as they are ideologically. Nor am I arguing for the legitimisation of the notion of nativism – the modern politics of birthplace, land and language. However, we are forced in the modern era to consider the way in which identities such as Britishness, and perhaps especially Englishness, have become problematic. We live in a world where many societies, not just Western ones, are characterised by the seemingly contradictory nature of the constant flux of migration on the one hand and the saturating impact of globalised media that purveys an apparently homogenised culture on the other.

Here, I find my subscription to the idea of a covenantal relationship to society (with its roots in religious tradition) allied with civic patriotism (rooted in secular tradition) very useful. A covenantal civic patriotism is one which:

- Builds community and societal cohesion – encompassing a responsible commitment to each other based on respect for history, heritage and traditions.
- Promotes a sense of belonging to a place and a community, but whose love for the place where you are born (or the place you have chosen to live) is welcoming and transforms 'outsiders' into 'insiders'.
- Affords mutual respect for diverse opinions and gives every voice a hearing, acknowledging that some opinions will be favoured over others.
- Builds resilience against the temptations of resorting to extremism and fascism.
- Promotes a sense of charity that begins at home but does not end there, and gives special concern to those in need.
- Develops bonds of trust and loyalty, which are reflected in an inclusive national identity and affords special honour to those who serve and have sacrificed.[30]

Civic patriotism, therefore, has an ethically and morally robust basis for the promotion of fundamental British values through spiritual, moral, social and cultural education, to which we will turn in Appendix C.

30 Compiled from ideas expressed by: David Goodhart, *Analysis: Conservative Muslims, Liberal Britain*, [radio programme], BBC Radio 4 (16 November 2016). Available at: https://www.bbc.co.uk/programmes/b04nrqsm; and Sacks, *Morality: Restoring the Common Good*, pp. 334–335.

Appendix B

MULTICULTURALISM AND A MULTICULTURAL SOCIETY

Multiculturalism is a range of ideas and practices introduced widely from the late 1970s across Western societies at national and local level, which sought to better integrate and respect the cultural, religious and ethnic backgrounds of minority immigrant groups. While its popularity as an idea has waned in recent years, its legacy is still very evident in schools and across public policy. There are signs that in some areas of education it is making a comeback. Although multiculturalism was introduced with the best moral and ethical intentions, there is now strong evidence that it has led to unintended negative outcomes, such as entrenched forms of segregation. In recent years, many political and social commentators from both the right and left have voiced criticisms – for example, the former Chief Rabbi Jonathan Sacks wrote that multiculturalism has 'turned society from a home into a hotel, in which each group has its own room but there is little sense of collective belonging'.[1]

Concrete evidence of its negative impact comes from a number of sources. Firstly, a recent Dutch study (the Netherlands has been one of the pioneers and most ardent advocates of the multicultural experiment) showed that a majority of Dutch respondents felt there had been a fundamental mismatch between the notions of 'tolerance' on the one hand and 'multiculturalism' on the other. The views of respondents were summed up in phrases like: 'tolerance means ignoring differences, multiculturalism means making an issue of them'; 'the benefits of tolerance are large and the costs negligible. By contrast, the material benefits of multiculturalism appear negligible and the costs high'; and 'sharing a common identity builds support for inclusion, bringing differences of ethnic and religious identity to the fore evokes an exclusionary reaction it is meant to avoid'. The critical fault line of the multiculturalism experiment has therefore been the attempt to square a very difficult if not impossible circle, in that it asserts simultaneously: 'You must understand me' and 'You cannot understand me'.[2]

As a teacher, I was an enthusiastic standard-bearer for multiculturalism in schools and universities throughout the 1980s and 1990s. Like the experiment itself, I acted with the best moral motives in mind, and I saw some important areas of public life change for the better. Indeed, at the time, I didn't view multiculturalism as an 'experiment'; I merely saw it as the natural and desirable outcome of people with different cultures living together. However, I look back now and realise that I was guilty of 'a fatal

1 Sacks, *Morality: Restoring the Common Good*, p. 140.

2 Quoted in Sacks, *Morality: Restoring the Common Good*, pp. 140–141.

conceit'[3] – when we believe with absolute certainty that a development is safe, not realising that it may be years before the real danger emerges, and then, even worse, not acknowledging it when it does.

I fear that as teachers and wider society, we are doing the same with diversity – that it is being used to uncritically endorse educational and social policies that are non-integrative and disharmonising. I am increasingly dismayed and sometimes alarmed at how often I see examples in the UK (and other countries) where suspicion of motive and an inclination to separate, if not exclude, has replaced a respectful tolerance for difference and the responsibility we all have to seek common ground. Such behaviour is justified on the basis of 'protecting minority cultures' or 'creating safe spaces', and an over-zealous inclination to embrace victimhood is laying claim to what the great philosopher Bertrand Russell called 'the superior virtue of the oppressed'.[4]

I have spent my professional life working to combat prejudice and bigotry, both that which is clearly evident and that which is covert, that which blatantly oppresses and that which furtively victimises minority groups. But victimisation and victimhood are not the same thing. Victimisation is an assault on the person from without. Victimhood is a chosen or adopted attitude – an assault on the psyche from within. One of the main legacies of multiculturalism is that we have allowed a cult of victimhood to become an established norm in our educational and political discourse.

There are two further dangers looming from the legacy of multiculturalism. The first is particular to schools and teachers: we fail to recognise the mistakes that former generations of teachers (like me) made, and in doing so we allow the negative aspects of multiculturalism to masquerade as diversity and become entrenched. The second is that as a liberal-democratic society, we have failed to respond to the growing popularity of exclusionary and divisive identity politics and the populist memes of far-right communitarianism and nationalism. A tolerant and patriotic society is about promoting the fundamental values to which we all subscribe, share and love. It is about the kind of patriotism described by George Orwell as a 'devotion to a particular place and a particular way of life, which one believes to be the best in the world but has no wish to force on other people'.[5]

Other evidence that multiculturalism has led to forms of segregation and separate identities comes from the writing and studies of journalists and social commentators from the political left who once, like me, wholeheartedly supported the idea. One such

3 A term coined by the neoliberal Austrian-British economist and philosopher Friedrich Hayek: *The Fatal Conceit: The Errors of Socialism* (London & New York: Routledge, 1988).

4 Bertrand Russell, The Superior Virtue of the Oppressed, in *Unpopular Essays* (Abingdon and New York: Routledge, 2009 [1950]), pp. 56–62.

5 George Orwell, Notes on Nationalism, *Polemic*, 1 (1945). Available at: https://www.orwellfoundation.com/the-orwell-foundation/orwell/essays-and-other-works/notes-on-nationalism.

example is David Goodhart.[6] He has reported how contemporary senior Muslim scholars in the UK have conceded that as a result of the multicultural model, Muslim communities in towns and cities across the UK (like Bradford, Birmingham, Luton, Leicester and elsewhere) are more segregated now than their forebears were who came to Britain in the 1950s, 1960s and 1970s. They also acknowledge that the current, largely British born-and-bred, generation is more religiously and socially conservative than previous generations who were the initial migrants. Even more surprising, Muslim communities in Britain are likely to be more religiously and socially conservative than their kith and kin who reside in Pakistan and Bangladesh.[7] After decades of socialising, schooling and education in a society with twenty-first century liberal values, how has this happened?

Goodhart asks a series of uncomfortable but pertinent questions that force us to examine the nature and extent of our tolerance. Moreover, they relate not just to conservative Muslim communities in places like Bradford and Luton, but also to orthodox Jewish communities in Stamford Hill in London, Prestwich or Cheetham Hill in Manchester and long-established Chinese communities in places like London, Liverpool and Manchester.

Discuss and reflect

- Is it intolerant to have reservations that parts of some British cities might become so culturally distinct that significant numbers of their residents no longer share the values, customs and language of the country as a whole?
- Is a high degree of ethnic separateness (as pertains in most US cities) compatible with a Britain at ease with itself? Is it a cause for celebration of the liberal ideal or a threat to it?
- Is it a liberal value to tolerate illiberalism? Should we be intolerant of intolerance?

These conundrums are not merely for public policymakers to solve. They are highly pertinent for teachers in schools who are facing such testing questions on a regular basis. Is it beneficial for children, and ethically acceptable for teachers, that Muslim parents and governors at state-funded primary schools can, for example, restrict the teaching of subjects like music, dance, PE and humanities (as has happened in some Luton secondary schools)? Is it a positive social development, let alone educational,

6 David Goodhart is the founder and former editor of the left-leaning, although largely contrarian, *Prospect* magazine.
7 Goodhart, *Analysis: Conservative Muslims.*

that the teaching of RE has been approved only from an Islamic perspective and authorised on the basis of gender (as has happened in some Birmingham schools)? The legacies of multiculturalism are not restricted to elements of the Muslim community: for most of my time teaching in Hackney, independent schools run by the orthodox Jewish community in Stamford Hill had their applications for state funding turned down because they refused to provide the full breadth of the national curriculum to girls.

However, as we have found in our discussion of aspects of identity, the picture is highly complex and we must always be wary of characterising a single group on the basis of its conservative or orthodox members. It is self-evident that not all ethnic groups are the same. Similarly, racism is not a homogeneous experience, and our analysis of it and responses to it need to be contextualised. A survey by the think tank Policy Exchange in 2016 reported (among a wide range of positive developments) that young Muslim people are much more likely to go on to university and into established professions (particularly medicine) than their white counterparts.[8] The social mobility of the rapidly expanding Muslim middle class is far more dynamic than almost every other ethnic group.

Conservatism in social values is not new and nor is it a feature of life unique to Muslims. There are plenty of upper-middle-class women in predominantly 'white society' who choose to stay at home and bring up their children. There are many conservative Christians who do not believe that women should become priests or are opposed to same-sex marriage. There are evangelical and Pentecostal Christians who believe that homosexuality is a mortal sin. Positive trends in some areas and in some communities do not necessarily extend to all. Where this includes a divergence from the fundamental values we have been discussing, then there are likely to be problematic issues for us all, especially when we are uncritical of social and educational policies like multiculturalism that exacerbate such trends.

Discuss and reflect

- Children should rightly have the individual liberty to choose their own friends. Would you be content to acquiesce to a state of affairs where children do not choose friends outside of their own ethnic group in school?
- Do you think the school should respond to such a situation? Why? How? And what practically might the school do?

8 Martin Frampton, David Goodhart and Khalid Mahmood, *Unsettled Belonging: A Survey of Britain's Muslim Communities* (London: Policy Exchange, 2016), ch. 4. Available at: https://policyexchange.org.uk/publication/unsettled-belonging-a-survey-of-britains-muslim-communities.

A third body of evidence on the negative outcomes of multiculturalism comes from the political columnist and former Labour Party advisor Sonia Sodha.[9] She claimed that councils, like Leicester, Tower Hamlets and others around the UK, were not only vulnerable to but also colluded with a system of 'patron–client politics'. Mainstream political parties (in particular the Labour Party) approached 'community leaders' (often self-appointed) to access temples, mosques and gurdwaras. These spurious leaders effectively became community gatekeepers, with the power to allow or disallow access to the community and to deliver (or deny) the block vote to particular politicians or parties who best patronised them. Local politicians actively colluded in this process and granted favours, such as dedicated community or sports centres or preferential housing allocations, wittingly or unwittingly allowing the process of self-segregation to grow.

The notion of so-called community leaders is, of course, blatantly racist. If we were to ask: 'Who are the community leaders of the white community?' the obvious answer would be the people who are either democratically elected, like local councillors and MPs, or appointed faith leaders, like priests, vicars, imams and rabbis. The irony is that this process distorted, if not corrupted, a legitimate demand for increased participation and a voice for marginalised ethnic minorities. However, once the practice of funding community projects for particular ethnic minorities became entrenched, so did a sense of entitlement based on ethnicity, which began to displace projects dedicated to the common good. It is possible to argue that if citizens in a liberal society choose to self-segregate, then that is their choice, but where public funds are being allocated, the criteria should be based strictly on ethical, not ethnic, grounds. Democratic accountability must be transparent. Community leaders are elected, not self-appointed. People should be treated as voters, not ethnic minorities.

By contrast, Newham Council in East London, one of the most diverse boroughs in the UK, followed the multiculturalism model for many years, but in the early 2000s began to reassess these practices and became a leading proponent for promoting community projects that are funded only when they can be seen to serve the needs of more than one religious or ethnic group. They have since become a model for integrationist and ethical approaches to local civic policy. Newham Council still values and celebrates difference and diversity, but not in exchange for the greater good – which is the common good.

As teachers, we must ensure that we have a similar philosophy to promoting civic values in schools. In order to acquire a strong sense of civic society – loving the place we live, respecting each other, tolerating difference and engaging in positively reconstructing a *shared* culture – we must:

9 Sonia Sodha, *Analysis: Multiculturalism: Newham v Leicester* [radio programme], BBC Radio 4 (28 February 2016). Available at: https://www.bbc.co.uk/programmes/b071459c.

- *articulate* – that is, give children the appropriate language and vocabulary
- *demonstrate* – show them how civic values work, and
- *model* – show them what civic values looks like.

Multiculturalism might have encouraged (and perhaps even succeeded) people being nicer to each other, but it has discouraged (and perhaps even prevented) people being critical of each other. I would urge the current generation of teachers not to make the same mistakes I made with the apparently innocent discourse of diversity and inclusion. Examine these terms and don't take them at face value. I am for diversity but against fragmentation. I am no longer in favour of multiculturalism. However, I am still, and hope I always will be, a huge and passionate advocate for the benefits of a multicultural society.

Appendix C

SPIRITUAL, MORAL, SOCIAL AND CULTURAL EDUCATION ACTIVITIES

The teaching of virtues, fundamental British values and civic patriotism is enabled through spiritual, moral, social and cultural education. This might include activities such as:

1. A school debating society: use established formats and methods to debate topical issues (e.g. the global climate crisis, the migrant crisis, a tax on sugar).
2. Circle Time: a well-established format (pioneered by Jenny Mosley) for conflict resolution and group discussion of personal and emotional issues in class.
3. A philosophy society: discuss and debate philosophical issues such as: 'Why am I not allowed to swear?' and 'Why am I not free to learn what I want?'
4. Recognition or celebration of religious festivals: such as Christmas, Easter, Passover, Hanukkah, Diwali, Eid, Vaisakhi and so on.
5. Visits to places of worship: such as churches, synagogues, mosques and temples.
6. Organising yoga, Pilates or mindfulness classes after school: involve the children in teaching, demonstrating or administering.
7. Involving pupils in organising visits to the school by local politicians: writing letters of invitation to MPs, candidates of political parties or serving councillors to talk about what they stand for, what they do and so on; organising a social event; organising a 'Question Time' event and so on.
8. Involving pupils in arranging a visit to the local (town, city or county) council chamber: request a tour with the school's local councillor; ask for an explanation of how the council works; organise a Q&A with, for example, the lead member for the environment or other concern.
9. Corresponding with local MPs or councillors: on a school or local issue arising out of the School Council, the school governing body and so on.

10. Involving children in elections for a school council: nominating candidates, devising a manifesto, organising political parties, writing and making speeches, a 'Question Time' event, organising the election, voting in a secret ballot, the count, the declaration and so on.

11. School awards system: involve the children in deciding what categories and kinds of awards (e.g. school citizen of the term), how often they are awarded and so on.

12. Organising joint governor and pupil focus group meetings: discuss and consult on matters of school governance, building maintenance or curriculum issues.

13. Involving students in mock elections for a General Election: devising a manifesto for children, choosing policies, affiliating to political parties, how to make speeches and stage debates, 'Any Questions' event, organising an election, secret ballots, the count, the declaration and so on.

14. Engaging in local politics: such as local council elections, mayoral elections, local pressure groups and issues.

15. Involving pupils in focus groups: consultations for introducing new school systems (e.g. new lunch menus, reorganising the playground, school rewards and awards, sanctions and punishments).

16. Advocacy assemblies and campaigns: involve children in organising appeals for local charities or supervised volunteering; fundraising for local, national or international charities (e.g. local environmental and children's charities, Comic Relief, Children in Need).

17. Home–school agreements or contracts: involve the school council in a consultative way on drawing up the terms of the contract, how parents can be involved, how often it is reviewed and so on.

18. Involving pupils in devising or reviewing school behaviour policies: such as 'the five Cs' class rules, golden rules, the school's behaviour policy and so on.

19. Involving pupils in the recruitment and selection of staff: a consultation group selected from the school council to conduct a consultative interview with teaching candidates.

20. Anti-bullying week: get pupils involved in devising activities and ideas to combat bullying, organise a pupil conference on harassment and intimidation with invited outside speakers.

21. Playground buddies: involve the children in nominating and appointing pupils who will befriend lonely and marginalised pupils.

22. Achievement assemblies: involve the children in nominating others (other than friends) for weekly recognition in various categories (e.g. citizen of the week).

23. Reviewing the school's curriculum policies: consult the children at the draft stage of reviewing school policies, such as the religious education curriculum, anti-bullying policy and so on.

24. Engaging with how the law is made and applied: establish school links and visit local law courts, arrange visits from lawyers to discuss their work, involve children in role-play in mock law courts, involve the school council in resolving civil disputes, compare the way Beth Din (Jewish) and Sharia (Islamic) communities settle disputes.

25. Competitive team sports clubs in school: start a new sports team or club, involve the children in how they are organised (e.g. selecting teams and captains, administering fixtures, taking responsibility for accounting).

26. Engaging in, supporting or celebrating local social events: selling at local markets, promoting the school at high street events or country fairs, joining fun runs, volunteering at marathons, engaging with local literary/film/music festivals.

27. Cultural school club: involve the children in running and managing a club (e.g. film, theatre, music, literary); invite actors, directors and authors; publish critical reviews and so on.

28. Local social volunteering: at food banks and homeless shelters, visits to old people's homes, helping with Christmas parties in special schools, volunteering on local environmental and wildlife projects.

29. Involving children in the local wildlife trust: visit wetlands, sanctuaries and reserves; invite speakers into school to demonstrate conservation methods; establish a conservation or wildlife reserve in the school grounds.

30. Involving pupils in running and managing a school shop (e.g. bookshop): organising applications and interviews for the posts of managers and assistants, choosing stock, stocktaking, accounting, marketing and so on.

31. Start a local environmental group: engage with local green and sustainable energy groups, volunteer for local environment projects, form or join local litter-picking groups, organise local volunteering opportunities.

32. Cubs/Scouts/Girl Guides/Woodcraft Folk/Sea, Air, Army Cadets: set up a group based at the school or link with a local group to share facilities, activities and resources.

33. Make links with a local historical society: invite local historians, visit sites of historical interest and examine documents of local historical significance.

34. Make links with local sports clubs (such as the junior sections of rugby, sailing or golf clubs): negotiate use of their facilities, organise access to coaching and so on.

35. Start a bird protection club: to observe and protect local birdlife, link with local and national groups, invite experts and activists to the school.

36. Start an outdoor society: to walk and explore local areas of outstanding natural beauty, National Parks, engage in other local outdoor activities, affiliate to the Ramblers or the Youth Hostel Association.

37. Links or visits to (or from) local civic services: promoting understanding of the role and work of police, fire and ambulance services; raising awareness of keeping safe; equality in career options and so on.

38. Involving pupils in organising visits to national institutions: such as the Houses of Parliament and regional assemblies in Scotland, Wales and Northern Ireland; national museums and galleries, such as the National Maritime Museums in Liverpool, Hull or Falmouth; the Imperial War Museums in London and Salford; the Slavery Museum in Liverpool; the Wilberforce House Museum in Hull; the Amgueddfa Genedlaethol in Cardiff; the National Galleries of Scotland in Edinburgh; the Royal Courts of Justice; and so on.

39. Celebrating or engaging with national events: such as the UK General Election, Guy Fawkes Night, Burns Night, the FA Cup Final, the Grand National, St George's Day, St Andrew's Day, St David's Day, St Patrick's Day, Remembrance Sunday, Commonwealth Day, Pride and so on.

40. Recognising or engaging with European-wide events: such as the Eurovision Song Contest, Six Nations Championship, Tour de France, UEFA European Championship, European Day of Languages and so on.

41. Recognising or engaging with international or world events: such as International Women's Day, Olympic Games, FIFA World Cup, Holocaust Memorial Day, US presidential election, climate treaties, issues debated at the United Nations and so on.

Let's take a few examples to better illustrate the process.

1. A school debating society

When I was at school, which was an inner-city comprehensive in Liverpool, my English teacher, Mr LeRoi, introduced a debating society. We didn't know what it was or how it worked, but once he had started it off, we learned to manage it ourselves. We could come up with motions about anything we liked – abortion, immigration, racial prejudice, unilateral nuclear disarmament – nothing seemed to be off limits. Indeed, it was almost impossible to conceive of any discussion that was deemed too contentious once we had learned the rules, which were rigidly applied to ensure there was no uncivil behaviour – abuse, threats or incitement. Within weeks, our debating society, which met at lunchtimes, was attracting audiences of scores.

The rules of debating require a fixed motion to be proposed and seconded, then two proponents and two opponents make prepared speeches stating their case on either side. Each gets their turn to speak without interruption for a fixed period while their opponents – and the audience – have to listen. At the end of the formal debate, there are questions from the audience managed by a chairperson. After a period during which the audience tests the arguments, there is a show of hands or the chair asks for those supporting the motion to say 'aye' and those opposing the motion to say 'no'.

To many, the idea of a debating society might seem archaic and insufferably middle class, conjuring up images of Eton, Harrow or the Oxford Union. Actually, these formats challenge young people to acquire a range of oratorical and intellectual skills (as the head teacher of a primary school, I had a monthly debating society with children as young as 10 and 11 years of age). From it, they learn to:

- Structure arguments: 'My first point is … My second point is … Finally, my third point is …'
- Use persuasive techniques: 'Think how you would feel if such a thing happened to you …'
- Exhibit rhetorical flourishes: 'My priorities are education, education, education …'

The convention requires young people to listen to assertions and opinions without interruption, ones that they might fundamentally disagree with or that they may find offensive, even odious. Once the arguments have been stated, the audience tests the logic or moral justification with questions that might expose flaws, raise counterpoints or more compelling counter-narratives. The debating society format is an exercise in competitive rhetoric, so at the end the audience is not being asked to vote on the opinion they held when they entered the room but which side of the argument made the most compelling and persuasive case. This challenges all participants to keep an open mind and allow themselves to be amenable to persuasion and reasonable disagreement.

Reasonable disagreements are based on the idea that arguments would be pointless if we did not recognise that there is some truth in an opposing position. For example, take the arguments presented when debating abortion. They are based on the premise – an essential truth – that both human life and human choice should be respected. Without participants accepting the premise of the other perspective, there could be no argument. For me, this example illustrates better than most how mutual respect and individual liberty are fundamental moral values.

The way to teach children about reasonable disagreements in morality is not to disguise or avoid controversial issues, but to teach controversial standards alongside justified standards and controversial arguments alongside sound arguments. This is the basis of human enquiry – how our knowledge is driven forward not by the assertion of certainty but by proposal and counterproposal, speculation and disputation, argument and criticism.[1] The outcome is, hopefully, greater wisdom and the development of character.

Former Labour cabinet minister Douglas Alexander has come up with four propositions for tackling apparently irreconcilable moral standards, beliefs and opinions.[2] He says:

1. Don't assume you know other people's motives. Contempt is a killer in any kind of relationship development, discussion or debate.

2. Don't split the difference and say you will compromise on something that you simply cannot compromise about. Alternatively, search for what common ground there is.

3. Be brave enough to display respectful but radical honesty – not just civility – towards one another.

4. Listen and try to establish empathy, imagining what it is like to be in your adversary's position.

Clearly, then, apart from the obvious oratorical and intellectual skills it can develop, regular meetings of debating societies enable young people 'to develop their self-knowledge, self-esteem and self-confidence', 'encourage respect for other people' and 'encourage respect for democracy and support for participation in the democratic

1 See Hand, *A Theory of Moral Education*, p. 84.
2 Douglas Alexander, *Seriously: A Guide to Disagreeing Better* [radio programme], BBC Radio 4 (17 December 2019). Available at: https://www.bbc.co.uk/programmes/p07y3d18.

processes'.[3] Activities such as these are the way fundamental British values should be promoted. They are also the way to inculcate wider interpretations of virtues, values and the development of character, not as a taught subject but caught and embedded in the life and fabric of the school.

10. School councils

At most of the schools I have worked in we had a school council. I have to admit that they often didn't function very well, but that wasn't the fault of the children as much as it was the fault of the teachers who managed them. The problem was that we didn't scope them properly. If you tell children they can have a school council without managing their expectations, they will suddenly think they can abolish all the horrible subjects they don't like or build a new swimming pool in the staff car park. When they discover they can't, they soon lose interest. If you want to set up and run a successful school council (and there are lots of resources and advice available – see Appendix F), start by explaining what the council can and cannot do.

School councils work best when the children understand that they can do things like:

- Liaise with the school cook on deciding lunch menus.
- Consult with school governors on reviewing school policies – for example, the discipline and behaviour policy.
- Interview candidates for playground buddies or the bookshop manager.
- Make decisions on how the school playground is designed or how it is managed to facilitate diverse interests.

Managing expectations will be a constant challenge, though, as children enthusiastically bring to you all kinds of ideas that they think might be within the remit of the school council. Explain how the boundaries of all democratic decision-making bodies have a limited jurisdiction – a parish council does not have the same scope as a town council, a town council does not have the same scope as a county council, a regional assembly does not have the same scope as the national Westminster parliament. Just because the school council can only make decisions about school dinners or bullying sanctions, it doesn't mean that the children are not starting to understand and participate in democratic processes – they are.

---

3 Department for Education, *Promoting Fundamental British Values as Part of SMSC in Schools*, p. 5.

In my experience, the most benefit (and the most fun) children get from school councils is electing them – nominating and seconding candidates, writing manifestos, delivering speeches and so on. When such activities are managed well (and children will need support and encouragement to do so), they learn 'respect for democracy and support for participation in the democratic processes, including respect for the basis on which the law is made and applied in England'. They also 'develop self-knowledge, self-esteem and self-confidence'. Such activities are also likely to 'encourage respect for other people' and contribute to their acquisition of 'a broad general knowledge of and respect for public institutions and services in England'.[4]

25. Competitive team sports

I don't intend to expand on all the virtues inherent in team sport, particularly as we have considered other dimensions of it elsewhere in the book, but there are some crucial aspects that I want to expand on in relation to the way we acquire fundamental values through spiritual, moral, social and cultural education.

First of all, what is sport? If you were to look up a dictionary definition, you would probably find something like 'rule-governed play involving competition'. When I think of how I learned to play as a young child, I remember crawling about on the floor with my collection of Dinky Toys, playing at garages or police car chases or Formula One races, and getting under my poor mother's feet. That is 'play', but it isn't the kind of rule-governed play we mean when we refer to 'sport'. It is imaginative play, where I was the sole arbiter of the rules that I made up as I went along.

When I was old enough to go to school, I saw other kids in the playground playing games like football (soccer), cricket, rounders (baseball) and bulldog. In order to participate, I had to learn the rules. I didn't do that by being instructed but by being inducted. I learned the rules as I participated. I soon discovered that not playing by the rules came with repercussions or penalties. If I handled the ball in football, the game would stop and a free kick would be awarded to the other team. The same would apply if I pushed someone aside or tripped them wilfully or clumsily. If I infringed the rules seriously or too often, I would be sent off the pitch and ruled out of the game. The lesson I was learning in sport – as in life – was to play by the rules.

4 Department for Education, *Promoting Fundamental British Values as Part of SMSC in Schools*, p. 5.

What makes sport so gripping for most of us is that it is also about loyalty, courage, hard work, practice, team spirit and the power to inspire others to greatness. Team sports and the passion with which they are followed also reflects an aspect of the human condition, which is the need to identify and belong to something greater than the individual self: the wider group, the 'we' and the 'us'.[5]

From the earliest days of the English public school, sports and games have been considered central to 'moulding the character of the English gentleman' and to developing and inspiring the virtues of fairness, loyalty, moral courage, physical courage and co-operation. In other words, the English public school provided 'a course in practical ethics'.[6]

Sport is a hugely important metaphor for civilised participation in society. Children need to learn that the landscape of our lives is like that of the sports pitch: we must know the boundaries and learn to play by the rules in order to join in and get on. When we do, we enjoy the benefit of others' company, we build relationships based on mutual reliance, we promote good physical and mental health, and we flourish. If we don't play by the rules, there are penalties, sometimes serious ones, which include exclusion, ostracism and banishment. From early beginnings, children learn to cope with gain and loss, success and disappointment, glory and despair. They learn about motivation, determination, resilience, self-reliance, team building and so on.

Sporting values also contribute to fundamental civic values. They provide the beginnings of understanding and imbibe a respect for the rule of law. They can enable children 'to develop their self-knowledge, self-esteem and self-confidence' and to 'distinguish right from wrong'. They can also encourage pupils 'to accept responsibility for their behaviour, show initiative, and to understand how they can contribute positively to the lives (of others)' and can 'encourage respect for other people'.[7]

This perhaps begs the question: are sporting values fundamental British values? In my view, yes, they are. Although they are not exclusively British and sport itself is not exclusively British, of course, it is interesting that British social and political history has played a huge part in introducing the rule-governed behaviour that we now recognise as formalised sport. This is true for many, if not most, games appropriated and made popular around the world – football (soccer), golf, tennis, boxing, rugby, cricket, hockey, horse racing and many more. All acquired their rules because of a peculiarly British preoccupation with bequeathing rules, if not law, through trade, imperialism and colonialism.[8]

5 See Sacks, *Morality: Restoring the Common Good*, p. 110.

6 See Arthur et al., *Teaching Character and Virtue in Schools*, p. 23.

7 Department for Education, *Promoting Fundamental British Values as Part of SMSC in Schools*, p. 5.

8 Consider the history of how various sports spread around the world largely as a result of Britain's trading and imperial past.

We only have to look at the performances of our national football teams in competitions over the last fifty years to see how countries like Italy, Brazil, Germany and Argentina have not only appropriated the game but also largely outperformed us at it. The same goes for other sports, like cricket, rugby, golf and so on. Irrespective of whether the British invented them or what our international ranking is, I think that sport is a fundamental British value. If the school you are working in does not have team games and clubs (with competition from an appropriate age), then once you are established in the school, I urge you to initiate them.

Appendix D

VIRTUES AND VALUES EDUCATION ACTIVITIES

Virtues can be categorised as:

- Moral virtues – such as courage, integrity, justice, respect, honesty, compassion, empathy, humility, self-regulation, responsibility, kindness, optimism, fairness, trustworthiness, gratitude.
- Performance virtues – such as resilience, teamwork, leadership, independence, confidence, determination, communication, motivation, diligence, adventurousness, perseverance, grit.
- Civic virtues – such as citizenship, civility, community awareness and neighbourliness, patriotism, socially oriented action, building on links with civic institutions, public service, volunteering.
- Intellectual virtues – such as curiosity, reasoning, analysis, judgement, autonomy, reflection, resourcefulness, critical thinking.[1]

You can do the following exercises with a group of your fellow trainees, your school colleagues or with the pupils in your class.

1 For more of a discussion on this, see Chapter 6; and Arthur et al., *The Good Teacher*. The Jubilee Centre also offer an online CPD course called 'Leading Character Education in Schools' – see www.jubileecentre.ac.uk.

Activity

What virtues make up your character? Put a circle around each virtue that you consider particularly reflects your own character and personality.

Accuracy	Acceptance	Achievement	Adaptability
Adventure	Affection	Altruism	Ambition
Assertiveness	Attractiveness	Bravery	Boldness
Balance	Beauty	Charm	Clarity
Calmness	Charity	Compassion	Completion
Cleanliness	Commitment	Consistency	Creativity
Cooperation	Contentment	Courage	Curiosity
Dignity	Dependability	Determination	Daring
Diversity	Diligence	Discipline	Devotion
Duty	Education	Effectiveness	Efficiency
Elegance	Empathy	Endurance	Enjoyment
Enthusiasm	Experience	Fidelity	Fairness
Fame	Family	Flexibility	Financial independence
Friendliness	Frugality	Fun	Freedom
Generosity	Grace	Gratitude	Growth
Honesty	Humour	Happiness	Harmony
Humility	Independence	Integrity	Intelligence
Imagination	Justice	Kindness	Leadership
Liberty	Loyalty	Neatness	Making a difference
Mastery	Obedience	Open-mindedness	Optimism
Originality	Organisation	Passion	Popularity
Peace	Perfectionism	Perseverance	Professionalism
Pleasure	Power	Privacy	Resilience
Reason	Resourcefulness	Reliability	Respect

Security	Sacrifice	Selflessness	Self-reliance
Spirituality	Service	Sincerity	Stability
Spontaneity	Success	Support	Sympathy
Strength	Truth	Teamwork	Temperance
Understanding	Uniqueness		

Notes and ideas for using this activity with your pupils:

- Of the virtues you have circled, choose the *five* most fundamental ones that reflect the essence of your character and personality. Discuss with a partner why you chose them. Are they really true? Or are they aspirations?
- How you would adapt this activity for the children you teach, given their age and maturity?

Some other suggestions:

- Make a selection and write or print them on cards. Form the children into small groups to collaboratively put the cards in order of their perceived importance.
- Choose some as topics for the school debating society – for example, 'This house believes that liberty is more important than peace.'
- Choose the virtues/values that are inherent to the teaching of your subject. For example, if you are a science teacher, these might be: accuracy, curiosity, cooperation, diligence, integrity, perseverance, truth and so on.
- Ask the children to design a crest or a coat of arms based on 'My five fundamental values'. What art forms or materials might they use?
- Ask the children: 'What virtues/values do you think reflect the character of our school? Are they true to your experience?'

Activity

How do we judge how to do the right thing, at the right time, in the right way and in the right measure?

Here are twenty questions about competing virtues and values. They will push you (and the children you teach) into considering the weight of one virtue against another.

1. What is the one thing you would most like to change about the world?
2. Do you always do what you believe in, or do you follow your family and friends?
3. If life is so short, why do we do so many things we don't like and like so many things we don't do?
4. If human life were limited to thirty years, how would you live yours?
5. Are you more worried about doing things right or doing the right things?
6. If you could offer your parents one piece of advice, what would it be?
7. Would you break the law to protect a loved one?
8. How come the things that make you happy don't make everyone happy?
9. What one thing have you not done that you really want to do? Why not?
10. If you were forced to flee this country, which country would you go to?
11. Why are you, you?
12. Have you been the kind of friend to others that you want as a friend?
13. What are you most grateful for?
14. How do you know something is true?
15. Would you break the law to achieve your ambition?
16. Is it possible to know, without any doubt, what is good and what is evil?
17. Would you be willing to reduce your life by ten years to become very attractive or very famous?

18. If we learn by our mistakes, why are we so afraid to make them?

19. Would you be different if you knew nobody would judge your actions?

20. Who or what do you love? How have recent actions of yours expressed this love?

Notes and ideas for use with your pupils in class:

- Select the questions that you think are most relevant to the age of your children or your specialist subject – for example: discuss the relevance of question 14 to learning about maths, science or history; or discuss question 17 in relation to music, sport, dance or drama.

- How you would organise a discussion with your pupils so that it maximises activity, discussion, reflection and thought? For example, you could use one question for school assembly, another at reflection time with your tutor group or one at each session of Circle Time.

- Select questions to inspire writing – for example: a speech about question 1 (The biggest change I would like to make to the world is …); a short drama about question 7 (My best friend broke the law – now what do I do?); or a poem about question 10 (choosing a country to flee to if you were a refugee).

The right response in the right measure

In Aristotle's lecture notes, he made (something similar to) a chart setting out a range of actions and feelings that require a virtuous response. Responses might be considered as either deficient (too little), in excess (too much) or as the right response in the right measure.

Activity

Choose from the 'right' virtues listed at the bottom and sort them between those that are 'too little' and those that are 'too much'. The first one (*courage*) is done for you.

Action or feeling	**Too little**	**The right response in the right measure**	**Too much**
Fear and daring	Cowardice	*Courage*	Rashness
Pleasures of touch/ taste	Insensibility		Self-indulgence
Giving and receiving	Stinginess		Extravagance
Self-presentation	Smallness		Vanity
Anger	Lack of spirit		Crankiness
Self-expression	Mock modesty		Boastfulness
Conversation	Boorishness		Buffoonery
Social conduct	Cantankerousness		Obsequiousness
Magnanimity *Truthfulness* ~~*Courage*~~ *Friendliness* *Gentleness* *Temperance* *Wit* *Generosity*			

The balance of virtue from A to Z (well, almost)

Ideas around achieving a balance of virtue was not the preserve of Aristotle or the Greeks; the list below has been compiled from sources in Buddhist, Christian, Hindu, Islamic, Jewish, as well as Greek and Roman writings.

Activity

Select from the virtues listed in the box that follows the table to find the ideal balance between the deficiencies (in the left column) and the excesses (on the right). The first one (*mercy*) is done for you.

Deficient in the virtue	The ideal balance	An excess of the virtue
Pitilessness	*Mercy*	Leniency
Ugliness		Gaudiness
Cruelty		Indulgence
Indifference		Mania
Scepticism		Fundamentalism
Violence		Spinelessness
Meanness		Ostentatiousness
Despair		Fantasy
Bias		Ineffectual
Compliance		Aggression
Indiscipline		Slavishness
Unfairness		Prescriptiveness
Dirtiness		Sterility
Treachery		Bondage
Apathy		Infatuation

Deficient in the virtue	**The ideal balance**	**An excess of the virtue**
Irreverence		Awe
Weakness		Brutality
Wastefulness		Austerity
Discord		Uniformity
Lifelessness		Mania
Ignorance		Bookishness

Devotion ~~*Mercy*~~ *Unity* *Enthusiasm*
Respect *Kindness* *Peacefulness* *Wisdom*
Hope *Faith* *Assertiveness* *Impartiality*
Justice *Strength* *Generosity* *Beauty*
Thrift *Obedience* *Vitality* *Cleanliness* *Loyalty*

The seven deadly sins

In Dante's *Divine Comedy*, Dante has Virgil accompany him on a journey to diagnose and heal a broken heart. He argues that every virtue and every vice springs from love, so that even sin itself is love that has wandered from the proper path and become misdirected. An example of misdirected love is to desire it too much and in the wrong way, and thereby exhibit *lust*. In order to redirect and temper this vice, we must display an opposing virtue – *courtly love*.

Activity

Fill in the examples of 'misdirected love' (from the list at the bottom) between the vice (in the column on the left) and the appropriate opposing virtue (in the column on the right). The first one (*excessive love of sex*) is done for you.

Vice	Misdirected love	Opposing virtue
Lust	*Excessive love of sex*	Courtly love
Gluttony		Temperance
Greed		Generosity
Sloth		Zeal
Wrath		Patience
Envy		Kindness
Pride		Humility

Perverted love of revenge *Excessive love of material possessions*
Perverted love of oneself *~~Excessive love of sex~~*
Inadequate love of beginning anything *Excessive love of food*
Perverted love of another's possessions

Appendix E

RESPONDING TO CHALLENGING REMARKS AND INCIDENTS[1]

One day a child in your class says: 'I don't like Muslims.' Given their right to free speech and the limits to it we discussed in Chapter 5 (that they must not abuse, threaten or incite violence), is this an acceptable thing to say? Let's take ourselves through some of these arguments.

Ask yourself: has the child abused, threatened or incited violence or hatred in their stated remark, 'I don't like Muslims'? No, they haven't, at least not in the way the law would define abuse, threat or incitement. While they may have expressed an opinion that is odious, bigoted or morally unjustifiable in general, it is not a remark that falls outside the category of free speech. You will have gathered by now that my position on free speech is that there is nothing so foolish a fool should not be allowed to utter. In demonstrating that we are, indeed, a tolerant society, we must tolerate the expression of opinions and beliefs with which we fundamentally disagree (given the relevant legal constraints). However, it is our moral duty to challenge such speech and our ethical duty to educate children to do so.

However, this child has expressed an opinion that is likely to be deeply offensive to the great majority of the population, so the appropriate response is not to say: 'You mustn't say that' or 'You can't say that', because the child will ask: 'Why not?' either directly or, more likely (to avoid conflict), inwardly to themselves. Given that you have tried to establish the fundamental value of free speech in school (within the limits we have noted), the child's question is reasonable. You will therefore find it a challenge to provide a justified response given the scope of free speech you have already outlined and endorsed.

The appropriate response is to continue to engage the child by challenging the remark with questions that will get her (or him) to reflect on her own moral justification and the soundness of her view, pointing particularly to the fundamental values of 'mutual respect' and 'individual liberty' (we will come to 'tolerance of those with different faiths and beliefs' shortly).[2] Your challenge should avoid confrontation, of course (not least because, on the face of it, you might lose your dignity, decorum or authority

---

1 Look again at the sections on cardinal and social virtues in Chapter 6 when considering how best to equip yourself with the tools to confidently respond to challenging remarks and incidents.

2 Department for Education, *Teachers' Standards*, p. 14.

if it escalates in front of the whole class), and you should also avoid a judgemental and moralising tone (to which most children soon tune out). However, you should put her viewpoint to the test. You might therefore ask: 'If you accept mutual respect as a fundamental value, how can your statement, "I don't like Muslims", be compatible with your values?'

You might also point out to her that while you respect her individual liberty to like and dislike whomsoever she wishes, as her teacher and as a fellow citizen you have a right to challenge her to justify the moral soundness of her opinions and preferences. In other words, she has a right to express herself, but you have a right to challenge her assertions. If she is unwilling to morally justify her argument (by offering a rational case as to why it is right) or is unable to do so, then while she is still at liberty to continue to make her claims, your kindly advice to her as her teacher (with an interest in her moral well-being) and as her fellow citizen (with an interest in the common good) is that she should reflect on her contentions because they do not cohere with her own values to respect other people in the way that she would like to be respected – mutual respect.

You may – if you are lucky – get her to accept the principle we discussed in Appendix A that we don't have to respect ideas, but we do have to respect people. If that is the case, then you have made considerable progress. Congratulate yourself. If you haven't, don't beat yourself up about it. Changing people's minds can be a long process, especially those whose moral formation has been undermined by neglectful parenting or whose moral subscriptions have been corrupted by exposure to unprincipled or nefarious influences. She may come round to accepting your principles later, after months or even years of reflection.

'Yeah but, no but ...'

Let's imagine that sometime later, the same child, not yet having reflected deeply on what you have said, comes back on a different tack. She says to you: 'OK, I accept that I have to respect people. I respect Muslims as *people*, it's their *religion* I don't like. I don't like the way Islam as a religion treats women ... or the cruelty of halal ritual slaughter ... or Sharia law.' Checkmate? No, not at all.

You may suspect that the child is using this argument as a ploy to mask her morally unjustifiable prejudice – her racism against Muslims – which is sitting behind an apparently rational attack on religious values and practice. My advice is, don't assume that this is their starting point, but once again, gently challenge the child. Remember that you need to demonstrate and model the moral behaviour you ultimately want them to adopt, so – respectfully but firmly – ask her to justify herself. For example, is she claiming to uphold a moral standard for Muslim women (dress styles and codes, for instance) that she may not be upholding for others? Does she know enough about Islam to be sure that the religion itself invokes ill treatment or prejudice against women? Or are these assumptions? Is she confusing religious, cultural and patriarchal practices? Is the moral standard to which she is holding Muslims to account (e.g. in the ritual slaughter of animals) different from what she is holding others? Does she know what Sharia law actually is? What it does and does not allow? What civil and legal claims it makes? Are there parallels with other religious groups (including the way civil disputes are resolved without resorting to the courts)?

She may not be honest with herself in the answers she gives to you. That doesn't necessarily matter. You are not going to change her attitudes overnight, but gentle nudges in the right direction – that is, towards rationality and away from irrational prejudice – are likely to provoke further thought and reflection, often away from the immediacy of your challenge. This can be much more productive than a demand to justify herself, which may feel more like an argumentative confrontation that is inevitably intellectually weighted against her.

When Boris Johnson wrote that he thought Muslim women who wore burkas looked like 'bank robbers' and 'letter boxes', he was doing so in the wider context of defending the right of (all) women to wear whatever they choose, even if he thought it looked 'ridiculous'.[3] However, what many people would have liked to ask him is whether the expression of such an opinion, lawful though it is, can be squared with a commitment to demonstrate mutual respect, if not tolerance. Johnson should not be told he 'must not say' such things, but rather to reflect on whether such remarks are compatible with the values of mutual respect to which he claims to subscribe and commit to, and as a national leader is duty-bound to demonstrate and model on our behalf. Just because we have a legal right and an individual liberty to make offensive comments, does not mean we ought to. We all have a duty – especially leaders in society, and that means teachers – to subscribe and commit to conflict-averting and cooperation-sustaining moral standards. The stability, cohesion and flourishing of society depends on it.

3 Johnson, Denmark Has Got It Wrong.

Appendix F

USEFUL LINKS AND RESOURCES FOR SUPPORTING SPIRITUAL, MORAL, SOCIAL AND CULTURAL EDUCATION

Amnesty International
www.amnesty.org.uk/primary-schools-education-resources

Anne Frank Trust UK
www.annefrank.org.uk

AQA Citizenship Resource Bank
https://citizenshipresources.aqa.org.uk

Association for Citizenship Teaching
www.teachingcitizenship.org.uk

Black Curriculum
https://theblackcurriculum.com

Black History 365
www.blackhistorymonth.org.uk

Citizens UK
www.citizensuk.org

Disability Rights UK
www.disabilityrightsuk.org

Duke of Edinburgh's Award Scheme
www.dofe.org

English Schools Cricket Association
www.escaonline.co.uk

English-Speaking Union
www.esu.org
Advice and resources on how to set up a debating society.

Equality and Human Rights Commission
www.equalityhumanrights.com

Equality UK
www.equalityuk.org

Gender Identity Research and Education Society
www.gires.org.uk/resources

Generation United Nations (UNA)
www.una.org.uk/GenUN-schools

Heritage Calling
www.heritagecalling.com
Historic England's blog.

Kick It Out
www.kickitout.org

Lawyers in Schools
www.lawyersinschools.org.uk
Offer free school visits from lawyers and resources to promote legal and justice issues.

Lyfta
www.lyfta.com
An initiative that supports schools to learn about global themes, centred on the UN's Sustainable Development Goals.

National Justice Museum

www.nationaljusticemuseum.org.uk

The NJM aims to increase understanding of career opportunities in the legal profession, explain the different types of courts and how they work, stage mock trials, show how appearing in court can affect people and encourage an interest in the law.

Parliament Education Service

https://learning.parliament.uk/en

Philosophy for Children (P4C)

www.p4c.com

www.sapere.org.uk

Philosophy Foundation

www.philosophy-foundation.org

Rugby Football Union

www.englandrugby.com/participation/education/schools

Show Racism the Red Card

www.theredcard.org

Sported

www.sported.org.uk

Supports the setting up of sports clubs for disadvantaged young people.

Standing Advisory Council on Religious Education (SACRE)

Each local authority has one and usually they have excellent SMSC resources including on global citizenship. Search SACRE and your local authority.

Stonewall

www.stonewall.org.uk/our-work/education-resources

United Nations Convention on the Rights of the Child

www.unicef.org/rightsite/files/uncrcchilldfriendlylanguage.pdf

Young Citizens

www.youngcitizens.org

Youth for Human Rights

www.youthforhumanrights.org

Useful links for tackling extremism

Educate Against Hate

www.educateagainsthate.com

P4S Prevent for Schools

www.preventforschools.org

Primary and secondary resources.

Since 9/11

www.since911.com/education-programme

Small Steps

www.smallstepsconsultants.com

UKEdChat

www.ukedchat.com/2015/09/18/resources-to-help-teach-about-extremism

Appendix G

CODES FOR PROFESSIONAL PRACTICE AND STANDARDS IN THE UK: ENGLAND, SCOTLAND, WALES AND NORTHERN IRELAND

England

Teachers' Standards – Department for Education

Preamble

Teachers make the education of their pupils their first concern, and are accountable for achieving the highest possible standards in work and conduct. Teachers act with honesty and integrity; have strong subject knowledge, keep their knowledge and skills as teachers up to date and are self-critical; forge positive professional relationships; and work with parents in the best interests of their pupils.

Part One: Teaching

A teacher must:

1. Set high standards which inspire, motivate and challenge pupils

   - establish a safe and stimulating environment for pupils, rooted in mutual respect
   - set goals that stretch and challenge pupils of all backgrounds, abilities and dispositions
   - demonstrate consistently the positive attitudes, values and behaviour which are expected of pupils.

2. Promote good progress and outcomes by pupils

    - be accountable for pupils' attainment, progress and outcomes
    - be aware of pupils' capabilities and their prior knowledge, and plan teaching to build on these
    - guide pupils to reflect on the progress they have made and their emerging needs
    - demonstrate knowledge and understanding of how pupils learn and how this impacts on teaching
    - encourage pupils to take a responsible and conscientious attitude to their own work and study.

3. Demonstrate good subject and curriculum knowledge

    - have a secure knowledge of the relevant subject(s) and curriculum areas, foster and maintain pupils' interest in the subject, and address misunderstandings
    - demonstrate a critical understanding of developments in the subject and curriculum areas, and promote the value of scholarship
    - demonstrate an understanding of and take responsibility for promoting high standards of literacy, articulacy and the correct use of standard English, whatever the teacher's specialist subject
    - if teaching early reading, demonstrate a clear understanding of systematic synthetic phonics.
    - if teaching early mathematics, demonstrate a clear understanding of appropriate teaching strategies.

4. Plan and teach well structured lessons

    - impart knowledge and develop understanding through effective use of lesson time
    - promote a love of learning and children's intellectual curiosity
    - set homework and plan other out-of-class activities to consolidate and extend the knowledge and understanding pupils have acquired
    - reflect systematically on the effectiveness of lessons and approaches to teaching

- contribute to the design and provision of an engaging curriculum within the relevant subject area(s).

5. Adapt teaching to respond to the strengths and needs of all pupils

   - know when and how to differentiate appropriately, using approaches which enable pupils to be taught effectively
   - have a secure understanding of how a range of factors can inhibit pupils' ability to learn, and how best to overcome these
   - demonstrate an awareness of the physical, social and intellectual development of children, and know how to adapt teaching to support pupils' education at different stages of development
   - have a clear understanding of the needs of all pupils, including those with special educational needs; those of high ability; those with English as an additional language; those with disabilities; and be able to use and evaluate distinctive teaching approaches to engage and support them.

6. Make accurate and productive use of assessment

   - know and understand how to assess the relevant subject and curriculum areas, including statutory assessment requirements
   - make use of formative and summative assessment to secure pupils' progress
   - use relevant data to monitor progress, set targets, and plan subsequent lessons
   - give pupils regular feedback, both orally and through accurate marking, and encourage pupils to respond to the feedback

7. Manage behaviour effectively to ensure a good and safe learning environment

   - have clear rules and routines for behaviour in classrooms, and take responsibility for promoting good and courteous behaviour both in classrooms and around the school, in accordance with the school's behaviour policy
   - have high expectations of behaviour, and establish a framework for discipline with a range of strategies, using praise, sanctions and rewards consistently and fairly
   - manage classes effectively, using approaches which are appropriate to pupils' needs in order to involve and motivate them

- maintain good relationships with pupils, exercise appropriate authority, and act decisively when necessary.

8. Fulfil wider professional responsibilities

   - make a positive contribution to the wider life and ethos of the school
   - develop effective professional relationships with colleagues, knowing how and when to draw on advice and specialist support
   - deploy support staff effectively
   - take responsibility for improving teaching through appropriate professional development, responding to advice and feedback from colleagues
   - communicate effectively with parents with regard to pupils' achievements and well-being.

Part Two: Personal and Professional Conduct

A teacher is expected to demonstrate consistently high standards of personal and professional conduct. The following statements define the behaviour and attitudes which set the required standard for conduct throughout a teacher's career.

- Teachers uphold public trust in the profession and maintain high standards of ethics and behaviour, within and outside school, by:

  - treating pupils with dignity, building relationships rooted in mutual respect, and at all times observing proper boundaries appropriate to a teacher's professional position
  - having regard for the need to safeguard pupils' well-being, in accordance with statutory provisions
  - showing tolerance of and respect for the rights of others
  - not undermining fundamental British values, including democracy, the rule of law, individual liberty and mutual respect, and tolerance of those with different faiths and beliefs
  - ensuring that personal beliefs are not expressed in ways which exploit pupils' vulnerability or might lead them to break the law.

- Teachers must have proper and professional regard for the ethos, policies and practices of the school in which they teach, and maintain high standards in their own attendance and punctuality.
- Teachers must have an understanding of, and always act within, the statutory frameworks which set out their professional duties and responsibilities.

Scotland

The Standard for Full Registration – General Teaching Council for Scotland (GTCS)

1. Being a Teacher in Scotland

Our increasingly interconnected and rapidly changing world faces many social, environmental and economic challenges, and an effective, responsive and inclusive education system is vital if we are to address these. Engaged, reflective, empowered and skilled teachers and learners acknowledge Scotland's place in the world, our history, our differences and diversity, our unique natural environment, and our culture based on social justice. Scotland's teachers help to embed sustainable and socially just practices in order to flourish as a nation.

The **Professional Standards** outline what it means to become, to be and to grow as a teacher in Scotland. A commitment to the **professional values** of **social justice, trust and respect and integrity** are at the heart of the Professional Standards and underpin our relationships, thinking and professional practice in Scotland.

The educational experiences of all our children and young people are shaped by the professional values and dispositions of all those who work to educate them. Values are complex: they are the ideals by which teachers shape their practice as professionals. Starting with teachers as individuals, values extend to our learners, our colleagues and community and to the world in which we live.

1.1 Professional Values

Professional values help to develop our professional identity and underpin a deep commitment to all learners' cognitive, social and emotional growth and wellbeing. They provide the foundation to support and encourage teachers to see the whole child or young person and their needs. They are integral to, and demonstrated through, all our professional relationships, thinking and actions and all that we do to meet our **professional commitment** as teachers registered with GTC Scotland.

As part of **teacher professionalism**, professional values are required to be enacted in everyday practice both within and outwith the educational establishment. They support us to ask critical questions of educational theories, policies and practices and to examine our own attitudes and beliefs. Values, and the connections between values and actions, require regular reflection over the course of teachers' careers as society and the needs of learners change and as understanding develops. Our commitment to career-long professional learning is a critical part of developing our professionalism. Enquiring and collaborative professionalism is a powerful force in developing teachers' agency and delivering our commitment to engaging children, young people, their families and communities in the education process.

Social Justice

Social justice is the view that everyone deserves equal economic, political and social rights and opportunities now and in the future.

Trust and Respect

Trust and respect are expectations of positive actions that support authentic relationship building and show care for the needs and feelings of the people involved and respect for our natural world and its limited resources.

Integrity

Integrity is the practice of being honest and showing a consistent and uncompromising adherence to strong moral and ethical principles and values.

1.2 Professional Commitment

Making a professional commitment to learning and learners that is compatible with the aspiration of achieving a sustainable and equitable world embodies what it is to be a teacher in Scotland. This means teachers commit to living the professional values and engage in lifelong learning, reflection, enquiry, leadership of learning and collaborative practice as key aspects of their professionalism. This commitment to professional learning and growth, to the growth of learners, and to helping support that of colleagues, is demonstrated through engagement with all aspects of professional practice. It is demonstrated by working collegially, in English or Gaelic medium with all members of our learning communities with enthusiasm, adaptability, critical thinking and associated constructive, professional dialogue.

A core component of teachers' professional commitment is understanding the needs of all learners. Some children and young people may have a barrier to wellbeing and learning associated with a range of circumstances such as the learning environment, family circumstances, disability or health need, and social and emotional factors. This includes learners with additional support needs such as: Attention Deficit Hyperactivity Disorder (ADHD) and Attention Deficit Disorder (ADD); Autism; Developmental Coordination Disorder (Dyspraxia) (DCD); Dyslexia; and Tourette syndrome. Teachers recognise, see and acknowledge the value in everyone and have a deep awareness of the need for culturally responsive pedagogies. They promote equality and diversity, paying careful attention to the needs of learners from diverse groups and in upholding children's rights.

Upholding the professional values of social justice, trust and respect and integrity requires a commitment to leadership that inspires confidence and encourages aspiration. This commitment underpins leadership of learning in all contexts and change for improvement. It values the contribution of others, challenges biases and assumptions and applies critical thinking to make effective decisions, in the interests of maintaining and improving the quality of education and leading to improved outcomes for all children and young people in Scotland.

The professional commitment of teachers in Scotland is to lead learning through:

- developing deep knowledge of learning and teaching;
- critically examining how our teaching impacts on learners; and
- using evidence collaboratively to inform teacher judgement and next steps for learners.

1.3 Standard for Full Registration

Professional Values and **Professional Commitment** are at the core of the **Standard for Full Registration**. They are integral to, and demonstrated through, all our professional relationships and practices. They are central to the delivery of high-quality learning and teaching, aimed at improving outcomes for all learners and contributing to efforts to achieve a sustainable and equitable world. The personal and professional qualities of sustainability and social justice, integrity, trust and respect and professional commitment are crucial if we are to inspire and prepare learners for success in our increasingly complex, interdependent and rapidly changing world.

'Learning for Sustainability' is a whole-school commitment that helps the school and its wider community develop the knowledge, skills, attitudes, values and practices needed to take decisions which are compatible with a sustainable future in a just and equitable world. Learning for Sustainability has been embedded within the Standard for Full Registration to support teachers in actively embracing and promoting principles and practices of sustainability in all aspects of their work.

All teachers are leaders of and for learning. They lead learning of, and with, all learners with whom they engage. They also work with and support the development of colleagues and other partners. The Standards for Registration include a focus on leadership of and for learning.

The **Standard for Full Registration** is the gateway to the profession and the benchmark of teacher competence for all teachers. It must therefore constitute standards of capability in relation to teaching, with reasonable adjustments as required, in which learners, parents, the profession itself and the wider community can have confidence.

The scope of this document is limited to defining expectations of teachers and does not address in detail how judgements will or should be made. It is not intended that the **Professional Actions** should be used as a checklist. In broad terms, the person reviewing the work of a teacher needs to be reassured that the capabilities described by the Professional Standard are achieved. Where it is thought that further development is needed, the Professional Actions provide a focus for what needs to be done.

Having attained the **Standard for Full Registration** teachers will continue to develop their expertise and experience across all areas of their professional practice through appropriate and sustained career-long professional learning. The **Standard for Career-Long Professional Learning** has been developed to support professional teacher growth and to identify, plan and develop their own professional learning needs and to ensure continuing development of professional practice.

The purposes of the **Standard for Full Registration** are:

- a clear and concise description of the professional qualities and capabilities probationer teachers are expected to attain;
- a professional standard against which reliable and consistent recommendations and decisions can be made on the fitness of new teachers for full registration with GTC Scotland;
- a clear and concise description of the professional qualities and capabilities fully registered teachers are expected to maintain and enhance throughout their careers;
- a benchmark standard of professional competence which applies to teachers throughout their careers.

The Professional Standards are organised into interrelated categories with **Professional Values** and **Professional Commitment** at the heart. These categories are inherently linked to each other in the development of teachers, and one aspect does not exist independently of the others. It is this inter-relationship among all of the categories which develops a teacher's understanding, practice and professionalism. Effective and systematic **Professional Review and Development** (PRD) and **Professional Update** processes support fully registered teachers' ongoing learning.

2. Professional Knowledge and Understanding

2.1 Curriculum and Pedagogy

2.1.1 Have a depth of knowledge and understanding of Pedagogical Theories and Professional Practice

2.1.2 Have a depth of knowledge and understanding of Research and Engagement in Practitioner Enquiry

2.1.3 Have a depth of knowledge and understanding of Curriculum Design

2.1.4 Have a depth of knowledge and understanding of Planning for Assessment, Teaching and Learning

2.2 Professional Responsibilities

2.2.1 Have a depth of knowledge and understanding of Education Systems

2.2.2 Have a depth of knowledge and understanding of Learning Communities

3. Professional Skills and Abilities

3.1 Curriculum and Pedagogy

3.1.1 Plan effectively to meet learners' needs

3.1.2 Effectively utilise pedagogical approaches and resources

3.1.3 Effectively utilise partnerships for learning and wellbeing

3.1.4 Effectively employ assessment, evaluate progress, recording and reporting as an integral part of the teaching process to support and enhance learning

3.2 The Learning Context

3.2.1 Effectively organise and manage learning

3.2.2 Effectively engage learner participation

3.2.3 Build positive, rights respecting relationships for learning

3.3 Professional Learning

3.3.1 Engage critically with literature, research and policy

3.3.2 Engage in reflective practice to develop and advance career-long professional learning and expertise.

With thanks to the General Teaching Council for Scotland for their permission to reproduce the Standard for Full Registration.

Wales

The Code of Professional Conduct and Practice – Education Workforce Council (EWC)

The Five Key Principles

Registrants, including those registered on a provisional basis, commit to upholding the key principles of Personal and **Professional Responsibility, Professional Integrity, Collaborative Working, Professional Knowledge and Understanding and Professional Learning**.

A. Professional Conduct

1. Personal and Professional Responsibility

Registrants:

1.1 recognise their personal responsibility as a role model and public figure, to uphold public trust and confidence in the education professions, both in and out of the workplace;

1.2 conduct relationships with learners professionally by:

- communicating with learners respectfully, in a way which is appropriate for them;
- using all forms of communication appropriately and responsibly, particularly social media;
- ensuring any physical contact is necessary, reasonable and proportionate;
- contributing to the creation of a fair and inclusive learning environment by addressing discrimination, stereotyping and bullying;
- maintaining professional boundaries.

1.3 engage with learners to encourage confidence, empowerment, educational and personal development;

1.4 have a duty of care for learners' safety, physical, social, moral and educational well-being:

- acting on anything which might put a learner's safety or welfare at risk;
- reporting, in line with 4.3 below, any safeguarding issue, or any other issue which may potentially harm a learner's safety or welfare.

1.5 are mindful of their professional responsibility for the health, safety and well-being of colleagues, and themselves;

1.6 demonstrate a commitment to equality and diversity.

2. Professional Integrity

Registrants:

2.1 are accountable for their conduct and professional competence;

2.2 behave honestly, and with integrity, particularly with regard to:

- finances and funds in the workplace;
- personal credentials, experience and qualifications;
- references, declarations made and signing documents;
- assessment and examination related tasks;
- use of property and facilities provided by their employer;

- communications with the EWC, informing it of any recordable criminal conviction or caution, or restriction placed on their practice by any other body;
- their employer, and report any matter which is required by their terms and conditions of employment.

2.3 handle information and data appropriately, applying the necessary protocols to matters relating to confidentiality, sensitivity and disclosure;

2.4 adhere to lawful standards of behaviour, in a manner in keeping with their position as a member of the education profession.

3. Collaborative Working

Registrants:

3.1 respect, support and collaborate with colleagues, learners and others to achieve the best learning outcomes;

3.2 share experience and knowledge to help themselves and other practitioners develop and maintain best practice (see Section B);

3.3 aim to develop and maintain professional working relationships with parents, guardians, carers and other stakeholders;

3.4 communicate appropriately and effectively with all involved in the education of learners.

B. Professional Practice

4. Professional Knowledge and Understanding

Registrants:

4.1 know, use and take responsibility for the relevant professional standards for their particular profession throughout their career;

4.2 know, understand and comply with current policies, procedures and guidelines which are relevant to their practice;

4.3 know, understand and comply with current safeguarding policies, procedures and guidelines which are relevant to their practice;

4.4 where necessary, seek support, advice and guidance and are open to feedback, responding to it positively and constructively.

5. Professional Learning

Registrants:

5.1 demonstrate a shared commitment to their continuing professional learning by reflecting upon and evaluating their practice, keeping their professional knowledge and skills up to date and taking steps to improve their practice where necessary.

With thanks to the Education Workforce Council for their permission to reproduce their code.

Northern Ireland

Core Values – General Teaching Council for Northern Ireland (GTCNI)

The core values of the teaching profession in Northern Ireland are as follows:

- Trust
- Honesty
- Commitment
- Excellence
- Respect
- Fairness
- Equality
- Dignity
- Integrity
- Tolerance
- Service

A commitment to serve lies at the heart of professional behaviour. In addition, members of the profession will exemplify the values listed above in their work and in their relationships with others; recognising, in particular, the unique and privileged relationship that exists between teachers and their pupils. In keeping with the spirit of professional service and commitment, teachers will at all times be conscious of their responsibilities to others: learners, colleagues and indeed the profession itself.

Many of the commitments that follow are also underpinned by legislation and the profession will always seek, as a minimum, to comply with both the spirit and detail of relevant legislative requirements.

Commitment to Learners

Teachers:

- maintain professional relationships with those pupils entrusted to their care which respect the learner as a person and encourage growth and development;
- acknowledge and respect the uniqueness, individuality and specific needs of each pupil and thus provide appropriate learning experiences; and
- aim to motivate and inspire pupils with a view to helping each realise his/her potential.

Commitment to Colleagues and Others

Teachers:

- work with colleagues and others to create a professional community that supports the social, intellectual, spiritual/moral, emotional and physical development of pupils;
- promote collegiality among colleagues by respecting their professional standing and opinions and, in that spirit, be prepared to offer advice and share professional practice with colleagues;
- cooperate, where appropriate, with professionals from other agencies in the interests of pupils;
- ensure that relationships with the parents, guardians or carers of pupils, in their capacity as partners in the educational process, are characterised by respect and trust; and
- respect confidential information relating to pupils or colleagues gained in the course of professional practice, unless the well-being of an individual or legal imperative requires disclosure.

Commitment to the Profession

Teachers:

- as reflective practitioners, contribute to the review and revision of policies and practices with a view to optimising the opportunities for pupils or addressing identified individual or institutional needs; and
- in keeping with the concept of professional integrity assume responsibility for their ongoing professional development needs as an essential expression of their professionalism.

With thanks to the General Teaching Council for Northern Ireland for their permission to reproduce their code.

Appendix H

CODES FOR PROFESSIONAL PRACTICE AND STANDARDS IN THE UNITED STATES, CANADA, SOUTH AFRICA, AUSTRALIA AND NEW ZEALAND

United States

Code of Ethics for Educators – Association of American Educators

Overview

The professional educator strives to create a learning environment that nurtures to fulfilment the potential of all students.

The professional educator acts with conscientious effort to exemplify the highest ethical standards.

The professional educator responsibly accepts that every child has a right to an uninterrupted education free from strikes or any other work stoppage tactics.

Principle I: Ethical Conduct Toward Students

The professional educator accepts personal responsibility for teaching students character qualities that will help them evaluate the consequences of and accept the responsibility for their actions and choices. We strongly affirm parents as the primary moral educators of their children. Nevertheless, we believe all educators are obligated to help foster civic virtues such as integrity, diligence, responsibility, cooperation, loyalty, fidelity, and respect for the law, for human life, for others, and for self.

The professional educator, in accepting his or her position of public trust, measures success not only by the progress of each student toward realization of his or her personal potential, but also as a citizen of the greater community of the republic.

1. The professional educator deals considerately and justly with each student, and seeks to resolve problems, including discipline, according to law and school policy.

2. The professional educator does not intentionally expose the student to disparagement.

3. The professional educator does not reveal confidential information concerning students, unless required by law.

4. The professional educator makes a constructive effort to protect the student from conditions detrimental to learning, health, or safety.

5. The professional educator endeavors to present facts without distortion, bias, or personal prejudice.

Principle II: Ethical Conduct Toward Practices and Performance

The professional educator assumes responsibility and accountability for his or her performance and continually strives to demonstrate competence.

The professional educator endeavors to maintain the dignity of the profession by respecting and obeying the law, and by demonstrating personal integrity.

1. The professional educator applies for, accepts, or assigns a position or a responsibility on the basis of professional qualifications, and adheres to the terms of a contract or appointment.

2. The professional educator maintains sound mental health, physical stamina, and social prudence necessary to perform the duties of any professional assignment.

3. The professional educator continues professional growth.

4. The professional educator complies with written local school policies and applicable laws and regulations that are not in conflict with this code of ethics.

5. The professional educator does not intentionally misrepresent official policies of the school or educational organizations, and clearly distinguishes those views from his or her own personal opinions.

6. The professional educator honestly accounts for all funds committed to his or her charge.

7. The professional educator does not use institutional or professional privileges for personal or partisan advantage.

Principle III: Ethical Conduct Toward Professional Colleagues

The professional educator, in exemplifying ethical relations with colleagues, accords just and equitable treatment to all members of the profession.

1. The professional educator does not reveal confidential information concerning colleagues unless required by law.
2. The professional educator does not wilfully make false statements about a colleague or the school system.
3. The professional educator does not interfere with a colleague's freedom of choice, and works to eliminate coercion that forces educators to support actions and ideologies that violate individual professional integrity.

Principle IV: Ethical Conduct Toward Parents and Community

The professional educator pledges to protect public sovereignty over public education and private control of private education.

The professional educator recognizes that quality education is the common goal of the public, boards of education, and educators, and that a cooperative effort is essential among these groups to attain that goal.

1. The professional educator makes concerted efforts to communicate to parents all information that should be revealed in the interest of the student.
2. The professional educator endeavours to understand and respect the values and traditions of the diverse cultures represented in the community and in his or her classroom.
3. The professional educator manifests a positive and active role in school/ community relations.

With thanks to the Association of American Educators for their kind permission to reproduce their Code of Ethics for Educators for which they hold the copyright.

The Association of American Educators is a national, non-governmental, non-partisan, non-union organisation established in 1994 to foster greater professionalism in the teaching profession in the United States and to promote the interests of learners. It is a voluntary membership body (not a federal professional body) for regulating the teaching profession in the United States.

This code is just one of the examples of voluntary, non-regulatory codes of ethics to which American teachers can refer. Others include:

American Association for Colleges of Teacher Education – www.aacte.org

Association for Advancing Quality in Educator Preparation – www.aaqep.org/standards

Association of Teacher Educators – https://ate1.org/standards-for-teacher-educators

Council for the Accreditation of Educator Preparation – http://caepnet.org/standards/2013/introduction

Council of Chief State School Officers – www.ccsso.org

Many individual states have their own codes of ethics for teachers working in public schools, such as this one for Virginia: www.doe.virginia.gov/about/code-ethics.shtml.

Canada

The Ethical Standards for the Teaching Profession and the Standards of Practice for the Teaching Profession – Ontario College of Teachers (OCT)

The Ethical Standards for the Teaching Profession

The *Ethical Standards for the Teaching Profession* represent a vision of professional practice. At the heart of a strong and effective teaching profession is a commitment to students and their learning. Members of the Ontario College of Teachers, in their position of trust, demonstrate responsibility in their relationships with students, parents, guardians, colleagues, educational partners, other professionals, the environment and the public.

The Purposes of the Ethical Standards for the Teaching Profession are:

- to inspire members to reflect and uphold the honour and dignity of the teaching profession

- to identify the ethical responsibilities and commitments in the teaching profession
- to guide ethical decisions and actions in the teaching profession
- to promote public trust and confidence in the teaching profession.

The Ethical Standards for the Teaching Profession are:

Care

The ethical standard of *Care* includes compassion, acceptance, interest and insight for developing students' potential. Members express their commitment to students' well-being and learning through positive influence, professional judgment and empathy in practice.

Trust

The ethical standard of *Trust* embodies fairness, openness and honesty. Members' professional relationships with students, colleagues, parents, guardians and the public are based on trust.

Respect

Intrinsic to the ethical standard of *Respect* are trust and fair-mindedness. Members honour human dignity, emotional wellness and cognitive development. In their professional practice, they model respect for spiritual and cultural values, social justice, confidentiality, freedom, democracy and the environment.

Integrity

Honesty, reliability and moral action are embodied in the ethical standard of *Integrity*. Continual reflection assists members in exercising integrity in their professional commitments and responsibilities.

The Standards of Practice for the Teaching Profession

The *Standards of Practice for the Teaching Profession* provide a framework of principles that describes the knowledge, skills, and values inherent in Ontario's teaching profession. These standards articulate the goals and aspirations of the profession. These standards convey a collective vision of professionalism that guides the daily practices of members of the Ontario College of Teachers.

The Purposes of the Standards of Practice for the Teaching Profession are:

- to inspire a shared vision for the teaching profession
- to identify the values, knowledge and skills that are distinctive to the teaching profession
- to guide the professional judgment and actions of the teaching profession
- to promote a common language that fosters an understanding of what it means to be a member of the teaching profession.

The Standards of Practice for the Teaching Profession are:

Commitment to Students and Student Learning

Members are dedicated in their care and commitment to students. They treat students equitably and with respect and are sensitive to factors that influence individual student learning. Members facilitate the development of students as contributing citizens of Canadian society.

Leadership in Learning Communities

Members promote and participate in the creation of collaborative, safe and supportive learning communities. They recognize their shared responsibilities and their leadership roles in order to facilitate student success. Members maintain and uphold the principles of the ethical standards in these learning communities.

Ongoing Professional Learning

Members recognize that a commitment to ongoing professional learning is integral to effective practice and to student learning. Professional practice and self-directed learning are informed by experience, research, collaboration and knowledge.

Professional Knowledge

Members strive to be current in their professional knowledge and recognize its relationship to practice. They understand and reflect on student development, learning theory, pedagogy, curriculum, ethics, educational research and related policies and legislation to inform professional judgment in practice.

Professional Practice

Members apply professional knowledge and experience to promote student learning. They use appropriate pedagogy, assessment and evaluation, resources and technology in planning for and responding to the needs of individual students and learning communities. Members refine their professional practice through ongoing inquiry, dialogue and reflection.

With thanks to the Ontario College of Teachers for their kind permission to reproduce the Standards of Practice for the Teaching Profession in Ontario, Canada.

The Ontario College of Teachers is the professional, regulatory body for teaching in the province of Ontario. Its mission is to place students' interests and well-being first by regulating and promoting excellence in teaching. Established in 1997, it is the largest such body in Canada. The college's mandate is to license, govern and regulate the practice of teaching in the province of Ontario, although there are similar bodies in Canada's other provinces.

South Africa

Professional Teaching Standards – South African Council for Educators (SACE)

1. Teaching is based on an ethical commitment to the learning and wellbeing of all learners.

1.1. Teachers believe in the capacity of all learners to achieve and make progress both inside and outside the classroom.

1.2. Teachers understand the different challenges that confront learners and their families and consider how these challenges may affect their behaviour and learning.

1.3. Teachers respect different aspects of learners' identities (including gender, race, language, culture, sexual orientation and dis/ability), and believe that these diversities can be a strength and resource for teaching and learning.

2. Teachers collaborate with others to support teaching, learning and their professional development.

2.1. Teachers conduct themselves in ways that earn the respect of those in their communities and uphold the dignity of the teaching profession.

2.2. Teachers understand that the wellbeing of learners and the support of their learning requires communication and collaboration between teachers, parents, caregivers, other professionals, and the community.

2.3. Teachers are responsible for their ongoing personal, academic and professional growth through reflection, study, reading, and research.

2.4. Teachers participate in endorsed continuing professional teacher development activities/programmes organised by their subject associations, professional learning communities (PLCs), higher education institutions, teacher unions and private providers.

2.5. Teachers provide supportive environments for the induction and mentoring of colleagues who are new to their school, as well as for pre-service and newly-qualified teachers.

2.6. Teachers actively involve themselves in educational debates, curriculum development initiatives, and educational issues that affect them.

3. Teachers support social justice and the redress of inequalities within their educational institutions and society more broadly.

3.1. Teachers are committed to ensuring that learners are given the support they need for inclusive access to learning opportunities.

3.2. Teachers have a responsibility to identify and challenge policies and practices that discriminate against, marginalise or exclude learners.

4. Teaching requires that well-managed and safe learning environments are created and maintained within reason.

4.1. Teachers are in class and teaching during scheduled teaching time.

4.2. Teachers establish class routines to make the most of the available teaching and learning time.

4.3. Teachers use fair and consistently-applied rules to promote respectful behaviour in their working environments.

5. Teaching is fundamentally connected to teachers' understanding of the subject/s they teach.

5.1. Teachers understand the subject/s they teach as bodies of knowledge in which important concepts are connected to one another.

5.2. Teachers understand how learners process and present information in the subject/s they teach.

5.3. Teachers understand how subject knowledge can be applied to interpret and address real-world issues.

5.4. Teachers keep themselves informed of new developments and research in their subject/s.

6. Teachers make thoughtful choices about their teaching that lead to learning goals for all learners.

6.1. Teachers consider how learners develop and learn when choosing teaching and learning strategies.

6.2. Teachers seek to understand how theoretical concepts and evidence-based research can inform the choices they make in their classroom practices.

6.3. Teachers can account for the design, delivery and assessment of lessons to themselves, their colleagues and to other stakeholders.

6.4. Teachers improve their teaching by reflecting on what has worked and what has not worked in the learning experiences they have created.

7. Teachers understand that language plays an important role in teaching and learning.

7.1. Teachers create opportunities for learners to develop their vocabulary, their command of the Language of Learning and Teaching (LoLT), and to develop their reading and writing skills in the lessons they teach.

7.2. Teachers draw on other languages, when necessary, to enhance learners' understanding of the important concepts in their lessons.

7.3. Teachers enable learners to understand and use the specialist terminology and language of their subject/s.

7.4. Teachers provide learners with ongoing opportunities to read, interpret, and respond to different kinds of written, graphical and visual texts.

7.5. Teachers recognise that all learners need to acquire and hone foundational skills in language and numeracy, and that there is a strong interrelationship between language and numeracy.

8. Teachers are able to plan coherent sequences of learning experiences.

8.1. Teachers use the national curriculum to identify what learners are required to know and do.

8.2. Teachers use the national curriculum and knowledge of their subject/s to understand how important ideas and skills are built up across different years of learning.

8.3. Teachers base their planning on what learners know and understand in order to design coherent units of lessons with meaningful learning activities and assessments.

9. Teachers understand how their teaching methodologies are effectively applied.

9.1. Teachers explain content knowledge to learners in ways that are understandable and accurate.

9.2. Teachers devise tasks that give learners opportunities to consolidate new knowledge learnt and to practise skills.

9.3. Teachers learn to anticipate what learners will find difficult to understand and develop effective ways to address common misunderstandings.

9.4. Teachers find, develop or modify carefully chosen physical, graphic, digital and text-based resources to enhance learning.

9.5. Teachers engage their learners to stimulate their curiosity about a subject and motivate them to learn more.

10. Teaching involves monitoring and assessing learning.

10.1. Teachers use assessment tasks that give learners opportunities to show what they have learnt, and what they can do with that knowledge.

10.2. Teachers provide learners with constructive feedback that helps them understand how they can improve their learning.

10.3. Teachers analyse learner contributions, their questions and their errors as important data that shows what the learners do and do not yet understand to inform future planning.

10.4. Teachers keep accurate records of assessments that track learner achievement and can report to stakeholders on the progress of learners.

With thanks to the South African Council for Educators for their kind permission to reproduce their Professional Teaching Standards.

The mission of the South African Council for Educators is to register fit-to-practise educators and lecturers, promote their continuing professional development, and maintain the profession's professional teaching and ethical standards across South Africa.

Australia

The Victorian Teaching Profession's Code of Conduct and Code of Ethics – Victorian Institute of Teaching (VIT)

Code of Conduct

Section 1: Professional conduct

Teachers' professional conduct is characterised by the quality of the relationships they have with their learners, the parents/carers/families of their learners, their communities and their colleagues.

PRINCIPLE 1.1 Teachers provide opportunities for all learners to learn

The main focus of teaching is the learning of those being taught.

Teachers demonstrate their commitment to their learners by

- knowing their learners and how they learn, respecting individual differences and catering for individual abilities
- maintaining a safe and challenging learning environment
- accepting professional responsibility for the provision of quality teaching
- having high expectations of every learner, and recognising and developing individuals' abilities, skills and talents
- approaching the teaching and understanding of each individual learner without judgment or prejudice
- demonstrating cultural sensitivity
- communicating effectively and appropriately with their learners
- engaging with parents/carers/families and colleagues to consult about their learners' needs.

PRINCIPLE 1.2 Teachers treat their learners with courtesy and dignity, and promote participation and empowerment

Teachers

- work to create an environment that promotes respect for everyone
- model and engage in respectful and impartial language and behaviour
- protect learners from intimidation, embarrassment, humiliation and harm
- display an understanding of a learner's individual context and specific vulnerabilities when they interact with them
- consider the cultural safety of Aboriginal and Torres Strait Islander learners
- enhance learner autonomy by seeking to ensure they
    - have the opportunity to express their views
    - are confident and creative individuals
    - are successful lifelong learners
    - are active and informed members of the community
- respect a learner's privacy in sensitive matters – such as health or family issues – and only reveal confidential matters when appropriate, necessary or required by law, such as
    - if the learner has consented to the information being used in a certain way
    - to prevent or lessen a serious threat to life, health, safety or wellbeing of a person (including the learner)
    - part of an investigation into unlawful activity
    - if the disclosure is required or mandated by law
    - to prevent a crime or enforce the law
    - to manage any risk to a child or young person
- use behaviour management strategies and consequences appropriate for a learner's individual context and actions, aimed at supporting positive change.

PRINCIPLE 1.3 Teachers work within the limits of their professional expertise

In fulfilling their role, teachers have a wide range of responsibilities. They support learning by knowing the strengths and the limits of their professional expertise.

Teachers

- seek to ensure they have the physical, mental and emotional capacity to carry out their professional responsibilities
- are aware of the role of other professionals and agencies, and know when learners should be referred to them for assistance
- are truthful when making statements about their qualifications and competencies, and can provide evidence to support these statements, if required to do so by VIT.

PRINCIPLE 1.4 Teachers maintain objectivity in their relationships with learners

In their professional role, teachers do not behave as a friend or parent/guardian.

They

- interact with learners without displaying bias or preference
- make decisions in learners' best interests
- keep their personal agendas separate from their learning environment.

PRINCIPLE 1.5 Teachers are always in a professional relationship with their learners, whether at the education setting where they teach or not

Teachers hold a unique position of influence and trust that should not be violated or compromised. They exercise their responsibilities in ways that recognise there are limits or boundaries to their relationships with learners.

Teachers should consider how their decisions and actions may be perceived by others. Teachers should be aware of the specific vulnerabilities of learners when determining appropriate professional boundaries. The following examples outline some of those limits.

A professional relationship will be violated if a teacher

- has a sexual relationship with a learner

- engages in sexual misconduct which includes behaviour, physical contact, speech or other communication of a sexual nature; inappropriate touching; grooming type behaviour; and voyeurism
- touches a learner without a valid reason
- engages in communications with a learner beyond the boundaries of a professional relationship without a valid reason, including via written/electronic/online means (including social media)
- accepts gifts, which could be reasonably perceived as being used to influence them, from learners or their parents/carers/families
- gives gifts to learners or their parents/carers/families that could be reasonably perceived as showing bias or favouritism.

A professional relationship may be compromised if a teacher

- socialises with learners (including online and via social media) outside of a professional context
- invites learners back to their home
- has a sexualised relationship with a former learner within two years of the learner completing their senior secondary schooling or equivalent. In all circumstances, the former learner must be at least 18 before a relationship commences.

PRINCIPLE 1.6 Teachers maintain a professional relationship with parents/carers

Teachers should be respectful of, and courteous to, parents and carers.

Teachers

- understand that in some circumstances a relationship with parents/carers outside of the education setting may compromise, or be perceived to compromise, the professional relationship
- consider parents'/carers' perspectives when making decisions which have an impact on the education or wellbeing of a learner
- communicate and consult with parents/carers in a timely, understandable and sensitive manner

- use appropriate communication methods with parents/carers when discussing the education or wellbeing of a learner
- take appropriate action when responding to parent/carer concerns.

PRINCIPLE 1.7 Teachers work in collaborative relationships with learners' families and communities

Teachers recognise their learners come from a diverse range of backgrounds, personal circumstances, values and beliefs, contexts and cultures, and seek to work collaboratively and respectfully with learners' families and communities.

PRINCIPLE 1.8 Collegiality is an integral part of the work of teachers

Teachers demonstrate collegiality by

- treating each other with courtesy and respect
- valuing the input of their colleagues
- using appropriate forums for constructive debate on professional matters
- sharing expertise and knowledge in a variety of collaborative contexts
- respecting different approaches to teaching
- providing support for each other, particularly those new to the profession
- sharing information to support the teaching, wellbeing and safety of learners.

Section 2: Personal conduct

The personal conduct of a teacher will have an impact on the professional standing of that teacher and the profession as a whole.

PRINCIPLE 2.1 The personal conduct of a teacher has an impact on the professional standing of that teacher and on the profession as a whole

Although there is no definitive boundary between the personal and professional conduct of a teacher, teachers reflect community expectations in their personal conduct by

- being positive role models in education settings, in the community and online
- respecting and complying with the law
- not exploiting their position for an inappropriate personal or financial benefit

- ensuring their personal or financial interests do not interfere with the performance of their duties
- acting with discretion and maintaining confidentiality in all communications concerning their professional teaching responsibilities
- being aware of the potentially serious impact that any demonstration of intolerance or prejudice could have on the safety and wellbeing of children, their standing as a teacher or the profession as a whole.

Section 3: Professional competence

Teachers are cognisant of their legal and professional requirements and value their professionalism. They set and maintain high standards of professional competence.

PRINCIPLE 3.1 Teachers value their professionalism, and set and maintain high standards of competence

Teachers

- are knowledgeable in their areas of expertise
- are committed to pursuing their own professional learning
- engage in reflective practice and identify professional learning needs
- are able to demonstrate how their practice meets the Australian Professional Standards for Teachers
- complete their duties in a responsible and thorough manner.

PRINCIPLE 3.2 Teachers are aware of, and comply with, the legal requirements that pertain to their profession

Teachers must comply with the requirements of

- mandatory reporting and other reporting obligations
- the principle of negligence, which includes duty of care
- laws preventing discrimination, harassment and vilification
- protection of privacy
- occupational health and safety
- teacher registration.

Teachers should be aware of

- child safe standards
- reportable conduct
- United Nations Convention on the Rights of the Child
- any other relevant legislation, policies or regulations that pertain to the role of a teacher in child safety and wellbeing.

Code of Ethics

As teachers, we use our expert knowledge to provide experiences that inspire and facilitate the learning of those we teach.

We are a significant force in developing a knowledgeable, creative, productive and democratic society. The values that underpin our profession are **integrity**, **respect** and **responsibility**.

We hold a unique position of trust and influence, which we recognise in our relationships with learners, parents/carers, colleagues and the community.

The purpose of this Code is to

- state the value that guides our practice and conduct
- enable us as a profession to affirm our public accountability
- promote public confidence in our profession.

We demonstrate our integrity by

- acting in the best interest of learners
- maintaining a professional relationship with learners, parents/carers, colleagues and the community
- behaving in ways that respect and advance the profession

We demonstrate our respect by

- acting with care and compassion
- treating learners fairly and impartially

- holding our colleagues in high regard
- acknowledging parents and carers as partners in the education of their children.

We demonstrate our responsibility by

- providing quality teaching
- maintaining and developing our professional practice
- working cooperatively with colleagues in the best interest of our learners.

With thanks to the Victorian Institute of Teaching for their kind permission to reproduce the Victorian Teaching Profession's Codes of Conduct and Ethics.

The Victorian Institute of Teaching was established in 2002 as an independent statutory authority for the teaching profession in the Australian state of Victoria, whose primary function is to regulate for a highly qualified, proficient and reputable teaching profession.

Aotearoa New Zealand

Code of Professional Responsibility and Standards for the Teaching Profession – Teaching Council of Aotearoa New Zealand (TCANZ)

Our values

These values underpin Our Code, Our Standards. They define, inspire and guide us as teachers.

WHAKAMANA: empowering all learners to reach their highest potential by providing high-quality teaching and leadership.

MANAAKITANGA: creating a welcoming, caring and creative learning environment that treats everyone with respect and dignity.

PONO: showing integrity by acting in ways that are fair, honest, ethical and just.

WHANAUNGATANGA: engaging in positive and collaborative relationships with our learners, their families and whānau, our colleagues and the wider community.

Our Commitment to Te Tiriti o Waitangi

Signed in 1840 by leaders of hapū and the Crown, Te Tiriti o Waitangi affirmed Māori rights as tangata whenua and provided a place and a shape of governance for Pākehā in Aotearoa.

Te Tiriti o Waitangi provided a basis for ongoing, peaceful power-sharing relationships between the first peoples and all others who would come in later years.

Today, Te Tiriti o Waitangi is seen as a commitment under which Māori and all other New Zealanders may live together in the spirit of honourable relationships, with the promise to take the best possible care of each other. This requires the injustices caused by colonisation to be addressed and all New Zealanders to engage in creating a positive future that honours Te Tiriti o Waitangi.

New Zealand is an increasingly multicultural nation, and Te Tiriti o Waitangi is inclusive of today's new settlers. As with earlier immigrants, their 'place to stand' comes with an expectation that they will live here in a way that respects the commitments of Te Tiriti o Waitangi and the position of Māori as tangata whenua.

As teachers, we are committed to honouring Te Tiriti o Waitangi and we understand this has implications in all of our practice.

The Code of Professional Responsibility

1. Commitment to the teaching profession

I will maintain public trust and confidence in the teaching profession by:

1. demonstrating a commitment to providing high-quality and effective teaching
2. engaging in professional, respectful and collaborative relationships with colleagues
3. demonstrating a high standard of professional behaviour and integrity
4. demonstrating a commitment to tangata whenuatanga and Te Tiriti o Waitangi partnership in the learning environment

5. contributing to a professional culture that supports and upholds this Code.

2. Commitment to learners

I will work in the best interests of learners by:

1. promoting the wellbeing of learners and protecting them from harm
2. engaging in ethical and professional relationships with learners that respect professional boundaries
3. respecting the diversity of the heritage, language, identity and culture of all learners
4. affirming Māori learners as tangata whenua and supporting their educational aspirations
5. promoting inclusive practices to support the needs and abilities of all learners
6. being fair and effectively managing my assumptions and personal beliefs.

3. Commitment to families and whānau

I will respect the vital role my learners' families and whānau play in supporting their children's learning by:

1. engaging in relationships with families and whānau that are professional and respectful
2. engaging families and whānau in their children's learning
3. respecting the diversity of the heritage, language, identity and culture of families and whānau.

4. Commitment to society

I will respect my trusted role in society and the influence I have in shaping the future by:

1. promoting and protecting the principles of human rights, sustainability and social justice
2. demonstrating a commitment to Te Tiriti o Waitangi based Aotearoa New Zealand

3. fostering learners to be active participants in community life and engaged in issues important to the wellbeing of society.

Standards for the Teaching Profession

Standard	Elaboration of the standard
Te Tiriti o Waitangi partnership Demonstrate commitment to tangata whenuatanga and Te Tiriti o Waitangi partnership in Aotearoa New Zealand.	■ Understand and recognise the unique status of tangata whenua in Aotearoa New Zealand. ■ Understand and acknowledge the histories, heritages, languages and cultures of partners to Te Tiriti o Waitangi. ■ Practise and develop the use of te reo and tikanga Māori.
Professional learning Use inquiry, collaborative problem- solving and professional learning to improve professional capability to impact on the learning and achievement of all learners.	■ Inquire into and reflect on the effectiveness of practice in an ongoing way, using evidence from a range of sources. ■ Critically examine how my own assumptions and beliefs, including cultural beliefs, impact on practice and the achievement of learners with different abilities and needs, backgrounds, genders, identities, languages and cultures. ■ Engage in professional learning and adaptively apply this learning in practice. ■ Be informed by research and innovations related to: content disciplines; pedagogy; teaching for diverse learners, including learners with disabilities and learning support needs; and wider education matters. ■ Seek and respond to feedback from learners, colleagues and other education professionals, and engage in collaborative problem solving and learning-focused collegial discussions.

Standard	Elaboration of the standard
Professional relationships Establish and maintain professional relationships and behaviours focused on the learning and wellbeing of each learner.	■ Engage in reciprocal, collaborative learning-focused relationships with: ● learners, families and whānau ● teaching colleagues, support staff and other professionals ● agencies, groups and individuals in the community. ■ Communicate effectively with others. ■ Actively contribute, and work collegially, in the pursuit of improving my own and organisational practice, showing leadership, particularly in areas of responsibility. ■ Communicate clear and accurate assessment for learning and achievement information.
Learning-focused culture Develop a culture that is focused on learning, and is characterised by respect, inclusion, empathy, collaboration and safety.	■ Develop learning-focused relationships with learners, enabling them to be active participants in the process of learning, sharing ownership and responsibility for learning. ■ Foster trust, respect and cooperation with and among learners so that they experience an environment in which it is safe to take risks. ■ Demonstrate high expectations for the learning outcomes of all learners, including for those learners with disabilities or learning support needs. ■ Manage the learning setting to ensure access to learning for all and to maximise learners' physical, social, cultural and emotional safety. ■ Create an environment where learners can be confident in their identities, languages, cultures and abilities. ■ Develop an environment where the diversity and uniqueness of all learners are accepted and valued. ■ Meet relevant regulatory, statutory and professional requirements.

Standard	Elaboration of the standard
Design for learning Design learning based on curriculum and pedagogical knowledge, assessment information and an understanding of each learner's strengths, interests, needs, identities, languages and cultures.	■ Select teaching approaches, resources, and learning and assessment activities based on a thorough knowledge of curriculum content, pedagogy, progressions in learning and the learners. ■ Gather, analyse and use appropriate assessment information, identifying progress and needs of learners to design clear next steps in learning and to identify additional supports or adaptations that may be required. ■ Design and plan culturally responsive, evidence-based approaches that reflect the local community and Te Tiriti o Waitangi partnership in New Zealand. ■ Harness the rich capital that learners bring by providing culturally responsive and engaging contexts for learners. ■ Design learning that is informed by national policies and priorities.
Teaching Teach and respond to learners in a knowledgeable and adaptive way to progress their learning at an appropriate depth and pace.	■ Teach in ways that ensure all learners are making sufficient progress, and monitor the extent and pace of learning, focusing on equity and excellence for all. ■ Specifically support the educational aspirations for Māori learners, taking shared responsibility for these learners to achieve educational success as Māori. ■ Use an increasing repertoire of teaching strategies, approaches, learning activities, technologies and assessment for learning strategies and modify these in response to the needs of individuals and groups of learners. ■ Provide opportunities and support for learners to engage with, practise and apply learning to different contexts and make connections with prior learning.

Standard	Elaboration of the standard
	■ Teach in ways that enable learners to learn from one another, to collaborate, to self-regulate and to develop agency over their learning. ■ Ensure learners receive ongoing feedback and assessment information and support them to use this information to guide further learning.

With thanks to the Teaching Council of Aotearoa New Zealand for their kind permission to reproduce their Code of Professional Responsibility and Standards for the Teaching Profession.

The Teaching Council of Aotearoa New Zealand/Matatū Aotearoa is the professional body for, and voice of, the New Zealand teaching profession. They represent over 100,000 registered teachers in New Zealand from early childhood education through to primary and secondary schooling, in English and Māori medium settings. Their role is to promote all that is best about teaching – good practice, new ideas and inspirational leadership – and to boost the status of teaching, strengthening accountability and bringing consistently high standards across the education system, providing leadership and working to strengthen the regulatory and disciplinary framework for teaching.

GLOSSARY OF TERMS AND ABBREVIATIONS

A level

Advanced level examinations, taken by pupils in most parts of the UK at age 18, and the usual benchmark for university entry.

BAQTS

Bachelor of Arts Qualified Teacher Status – a three- or four-year undergraduate degree course that combines the academic study of education and teaching with the professional qualification to qualify as a teacher.

ChildLine

A counselling service for children and young people in the UK up to their nineteenth birthday.

Class A drugs

A category of controlled drugs defined under the UK's Misuse of Drugs Act 1971 as the most dangerous substances, most of which are natural or synthetic opioids but also include some hallucinogens. The category also includes cocaine, heroin, LSD, MDMA, mescaline, methadone, methamphetamine and PCP.

Class B drugs

A category of controlled drugs under the UK's Misuse of Drugs Act 1971 which are less dangerous than Class A drugs but more so than Class C. They include sedatives, stimulants, opioids, amphetamine, cannabis and codeine.

CPD

Continuing (or continuous) professional development is training and development that professional people are expected and often required to undertake to maintain their standing.

DBS

The Disclosure and Barring Service is a body that enables organisations in the public, private and voluntary sectors to make safer recruitment decisions by identifying candidates who may be unsuitable for certain work, especially involving children or vulnerable adults, and provides wider access to criminal record information through its disclosure service for England and Wales.

DfE

The Department for Education is the government department responsible for education, child protection, apprenticeships and wider skills in England. Education is a devolved responsibility to other UK governments in Scotland, Wales and Northern Ireland.

DSL

A designated safeguarding lead is a senior member of school staff who has responsibility for safeguarding and child protection, including online safety. A DSL will take part in strategy discussions and inter-agency meetings, and support other staff to do so, and contribute to the assessment of children. This should be explicit in their job description.

ECF

The Early Career Framework sets out what professional development new teachers are entitled to in their first two years of teaching. It is designed to help new teachers develop their practice, knowledge and working habits.

ECT

Early career teacher replaces newly qualified teacher (NQT) and recently qualified teacher (RQT) as a catch-all term for new entrants into the teaching profession.

GCSE

The General Certificate of Secondary Education is a qualification in a specific subject usually taken by pupils aged between 14 and 16, at a level below A level.

Institute of Teaching

From 2022, this will provide training and development to teachers and school leaders in England throughout their career. It will be delivered through a mix of regional campuses and school-based means, both face-to-face and online.

ITT (or ITE)

Initial teacher training (or initial teacher education in some countries) refers to the way that student or trainee teachers are prepared with the knowledge, professional attitudes and behaviours, skills and qualifications required to perform effectively in their classrooms, schools and wider community.

MA

A Master of Arts is a type of master's degree awarded by universities in many countries. It is not required in order to practise as a teacher in the UK, although it is increasingly encouraged. Some states in the United States require teachers to work towards attaining an MA as a supplementary qualification to a teacher's licence.

NPQML

National Professional Qualification for Middle Leadership – a middle-management qualification available to UK school teachers.

NQT

Newly qualified teacher. A term now replaced by early career teacher (ECT).

NSPCC

The National Society for the Prevention of Cruelty to Children is a charity campaigning and working for child protection in the UK.

Ofsted

Office for Standards in Education – the body charged with inspecting the quality of teaching in schools in England, with equivalent bodies in other parts of the UK.

The equivalent bodies in Scotland, Wales and Northern Ireland are, respectively, Education Scotland, Estyn and the Education Training Inspectorate.

ONS

The Office for National Statistics is the UK's independent producer of official statistics. It is responsible for collecting and publishing statistics relating to the economy, population and society at national, regional and local levels, and conducts the census in England and Wales every ten years.

PGCE (or PGDE)

Post-Graduate Certificate (or Diploma) in Education is a one- or two-year higher education course in the UK which provides professional training in order to allow graduates to become qualified teachers within maintained schools. A similar qualification exists in Australia, New Zealand, the Republic of Ireland, Hong Kong and Singapore.

Prevent duty

The Counter-Terrorism and Security Act 2015 includes the Prevent duty. This is a duty placed on specified authorities, such as schools, to have due regard for the need to prevent individuals from being drawn into terrorism. In schools, it is intended to keep young people safe from the threat of terrorism, not to prevent them from discussing controversial or sensitive issues. All school staff receive Prevent duty training.

QTS

Qualified teacher status is required in England and Wales to work as a teacher of children in a state school. A similar status exists under a different name in Scotland and Northern Ireland.

RQT

Recently qualified teacher. A term now replaced by early career teacher (ECT).

SCITT

School-centred initial teacher training is a teacher training programme in England which enables graduates to complete their training and qualifications within a school environment. Some SCITT programmes also award a Post-Graduate Certificate in Education (PGCE) qualification.

SEND Code of Practice

Statutory guidance provided for those with special educational needs under the Children and Families Act 2014. It describes the duties and requirements that teachers and schools must follow by law, unless there is a good reason not to do so.

SMSC

Spiritual, moral, social and cultural education is an overarching but non-specific requirement of schools since the introduction of the Education Reform Act 1988. It is intended to be the general foundation for teaching civic and fundamental British values.

STPCD

The School Teachers' Pay and Conditions Document is an annually published document that forms part of the contract of all teachers in schools in England and Wales. It is binding on all maintained schools and local authorities.

TRA

The Teaching Regulation Agency is responsible for regulating the teaching profession in England. It conducts misconduct hearings and has the power to suspend and prohibit teachers from practice.

Teachers' Standards

A framework of descriptors of professional standards for teachers in England. Part One describes more the technical competencies required of a teacher, while Part Two focuses on the professional and personal qualities and attributes.

Teaching School Hubs

A network of over eighty centres of excellence for teacher training and development across England, providing CPD to teachers at all stages of their career, in particular delivering initial teacher training and early career development.

TES

A popular education journal based in the UK, formerly known as the *Times Educational Supplement*.

Western values

The values emerging from Western philosophy and generally referring to the philosophical thought and work beginning with the ancient Greek philosophy of the pre-Socratics and culminating in the European Enlightenment of the eighteenth and nineteenth centuries. Commonly, it refers to values like freedom of the individual, democracy, free speech and the rule of law.

WRAP

Workshop to Raise Awareness of Prevent is a free specialist workshop, designed by the UK government, to give an introduction to the Prevent duty and provide support to teachers, schools and others in safeguarding vulnerable people.

BIBLIOGRAPHY AND FURTHER READING

Al-Hothali, Huda M. (2018) Ethics of the Teaching Profession Among Secondary School Teachers from School Leaders' Perspective in Riyadh, *International Education Studies* 11(9): 47–63. Available at: http://www.ccsenet.org/journal/index.php/ies/article/view/76845.

Alexander, Douglas (2019) *Seriously: A Guide to Disagreeing Better* [radio programme], BBC Radio 4 (17 December). Available at: https://www.bbc.co.uk/programmes/p07y3d18.

Appiah, Kwame Anthony (2016) *The Reith Lectures: Mistaken Identities* [radio series], BBC Radio 4. Available at: https://www.bbc.co.uk/programmes/b080twcz.

Arthur, James; Kristjánsson, Kristján; Cooke, Sandra; Brown, Emma; and Carr, David (2015) *The Good Teacher: Understanding Virtues in Practice. Research Report*. Birmingham: University of Birmingham Press and Jubilee Centre for Character and Virtues. Available at: https://www.jubileecentre.ac.uk/1568/projects/virtues-in-the-professions/the-good-teacher.

Arthur, James; Kristjánsson, Kristján; Harrison, Tom; Sanderse, Wouter; and Wright, Daniel (2017) *Teaching Character and Virtue in Schools*. Abingdon and New York: Routledge.

Aristotle (1912) *Politics: A Treatise on Government*, tr. William Ellis. London: J.M. Dent & Sons. Available at: http://www.gutenberg.org/ebooks/6762.

Aristotle (2009) *The Nicomachean Ethics*, tr. David Ross. New York: Oxford University Press.

Association of American Educators (n.d.) Code of Ethics for Educators. Available at: https://www.aaeteachers.org/index.php/about-us/aae-code-of-ethics.

Barnes, Jonathan (2000) *Aristotle: A Very Short Introduction*. Oxford: Oxford University Press.

BBC News (2017) Baroness Warsi: Prevent Scheme Should Be Paused (26 March). Available at: https://www.bbc.co.uk/news/av/uk-39399011.

Beabout, Gregory R. (2016) *Ethics: The Art of Character*. Glastonbury: Wooden Books.

Berry, Jon (2013) *Teachers' Legal Rights and Responsibilities: A Guide for Trainee Teachers and Those New to the Profession*. St Albans: University of Hertfordshire Press.

Blackburn, Simon (2001) *Ethics: A Very Short Introduction*. Oxford: Oxford University Press.

Bragg, Melvyn (1998) *In Our Time: The British Empire's Legacy* [radio programme], BBC Radio 4 (31 December). Available at: https://www.bbc.co.uk/programmes/p005459p.

Bragg, Melvyn (2018a) *A History of Ideas: How Can I Tell Right from Wrong?* [radio programme], BBC Radio 4 (12 November). Available at: https://www.bbc.co.uk/programmes/b04prhq3.

Bragg, Melvyn (2018b) *A History of Ideas: How Do I Live a Good Life?* [radio programme], BBC Radio 4 (10 September). Available at: https://www.bbc.co.uk/programmes/b05nt099.

Bragg, Melvyn (2018c) *A History of Ideas: What Does It Mean to Be Free?* [radio programme], BBC Radio 4 (13 August). Available at: https://www.bbc.co.uk/programmes/b04bwyf8.

Brooks, David (2016) *The Road to Character*. London: Penguin.

Campbell, Elizabeth (2003) *The Ethical Teacher*. Milton Keynes: Open University Press.

Carr, David (1999) *Professionalism and Ethics in Teaching*. Abingdon and New York: Routledge.

Cave, Peter (2015) *Ethics: A Beginner's Guide*. London: Oneworld.

Commission on Race and Ethnic Disparities (2021) *The Report* (March). Available at: https://www.gov.uk/government/organisations/commission-on-race-and-ethnic-disparities.

Curry, Oliver S.; Mullins, Daniel A.; and Whitehouse, Harvey (2019) Is It Good to Cooperate? Testing the Theory of Morality-as-Cooperation in 60 Societies, *Current Anthropology* 60(1): 47. Available at: https://doi.org/10.1086/701478.

Department for Education (2011a) *Teachers' Standards: Guidance for School Leaders, School Staff and Governing Bodies* (July; introduction updated June 2013). Available at: https://www.gov.uk/government/publications/teachers-standards.

Department for Education (2011b) *Teachers' Standards: Overview*. Available at: https://www.gov.uk/government/publications/teachers-standards.

Department for Education (2013) *Use of Reasonable Force: Advice for Headteachers, Staff and Governing Bodies* (July). Available at: https://www.gov.uk/government/publications/use-of-reasonable-force-in-schools.

Department for Education (2014) *Promoting Fundamental British Values as Part of SMSC in Schools: Departmental Advice for Maintained Schools* (November). Available at: https://www.gov.uk/government/publications/promoting-fundamental-british-values-through-smsc.

Department for Education (2015) *The Prevent Duty: Departmental Advice for Schools and Childcare Providers* (June). Available at: https://www.gov.uk/government/publications/protecting-children-from-radicalisation-the-prevent-duty.

Department for Education (2018a) *Searching, Screening and Confiscation: Advice for Headteachers, School Staff and Governing Bodies* (January). Available at: https://www.gov.uk/government/publications/searching-screening-and-confiscation.

Department for Education (2018b) *Teacher Misconduct: The Prohibition of Teachers. Advice on Factors Relating to Decisions Leading to the Prohibition of Teachers from the Teaching Profession* (October). Available at: https://www.gov.uk/government/publications/teacher-misconduct-the-prohibition-of-teachers--3.

Department for Education (2019) *ITT Core Content Framework* (November). Available at: https://www.gov.uk/government/publications/initial-teacher-training-itt-core-content-framework.

Department for Education (2020a) *Keeping Children Safe in Education (2020): Statutory Guidance for Schools and Colleges* (updated January 2021). Available at: https://www.gov.uk/government/publications/keeping-children-safe-in-education--2.

Department for Education (2020b) *School Teachers' Pay and Conditions Document 2020 and Guidance on School Teachers' Pay and Conditions* (September). Available at: https://www.gov.uk/government/publications/school-teachers-pay-and-conditions.

Department for Education (2021) *Early Career Framework* (March). Available at: https://www.gov.uk/government/publications/early-career-framework.

Department for Education and Department of Health (2015) *Special Educational Needs and Disability Code of Practice: 0 to 25 Years* (January). Available at: https://www.gov.uk/government/publications/send-code-of-practice-0-to-25.

Department for Education and Employment (1998) *Circular 10/98: Section 550A of the Education Act 1996. The Use of Force to Control or Restrain Pupils*. London: HMSO.

Department for Education and York Consulting LLP (2012) *Allegations of Abuse Against Teachers and Non-Teaching Staff*. Research Report DFE-RR192. Available at: https://assets.publishing.service.gov.uk/government/uploads/system/uploads/attachment_data/file/361444/DFE-RR192.pdf.

Disraeli, Benjamin (1880) *Endymion*. London: Longmans & Green. Available at: https://www.gutenberg.org/ebooks/7926.

Education Workforce Council (2019) *Code of Professional Conduct and Practice for Registrants with the Education Workforce Council (EWC)* (1 September). Available at: https://www.ewc.wales/site/index.php/en/fitness-to-practise/code-of-professional-conduct-and-practice-pdf.html.

Evans, Richard L. (1971) *Richard Evans' Quote Book*. Salt Lake City, UT: Publishers Press.

Frampton, Martin; Goodhart, David; and Mahmood, Khalid (2016) *Unsettled Belonging: A Survey of Britain's Muslim Communities*. London: Policy Exchange. Available at: https://policyexchange.org.uk/publication/unsettled-belonging-a-survey-of-britains-muslim-communities.

Frankl, Viktor E. (2004 [1959]) *Man's Search for Meaning*, tr. Ilse Lasch. London: Random House.

Gardner, Howard; Csikszentmihalyi, Mihaly; and Damon, William (2001) *Good Work: When Excellence and Ethics Meet*. New York: Basic Books.

Garton Ash, Timothy (2016a) *Free Speech: Ten Principles for a Connected World*. London: Atlantic Books.

Garton Ash, Timothy (2016b) *Free Speech* [radio series], BBC Radio 4. Available at: https://www.bbc.co.uk/programmes/b077ndw5.

Garton Ash, Timothy (2016c) *Free Speech: Respect Me, Respect My Religion* [radio programme], BBC Radio 4 (13 April). Available at: https://www.bbc.co.uk/programmes/b076zxyt.

General Teaching Council for England (2004) *Code of Conduct and Practice for Registered Teachers: Setting Minimum Standards for the Regulation of the Profession*. Available at: https://dera.ioe.ac.uk/8257/3/conduct_code_practice_for_teachers.pdf.

General Teaching Council for Northern Ireland (2018) *GTCNI Digest of the Teachers Competences*. Available at: https://gtcni.servers.tc/cmsfiles/Resource365/Resources/Publications/DIGEST_OF_TEACHER_COMPETENCES.pdf.

General Teaching Council for Scotland (2021) *The Standard for Full Registration: Mandatory Requirements for Registration with the General Teaching Council for Scotland* (August). Available at: https://www.gtcs.org.uk/professional-standards/professional-standards-2021-engagement.aspx.

Goodhart, David (2016) *Analysis: Conservative Muslims, Liberal Britain* [radio programme], BBC Radio 4 (16 November). Available at: https://www.bbc.co.uk/programmes/b04nrqsm.

Goodhart, David (2017) *The Road to Somewhere: The Populist Revolt and the Future of Politics*. London: Hurst and Co.

Guardian, The (2019) The 100 Best Male Footballers (20 December). Available at: https://www.theguardian.com/global/ng-interactive/2019/dec/17/the-100-best-male-footballers-in-the-world-2019.

Haidt, Jonathan (2002) *The Righteous Mind: Why Good People are Divided by Politics and Religion*. London: Penguin.

Hall, Catherine (2013) Britain's Massive Debt to Slavery, *The Guardian* (27 February). Available at: https://www.theguardian.com/commentisfree/2013/feb/27/britain-debt-slavery-made-public.

Hand, Michael (2018) *A Theory of Moral Education*. Abingdon and New York: Routledge.

Harari, Yuval Noah (2011) *Sapiens: A Brief History of Humankind*. London: Penguin.

Harari, Yuval Noah (2015) *Homo Deus: A Brief History of Tomorrow*. London: Penguin.

Harari, Yuval Noah (2018) *21 Lessons for the 21st Century*. London: Jonathan Cape.

Harris, Naomie (2019) *Who Do You Think You Are?* [TV programme], BBC One (29 July). Available at: https://www.bbc.co.uk/programmes/m00077q4.

Hayek, Friedrich A. (1988) *The Fatal Conceit: The Errors of Socialism* (London & New York: Routledge).

HM Government (2011) *Prevent Strategy* (June). Available at: https://www.gov.uk/government/publications/prevent-strategy-2011.

HM Government (2018) *Working Together to Safeguard Children: A Guide to Inter-Agency Working to Safeguard and Promote the Welfare of Children* (July). Available at: https://www.gov.uk/government/publications/working-together-to-safeguard-children--2.

HM Government (2020) Initial Teacher Training Census – Academic Year 2020–21 (3 December). Available at: https://explore-education-statistics.service.gov.uk/find-statistics/initial-teacher-training-census/2020-21.

HM Government (2021) School Teacher Workforce (18 February). Available at: https://www.ethnicity-facts-figures.service.gov.uk/workforce-and-business/workforce-diversity/school-teacher-workforce/latest#by-ethnicity.

Hobbs, Angie (2018) *A History of Ideas: Philosopher Angie Hobbs on Beauty and Morality* [radio programme], BBC Radio 4 (24 August). Available at: https://www.bbc.co.uk/programmes/b04pc7w4.

House of Commons (2009) *Allegations Against School Staff. Children, Schools and Families Committee – Fifth Report*. Available at: https://publications.parliament.uk/pa/cm200809/cmselect/cmchilsch/695/69502.htm.

House of Commons Health Committee (2003) *The Victoria Climbié Inquiry Report: Sixth Report of Session 2002–03*. HC 570. Available at: https://publications.parliament.uk/pa/cm200203/cmselect/cmhealth/570/570.pdf.

Johnson, Boris (2018) Denmark Has Got It Wrong. Yes, the Burka is Oppressive and Ridiculous – But That's Still No Reason to Ban It, *The Telegraph* (5 August).

Kaur-Ballagan, Kully (2020) Attitudes to Race and Inequality in Great Britain, *Ipsos MORI* (15 June). Available at: https://www.ipsos.com/ipsos-mori/en-uk/attitudes-race-and-inequality-great-britain.

King Jr, Martin Luther (1963) Letter from a Birmingham Jail (16 April), *Center for Africana Studies – University of Pennsylvania*. Available at: https://www.africa.upenn.edu/Articles_Gen/Letter_Birmingham.html.

Long, Robert and Danechi, Shadi (2019) *Faith Schools in England: FAQs*. Briefing Paper Number 06972 (20 December). London: House of Commons Library. Available at: https://commonslibrary.parliament.uk/research-briefings/sn06972.

Lough, Catherine (2020) Third of Teachers Leaving the Profession Within Five Years, *TES* (25 June). Available at: https://www.tes.com/news/recruitment-third-teachers-leaving-profession-within-5-years.

Lukianoff, Greg and Haidt, Jonathan (2018) *The Coddling of the American Mind: How Good Intentions and Bad Ideas Are Setting Up a Generation for Failure.* London: Penguin.

Myers, Kate; with Clayton, Graham; James, David; and O'Brien, Jim (2004) *Teachers Behaving Badly: Dilemmas for School Leaders.* Abingdon: RoutledgeFalmer.

National Education Union (2019) *Lecture Notes 2019–20: Education, the Law and You.* Available at: https://neu.org.uk/media/596/view.

Office for National Statistics (2011) 2011 Census: Key Statistics for England and Wales (March). Available at: https://www.ons.gov.uk/peoplepopulationandcommunity/populationandmigration/populationestimates/bulletins/2011censuskeystatisticsforenglandandwales/2012-12-11#ethnic-group.

Ofsted (2019) *The Education Inspection Framework* (May). Available at: https://www.gov.uk/government/publications/education-inspection-framework.

Olusoga, David (2017) *Black and British: A Forgotten History*. London: Pan Books.

O'Neill, Onora (2002) *The Reith Lectures: A Question of Trust* [radio series], BBC Radio 4. Available at: https://www.bbc.co.uk/programmes/p00ghvd8.

Ontario College of Teachers (n.d.) The Ethical Standards for the Teaching Profession and the Standards of Practice for the Teaching Profession. Available at: http://teachercodes.iiep.unesco.org/teachercodes/codes/America/Canada/Canada_Ontario_Standards.pdf.

Orwell, George (1945) Notes on Nationalism, *Polemic*, 1. Available at: https://www.orwellfoundation.com/the-orwell-foundation/orwell/essays-and-other-works/notes-on-nationalism.

Perraudin, Frances (2016) Andy Burnham Calls for 'Toxic' Prevent Strategy to Be Scrapped, *The Guardian* (9 June). Available at: https://www.theguardian.com/politics/2016/jun/09/andy-burnham-calls-for-toxic-prevent-strategy-to-be-scrapped.

Peters, Richard S. (1974) *Ethics and Education*. London: Unwin.

Peterson, Jordan (2018) *12 Rules for Life: An Antidote to Chaos*. London: Penguin.

Plato (1871) *Laws*, tr. Benjamin Jowett. Available at: https://www.gutenberg.org/files/1750/1750-h/1750-h.htm.

Putnam, Robert (2001) *Bowling Alone: The Collapse and Revival of American Community*. New York: Simon & Schuster.

Rosney, Daniel and Hastie, Roisin (2018) Dating Apps: Tinder, Chappy and Bumble 'Least Preferred' Way to Meet People, *BBC Newsbeat* (3 August). Available at: https://www.bbc.co.uk/news/newsbeat-45007017.

Russell, Bertrand (2009 [1950]) The Superior Virtue of the Oppressed, in *Unpopular Essays*. Abingdon and New York: Routledge, pp. 56–62.

Sacks, Jonathan (2016) The Danger of Outsourcing Morality [speech delivered on being awarded the Templeton Prize] (27 May). Available at: https://rabbisacks.org/danger-outsourcing-morality-read-rabbi-sacks-speech-accepting-templeton-prize.

Sacks, Jonathan (2018a) *Morality in the 21st Century* [radio series], BBC Radio 4. Available at: https://www.bbc.co.uk/programmes/b0bh7jkp.

Sacks, Jonathan (2018b) *Morality in the 21st Century: Noreena Hertz* [podcast], BBC Radio 4 (3 September). Available at: https://www.bbc.co.uk/programmes/p06k3v6v.

Sacks, Jonathan (2018c) *Morality in the 21st Century: Robert Putnam* [radio programme], BBC Radio 4 (3 September). Available at: https://www.bbc.co.uk/programmes/p06k4t86.

Sacks, Jonathan (2020) *Morality: Restoring the Common Good in Divided Times*. London: Hodder & Stoughton.

Schama, Simon (2009a) *A History of Britain. Vol. 1: At the Edge of the World? 3000 BC–AD 1603*. London: Bodley Head.

Schama, Simon (2009b) *A History of Britain. Vol. 2: The British Wars 1603–1776*. London: Bodley Head.

Schama, Simon (2009c) *A History of Britain. Vol. 3: The Fate of the Empire 1776–2000*. London: Bodley Head.

Scruton, Roger (2001) *Kant: A Very Short Introduction*. Oxford: Oxford University Press.

Sodha, Sonia (2016) *Analysis: Multiculturalism: Leicester v Newham* [radio programme], BBC Radio 4 (28 February). Available at: https://www.bbc.co.uk/programmes/b071459c.

South African Council for Educators (2017) *Professional Teaching Standards*. Available at: https://www.sace.org.za/assets/documents/uploads/sace_31561-2020-10-12-Professional%20Teaching%20Standards%20Brochure.pdf.

Teaching Council of Aotearoa New Zealand (2017) *Our Code, Our Standards: Code of Professional Responsibility and Standards for the Teaching Profession/Ngā Tikanga, Matatika Ngā Paerewa: Ngā Tikanga Matatika mō te Haepapa Ngaiotanga me ngā Paerewa mō te Umanga Whakaakoranga*. Available at: https://teachingcouncil.nz/assets/Files/Code-and-Standards/Our-Code-Our-Standards-Nga-Tikanga-Matatika-Nga-Paerewa.pdf.

TES (2004) Lost Age of the Discreet Dalliance (30 January). Available at: https://www.tes.com/news/lost-age-discreet-dalliance.

Thompson, Meryl (1997) *Professional Ethics and the Teacher.* Stoke-on-Trent: Trentham Books.

University of Bristol (2020; revised and published annually) *Handbook for Education Professionals: The Bristol Guide 2020/21*. Bristol: University of Bristol Press.

Victorian Institute of Teaching (n.d.) *The Victorian Teaching Profession's Code of Conduct*. Available at: https://www.vit.vic.edu.au/__data/assets/pdf_file/0004/137911/Code-of-Conduct.pdf.

Victorian Institute of Teaching (n.d.) *The Victorian Teaching Profession's Code of Ethics*. Available at: https://www.vit.vic.edu.au/__data/assets/pdf_file/0007/137914/Code-of-ethics.pdf.

Williams, Hugh (2008) *Fifty Things You Need to Know About British History.* London: Collins.

ABOUT THE AUTHOR

Alan Newland has spent over forty years working in education – as a primary school teacher, a lecturer at a London university, a head teacher at an inner-city primary school in East London, and as an advisor to the UK's Department for Education and the General Teaching Council for England. In recent years, he has been writing and lecturing on ethics and professional values in teaching. He has presented hundreds of lectures and seminars at universities and teacher training institutions, meeting thousands of trainee teachers about to enter the teaching profession every year.

INDEX

D

E